Anthropology at War

Anthropology at War

World War I and the Science of Race in Germany

ANDREW D. EVANS

The University of Chicago Press
Chicago and London

Andrew D. Evans is assistant professor of history at the State University of
New York at New Paltz.

The University of Chicago Press, Chicago 60637
The University of Chicago Press, Ltd., London
© 2010 by The University of Chicago
All rights reserved. Published 2010
Printed in the United States of America

18 17 16 15 14 13 12 11 10   1 2 3 4 5

ISBN-13: 978-0-226-22267-7 (cloth)
ISBN-13: 978-0-226-22268-4 (paper)
ISBN-10: 0-226-22267-5 (cloth)
ISBN-10: 0-226-22268-3 (paper)

Library of Congress Cataloging-in-Publication Data
Evans, Andrew D. (Andrew David), 1968–
    Anthropology at war : World War I and the science of race in Germany /
Andrew D. Evans.
        p. cm.
    Includes bibliographical references and index.
    ISBN-13: 978-0-226-22267-7 (cloth : alk. paper)
    ISBN-13: 978-0-226-22268-4 (pbk. : alk. paper)
    ISBN-10: 0-226-22267-5 (cloth : alk. paper)
    ISBN-10: 0-226-22268-3 (pbk. : alk. paper)   1. Anthropology—Germany—
History—20th century. 2. Racism in anthropology—Germany—History—
20th century.   I. Title.
    GN17.3.G3E93 2010
    301.0943'09041—dc22   2009051469

CONTENTS

ACKNOWLEDGMENTS

I am pleased to be able to express my thanks, at long last, to the many individuals and institutions that helped make this book a reality. At Indiana University I was blessed to work with scholars who communicated the delight of doing academic work. James M. Diehl showed me how to navigate the archives, and reacted to every draft that I gave him with gentle encouragement and good humor. The late William B. Cohen pushed me to trust my sources and follow through on my conclusions. These two scholars served as my intellectual role models, and I am profoundly grateful that I was able to learn from them. Ann Charmichael, Della Cook, and Albrecht Holschuh provided excellent suggestions and saved me from many errors. Other members of the faculty at Indiana—especially Carl Ipsen, Larry Friedman, and George Alter—offered advice and support at key junctures. My research was supported by grants from the College of Arts and Sciences, Graduate School, and Department of History at Indiana University.

After Indiana, I found an intellectual home in the Department of History at the State University of New York at New Paltz. My colleagues in the department and within the wider institution have been an unflagging source of support. I am particularly indebted to Katherine French, Susan Lewis, and Louis Roper, who have been instrumental in supporting my writing and research. Lee Bernstein gladly (and promptly) read everything I gave him and provided valuable critiques. Bruce Milem gave excellent advice over instant coffee and reminded me that, according to Gilles Deleuze, "complaining is an affirmation of life." My students at New Paltz, particularly those in my World War I seminar, continue to invigorate me with their enthusiasm and curiosity. A Creative Projects Award and a pre-tenure fellowship leave from SUNY New Paltz also aided in the completion of this project.

Beyond Indiana and New York, I have also benefited from the aid and generosity of colleagues far and wide. I especially would like to thank the many people who read and commented on sections of the work in various forms, including Tim Schmitz, Kay McAdams, Patrick Ettinger, Timothy Pursell, Katherine Clark, Brian Els, John Tomasic, Marina Mogilner, Monique Scheer, Reinhard Johler, Christian Marchetti, Eleanor Hight, Gary Sampson, Glenn Penny, Andy Donson, Lynn Nyhart, Belinda Davis, and Sara Pugach. I am especially grateful to Jeff Wilson, Sue Marchand, Henricka Kuklick, and an anonymous reviewer for the University of Chicago Press, each of whom provided pointed and judicious comments on the entire manuscript. Matti Bunzl deserves special thanks for his repeated reading of the manuscript and his excellent critiques. I am deeply thankful to Andre Gingrich, who provided shrewd and lively guidance at a key juncture in the process of preparing the manuscript. In addition, I owe a particular debt of gratitude to David Brent at the University of Chicago Press for his continual support of the project. His assistant Laura Avey was also critical in seeing this book to fruition, as was my manuscript editor, Renaldo Migaldi. Mark Seidl has my sincere thanks for preparing the index. I also benefited from conversations and correspondence with Niels Lösch, Wolfgang Wippermann, Rainer Buschmann, Marion Melk-Koch, Margot Kahyless, Sierra Bruckner, Andrew Zimmerman, John David Smith, Brent Maner, and Diethelm Prowe.

Librarians and archivists also provided invaluable guidance and helped to make my time with the sources profitable. I want to thank the staff at the Indiana University Library, the Sojourner Truth Library at SUNY New Paltz, the Vassar Library, and the New York Public Library for their assistance. In Germany I benefited from the help and expertise of staff at a variety of archives, but several individuals deserve special mention. I am particularly indebted to Horst Junker at the archive of the Berliner Gesellschaft für Anthropologie, Ethnologie, und Urgeschichte; Dr. Elisabeth Tietmeyer at the Berlin Museum für Völkerkunde; and Dr. Heidelies Wittig-Sorg at the Staatsarchiv in Hamburg. Staff members at the Handschriftenabteilung of the Staatsbibliothek in Berlin cheerfully filled my endless requests.

Some of the material in this book appeared first in other venues. These earlier versions include "Race Made Visible," *German Studies Review* 31/1 (2008): 87–108; "A Liberal Paradigm? Race and Ideology in Late-Nineteenth-Century German Physical Anthropology," *Ab Imperio: Studies of New Imperial History and Nationalism in the Post-Soviet Space* 8 (1/2007): 113–38; "Anthropology at War: Racial Studies of POWs during World War I," in *Worldly Provincialism: German Anthropology in the Age of Empire*, edited by H. Glenn Penny and Matti Bunzl (Ann Arbor: University of Michigan

Press, 2003), 198–229; "Capturing Race: Anthropology and Photography in German Prisoner-of-War Camps during World War I," in *Colonialist Photography: Imag(in)ing Race and Place*, edited by Eleanor Hight and Gary Sampson (New York: Routledge, 2002), 226–56. I am grateful to the editors of these publications for their support, and to the publishers for permission to reuse the material in this book.

Finally, I would like to thank friends and family for their continued support. I am indebted to Jeff Fleisher, Tom Berger, Stephen Kingsley, Kazaan Viveiros, Debbie Gershenowitz, Paul Murphy, Dean Kotlowski, Adrienne Russell, Ellen Willow, David Kelly, and Catherine Lerat for their friendship and intellectual comaraderie. The friendship and support of the Schoeller family—Ina, Jochen, Christina, Bernd, and Dieter—has sustained me since my first visit to Germany as a college student. Likewise, the hospitality of Tom and Elke Seel made me feel at home in Germany when I was far from my own home. I give my deepest thanks to the members of my family for their continued encouragement: Carolyn Evans, Peter Evans, Kammi Evans, Daniel Evans, Deborah Murdock, Robert Bryan, Angus Murdoch, Alice Wakefield, Alec Murdoch, and Kris Parker. My sons Christopher and Henrik kept me grounded in the small delights of life. More than anyone else, however, my partner, spouse, and intellectual companion Lydia Murdoch deserves special gratitude. She continually inspired me with her own work and showed me, by her example, how scholarship should be done. At every stage in this project and in our crowded daily lives, I have depended on her sound counsel, humor, and love.

This book is dedicated to the memory of my father, David C. Evans, who was also a professional historian and teacher. In his wry and modest way, he introduced me the joys of intellectual work without ever seeming to do so. Even more important, he quietly provided a model for how to live in the world. For these things, I am forever grateful.

ABBREVIATIONS

AA   *Archiv für Anthropologie*

BAL   Bundesarchiv Lichterfelde, Berlin

BAUG   *Beiträge zur Anthropologie und Urgeschichte Bayerns*

BGAEU   Archive der Berliner Gesellschaft für Anthropologie, Ethnologie, und Urgeschichte

BHSTA   Bayerische Hauptstadtsarchiv, Munich

CBDAG   *Correspondenz-Blatt der Deutschen Anthropologischen Gesellschaft*

GStA PK   Geheimes Staatsarchiv Preußischer Kulturbesitz, Berlin

HAS   Staatsarchiv der Freien und Hansestadt Hamburg

HU   Archiv der Humboldt Universität zu Berlin

LMU   Ludwig-Maximilian Universitätsarchiv München

MAGW   *Mitteilungen der Anthropologischen Gesellschaft Wien*

MfVB   Archiv des Museums für Völkerkunde, Berlin

MfVH   Archiv des Museums für Völkerkunde, Hamburg

NL Bode   Nachlass Wilhelm von Bode, Zentralarchiv, Staatliche Museen Preussischer Kulturbestiz

NL Luschan Nachlaß Felix Luschans, Handschriftenabteilung, Staatsbibliothek zu Berlin - Preußischer Kulturbesitz

PSS   Prähistorische Staatssammlung, Museum für Vor- und Frühgeschichte, München

ZfE   *Zeitschrift für Ethnologie*

ILLUSTRATIONS

In 1917, with Europe in the grip of World War I, a publishing house in Berlin released a tiny book, *Prisoners of War: A Contribution to Ethnology in Wartime*. This unusual volume contained dozens of charcoal drawings of prisoners in German POW camps by Hermann Struck. Readers found not only portraits of Russian, English, and French soldiers, but also depictions of men serving in the colonial armies of the Entente powers: Sikhs with long turbans, west Africans in military uniforms, bearded Algerians. Captions beneath each portrait detailed the subject's name, ethnic group, country of origin, and military unit. By themselves, such pictures were not particularly unusual, as similar images of prisoners of war had already appeared in the German popular press.[1] What made them unique was their purpose.

In addition to the portraits, the book included an essay, "Introduction to the Foundations of Anthropology," by Felix von Luschan (1854–1924), the gruff and opinionated professor of anthropology at the University of Berlin. In the essay, Luschan explained that he considered the drawings to have "scientific" value both to anthropologists and the wider public. He had agreed to write an introduction for the volume because, "More than ever before even the layperson is thinking of the great connections within humanity"—a topic that he claimed his discipline, anthropology, could illuminate.[2] The global nature of the war, as well as the presence of colonial troops in the armies of the enemy, had increased public interest in the peoples of the world. Luschan pointed out that POW camps in Germany contained "an almost incalculable quantity of the most different races" and that "now many human groups can be better and more comfortably studied here than in their homeland."[3] In his view, POW camps served as a kind of laboratory for the study of the cultural and physical variations of humanity. Luschan's introduction to the volume not only framed Struck's drawings as scientific documents that might reveal clues to the mysteries of race, but also implicitly positioned his discipline as illuminating the dynamics of a world at war.

Anthropology was still in its youth as an established area of study when the war broke out in 1914. The discipline, which claimed to be pursuing the "science of man," began to take formal institutional shape in the late nineteenth century. In Germany it encompassed three distinct but related disciplines: ethnology, physical anthropology, and prehistoric archeology. The terminology and shape of these fields in the German-speaking context differed from similar areas of study in England and the United States. In German, the term *Anthropologie* referred not to cultural anthropology but to physical anthropology, a discipline concerned with the classification of human physical forms and the systematic study of the origin of the human species. By using the empirical methods of the natural sciences, physical anthropologists sought to discover the bodily characteristics that differentiated humans from each other. Race, as a category of physical variation, was often a central focus of their discipline. *Ethnologie*, or *Völkerkunde*, on the other hand, referred to the comparative study of the cultures and psychology of the world's peoples.[4] This field was an early forerunner of today's cultural anthropology. In this book, the term "anthropologist" refers to physical anthropologists and "ethnologist" refers to cultural anthropologists. As experts studying the peoples of the world in all their forms, both groups felt that they had a great deal to contribute to the German war effort, which was being fought against a so-called "world of peoples."

The subject of Luschan's introductory essay to *Prisoners of War* was physical anthropology, rather than ethnology. Trained in both fields, Luschan had begun to devote most of his energies to physical anthropology by 1914. He was a central figure in organizing the major anthropological project of World War I: racial studies of enemy soldiers captured by German and Austrian armies. Beginning in 1915, the chief venue for anthropological work in Germany was the prisoner-of-war camp, where teams of scientists investigated the physical makeup, languages, and cultural practices of the prisoners.[5] This project represented the largest anthropological undertaking of the war years, and young scientists lobbied hard to take part. Working closely with anthropologists in Vienna, Luschan coordinated the physical anthropologists who entered the camps to interview, measure, and photograph prisoners. Scientists traveled to camps throughout Germany and the Austrian empire, investigating enemy soldiers from Africa, Asia, and Europe. With the blessing and support of the state and military authorities, anthropologists sought to harness the "opportunity" provided by the camps and, by extension, the war itself.

Luschan's essay was an example of a larger phenomenon in the German-speaking anthropological community during World War I: the effort to link anthropological science to the war effort. The POW studies represented a perfect opportunity for anthropologists because they involved state support for anthropological work, promised wider political and social relevance for the discipline, and ensured the collection of data that would otherwise be impossible during wartime. Rather than limiting opportunities for anthropological work, as many feared, the war ironically offered more. Moreover, the POW camp appeared to be an ideal venue for the collection of data. The prisoners, held under the authority of the German and Austrian armies, were at the disposal of the scientists, available for investigation. Anthropological work thus continued during the war, but in a context unique in the history of the discipline. In the end, physical anthropology could not escape the influence of the war raging around it.

This book is an intellectual and cultural history of anthropology during wartime. It contends that World War I played a crucial role in the transformation of German anthropology from the decidedly liberal discipline of the late nineteenth century into the racist and nationalistic race science of the 1920s. In the first decade of the twentieth century, a self-consciously liberal tradition had persisted in German anthropological circles based on the rejection of racial hierarchies and the repudiation of Germanic racial theories. In the early 1920s, however, this tradition was rapidly replaced by *Rassenkunde*, or racial science, an overtly racist brand of anthropology that embraced racial inequality and *völkisch* racial thought as foundational principles. How and why did German anthropology alter course so dramatically from the turn of the century to the early Weimar period? This study locates crucial elements of the change in the war years and their aftermath. From 1914 to 1918, anthropologists worked in a series of new contexts—ideological, political, and practical—in which the definitions and precepts of the liberal tradition quickly became unfashionable. Exploring the practice and discourse of anthropology during World War I thus sheds light on the trajectories of physical anthropology as a discipline, and on the larger history of race and racial thought in Germany.

Histories of German and European racism often include anthropology as part of a larger narrative tracing the origins of racial and biological concepts to their culmination in National Socialism, but until recently very few have undertaken a thorough investigation of trends within the discipline itself. In intellectual histories of the ideas leading "towards the Final Solution," the complexity of anthropological institutions, practice, and theory is often overlooked in favor of a grand narrative.[6] As recently as the 1990s, historians drew straight lines from the anthropological discourse of the nineteenth century to the Nazi period. Michael Burleigh and Wolfgang Wippermann, for example, cite the "racial-anthropological theories" of the nineteenth century as the beginning of Germany's "special path" in the development and diffusion of racial thought that led to the "racial state" created by the Nazis.[7] By their very nature, these teleological narratives often tend to obscure the diversity of anthropological thought in the nineteenth century by failing to investigate the discipline itself and ignoring the trends that did not culminate in Nazism. And yet the shadow of National Socialism certainly cannot be ignored in the larger history of German anthropology, since many German anthropologists participated enthusiastically in the racial policies of the Nazi regime during the 1930s and 1940s.[8] The first effort to write the history of German-speaking anthropology, in fact, was compromised by its author, Wilhelm Mühlmann, who was heavily implicated in Nazism himself.[9]

Several historiographical trends have combined to alter teleological narratives of German racism. First, Geoff Eley and David Blackbourne's revision of the famous Sonderweg (or special path) thesis in the early 1980s prompted historians to question teleological narratives in German history that led neatly from the nineteenth century to the Nazi seizure of power in 1933. Although they differed in many respects, proponents of the Sonderweg approach looked to events before 1900 to explain the conditions that prevented the development of a viable liberal democracy in Germany along the lines of France or Great Britain. The most influential variant of this idea was a social/structural explanation that located the roots of German exceptionalism in the lack of a liberal, bourgeois revolution and the continued hegemony of preindustrial, agrarian elites in an era of rapid modernization.[10] Eley and Blackbourne, however, questioned the use of Britain and France as the norm for Western political development and argued that the diverse German middle classes, rather than functioning as weak-willed imitators of reactionary elites, dominated German cultural, social, and economic life. Perhaps most important, they maintained that the late nineteenth century should not be "reduced to the anteroom of Nazism," a stance that prompted historians to take new approaches to the history of the Kaiserreich.[11] Second, historians of biological and racial thought in other national contexts became more willing to investigate strands of eugenic and biological thinking that did not end in 1945. Studies of eugenics in France and Britain, for example, explored forms of racial and biomedical thinking that were incorporated into the reasoning of the welfare state.[12] These studies demonstrated the multiple directions that racial and biomedical thought took in the twentieth century. Finally, the 1980s and 1990s saw a general rise of interest in the history of anthropology among both anthropologists and historians.[13] At first, scholars largely ignored German-speaking anthropology, concentrating instead on the history of Anglo-American anthropology, which held a dominant position in the discipline after World War II.

In recent years, however, the history of the German-language anthropological tradition has come into its own. An initial wave of works assessed the involvement of the German tradition in Nazism and colonialism.[14] A number of American scholars, led by George Stocking, also found their way to German anthropology as they explored the intellectual influences on the American anthropologist Franz Boas, who was educated in Berlin in the 1880s.[15] By the late 1990s, scholars from a variety of national backgrounds and disciplinary perspectives had begun to explore the history of German-speaking anthropology in the late nineteenth century on its own terms, without continual reference to the Anglo-American tradition or an explicit focus on Nazism. Such studies have motivated historians and anthropologists alike to place the history of the discipline within the larger political, ideological, and imperial contexts of German-speaking countries. The result has been a more complex picture of the development of German-speaking anthropology in the late nineteenth and early twentieth centuries.

One of the central issues in this scholarship is whether or not the discipline changed fundamentally between the late nineteenth and early twentieth century, and, if so, what caused such a transformation. Some scholars see clear lines of continuity connecting the anthropology of the *Kaiserreich* to the racial science of the 1920s and 1930s. Andrew Zimmerman maintains, for example, that the anthropology of imperial Germany emerged as a deliberate rebuke to humanist and historicist understandings of the world. In their place, anthropologists offered an empirical and non-narrative approach to humankind that, through its association with imperialism, forged an "anti-humanist worldview" in the study and representation of non-Europeans and laid the foundations for the anthropology of the Nazi period.[16] Focusing on the development of biological anthropology, Uwe Hoßfeld presents Weimar-era *Rassenkunde* as the continuation of trends that originated with Ernst Haeckel and other Darwinists in the late nineteenth century.[17]

Other scholars, including Robert Proctor, Woodruff Smith, Benoi Massin, Glenn Penny, and Matti Bunzl, have posited a fundamental shift between the anthropology of the two periods.[18] Many of these accounts highlight the dominance and subsequent decline of a liberal, anti-racist, humanitarian anthropology under the leadership of the renowned pathologist Rudolf Virchow (1821–1902) and his colleagues, especially the Munich anthropologist Johannes Ranke (1836–1916), the ethnologist Adolf Bastian (1826–1905), and the Swiss anatomist Julius Kollmann (1834–1918). In the late nineteenth century, these men maintained that no one race or people was superior to any other. They opposed anti-Semitism, rejected Germanic racial theories, and forcefully argued for the unity of the human species. By the twentieth century, however, this strain of liberal anthropology faded as a younger generation of scholars led by Eugen Fischer (1874–1967) readily accepted biological determinism and *völkisch* racism. By the 1920s, *Rassenkunde* replaced traditional physical anthropology with a brand of science that sought to link physical characteristics to mental and cultural faculty.[19]

Increasingly convinced that such a shift occurred, historians and anthropologists alike have been at great pains to provide convincing explanations as to how and why it took place.[20] Benoit Massin, whose groundbreaking work was crucial in identifying the contours of the transformation, looks mainly to events within the anthropological community to account for the change.[21] He pins his explanation primarily on the death of Virchow, arguing that the great scientist's passing in 1902 left a vacuum within the discipline that was quickly filled by virulent Darwinism and Germanic racial theories. In Massin's formulation, Nordic racial biology became the norm within anthropology as early as 1910, a mere eight years after Virchow's death. Yet this view not only overlooks the continued presence of liberal ideas in German anthropology, upheld during this period by scientists like Ranke, Luschan, and Rudolf Martin (1864–1925), but also often fails to take extra-disciplinary factors and outside events into account. In a similar vein, Robert Proctor sees the advance of racial hygiene and genetics as central to the transformation of the discipline.[22] Woodruff D. Smith, for his part, ties his explanation of the change to a teleological variant of the *Sonderweg* thesis, arguing that the erosion of "neo-liberal" anthropology was related to the wider decline in the salience of German liberalism in the 1880s and 1890s.[23] Glenn Penny argues that the shift in German ethnology was related to a rejection of the inductive method in the conceptualization of ethnographic museums.[24] Important works on both sides of the debate, however, often fail to link the history of the discipline in the late nineteenth century with developments in the field after 1914. Studies of German-speaking anthropology often end with the outbreak of World War I or begin with the Nazi period, ignoring the period in between. Moreover, despite the excellent work that has been done, the question about the causes of the discipline's shift in trajectory remains open. As Glenn Penny and Matti Bunzl have remarked, "we continue to know very little about what clearly was the contested road from liberal to Nazi anthropology."[25]

This study, then, examines the effects of the war on a discipline already in transition. When the war broke out in 1914, the future direction of anthropology was unclear. With the rediscovery of Gregor Mendel's studies of inheritance at the turn of the century, a move toward genetic approaches had begun within the discipline. Moreover, radically racist and *völkisch* approaches had made inroads into the discipline by the early twentieth century. Several prominent anthropologists, such as Gustav Schwalbe (1844–1916), publicly embraced the racial ideas of Arthur de Gobineau and other racial theorists in the first decade of the new century. In addition, many anthropologists increasingly looked to eugenics as an attractive way for the discipline to prove its worth to the state.

Despite these trends, elements of the older liberal paradigm also persisted within the discipline in the years leading up to World War I. Liberal anthropologists continued to maintain, for example, that the categories of race, nation, and *Volk* (translated roughly as "people" or ethnic group) were unrelated. Since Virchow's heyday, anthropologists in the liberal tradition had maintained that races were nothing more than physical variations, categories that were unrelated to culture or psychological makeup. This principle allowed anthropologists like Virchow, and later Felix von Luschan, Johannes Ranke, and Rudolf Martin, to argue that there was no connection between race and human faculty or mental ability. By the same token, this same conviction allowed anthropologists to argue against the construction of racial hierarchies. Since races were only morphological or physical variations, unrelated to cultural or mental ability, no one race could be considered superior to any other. Furthermore, by emphasizing the distinction between race, nation, and *Volk*, anthropologists were also able to maintain that European peoples were interrelated and racially indistinct. They drew on liberal notions of universalism and equality to argue for the unity of the human species, as well as for the inherently international nature of their science. These ideas, in particular the division of race, nation, and *Volk*, which was at the heart of Virchow's liberal anthropological project, still formed the foundation of the discipline in the years leading up to World War I, despite the encroachment of *völkisch* racial thought and eugenics.

It was during World War I that many anthropologists, particularly younger ones, fully abandoned the remaining elements of the liberal tradition.

The shift occurred as members of the discipline gradually accommodated their scientific goals and methods to the political and ideological contexts in which they worked. This process began around the turn of the century as anthropologists increasingly linked their science to the imperial exploits of the German state, but it came to full fruition during the war, when members of the discipline sought to transform their field into a tool that would serve the war effort. Virchow and the leading liberal anthropologists of the previous century had always maintained that anthropology was an empirical science that should remain detached from the day-to-day turmoil of politics, but in the context of an all-encompassing total war, this stance became highly unfashionable. During World War I, anthropologists made a series of changes in focus—sometimes without a full understanding of their consequences—to match their science to ideological fashion and the prevailing political climate. For example, members of the discipline undertook the study of Germany's European enemies, portraying them as racial "others" and directly assigning racial identities to nations and peoples. In the process, the distinctions between race, nation, and *Volk* that were central to the liberal tradition began to crumble. The practice of political accommodation encouraged a series of small moves and adjustments that eventually led to the creation of a racist, ideologically driven pseudoscience in the service of the state.

Analyzing how this change occurred illuminates the often dangerous relationship between politics and science. Historians of science have been concerned with the interaction between science and ideology since the early years of the cold war, when the history of science as an academic discipline expanded dramatically.[26] As Carola Sachse and Mark Walker have pointed out, however, much of the traditional work exploring the relationship between science and politics not only assumed that science was nonideological, but also that it became politicized only under pressure from the state.[27] Recently this has begun to change. Following Mitchell Ash, recent studies understand science and politics acting as resources for each other, with scientists situated not simply as passive agents or victims of the state, but as "self-confident actors."[28] This is particularly true for the history of science and war, which scholars now see as fundamentally intertwined and "mutually dependent activities, rather than opposing narratives."[29] Recent studies of Germany's Kaiser Wilhelm Gesellschaft during World War II, for example, portray the relationship between the state and scientific institutions as a two-way street: while the state mobilized scientific institutions for war, scientists also sought to use the culture of war to achieve their own professional goals.[30]

The story of German anthropology during World War I reveals that the political instrumentalization of a discipline can occur with minimal pressure from the state. The German government had only a passing interest in physical anthropology and certainly did not set out to mobilize it for war. Instead, the drive toward a politicized and nationalist anthropology came entirely from the scientists themselves. Anthropologists adjusted their science to be more relevant to the political world around them, and in the process they compromised the independence of their fields. Many of these adjustments were made out of disciplinary or personal self-interest, but others were less deliberate, growing instead out of the wartime context in which scientists lived and worked. Some anthropologists saw professional opportunities in the war while others, affected by what was happening around them, simply began to approach their work through a wartime lens, distorted by nationalism and wartime environments. Either way, the responsibility for the change in their discipline was entirely their own. The history of German anthropology during World War I demonstrates that change within a scientific discipline can occur through a series of political adjustments both large and small, many with unforeseen results, that add up to a major shift in direction.

A number of larger forces and motivations drove this shift. Professional and institutional dynamics, in particular, played a central role. Physical anthropologists were anxious to attract the attention and support of the state by 1914. Since the early 1870s, the institutional locus for anthropology in Germany had been the local anthropological society, where scientists, doctors, and enthusiasts pursued the science, usually as a sidelight to other professional interests. All three anthropological subfields were represented in the societies, but physical anthropology dominated in the initial decades after their founding. Local societies were an effective vehicle for getting the anthropological disciplines off the ground, but their membership consisted mainly of amateurs who saw the science as a hobby. Professionally-minded anthropologists wanted the legitimacy and support associated with the university system. In 1908, the biologist Emanuel Radl expressed the common perception among German academics: "He who says 'German science' means the universities."[31] Aside from a few successes, including the establishment of a chair in anthropology at the University of Munich in 1886, recognition for anthropology within the German university system was slow in coming. By the turn of the century, anthropologists began to feel that their discipline had still not found secure institutional foundations within the larger landscape of German academic life. Ethnology, by contrast, had carved out a stable institutional base in German ethnographic museums by 1900 and enjoyed ample flows of state funding. The processes of specialization and professionalization, which widened the distinctions and distance between physical anthropology and ethnology, worsened the feeling of institutional insecurity among the anthropologists. The war provided a way out of this quandary: the aggressive pursuit of political relevance and government support by bending the content and focus of the discipline to meet the concerns of the state and nation during a time of crisis.

Another critical driving force in the shift was nationalist ideology. Before the war, national chauvinism was on the rise within anthropological circles as scientists increasingly backed Germany's project of empire-building overseas, but it came to define the discipline during World War I. Compared with Britain, France, and Russia, Germany was still a young nation at the outbreak of the war, and the tone of its nationalist rhetoric—at turns aggressive and insecure—mirrored its "latecomer" status. Like those in other academic fields, anthropologists were susceptible to the patriotic enthusiasm that swept German intellectual life in 1914. Within the academy, professors and academics portrayed the war as a titanic struggle between the community-driven principles of German *Kultur* and the corrupt values of its enemies: the soulless materialism and rationalism of the West on the one hand and the Asiatic barbarism of the Russians on the other.[32] Anthropologists took part in this campaign, publicly condemning Germany's enemies, signing nationalist manifestos defending Germany's actions in Belgium, and proclaiming their support for German militarism. The tide of aggressive nationalism in anthropology buried the long tradition of internationalism within the field, cutting German anthropologists off from contacts abroad and leaving the discipline isolated during and after the war. Driven by a combination of nationalist conviction and a desire to insulate themselves from charges of disloyalty, German anthropologists crafted a political approach to their science, incorporating nationalist aims and concerns into their definition and pursuit of anthropological projects. This meant using the tools of their discipline—particularly concepts of race—to understand the war and its participant nations, a task that members of the discipline were eager to undertake. It was not simply that anthropologists became more nationalistic during the war, but that they took the further step of fashioning their science into an instrument to serve nationalist ends.

This development was aided by a third factor, the gradual process of socialization to wartime environments. Members of the discipline, in particular a younger group of anthropologists in the process of building their careers, found themselves pursuing their science in new, highly politicized settings. The jingoistic atmosphere of the German academy during wartime was certainly one of these, but even more important were new environments on the ground in which members of the discipline conducted anthropological work. These included the POW camp, where the lion's share of wartime anthropological investigation took place. The setting of the POW studies influenced those who participated, altering not only their understanding of their discipline's objectives but also their view of the subjects they were studying. The prisoners under investigation were controlled by military authorities and set off from their captors, a dynamic that served to enforce a dichotomy between Germans and everyone else. In this environment, the initial impulse to study colonial soldiers from Africa and Asia was supplemented by a desire to investigate European prisoners, who became anthropologically interesting precisely because they were the national enemies of the Central Powers. The unequal power relationships and the distancing between scientists and subjects in the camps combined with the anthropologists' growing nationalist convictions to lead toward the racialization of the European enemy and away from the liberal tradition.

Finally, generational factors also drove the wartime changes within the discipline. Age often influenced how individual anthropologists engaged the liberal tradition and understood the role of their science during wartime. Recent studies in the history of science have employed generational analyses to shed light on the intellectual dynamics within developing disciplines. In particular, Lynn Nyhart has convincingly used the generational theory of the sociologist Karl Mannheim to explain developments within biology over the course of the nineteenth century in Germany.[33] In her study of animal morphology she identifies six age cohorts, or professional generations, separated by fifteen- to twenty-year intervals and made up of individuals whose approach to their science was shaped by a common set of experiences, intellectual challenges, and institutional dynamics in early adulthood, particularly during their early professional years. Unlike in Mannheim's work, the generational groups in Nyhart's study are small, usually from six to twelve men, because the professoriate in each field remained a limited and circumscribed community with only a few members. Consequently, however, the influence of each professional cohort, in place for thirty years or more, was great. Nyhart convincingly charts the "flesh-and-blood dynamics of change" within biology by showing the ways in which events or ideas had alternate meanings to scientists in different age groups because of their different career stages and the different historical periods they had experienced.[34] She further points out, following Mannheim, that the intellectual frames of reference for many scientists were set early in their professional lives and tended to shape their approach to later events and ideas.

A similar dynamic can be seen in the history of physical anthropology in the late nineteenth and early twentieth century. A generational analysis reveals three distinct age cohorts, each shaped by different intellectual and institutional dynamics. The founding generation of anthropologists, led by Rudolf Virchow, Adolf Bastian, Johannes Ranke, and Julius Kollmann, created anthropological societies in the early 1870s and established a liberal brand of the science. For these men, born in the 1820s and 1830s, the political struggles between liberals and conservatives in the 1860s and the creation of the German empire in 1871 were formative experiences. Members of a second generation, born in the 1850s and 1860s and represented by Felix von Luschan, Georg Thilenius (1868–1937), Hermann Klaatsch (1863–1916), and Rudolf Martin, entered professorships and positions of institutional influence around the turn of the century. These men held university degrees in the anthropological sciences and professionalized in the atmosphere of aggressive nationalism that characterized public life during the Wilhelmine period (1890–1918). They generally supported the German imperial mission as a matter of course, unlike Virchow and his cohort, who remained ambivalent about Germany's imperial goals. They retained liberal principles in anthropology, but also proved more open to Darwinian ideas and nationalist directions in the pursuit of their science.

A third generational cluster in German-speaking anthropology, men born in the late 1870s to the early 1890s, gained positions of power in the 1920s, in the aftermath of the war. This group included Eugen Fischer, Otto Reche (1879–1966), Walter Scheidt (1895–1976), Egon von Eickstedt (1892–1965), Bernhard Struck (1888–1971), Theodor Mollison (1874–1952), Joseph Weninger (1886–1959), and Otto Schlaginhaufen (1879–1973). These men, whom Andre Gingrich has evocatively dubbed "hungry young hyenas," gained their professional experience in the hypernationalist contexts of empire and war.[35] Fischer, Schlaginhaufen, and Reche, for example, launched their professional careers by taking part in colonial expeditions. Eugen Fischer, one of the oldest members of this cohort, made his name professionally with a study of the offspring of European settlers and indigenous peoples in German Southwest Africa (today Namibia). Several of these younger anthropologists, particularly Fischer and Reche, began to move toward an illiberal brand of anthropology in the years leading up to 1914. Involvement in World War I, however, was perhaps the central experience for members of this generation. Nearly all—save Fischer and

Schlaginhaufen—served in the military during World War I. More importantly, the central participants in the POW studies came from this group,
and several of them, including Eickstedt, Weninger, and Reche, used the
data they collected as the foundation for their later careers. Shaped by experiences of colonial superiority and nationalist conflict, these men had
little patience for the pluralistic and cautious brand of anthropology championed by the fading members of the founding liberal generation and
their successors. During and after the war, they increasingly turned toward
an illiberal and racist science that could be used to legitimate nationalist
goals.

The rise of *Rassenkunde* or "racial science" as the new disciplinary paradigm in the 1920s thus reflected the ideological and conceptual shifts of
the war years. At its heart, *Rassenkunde* was based on the exploration of the
supposed connections between race, *Volk*, and nation, the very categories that
had remained distinct in the liberal tradition. Adherents of *Rassenkunde* also
focused intensely on the racial makeup of Europeans, particularly Germans,
as a result of the war experience. Fischer, Reche, and others unabashedly
accepted *völkisch* racial thought as a foundation of their new science, drawing
inspiration from writers like Arthur de Gobineau and Gustav de Lapouge,
the very figures whom Vichow and his generation had rejected. A highly
racialized version of eugenics also became the norm within German anthropological circles as anthropologists sought to connect their racial science to
social problems. These new conceptual directions were not solely the product
of changes within the discipline, such as the embrace of genetics or the
increased influence of Darwinism. Instead, these trends combined with the
ideological and conceptual shifts of the war years to create an atmosphere in
the postwar period that facilitated the abandonment of the categories and
concepts at the heart of the liberal tradition.

The impact of the war on other national anthropological traditions, however, was markedly different than in Germany and Austria. The elements of
the wartime pattern in German-speaking anthropology—lunging to exploit
the scientific "opportunity" of the POW camps, applying colonial and racial
discourses to the nation's enemies and allies, mobilizing the discipline as a
political tool in the war effort—were less common in other major traditions.
An examination of the activities and trends among anthropologists in the
other belligerent nations during World War I reveals the particular circumstances operating in the German case. In the other Western countries, where
anthropologists were enmeshed in different political, intellectual, and institutional contexts, the engagement with wartime themes was generally less
intense and the influence of the conflict on disciplinary development less

pronounced. In fact, rather than creating ruptures or breaks, the war years generally fostered continuity within the anthropological traditions of other nations.

This was true in the case of Great Britain, where the war had a minimal impact on the direction of the discipline. British anthropologists generally shied away from intense political engagement with the war, published very little with direct relevance to the conflict, and refrained from discussing the war in racial terms.[36] If anything, the war accelerated prewar trends in British anthropology. The outbreak of hostilities and his status as an alien citizen forced Bronislaw Malinowski to undertake his groundbreaking study of natives on the Tobriand islands rather than face internment by authorities in Australia, but this turn toward ethnographic fieldwork had prewar imperial antecedents in the British tradition, particular in the Torres Straits expedition of 1898 and the expedition in central Australia by Baldwin Spencer and F. J. Gillen in the late nineteenth century.[37] Wartime activities in physical anthropology also continued prewar trends. During the war, a panel of prominent British anthropologists recommended that military recruits be examined by medical boards, but their findings emphasized prewar conclusions: environmental, rather than racial, factors primarily determined the physical health of soldiers. Several British anthropologists conducted studies of German POWs during the war, but they did not characterize Germans as belonging to a particular race and even questioned the accuracy of their own data from the camps.[38] This is not to say that the British anthropological community was entirely free of wartime politicization. As we shall see in a later chapter, the prominent British anthropologist Arthur Keith created an international stir when he painted a racial portrait of Britain's enemies in a presidential address before the Royal Anthropological Institute, but this perspective was unusual within British anthropological circles. In Britain, the extreme nationalist tenor of wartime anthropology in Germany was absent, and institutional arrangements pushed the discipline in different directions. British physical anthropology was more directly tied to the study of evolution, a connection that encouraged its integration into the natural and life sciences after the war.[39]

In France, where the boundaries of anthropology and ethnology as disciplines were notoriously unclear, the war had little impact on their direction. Before 1914, the French anthropological tradition included several competing intellectual strands. The most dominant was Emile Durkheim's sociological approach, which was averse to the collection of ethnographic data and even the use of the term "anthropology" itself. The preponderance of theorists in the Durkheimian mold meant that the developing ethnographic strain in French anthropology remained underappreciated, but the seeds of a fieldwork tradition had begun to sprout. France also possessed a storied tradition in physical anthropology associated with Paul Broca, a pioneer in craniology and the founder of the major French anthropological society, the Société d'Anthropologie, in the mid-nineteenth century. Physical anthropology in France, however, was increasingly in crisis by 1900 because of methodological confusion over the concept of race. Major changes in the French anthropological tradition—particularly a move toward ethnographic fieldwork and a step away from racialist physical anthropology—began before the war, around the turn of the century, as the Société d'Anthropologie sought to reorient its research program away from race and toward Durkheimian social science.[40] The main effect of the war on French anthropology was to cause the death of many young sociologists and anthropologists at the front. After the war, Durkheim's nephew and chief follower, Marcel Maus, succeeded in training a new generation of anthropologists and sociologists in order to keep the Durkheimian approach alive.[41] There has been little research on the activities of French physical anthropologists during World War I, but it appears that the engagement with wartime themes in their science was minimal.[42]

The dynamic of continuity was similar in the two other major nations aligned against the Central Powers. The influence of the war on anthropology in the United States, which entered the conflict only in 1917, appears to have been negligible, although more research is needed on this question. Franz Boas had already begun to adapt the liberal ideals of his German mentors, especially Virchow and Bastian, to the American context by establishing a "four field" approach in anthropology that emphasized anti-racism and equality.[43] Boas opposed America's entry into the war, and this stance rankled many of his colleagues, who charged that his pro-German sympathies, rather than his staunch pacifism, explained his position. In 1919, the American Anthropological Association censured Boas after he accused several unnamed American anthropologists of spying for the United States in Central America during the war. George Stocking reads this incident as motivated not only by outraged patriotism but also by a backlash against the growing dominance of Boasian cultural anthropology by scientists who favored a more traditional, biological approach.[44] Despite this setback, however, Boas's influence in anthropological circles grew in the immediate postwar era.[45] Boasian anthropology may have received a boost from Wilson's ideals of self-determination and emphasis on cultural diversity, but the war itself apparently did little to alter the trajectory of American anthropology.

In Russia a great deal of anthropological work took place within the imperial army, and the war did not change this tradition.[46] Before and after 1914, graduates of the St. Petersburg Military-Medical Academy produced dissertations in physical anthropology with the support of the Russian War Ministry. These studies of army recruits served imperial purposes by addressing questions of nationality and documenting the ethnic diversity of the military as a model for an integrated empire. The outbreak of the war did not signal a moment of change for this brand of military anthropology, and anthropologists within the imperial army did not apply colonial discourses to Russia's enemies during the war. Rather, the turning point came with the Russian Civil War and early Soviet state-building, which marked a turn toward ethnography on the one hand and eugenicist projects on the other, as anthropologists conformed to the political realities of the new state.[47]

In comparison with these other national anthropological traditions, the involvement with the war in German-speaking anthropology was more intense, and the effect of the conflict on the discipline more significant. The specific institutional and ideological conditions within German anthropology explain these differences, but so too do the larger contexts of the wartime experience in Germany and Austria-Hungary. The hostile and defensive nationalism that encouraged involvement in wartime themes reflected the insecurities of a young German nation coming late to the race for influence among the Great Powers. (The intense engagement with the war among Austrian anthropologists, meanwhile, hinted at fears that their empire was falling behind in that competition.)[48] In addition, the effects of the geographical and intellectual isolation of German anthropologists during the war cannot be underestimated. With the British blockade in place and battlefronts surrounding the Central Powers, contact with other countries was difficult and foreign travel nearly impossible. Anthropologists reacted with a "turn inward," a move toward the POW camps as a site for scientific work. Finally, unlike in the Allied countries, the war ended in defeat for Germany and Austria-Hungary, a wrenching experience that highlighted the discipline's dislocation, isolation, and uncertainty in the aftermath of the conflict.

This book examines anthropologists and the impact of the war primarily within three institutional contexts: the anthropological society, the university, and the ethnographic museum. These were the sites in which much of the intellectual work of anthropology was conducted by both amateurs and professionals in the field. Anthropologists shared these institutions with ethnologists and representatives of other fields, often feeling that as a result they did not have a secure institutional home of their own in any of them. By expanding the study of anthropologists beyond the limits of anthropological society, this book seeks to gain a fuller picture of the place of the discipline within the larger world of German science and the larger context of the wartime experience. Second, the study examines the place and activities of anthropologists primarily in three cities: Berlin, Munich, and Hamburg. All three were major centers of anthropology, but the scientific work in each city took place in a different political and regional context. Anthropologists in the capital city of Berlin worked under the aegis of the Prussian authorities. The cases of Munich and Hamburg, meanwhile, provide examples of anthropological institutions in non-Prussian contexts, one operating under a state government and the other under a city administration. Despite the differences of setting and administrative structure in each case, this study shows the remarkable similarities of the wartime experience of the anthropologists in each city. Finally, close wartime cooperation between anthropologists in Germany and Austria-Hungary also necessitates the inclusion of the Viennese Anthropological Society and other Austrian institutions at key points in the narrative.

This study also takes great care not to reify the category of race, even while it demonstrates the constructed nature of race in the wartime context. Douglas Lorimer and others have pointed out the dangers in treating race as an absolute when writing about the history of racism and racial thinking.[49] Even as they deconstruct varieties of racism, historians must be careful not to accept race as a given, but rather must treat the category as a highly problematic and ambiguous concept whose meanings have changed over time. Thus, I refer to "race" throughout this study not as a concept with a basis in biological reality, but as a social and ideological construct shaped by the historical circumstances in which it is used. Following the lead of Nancy Stepan and others, this study seeks to understand the ways in which scientists of the period understood the term in the wider context of their era.[50] In the process, we can gain a fuller understanding of the process by which race is, in Shearer West's words, "socially created and thus historically variable," particularly in the context of wartime.[51]

The chapters of this book chart the arc of the change within the discipline from the turn of the century to the late 1920s. The first chapter explores the development of anthropological institutions in the late nineteenth century and their place within the wider world of Germany after 1900. During this period, physical anthropologists experienced difficulty establishing firm anchors in the German university system, which had little use for their science, or in ethnographic museums, where ethnology already dominated.

The dual processes of specialization and professionalization also served to highlight the dilemmas of anthropologists, so that on the eve of the war, members of the discipline were extremely eager to attract the notice and support of the state. Chapter 2 examines the pre-war ideological context in German anthropological circles. Despite the encroachment of *völkisch* and racist strains of thought around the turn of the century, the liberal precepts of Virchow and his followers continued to inform anthropological work in the laboratory, the field, and the lecture hall. Even as the liberal tradition slipped from its previous position as the dominant paradigm, it persisted within the discipline, often existing alongside competing and often contradictory modes of anthropological thought.

Chapter 3 begins the examination of the practice and discourse of anthropology during the war years, exploring the influence of the conflict on the day-to-day work of anthropologists. With normal avenues for anthropological work cut off, many anthropologists turned the focus of their science toward the conflict itself in an attempt to support the war effort and gain the recognition of the state. As a result, anthropologists fully mobilized their discipline for war, throwing their support behind the German government, signing patriotic decrees, and condemning the enemies of the Central Powers. Anthropologists gave lectures on the anthropological makeup of the enemy, undertook investigations of wartime nutrition in German schoolchildren, and commented on the Allied use of colonial troops. All the while, the shortages and limitations caused by the war affected the institutions in which they did their work. The new wartime context encouraged members of the discipline to practice an increasingly nationalistic anthropology and facilitated the erosion of the distinctions and precepts at the heart of the liberal tradition.

Chapter 4 investigates the major anthropological project of the war years: the study of foreign soldiers in German POW camps. The particular setting of the POW camp combined with the increasingly nationalist directions of the scientists working there to facilitate the racialization of the enemy, particularly the European foes of the Central Powers. As anthropologists in the camps implicitly carved out a specialized racial space for Germans in central Europe, they also blurred the distinctions between the liberal categories of race, nation, and *Volk*. Chapter 5 uses the methods of cultural history to analyze the photography of POWs as a further means of examining how anthropologists constructed the racial and colonial "other" in the context of war. In the camps, anthropologists went to great lengths to capture (and thus define) the racial makeup of the prisoners through the camera lens. In the process, they produced a series of propagandized images that not only racialized the enemy, but also emphasized the supposed power and cohesion of the Central Powers and Germany.

The final chapter examines anthropology in the aftermath of the conflict. The impact of the war continued to be felt long after 1918, not only through the hardships of difficult daily working conditions and financial strain, but also in the larger ideological directions of the discipline itself. The process of transforming anthropology into *Rassenkunde* or "racial science" was carried out primarily by a younger group of anthropologists, many of whom had professionalized at the very moment of World War I. Seeking to refashion their discipline, these men rejected the earlier morphological and liberal tradition of Virchow's generation as "the science out of which nothing is allowed to come."[52] Instead, they took inspiration from genetic approaches as well as *völkisch* racial theorists. Most important, they sought to explore the connections between race, nation, and *Volk*, the very categories that liberal anthropologists had argued were distinct and unrelated. With the rise of *Rassenkunde*, the liberal tradition in German anthropology faded from the scene, replaced by a form of racial science that paralleled the racial ideologies of the National Socialists in the 1930s.

By combining the study of anthropological discourse with the highly politicized practical contexts in which wartime science was pursued, this study reveals new perspectives on the history of anthropology as a discipline and the course of racial science in Germany. On the one hand, it demonstrates that the development of German anthropology did not proceed in a straight line to the Nazi racial science of the 1930s, but rather encompassed a variety of strands of anthropological thought that changed over time. On the other hand, it also proposes new answers as to why German anthropology quickly changed from a liberal version of the science around 1900 to the racial science of the 1920s. The final abandonment of liberal precepts by anthropologists was facilitated by a series of changing circumstances inside and outside the discipline, both environmental and ideological, created by the war itself. Changes in the direction of anthropology were thus at least partially contingent on the wider context in which anthropologists did their work. The history of the First World War should be incorporated into the larger story of German anthropology's turn toward the racist and *völkisch* science of the 1920s.

ONE

Institutionalizing the "Most Recent Science": Anthropology in the World of German Learning at the Fin de Siècle

In the fall of 1916, the Munich anthropologist Ferdinand Birkner sent a copy of his most recent anthropological work to a high-ranking Bavarian minister, as was the custom of the day. The book, entitled *The Races and Peoples of Humanity*, was a massive tome that he had worked on for many years and finally published in 1913. Despite its daunting size and heft, the volume was primarily designed to introduce the layperson to anthropological questions and to awaken a general interest in the discipline.[1] With the book, Birkner included a short note that read, "In order to show your Excellence that somatic anthropology has full justification alongside the older disciplines in the natural sciences, please allow me to present my work . . . . Your Excellence will see from it which problems fall in the area of anthropology."[2] The minister responded, perhaps disingenuously, that he would greatly enjoy the "fine hours" of reading over the work and absorbing its explication of "old and new research in the field of anthropology."[3]

In the life of the Bavarian bureaucracy, this exchange was wholly unremarkable, except perhaps for Birkner's tone. For the anthropologist, the presentation of the volume was an opening to affirm the worth of his discipline. In what would normally have been a trivial and unimportant message, Birkner felt it necessary to defend anthropology's right to take its place alongside the traditional disciplines in the natural sciences, such as physics, biology, and medicine. These were the fields that received a great deal of public attention and state support, and he sought to include anthropology among their ranks. Moreover, he hoped—probably in vain—that the minister would truly learn which issues fell into the purview of the discipline, or, in other words, what the disciplinary boundaries of anthropology really were. The note demonstrated a desire to increase anthropology's visibility within the world of German science and to attract the attention of the government. Birkner's short message exemplifies a larger theme in the history of German anthropology in the decades before World War I: the attempts of a new science to fashion itself as an independent and respected field of study with a strong line of state support.

In 1890, the anatomist and anthropologist Wilhelm Waldeyer (1836–1921) described anthropology as "one of the most recent sciences."[4] The discipline remained a relative newcomer in the world of German learning at the turn of the century. Anthropologists were still working not only to define their field, but also to gain its acceptance as a legitimate scholarly pursuit. In previous decades they had achieved only limited success in creating firm institutional anchors supported by the state. Leading figures in the discipline had managed to create anthropological societies and found ethnographic museums, but efforts to position anthropology as an established field in the German university system were less successful. Moreover, the forces of professionalization and specialization, increasing in intensity around 1900, had begun to alter the shape and goals of nearly every scientific enterprise, including anthropology. Specialization increased the pace of differentiation among the three anthropological subdisciplines—physical anthropology, ethnology, and prehistory—and highlighted the growing tensions between them. Professionalization contributed to the situation by creating a cadre of scientists trained specifically in one subfield, rather than two or three.

Taken together, these factors meant that the anthropological disciplines developed along a different path than the more established sciences in the Kaiser's Germany. The traditional historiography on the rise of German science in the nineteenth century has emphasized the tight connection between the university and the state in fostering scientific innovation.[5] Anthropology, however, developed almost entirely outside of the university and without a great deal of help from the state. The effect of anthropology's outsider status was to create an even greater desire in anthropological circles for state support and the establishment of solid institutional underpinnings. This was particularly true in the field of physical anthropology. As the anthropological subfields became increasingly distinct, the disparity between their institutional circumstances became clearer. In the last two decades of the nineteenth century, ethnology developed strong, state-supported institutional bases in ethnographic museums, which quickly became the conceptual and professional center of ethnological work. Physical anthropology, once the most dominant of the three fields in local anthropological societies, fell somewhere in between the university and the museum, failing to find a secure home in either institution or to tap into a consistent line of state support. The result of these pressures was institutional uncertainty within physical anthropology, whose proponents longed to prove the worth of their science, attract the attention and resources of the government, and carve out their own institutional and intellectual domain.

Feelings of institutional insecurity and the accompanying desire for greater professional opportunities proved to be major forces for change in German anthropology. The marginal position of the discipline within the larger landscape of German science gradually drove physical anthropologists to seek greater social and political relevance. This process began around 1900, as select members of the anthropological community slowly shifted their scholarly focus toward national and imperial themes in the hopes of attracting state support and more attention from society at large. Germany's colonial project, gathering force under Wilhelm II, appeared to be the perfect opportunity for the anthropological disciplines, since it required research into the peoples and places that Germans sought to rule. Here too, however, physical anthropologists found themselves eclipsed by ethnologists, who were more successful in arguing that their discipline would be useful in the nation's colonial efforts. In an era of scientific growth, anthropologists felt underappreciated. In the years leading up to 1914, the discipline was dominated by a creeping sense of institutional anxiety that later encouraged the transformation of the field into a political and nationalist tool during World War I.

The Changing World of German Science

Scholarship, especially in the natural sciences, played a crucial role in Wilhelm II's Germany. German science was entering a new era of unprecedented development in the first decade of the twentieth century, a period characterized by increasing levels of state support and heightened prestige for scientists. Spurred by its domination of the "second industrial revolution," Germany was fast becoming the most important industrial nation in the world, demonstrating a marked superiority in new sectors such as chemistry and electricity. Advances and innovations in the German natural sciences—from physics to pathology—fueled this new dominance. Hoping to continue Germany's industrial ascendancy, both state bureaucracies and private industry sought to encourage scientific research. In the 1880s, for example, dyestuff companies created their own scientific research units, designed to improve manufacturing and formulate new products.[6] Large industrial firms also began to compete for scientific talent like the German chemist and professor Fritz Haber, who developed the process of fixing nitrogen from the air in a laboratory run by the German chemical firm

BASF, which also gave him a large grant that effectively doubled his salary. Perhaps most important, government and industry alike recognized that the practical worth of scientific knowledge went well beyond the achievement of industrial or economic goals: advances in bacteriology and other medical sciences appeared to be leading the world into an age where epidemics and disease would be distant memories.[7]

Thus, in the first decade of the new century, science was more than simply a cause of industrial dominance or a force for social improvement; it was also a source of national prestige. Germany was internationally known as a leader in scientific research and innovation. German universities had become increasingly famous around the globe throughout the nineteenth century, and by 1900 they were the preeminent international centers for scientific education. As innovations in German science continued, the German language increasingly became the standard tongue of international scientific discourse. The top German scientists, such as Paul Ehrlich, Robert Koch, and Rudolf Virchow, were national and even international celebrities, the "new heroes" of the modern era.[8] In the eyes of many in Europe and around the world, Germany's scientific achievements even served to counterbalance the authoritarianism and militarism of the German Empire. By 1900, natural science was closely linked in the popular mind with modernity, an association that the Second Empire encouraged by placing the achievements of German scientists at the center of its self-representations as a modern nation-state. At the 1893 and 1904 World's Fairs, the German pavilions not only highlighted the central features of the Bismarckian social insurance system, but also trumpeted the achievements of German scholarship and education.[9] In the new Germany of the twentieth century, the natural sciences enjoyed an unprecedented level of national and international prestige.

The boom in German science was also accompanied by momentous changes in the German university system. Chief among these was massive growth. The number of university students nearly tripled from 1876 to 1908.[10] The size of academic staffs also increased over the same period, usually by hiring temporary teaching faculty. University budgets expanded rapidly. While Friedrich Althoff was in charge of Prussian higher education from 1882 to 1908, the portion of the state budget allocated to Prussian universities rose from 5.6 to 12.25 million marks.[11] In 1899, the government awarded technical colleges university status, allowing them to confer doctoral degrees. New fields proliferated, especially in the sciences. Chemistry, for example, soon splintered into a host of new subfields including physical chemistry, electrochemistry, pharmaceutical chemistry, and biochemistry.[12]

These changes had their detractors. To entrenched members of the professoriate, the proliferation of new fields and the advance of specialization appeared to threaten their power and prestige.[13] Full professors, or *Ordinarien*, wielded great power within the university system because they made up the corporate body at the heart of each institution and served as the heads of institutes, where research took place. By 1900, the German professoriate adopted a defensive stance toward specialization, generally opposing the addition of new fields, especially those associated with applied sciences like engineering. They likewise resisted the extension of university status to technical colleges. Disciplines that were either already well established at the university, such as clinical medicine and experimental physics, or that didn't require extensive laboratory facilities saw a good deal of growth, but newer experimental fields often had difficulty gaining a foothold in the academy.[14] The intransigence of the universities provoked strong reactions from state officials and scientists. State governments began to take a greater role in supporting scientific research, even forcing universities to accept new areas of study in some cases.[15] Other scientists decided to create centers for scientific research outside the university with the support of industry and the imperial government. The formation of the Physikalisch-Technische Reichsanstalt (Imperial Physical and Technical Institute or PTR) in 1887 and the Kaiser Wilhelm Society for Chemistry in 1912 provided new models for scientific production outside of the academy.

Despite the resistance of traditionalists, the forces of specialization and professionalization gained momentum throughout this period. As the pressure for innovative research increased and alliances with private industry became more common, scientists in fields such as chemistry, engineering, and pathology developed narrower specialties. Once removed from the university structure, scientists were able to abandon the Humboldtian scholarly ideal of uniting teaching with research.[16] In new institutional settings like the Kaiser Wilhelm Society, they focused solely on experimentation and innovation. Moreover, as the practical knowledge in the sciences and other academic disciplines increased exponentially around the turn of the century, experts were forced to specialize in order to keep up with the expanding production of knowledge in their fields. The related phenomenon of professionalization also accelerated in the first decade of the new century. By 1900, a rigorous system of academic training and credentials was in place in all the major sciences. In order to enter a field like chemistry, for example, a student needed an advanced degree from a university, which required the completion of a *Habilitation*, an original work of research, under the mentorship of an advising professor. With a degree in hand, one could embark on an academic career or find work with a chemical firm. Professional associations in fields like chemistry and medicine also increased in strength from 1900 to 1914 by enforcing further educational requirements and unifying professional standards.[17]

At the turn of the century, conditions in the late Wilhelmine Empire appeared promising for the further development of the anthropological sciences. The natural sciences in general were experiencing an unprecedented boom, lending clout to almost all kinds of scientific endeavor. The German government sought to exploit scientific research both for industrial gain and for national prestige, and state support for science was on the rise. Professional scientists in a myriad of specialized fields were in high demand. And yet these factors benefited ethnology much more than physical anthropology. Even in an era of scientific expansion, the institutional aspirations of physical anthropologists remained largely unfulfilled. Throughout this period, anthropologists sought the approval and support of the state without a great degree of success.

The Anthropological Disciplines in the Late Nineteenth Century

As they developed in the nineteenth century, the anthropological disciplines were notoriously difficult to define, and their boundaries shifted considerably over time. Generally understood as the "science of man," anthropology encompassed a wide range of methods and had different meanings in various intellectual contexts. In early nineteenth-century philosophy and history, the word often simply implied the general study of human nature. Even as late as 1850 in Germany, anthropology could refer to nearly any empirical study of humankind.[18] Scholars employed the term in a variety of other fields of knowledge such as sociology, cultural history, and linguistics. Even for those who defined anthropology as the comparative study of culture, several nascent and competing models for its creation as a specific field of knowledge existed, many of which drew on humanistic disciplines like history and geography.[19] The discipline only began to take formal shape with the foundation of anthropological societies in the late 1860s and early 1870s. Within these organizations, anthropology as a field of inquiry was organized around three subdisciplines: physical anthropology, ethnology, and prehistory. In theory each area had a distinct purview, but in reality a great deal of overlap existed between them in the first several decades of their existence.

Physical or "somatic" anthropology was understood to be a "natural science of humankind" or a "natural history of hominids." It aimed at the systematic classification of the human species, much like zoology sought to achieve for the animal kingdom.[20] Wilhelm Waldeyer explained in 1890 that physical anthropology was the field that "takes the physical composition of the human species as [its] subject, primarily pursues the study of race, and seeks to ascertain the differences and similarities which occur in the construction of humans across the globe."[21] The goal was to discover, by using the empirical methods of the natural sciences, the physical characteristics that differentiated humans from each other. Anthropologists understood their project as identifying and cataloging the myriad forms of human variation, which they classified as "races" or physical "types." The methods varied, but usually incorporated the measurement and quantification of anatomical attributes, with particular attention to the bones and skull. By investigating the bodily characteristics of individuals, anthropologists hoped to come to conclusions about the aggregate, especially the relations between peoples and regions. Anthropologists emphasized a lineage for their field reaching back to the eighteenth-century naturalist Johann Friederich Blumenbach (1752–1840), who published his foundational work, *On the Natural Varieties of Humankind*, in 1775.[22] Blumenbach, an anatomist and professor at the University of Göttingen, pioneered the field of craniometry, the study of the human skull as a method of classifying human "races."[23]

The anthropological attention to the human body made the discipline a natural area of interest for physicians, and anthropology was often studied as a substratum of medicine.[24] The major figures in the discipline were doctors. The dominant personality in anthropology throughout the late nineteenth century was Rudolf Virchow, professor of medicine at the University of Berlin and member of the Prussian Academy of Sciences who was internationally known as the founder of cellular pathology. Widely acknowledged as the founding father of anthropology in Germany, Virchow was the primary figure in the creation of the first anthropological societies and published over one thousand pieces related to anthropology before his death in 1902.[25] Other disciplinary leaders also came from a medical and anatomical background, including Johannes Ranke, Wilhelm Waldeyer, Felix von Luschan, and Eugen Fischer, to name just a few.[26] In practice, the study of physical anthropology usually required a medical education. On the first day of his classes on physical anthropology at the University of Berlin, Luschan stressed the need for an anatomical background and medical training to succeed in his course. In order to understand physical anthropology, he said, "anatomical knowledge is absolutely indispensable."[27] The deep connection to the medical tradition supplied physical anthropology with a claim to status as an empirical natural science.

The discipline of ethnology or *Völkerkunde* took a different set of issues as its subject. The primary figure in the foundation of ethnology as a discipline in the late nineteenth century was Adolf Bastian, who dominated the field until his death in 1905, much as Virchow did for physical anthropology. He came to his interest in ethnology through travel, serving as a ship's doctor on a number of worldwide voyages in the 1850s. Bastian made his reputation with the publication of *Der Mensch in der Geschichte*, a multivolume work based on his journeys abroad.[28] His primary position, however, was as the head of the Berlin Museum für Völkerkunde from 1873 to 1905, where he articulated a vision for his discipline that held sway for nearly twenty-five years. While other ethnologists, particularly the diffusionist Friedrich Ratzel, were important to German ethnology, Bastian more than anyone else determined the direction that the discipline took in Germany during the period of its institutionalization.[29]

Under Bastian's leadership, ethnology aimed at the comparative study of the culture and psychology of the world's peoples as a alternative means of exploring human history. Rejecting the philological tradition of constructing historical narratives only from written texts, ethnologists turned to the empirical study of material culture as method of learning about the past.[30] Conceived as a natural science that addressed historical and cultural questions, ethnology rested upon the description and comparison of the world's peoples. Unlike traditional historians, Bastian and his colleagues argued that the study of *Naturvölker* or "natural peoples," groups untouched by European culture and without recorded or written history, was crucial to an understanding of humankind, since all humans possessed a common psychological foundation. Bastian's notion of the "psychic unity of mankind" underpinned ethnological arguments that all peoples possessed a common set of "elementary ideas" that then took different forms in different historical and environmental contexts.[31] By analyzing the societal forms and material culture of the world's peoples, ethnologists hoped to identify the common elements of humanity. Thus, Bastian and his colleagues maintained that the study of "natural peoples" would also shed light on the history of "cultured peoples" (*Kulturvölker*). They believed that time was against them in this pursuit, since *Naturvölker* were being eradicated by the rapid advance of European technology and civilization. They argued that they needed to "save" the remnants of those cultures by engaging in a kind of so-called "salvage anthropology," the collection of rare ethnographic artifacts before it was too late. The overall goals of ethnology necessitated broad comparisons between cultures, and cultural artifacts provided the main source of evidence from which ethnologists worked. Under the influence of Bastian, ethnology was based on rigorous empiricism and an inductive methodology, placing it in the realm of the natural sciences.

Prehistory, the third anthropological discipline, entailed the excavation and analysis of prehistoric cultural artifacts and skeletal remains. In the first half of the nineteenth century, local German historical associations, hobby-ists, and antiquarians developed archeology as a field devoted to uncovering the history of ancient Germanic tribes.[32] In the 1850s, however, dramatic finds of prehistoric bones created an explosion of both academic and ama-teur interest in prehistoric archaeology and an accompanying demand for its foundation as a distinct discipline. In 1857, the remains of the so-called Neanderthal man were dug up in a cave near the Neander valley, not far from Düsseldorf.[33] Similar finds of human bones, prehistoric tools, and remains of extinct animals occurred along the Somme River in France and in Brixham Cave in England. These discoveries challenged the biblical chronology of human origins, suggesting instead that the world was millions of years old. They also engaged the interest of anthropologists, particularly Virchow, who came to believe that prehistoric archeology should function as a critical "as-sisting science" (*Hilfwissenschaft*) to physical anthropology in the search for information about the earliest forms of humankind. In opposition to local antiquarians, Virchow set about establishing prehistory as an empirical sci-ence, insisting on high standards of objectivity in the collection and interpre-tation of evidence.[34] As it developed in the anthropological societies of the late nineteenth century, the field of prehistory thus encompassed both cul-tural and bodily remains, and the proponents employed a variety of methods drawn from archaeology, anatomy, and physical anthropology in pursuit of their goals. In 1890, Wilhelm Waldeyer described the task of the field in the most basic terms: "There, where the past recognized and guaranteed by historical documents ends, begins our task, the research of prehistory."[35] The purview of prehistory was, by definition, extremely broad.

Throughout the late nineteenth century, there was a great deal of over-lap among the three anthropological disciplines. Describing the difficulties of teaching anthropology in 1892, Virchow argued that "the fields which must be attributed to anthropology are even now by no means so sharply defined. . . . Empirically, physical (or somatic) anthropology, ethnology, and prehistory belong. These three are not conveniently separated from one another."[36] Virchow recognized, for example, that prehistory hardly existed as a distinct discipline since the boundaries between it and physical anthro-pology were almost nonexistent. He worked in both fields himself. Physical anthropologists were as much interested in prehistoric human morphologies as they were in contemporary human forms, and this interest meant that the bones and skulls dug up at prehistoric sites were as much evidence for their discipline as they were for prehistory. In his discussion of the anthropological disciplines, Virchow wrote, ". . . sooner or later every 'physical anthropologist' brings a good amount of archeology into his pronouncements."[37] As a result, nearly every physical anthropologist also de facto worked in the field of prehistory. Ethnology and prehistory also overlapped. Ethnologists, concerned primarily with material culture, took a natural interest in prehistoric cultural artifacts. Archeological finds provided another means of exploring the past beyond what could be found in historical documents. In fact, archeological discoveries in the 1850s and 1860s actually inspired ethnologists like Bastian to pursue ethnographic analyses, as famous digs attracted more attention to the study of material culture in general and ethnology in particular.[38] Prehistory was a field in which anthropologists and ethnologists of all stripes participated. The annual yearly conference of the national German Society for Anthropology, Ethnology, and Prehistory, for example, included day trips to archeological sites, where anthropologists and ethnologists alike could find something of interest.[39]

The chief division between the anthropological subdisciplines in the late nineteenth century was between physical anthropology and ethnology, but even here there was a good deal of overlap, mainly in personnel. Many physical anthropologists worked in the field of ethnology as well as their own. Luschan, for example, worked as both an ethnologist and physical anthropologist for the majority of his career and taught in both fields at the University of Berlin. Ranke also taught in both fields at the Ludwig Maximilian University in Munich. Moreover, many important ethnologists, like physical anthropologists, were physicians. Bastian, for example, was a doctor who had studied medicine under Virchow. Furthermore, although the goals of the two fields differed, both shared an approach drawn from the natural sciences. Inductive empiricism formed the methodological basis upon which both subdisciplines conducted their work. Both fields took the study of the world's peoples as their primary focus, even though one focused on culture and the other on physical morphologies.

Despite these elements of overlap in personnel and even approach, proponents of both subdisciplines often sought to distinguish one field from the other. In the very first issue of the flagship journal of the Berlin Anthropological Society, Bastian went to great lengths to differentiate the two, arguing that although ethnology was an attempt to ground cultural psychology in the methods of natural science, categories from anatomy or craniometry had no place in this effort.[40] Other anthropologists explained the distinction between the two subdisciplines as one between "physical" and "psychological" anthropology.[41] As the decades progressed, the distinctions between physical anthropology and ethnology became sharper under the influence of specialization. Nowhere was this more apparent than in the institutions where anthropology, ethnology, and prehistoric archaeology sought to find their respective homes.

Physical Anthropology and the Search for an Institutional Locus

In the late nineteenth century, the anthropological disciplines were primarily represented in three institutions within the larger academic and scientific world: anthropological societies, universities, and ethnographic museums. Of these, the societies played the most crucial role at first, because anthropology, broadly defined, received relatively little support from the state and had no clear home at the university in the initial years of its existence. For this reason the anthropological disciplines initially developed within the societies, which provided an institutional locus, scientific networks, and forums for publication. Physical anthropology was the largest and most dominant of the three fields in the initial stage of disciplinary formation, but this dominance did not last. As ethnographic museums developed in the late nineteenth century, ethnology grew in importance. Physical anthropology, by contrast, was unable to secure a stable place in either the museum or the university, leaving it anchored primarily in the societies—institutions that it shared with the other two fields, and which received less support and attention from the state. After 1900, physical anthropology found itself in a quandary: it possessed no clear institutions of its own, while its sister discipline ethnology had carved out a clear institutional space in the museums.

Anthropological Societies

The local anthropological society was the primary institution for the development of anthropology as a science in the late nineteenth century. From 1869 to 1895, some twenty-five such societies were founded across Germany.[42] This expansion reflected the wider growth of scientific associations in Germany during the nineteenth century. Enthusiasts founded dozens of local associations dedicated to a wide range of natural sciences, from entomology to botany, between 1850 and 1880.[43] Businessmen, teachers, and bureaucrats flocked to these organizations as a means of acquiring *Bildung,* the intellectual and moral self-cultivation considered a crucial marker of membership in the educated middle-classes, or *Bildungsbürgertum.* The associations were also appealing because they allowed local citizens to participate in the cultural life of the community and engage in the rich social life of the German club, or *Verein*. In anthropological circles, learned societies created forums for scholarly work and popularized the newly developing science by sponsoring lectures, outings, and other scholarly events. They were an important first step in the institutionalization of anthropology as a discipline.

The foundation of the major German anthropological societies coincided with the foundation of the German empire, and Virchow was the crucial player. At the Congress of German Natural Scientists and Physicians in Innsbruck in 1869, he organized a special meeting devoted to anthropology and ethnology. With the aid of the zoologist Carl Vogt (1817–1895), Virchow convinced the participants that the creation of a national German anthropological society was long overdue, and he immediately declared the formation of a German Society for Anthropology, Ethnology, and Prehistory. The founding members had several motivations. Other nations in Europe had similar anthropological organizations, they reasoned, whereas the German states had none.[44] With the German Confederation already a reality and the complete unification of Germany seemingly imminent, the moment appeared ripe for a national anthropological society. In addition, the foundation of such an organization would serve as the crucial first step in establishing anthropology as a distinct discipline. The separation of newly forming fields from the Association of German Natural Scientists and Physicians was a common maneuver in the process of declaring disciplinary independence.[45] As the sciences became increasingly specialized in the late nineteenth century, fields such as botany, anatomy, and zoology were breaking away to establish their own independent societies.

When the initial momentum for the foundation of a national organization stalled after the meeting at Innsbruck, Virchow joined with Bastian to found the local Berlin Society for Anthropology, Ethnology, and Prehistory (*Berliner Gesellschaft für Anthropologie, Ethnologie und Urgeschichte*), the first of its kind in Germany. With the help of Bastian and others, Virchow eventually managed to put together a national German Anthropological Society in the following year, 1870. Virchow was the first president of the Berlin Society and served simultaneously as the head of the larger German Society. Declaring itself a branch of the larger German organization, the Munich Anthropological Society—which also took its inspiration from the Innsbruck meeting—was founded in 1870.[46] In the 1870s smaller, local anthropological societies were also established in Leipzig, Hamburg, Württemburg, Bonn, Würzburg, and Freiburg, all as branches of the larger German Anthropological Society.[47] Despite its official role as the umbrella association for these groups, however, the larger German organization never achieved the status of a true national institution. The real centers for anthropology remained the local and regional branches.[48] German anthropology was thus never truly centralized, and the science had multiple, competing centers.[49] The Berlin Society soon became the dominant anthropological organization in Germany, setting the tone for the other groups because of its size, the leading role of its most prominent members, and its location at the center of the empire.

Within the newly formed anthropological societies, physical anthropology was initially the strongest of the three subdisciplines. The driving force behind the societies' creation had come from medical men like Virchow who were primarily interested in physical anthropology. Moreover, the history of physical anthropology, reaching back to Blumenbach, appeared unambiguous, while the patrimony of ethnology was unclear in comparison. The dominance of physical anthropology was noticeable in the very names of the national and local societies: *Anthropologie* took up first position in the title of the Berlin Society for Anthropology, Ethnology, and Prehistory. Similarly, the yearly conference of the national German society was referred to as the *Anthropologentag*. The Austrian ethnologist Wilhelm Schmidt, writing in 1907, considered these titles clear indications of the dominance of physical anthropology in the early history of the societies.[50] The Anthropological Society in Munich concentrated primarily on prehistory and physical anthropology almost from the moment of its foundation.[51] The title of its journal, *Beiträge zur Anthropologie und Urgeschichte Bayerns*, omitted ethnology entirely, reflecting the focus on the other two fields within both the journal and the local branch itself.

What function did these organizations serve? They provided the anthropological sciences with an institutional framework and powerful internal networks that strengthened the three subdisciplines. Through them, those interested in anthropology were able to connect with one another at the local, national, and even international level. Within each local branch, the central events were monthly meetings at which members gave papers and presented their latest research. Each year the larger national organization also held an annual conference, which the members of local societies attended. Andrew Zimmerman has skillfully analyzed the ways in which the Berlin Anthropological Society drew on forms of sociability commonly found in clubs, or *Vereine*, traditional German forms of social organization.[52] In addition to lectures and scholarly gatherings, the societies often sponsored banquets and parties at which various forms of festivity, especially singing, were common. Brass bands, frequent toasts, and general conviviality marked the occasions as events of, as Zimmerman puts it, "clubby sociability." Moreover, the societies commonly organized day trips and excursions, often to archeological sites, as a means of generating interest and strengthening the bonds between members. With the societies as their institutional center, those interested in anthropology became acquainted with one another and established social bonds.

The societies also supported scholarly work in the field. The major local societies published journals, which quickly became crucial links in the organizational framework of anthropology and the source of the societies' considerable scholarly influence outside of Germany. The journal of the Berlin society, the *Zeitschrift für Ethnologie*, founded by Bastian in 1869, quickly achieved international status as the premier German anthropological publication. Similarly, the Munich society founded a journal expressly to serve as a forum for publishing the work of its members.[53] The larger German Anthropological Society also published a major journal, the *Archiv für Anthropologie*, as well as a monthly newsletter, the *Correspondenz-Blatt*. By 1896 the volume of publications in the field had increased to the point that a new bibliographic review of anthropological literature, Georg Buschan's *Centralblatt für Anthropologie, Ethnologie, und Urgeschichte*, could thrive.[54]

Anthropological societies in Germany, particularly the larger branches, were noticeably international in their orientation. Immediately after their foundation, the major local branches set up connections with anthropological societies in other countries, exchanging publications and accepting anthropologists abroad as "corresponding members." In 1870, for example, the Berlin Society forged ties with anthropological societies in London, Paris, and Moscow.[55] By 1900 the organization had some 119 corresponding members from throughout the world, including such influential figures in the field of anthropology as Franz Boas in New York, J. W. Powell in Washington, and Edward Tylor in Oxford.[56] Scholars from throughout Central Europe, including Switzerland, Austria, Hungary, Poland, and Bohemia, published in German anthropological journals.[57] The connections between German-speaking anthropologists in Germany, Austria-Hungary, and Switzerland were particularly strong. German scientists even created ties with anthropologists in France. Luschan studied in Paris, and Wilhelm von Waldeyer attended the fiftieth anniversary celebrations of the Paris Anthropological Society.[58]

Anthropological societies were also designed to promote anthropology as a field of study in Germany and, most importantly, to lobby private and public support for the discipline. In most cases, they were less than successful in securing state funding for anthropological endeavors and primarily relied on private money instead. The case of the Berlin society is instructive.

Beginning in the early 1870s, it received a small annual subsidy from the Prussian Cultural Ministry to support publications. This subvention usually made up only a fraction of the society's total income, however—most of which came from membership dues. In 1890, for example, the Prussian state offered the society a subvention of 1,800 marks, which amounted to twelve percent of the group's total intake.[59] Dues from members made up the other eighty-two percent of that year's income. By 1907 the state subvention had dropped to 1,500 marks, which accounted for ten percent of the society's income.[60] State support remained relatively constant for the next thirty years, staying at the same low level into the 1920s.[61] Moreover, the president of the Berlin society often had to make multiple requests and engage in a bureaucratic struggle with the cultural ministry to retain the funding.[62] Requests from the society for extraordinary state aid to cover the costs of the journal or other society expenditures were frequently denied.[63] The Prussian bureaucracy supported the Berlin society as an institution, but by no means made it a priority in its budget for scientific spending. Instead, most of the funding for research and projects came from private or outside sources. The Rudolf Virchow Foundation, a major endowment for the support of research anthropology, was established in 1881 entirely with money from a private donor.[64] The Berlin society created a "gold medal for scientific service" in 1909 that included a large monetary award, but again with private funding.[65]

Despite its failure to attract state funding, the Berlin society was more successful in promoting the recognition of anthropology, broadly defined, as a field of inquiry, and in developing itself as a consultative body on anthropological or ethnological issues. In the 1870s, before the formal foundation of a museum for *Völkerkunde* in Berlin, the Prussian state often sought advice from the society on the purchase of ethnographic collections.[66] The Prussian cultural ministry also frequently consulted the Berlin society on the protection and mapping of archeological sites. In addition, the state government also made archeological objects, such as artifacts found during the construction of a canal system in Berlin in 1875, available to society members for scientific work.[67] These moments of cooperation, however, hardly amounted to a deep commitment on the part of the Prussian state to any of the three anthropological subdisciplines.

In one major case—Virchow's 1876 anthropological survey of German schoolchildren, known as the *Schulstatistik*—anthropological societies did manage to attract the support and cooperation of state governments. Soon after the foundation of the German Reich and the establishment of the first anthropological societies in 1871, members of the newly emerging discipline proposed a nationwide study of the populations within the boundaries of the new state.[68] The idea originated within the German Anthropological Society, which served as the institutional locus for the project. Virchow took the leading role. From the moment that they proposed the idea, society members understood that such an undertaking would require the involvement of state authorities. After the Prussian military rejected the idea of measuring recruits, Virchow suggested surveying the eye and hair color of German schoolchildren. State governments across the Reich cooperated in the effort, and instructions were sent to schoolteachers across the country. To gain the support of state officials, Virchow emphasized the "scientific and in some senses even political uses of such work," without actually specifying what the political utility of such information might be.[69] In the materials sent to the teachers, however, the goals of the project were described in terms of "the research of the cultural history of humankind and the particular prehistory of every country."[70] The information was needed, in other words, to explain the relationships between prehistoric migrations into central Europe.

The project was extremely ambitious in its scope and took years to complete. Over six million German school children were surveyed and hundreds of thousands of data forms were produced. In 1875 the German Anthropological Society used the services of the Royal Prussian Statistical Bureau to tabulate the data from the study.[71] Virchow published his findings some ten years later. In the larger effort to attract state support for anthropology in the late nineteenth century, the *Schulstatistik* represented the discipline's greatest success. The problem was that the project did not translate into further collaboration with the state or an increased stream of funding for anthropology. An attempt to drum up support for another national anthropological survey in 1903, for example, died from lack of governmental interest.[72]

Despite the success of the school survey and the growth of anthropological societies in the years after unification, the overall level of professionalization within the discipline remained extremely low throughout the late nineteenth century. The overwhelming majority of the members of local anthropological societies were academics or private persons whose professional identities lay elsewhere. Most members of German anthropological societies were amateurs, people who possessed no formal training in the anthropological disciplines and who were interested in the field as a hobby. Analyses of the membership lists of the Berlin Anthropological Society by Benoit Massin and Andrew Zimmerman have revealed the diversity of the membership's occupational makeup.[73] In 1890, a significant number of the society's "full" (as opposed to corresponding) members were nonacademics and nonexperts from various walks of life.[74] Of the 577 members in 1890, 105 (approximately 18 percent) were listed as private businessmen, unconnected to the government or the academic world. These men came to anthropology from a variety of private and commercial endeavors. Among its members in 1890, the Berlin society counted engineers, factory owners, freelance writers, pharmacists, an architect, a photographer, a wine seller, and a hotel owner.

By far the largest group in the society, however, consisted of medical men. Of 577 members in 1890, 194 (almost 34 percent) were somehow connected to medicine as a profession. Over one hundred members had medical degrees, and thirty of these were listed as medical professors of some kind. This group also included doctors who worked for the military. Academics of various stripes outside of the medical field were also well represented. Of 577 members, 135 possessed some connection to academic life, whether a nonmedical doctorate, the title of professor, a job in a library or a nonanthropological museum, or a position teaching at a German secondary school or *Gymnasium*.[75] The exact number of government bureaucrats and state officials is more difficult to determine, but at least several dozen members worked for the government in some way, including one man who was the chief engineer of the Berlin water works. Fourteen members were military officers, while 52 members had no occupation or degree listed. Some of the full members lived outside of Germany and were not German citizens, but most lived in Germany, and more specifically in Berlin. The society was, of course, astoundingly male; only two of the 577 members were women. In social terms, the vast majority of the society's membership in 1890 belonged to the German *Bildungsbürgertum*, or educated middle class. Only twelve members held noble titles. Nine members owned a manorial estate. On the whole, the society's membership was representative of the rising upper middle class that was distinguished by its education and wealth.[76]

Professional anthropologists made up only a tiny fraction of the membership. Of the 577 members in 1890, only eight listed occupations that were directly linked to the anthropological disciplines, and only one of these worked outside Germany. Thus, only seven of the German members in the Berlin society could claim anthropology as their primary profession, and all of these were connected with the Museum für Völkerkunde in Berlin. In 1890, not a single German member of the Berlin society could list physical anthropology as his primary profession. This low level of professionalization was the result of the circumstances under which the anthropological disciplines had been founded. Most of the major figures in German physical anthropology at the founding of the local anthropological societies continued to derive their primary professional identity from medicine. Virchow, Wilhelm Waldeyer, and Gustav Fritsch (1838–1927) retained their positions as professors of medicine and anatomy while also working as the leading experts in physical anthropology within the Berlin society. On the whole, there were very few professional anthropologists among the members of German anthropological societies.

By the first decade of the twentieth century, the earlier dominance of physical anthropology had begun to fade in anthropological societies. Ethnology was becoming an important and distinct field with its own institutions; after 1900 it was increasingly the equal of physical anthropology within the Berlin Anthropological Society. Changes in the presidency of the Berlin society clearly demonstrate this trend. Physical anthropologists, chiefly Virchow, dominated the position of president in the late nineteenth century. From 1870 to his death in 1902, Virchow served as president of the society twenty-three times. By comparison, Bastian and several other ethnologists occupied the spot a mere seven times. Including Virchow, Waldeyer, and Abraham Lissauer, physical anthropologists occupied the position of society president from 1889 straight through to 1907 without a single ethnologist taking the spot. At the end of the first decade of the twentieth century, ethnologists began to occupy the presidency with more frequency: from 1908 to 1918 they took the job eight times while a physical anthropologist, Virchow's son Hans, held the post only three years. The increasing acceptance of ethnologists in the top administrative post after 1905 suggests that ethnology had achieved greater equality within the society. In 1906 Wilhelm Schmidt looked back at the foundation of the major German anthropological societies in the 1870s and commented on the gains that ethnology had made within those organizations since that time. After relating the story of the foundation of the Berlin society, he wrote, "Slowly, physical anthropology has shrunk back from many of the areas which it occupied since then, and ethnology has recovered."[77] One of the major reasons for the resurgence of ethnology by 1900 was the foundation of ethnographic museums.

Ethnographic Museums

In the institutional history of German anthropology, ethnographic museums provide a conspicuous example of success in the search for government funding and support. From the late 1880s to World War I, major cities throughout Germany added ethnographic museums to their civic and cultural landscape. Museums dedicated to *Völkerkunde* were founded in Berlin, Leipzig, Hamburg, Munich, Cologne, Dresden, Frankfurt, Kassel, and Darmstadt. H. Glenn Penny has convincingly shown that civic pride and self-promotion were central motivations behind the ethnographic museum movement. Cities grew rapidly in the late nineteenth century, and their governments often staked their claims to status as a *Weltstadt* ("world city") on the basis of their civic and cultural institutions. Through the support of ethnology, a science dedicated to the study of the world's peoples, cities hoped to gain reputations for cosmopolitanism and worldliness. Ethnologists were thus able to capitalize on this fierce intra-German competition to gain recognition and financial support from city and state governments.[78]

In the late nineteenth and early twentieth century, the museum stood at the center of both ethnographic theory and practice. Long before the first architectural plans for ethnographic museums were drafted or foundations for buildings were laid, the ethnologist Adolf Bastian conceived of the museum as a critical site for the empirical study of culture.[79] It was to function as a kind of laboratory in which ethnologists could formulate and test theories about human development. Bastian, steeped in the methods of inductive science, believed that by assembling and observing ethnographic collections next to one another, he could begin to determine patterns in the psychological makeup of humanity. In addition, the museum was to serve as the administrative center for the accumulation and storage of ethnographic objects. Ethnologists needed to collect and store particular pieces of material culture before they could begin to interpret them, and the museum served as both clearing house and center for the acquisition of ethnographic objects from abroad. In the race to "save" the traces of the cultures disappearing in face of civilization's encroachment, the museum was to play a key role. Bastian's vision for the ethnographic museum triumphed by the 1880s, as museums throughout Germany followed his model.[80] As Georg Thilenius put it in 1919, "The museums receive their tasks from *Völkerkunde* and provide [the field with] new ones."[81] Ethnographic museums were created with the goals of ethnology in mind. Physical anthropology played almost no role in their conceptualization and layout.

The Museum für Völkerkunde in Berlin provides an excellent example of the failure of physical anthropology to find a full and stable place in an ethnographic museum. The Berlin museum was officially founded in 1873, with Bastian as its director, but did not receive its own building until 1886, after seven years of construction in the Prinz-Albrecht-Strasse. As initially conceived, the museum was to house all three anthropological disciplines.[82] In its early stages it represented physical anthropology with an anthropological collection created by Luschan, then a low-level university lecturer in anthropology and assistant at the museum. The skulls and bones that made up the collection were the property of the museum, but compared to the ethnographic sections, they received very little space in the building and even less attention from the directors. They never received their own exhibit, despite frequent promises in the museum guidebooks that such a section was soon to open.[83] The guidebook from 1908, for example, makes no mention of the anthropological collection at all, while providing detailed descriptions of the ethnological sections and their organization by geographic regions.[84] Luschan officially became the "director" of the anthropological collection in 1911, but even then received no space for exhibition. The majority of the anthropological objects, 4,200 pieces by 1914, remained in storage until after World War I, inaccessible to the public.[85] A small anthropological collection owned by the Berlin Anthropological Society was located on the uppermost floor of the museum, next to the rooms which the society rented for its monthly meetings, but it took up only a fraction of the museum's floor space. By 1922, Luschan's anthropological collection had received some space but still took up a miniscule 144 square meters on the upper floor, while the ethnographic collections occupied several thousand square meters on the three lower floors.[86] Of course, lack of space was also a constant problem for the ethnographic collections, but hundreds of artifacts from each ethnological section were nevertheless on public display in the museum throughout the late nineteenth century. The anthropological collection remained, for the most part, hidden away.

Just as the Berlin museum provided no space for an anthropological exhibition, it also did not suit the research needs of physical anthropologists. While the ethnographic museum was conceptualized as a veritable laboratory for the practice of ethnology, it did not include the space or the facilities for the work of physical anthropology. In 1892, Rudolf Virchow commented on Felix von Luschan's difficulties within the Berlin museum and argued that an anatomical institute would be a better place for him to do his anthropological work. With space for physical anthropology at a minimum and many of the uppermost rooms rented to the Berlin Anthropological Society, Virchow argued that serious anatomical work, such as the dissection of cadavers and preservation of specimens in ethyl alcohol, was impossible.[87] To use the anthropological collection, Luschan was forced to descend into a "miserable room in the basement" where the thousands of skulls and bones were stored.[88] For his own part, Virchow did no anthropological work at the museum and stored his own collection of skeletons and skulls at the Pathological Institute of the University of Berlin. In his early years as an independent lecturer (*Privatdozent*) at the University of Berlin in the 1880s and 1890s, Luschan managed to teach his classes in the museum, using its anthropological collection in his instruction, but he often complained to state and university authorities that these materials were inadequate.[89] Luschan's main professional role at the Berlin museum was as an assistant and later director in the ethnographic collections, not as a physical anthropologist. In 1904 he became the head of the African and Oceanic section, one of the largest ethnographic departments in the museum, and in 1908 the director of the museum itself. But these positions still did not translate into a more prominent place for physical anthropology at the institution, where Luschan's anthropological interests were considered a mere sidelight to his ethnographic work. The question of the anthropological collection remained unresolved leading up to the war. In May of 1914 a liberal representative in the Prussian parliament deplored the state of anthropological collection, pointing out that four-fifths of the materials were packed away, unavailable for use.[90] The Berlin museum was a less than ideal environment for conducting research in physical anthropology.

Similar dynamics existed in Hamburg and Munich. Physical anthropology played a role in the Hamburg Museum für Völkerkunde, but was by no means equal to ethnology. The museum possessed a large collection of skulls and bones, but the director, Georg Thilenius, expressed doubt about its worth in public presentations: "A few museums possess such [anthropological] collections, but the question of their use in the exhibits is still open."[91] These materials played no role in the public displays at the museum until the 1920s. Otto Reche, a physical anthropologist, was hired in 1906, but his primary task was to take charge of the African section of the museum, since he was also trained as an ethnologist. In Munich, the Museum für Völkerkunde had little to do with physical anthropology and contained very few anthropological materials or artifacts.[92] Instead, anthropological collections in the city found their primary home in the Prehistoric Collection of the Bavarian State, founded in 1885 by Johannes Ranke, the professor of anthropology at the Ludwig Maximilian University. Here too, however, physical anthropology took a subordinate position to a sister discipline, this time prehistoric archeology. The prehistoric exhibit opened its doors to the public in 1889, but no section within its four-room display was devoted to somatic or physical anthropology.[93] From Berlin to Munich, anthropologists could not count on museums to provide them with stable institutional support.

Universities

Physical anthropology also struggled to find representation in the German university system. Despite some isolated successes, the discipline remained a marginal field with the academic establishment into the twentieth century. The same was generally true for ethnology, but it had a stable institutional home in museums. In many cases, physical anthropology fell into a gray area between the museum and the university, ending up with no institutional center aside from anthropological societies. The failures of physical anthropology to find a place in the university system further hindered the process of professionalization and frustrated the aspirations of physical anthropologists who sought increased stature and visibility for their science.

The establishment of university chairs and the creation of institutes were important milestones in the establishment of a new discipline, as well as measures of a new field's prestige and its level of support from the government. Chaired professorships were the positions through which power flowed in the academic world. Full professors (*Ordinarien*) directed university institutes, which served as centers for research and as training grounds for the next generation of scholars in a particular specialty. The rise of the institute as an institutional structure was directly related to increased specialization in all areas of scholarship, particularly in medical and scientific fields.[94] Establishing an institute became a means for governments to lavish money on rapidly developing new specialty by providing it with new buildings, equipment, and personnel. The Prussian minister of education, Friedrich Althoff, was particularly partial to medical and scientific fields, establishing eighty-six medical institutes and laboratories throughout the Prussian university system during his time in office. On the whole, 173 new institutes were founded at German universities between 1860 and 1914.[95] The representation of a new discipline at the university chiefly by the lower ranks of the professoriate, on the other hand, indicated that a field was still a marginal endeavor. Extraordinary professors and private docents, who did not have voting rights within the faculty, were usually hired as a means of adding new specialties without pledging money or commitment to a new field.

By this standard, physical anthropology was not well supported by state governments in the decades leading up to 1914. Before 1886, not a single chair of anthropology existed in Germany. Anthropology was taught in German universities, but usually by members of medical faculties and professors in other fields like anatomy or pathology. Virchow offered courses in anthropology at the University of Berlin nearly every year until his death in 1902, but his primary job was as a professor of pathology and head of the pathological institute. Then, in 1886, Ranke was named the first fully chaired professor in anthropology at the Ludwig Maximilian University in Munich, where he oversaw the foundation of the first anthropological institute in Germany. With the creation of Ranke's chair, Munich became a leading center of anthropology in Germany, but the position remained the only one of its kind for decades. In 1903 only six of Germany's twenty-one universities taught physical anthropology, and only one of the lecturers—Ranke—was a chaired professor.[96] In 1908, the University of Berlin created the second chair of anthropology in the country, but the position was a dual professorship that encompassed ethnology as well as physical anthropology. Luschan accepted the appointment. In 1910, only two full chairs in anthropology existed in Germany: Ranke's in Munich and Luschan's in Berlin.

The number of anthropological institutes remained similarly low throughout the nineteenth and into the twentieth century. The anthropological institute in Munich was the only such institution in Germany until 1907, when an anthropological section was created within the anatomical institute in Breslau. The physical anthropologist Hermann Klaatsch was appointed an extraordinary professor of anthropology at the university in Breslau in that year and simultaneously made the director of the anthropological section. While Klaatsch enjoyed the benefits of having his own institute, the anthropological subdivision he directed remained but one part of the larger anatomical institute. Perhaps more revealing was the case of the up-and-coming anthropologist Eugen Fischer, who began to collect anthropological materials at the anatomical institute in Freiburg after 1900. Fischer was able to conduct anthropological work within the anatomical institute, but he felt that his career as an anthropologist was languishing because of his position there.[97] Unlike other medical and scientific fields, physical anthropology did not benefit from the boom in the foundation of institutes within the German universities in the last decades of the empire.

The place of anthropology at the University of Berlin further reveals the struggle of the discipline to find institutional stability. The central figure in this effort was Luschan, whose progress toward a position of power at the University of Berlin was extremely slow. Luschan was an Austrian who had studied anthropology in Paris and taught the subject in Vienna before coming to Berlin for a position at the Museum für Völkerkunde in 1886. He taught both anthropology and ethnology in Berlin as a private docent in the 1890s and was named extraordinary professor of anthropology only in 1900. The creation of his chair in physical anthropology in 1908 was controversial. Several members of the faculty objected strenuously to the creation of a full professorship, and ten members voted against it in the final count.[98] Many members of the academy felt that anthropology was not a viable academic discipline. This understanding was also found in the Prussian Academy of Science, where members maintained that the discipline "lacked a secure basis and certain goal."[99] In addition, the creation of Luschan's position within the philosophical faculty reflected some confusion about whether the field belonged among the natural sciences or humanities. Students at the university studied anthropology as subfield of geography. Luschan's courses in ethnology and anthropology were listed under geography and history, but later shifted to the natural sciences.[100] A stand-alone doctorate in physical anthropology was offered only in 1915, and one for ethnology in 1922.[101]

Luschan's larger goal, however, was to establish an institute for physical anthropology in Berlin. Despite his strenuous efforts, no such institution was created in his lifetime. A major problem was the inability of state authorities and local scientists to decide whether such an institute should be anchored in the university or the museum. As early as the 1890s, Luschan agitated for an anthropological teaching "laboratory" in the museum, a request that was equivalent to asking for the rudiments of an anthropological institute.[102] The university faculty rejected the proposal, arguing that it could not approve anything until "the question of the future configuration of anthropological instruction at our university finds a conclusive solution."[103] At this stage, the future of anthropology at the university was still questionable enough to merit a rejection.

Luschan's efforts to create an institute in Berlin continued to meet with failure even after he was appointed an extraordinary professor for anthropology. Because of his connection with the museum he initially imagined that an anthropological institute would be housed there, but it soon became clear that many of his colleagues at the museum did not support such a move. When Wilhelm von Bode, the director of the royal museums in Berlin, raised the possibility of installing an institute on the museum's top floor, Luschan said that his colleagues in charge of the Asian ethnographic collection would never stand for the installation of an anthropological institute there, since "they want the whole house for themselves and in ten years will probably really need it."[104] The only solution, in his view, was to build a separate building in the suburbs of Berlin. Money was not forthcoming, however, and educational authorities continued to maintain that such an institute should be part of the museum, not the university. The museum authorities, for their part, suggested that the university should take over the anthropological collection.[105] Luschan pleaded and demanded, but the issue remained unresolved when the war broke out in 1914. After the war, he blamed the failure to establish fully developed anthropological institutions in Berlin on the "absolute indifference of the government, which despite my pressure never came forward to decide between the museum and the university for anthropology."[106]

Professionalization and Specialization after 1900

In the first decade of the twentieth century, professionalization and specialization accentuated the increasingly secondary and insecure position of physical anthropology. During this period, ethnology prospered in ethnographic museums staffed by a growing cadre of professionals. Physical anthropology, by contrast, granted very few advanced degrees and could offer few positions. The anthropological subdisciplines were also becoming more distinct as specialization proceeded. On the eve of the war, physical anthropologists had reason to feel uncertain about the institutional place of their discipline and its low level of governmental support.

With few full chairs or institutes, physical anthropology failed to produce more than a handful of new professionals. Over a forty-year period from 1870 to 1910, only three *Habilitation* degrees, which allowed one to teach as a private docent, were awarded in physical anthropology in Germany.[107] Luschan in Berlin and Emil Schmidt in Leipzig received their degrees in the 1880s, and Ferdinand Birkner was awarded his in 1904. The program in physical anthropology at the University of Zürich produced a number of habilitated professionals including Rudolf Martin, Theodore Mollison and Otto Schlaginhaufen, several of whom later found major teaching positions in the German empire, but the degrees these men held could not be counted as products of the discipline in Germany. Several others, including Eugen Fischer, received a *Habilitation* in anatomy that included training in physical anthropology, but even when counting these men, fewer than a dozen *Habilitation* degrees were awarded in the field over a forty-year period.[108] After the war, the ethnologist Karl Weule noted the inability of physical anthropology to produce new members: "It is painful to acknowledge that this discipline in Germany did not at all understand [the need to] enlist for itself, so that the next generation consists of hardly a half dozen people."[109]

Even if physical anthropology had produced more professionals, it is unclear where they would have found jobs. Specialists in anthropology were not in high demand, even in the booming scientific and academic world of Wilhelmine Germany. Positions for anthropologists in ethnographic or zoological museums were few, university positions equally scarce, and competition for available jobs was fierce. When a position for an anthropologist opened at the Dresden zoological museum in 1912, the director of the museum remarked that the "supply of anthropological specialists is much greater than the number of positions."[110] Often anthropologists had no choice but to work for very little pay, or even for free. In 1912, Luschan wrote to Ernst Frizzi, a young doctoral candidate at the anthropological institute in Munich, that he knew of no vacancies in the field, but that the young man was welcome to work in the anthropological collection of the Berlin Museum für Völkerkunde as an unpaid volunteer.[111] Unless one occupied a chair, university instruction in physical anthropology was hardly more lucrative. Private docents depended on student fees, and in a specialized field like physical anthropology, which usually required some medical training as a prerequisite, university courses did not attract hordes of students. Many anthropologists who continued to teach or work in the field lived primarily on independent means or private fortunes, while others left the university for jobs as librarians or schoolteachers.[112]

Ethnology, by contrast, experienced marked professional and institutional growth after 1900. Ethnographic museums prospered during this period, becoming serious scientific institutions with professionals at their helms. Before 1900, directors of ethnographic museums were largely dilettantes—officials, collectors, and natural science buffs—rather than professionals with advanced degrees. After the turn of the century, a new wave of directors, armed with university credentials, replaced the generalists of the earlier, founding generation. This group of professionals helped to boost the fortunes of their respective museums and ethnology in general. Georg Thilenius, who held advanced degrees in medicine, became the director of the Hamburg Museum für Völkerkunde in 1904 and quickly convinced the city government to construct a grand new building to house the ethnographic collection. The pattern was similar in Munich. Lucien Scherman, who received his *Habilitation* in the 1890s, became the museum's director in 1907 and was named to a professorship in ethnology at the Ludwig-Maximilian University in 1916. Scherman's appointment marked a new era for ethnology in Munich, during which the museum prospered as a scientific institution and ethnology became an established discipline at the university.[113] In the museums, professionals in ethnology not only found positions but were able to promote their discipline.

The membership lists of the Berlin Anthropological Society reveal not only the increasing pace of professionalization but also the growing disparity between physical anthropology and ethnology.[114] The number of professionals in the anthropological disciplines within the Berlin society was undoubtedly on the rise, particularly between 1900 and 1910. In 1880, six years before the foundation of an ethnographic museum in Berlin, only one member of the Berlin society was listed as an anthropological professional: Bastian, as the director of the ethnological collection of the Royal Museums in Berlin.[115] This number increased to eight in 1890 because of jobs in the new Museum für Völkerkunde.[116] In 1900, only ten German members of the society were specifically working in jobs connected to the anthropological disciplines.[117] By 1910, however, that number had jumped to twenty-six, primarily because of jobs in ethnographic museums located not only in Berlin but also in Hamburg and Leipzig.[118] Although still a small fraction of the overall membership, more members were actually working as ethnologists and anthropologists rather than taking up the field as a hobby or sideline to their other academic work.

The membership lists also demonstrate that the vast majority of the new professionals in the field were primarily connected to ethnology, rather than to physical anthropology or prehistory. Of the twenty-six clear anthropological professionals in 1910, sixteen worked primarily as ethnologists. Out of the same number of clear professionals, only five could be said to be working or to have at one time worked as physical anthropologists. And there are some important qualifications even to this low number. Of these five, two—Reche and Luschan—worked as *both* physical anthropologists and ethnologists. Klaatsch was the only member who was listed as holding a professorship solely in the field of physical anthropology.[119] While more ethnologists could claim professional status by 1910, the physical anthropologists who derived their professional identity solely from their subdiscipline were few indeed.

As the anthropological disciplines became more professional, they also became more specialized. The process of specialization picked up speed around the turn of the century. Anthropologists such as Virchow, who worked in multiple fields, increasingly became a rarity. In 1899, the Strasbourg anatomist Gustav Schwalbe founded a separate journal, the *Zeitschrift für Morphologie und Anthropologie*, devoted strictly to physical anthropology. At the University of Berlin, a group of ethnologists who included Eduard Seler and Paul Ehrenreich, became known for specializing in the cultures of one particular region: North and South America.[120] Specialization also increasingly became a topic of discussion and concern at the annual meeting of the German Anthropological Society, where it appeared in the form of impassioned appeals for the anthropological disciplines to work together. The need for "solidarity" among the disciplines was repeated like a mantra in the years around 1910, especially among senior anthropologists. In his opening address at the conference in 1912, Luschan complained about prehistoric archeologists who wanted to break away from physical anthropology: "It was certainly no accident when each of our [conference] chairmen in recent years . . . repeatedly emphasized the solidarity of the three disciplines that are united in our society. . . . The louder that a few prehistorians raised the cry of 'away from anthropology,' the more a few excellent men felt an inner duty . . . to recognize how deep the old solidarity was dear to their hearts."[121] He went on to praise the anthropologist Richard Andree for the "universality of his knowledge" in "our time of the splintering and ever-increasing specialization of all sciences." Luschan's idealization of the disciplinary solidarity and universalist pursuit of knowledge that had supposedly reigned several decades before was common. But by 1912 the "old solidarity" between the disciplines was indeed something old, a feeling and a trend that was quickly becoming part of the past. By the war, the view that "ethnology, like sociology, constitutes a completely independent field" could be found in anthropological journals.[122] In 1917, at his first meeting as president of the Berlin Anthropological Society, Karl Schuchhardt even felt it necessary to reaffirm that all three disciplines still belonged in the same society.[123] Although they did not completely disconnect from one another, the boundaries between them became firmer.

Imperial Opportunities

In light of ethnology's successes, anthropologists were eager to locate new professional opportunities to strengthen their own subdiscipline and shore up its institutional underpinnings. Some members of the field, especially younger scientists looking to establish a reputation, began to seek out projects that would forge tighter connections to the state and display a willingness to serve its interests. In the process, they hoped to demonstrate the field's practical utility for national and political goals. German colonialism seemed, on the surface, to offer anthropologists the perfect venue to pursue these aims.

As a rising industrial nation with ambitions to take its place alongside the great powers of Europe, Germany embarked on its imperial venture in 1884 when Otto von Bismarck declared several areas in west, southwest, and east Africa to be German protectorates.[124] Over the next fifteen years Germany added colonies in Micronesia, Samoa, and the Shantung peninsula in China. For much of the late nineteenth century, the goal of its colonial project was to encourage private investment in colonial areas by industrial and commercial firms. Initially, the German government did not seek direct administration of its new colonial territories, hoping that the private sector would do much of the heavy lifting. After 1900, however, the state's role in the colonial project increased dramatically. In 1904 and 1905, for example, the German government was forced to send an expeditionary force to Africa to crush two rebellions: the Herero revolt in German Southwest Africa and Maji Maji uprising in Tanganyika. Several years later, in 1907, the Germans also created a new Reich Colonial Office, headed by the reformer Bernhard Dernberg, who argued that the state should become the central initiator of development in the colonies. This new orientation was a response to the damaging uprisings of the preceding years, which, the argument ran, could have been avoided by a more effective colonial administration.[125] Dernberg's plan was to develop a brand of "scientific colonialism" based on extensive research into the colonies' geology, economics, and agriculture. Thus, although Germany had been involved in the imperial project since the 1880s, the first decade of the twentieth century marked a period of increased state involvement in the colonies.[126]

The relationship between anthropologists and colonialism was complex. Virchow publicly opposed Germany's acquisition of African colonies in the 1880s and continued to argue against imperial expansion until his death in 1902.[127] On the other hand, he and his fellow anthropologists benefited from the increased contact with non-European peoples that imperialism made possible. Virchow and other scientists depended on traveling troupes of ethnographic performers from the colonies—participants in so-called *Völkerschauen*, or "shows of peoples"—to conduct anthropological and ethnographic studies. These exhibitions featured indigenous peoples, often from parts of the German empire, performing cultural practices for mass audiences. Organized by private entrepreneurs like the Hamburg businessman Carl Hagenbeck, the events were endorsed by Virchow, who saw them not only as sources of anthropological data but also as educative venues in which the public could view peoples rarely seen on European soil.[128] Contradiction and opportunism also characterized Bastian's attitude; he opposed the characterization of Africans as "savage" throughout his life, but also made certain that the Berlin Museum für Völkerkunde became the central collection point for all ethnographic materials seized by government officials in the colonies.[129] By the time that the second generation of anthropologists and ethnologists began to take up positions of influence in the discipline after the turn of the century, ambivalence about empire had all but disappeared. Newly appointed heads of ethnographic museums after 1900—Thilenius in Hamburg, Karl Weule in Leipzig, Lucien Scherman in

Munich, and Luschan in Berlin—took imperial relationships for granted and assumed that colonies would remain the major source of materials for their studies. Luschan, in particular, voiced support for what he saw as the progressive, "civilizing" effects of European imperialism, particularly in the British empire.[130] These men saw opportunity for their disciplines in the intensifying colonial efforts of the German government.

Ethnologists took the lead in emphasizing the practical worth of their discipline in the imperial project, especially after the German government began to take a more direct role in administering the colonies after 1900. At the annual meeting of the German Anthropological Society in 1908, Richard Andree argued that ethnology deserved more university chairs and more support from the state, since the discipline was indispensable to the colonial effort.[131] Luschan was, of course, equally enthusiastic about the utility of ethnology in the imperial context, arguing that *Völkerkunde* was essential for political and economic success in the colonies:

> Like any other science, *Völkerkunde* also has an inner worth that is totally independent of the material uses that it can bring, although these too are not to be underestimated. Political successes can be consistently and universally achieved and expected only on the basis of ethnographic knowledge. . . . [And] how can one seek and achieve outlets for export goods in the African colonies and elsewhere without being instructed in the art and nature of the indigenous peoples to the most exact degree! Knowledge is power.[132]

Luschan clearly saw ethnology's potential both as an effective instrument of imperial rule and as a research tool for market capitalism. Judging by the titles of his courses at the University of Berlin, he sought to demonstrate the colonial utility of ethnology and anthropology in the classroom as well. He taught classes such as "*Völkerkunde* and Anthropology of East Africa with special consideration of the German Colonies," and his general courses in both anthropology and ethnology were crosslisted as "colonial" (*kolonial-wissenschaftlich*) in an annual catalog put together by the Seminar for Oriental Languages, an institute at the University of Berlin for the training of colonial officials.[133]

Ethnologists also associated themselves with the imperial project by taking part in colonial expeditions in the first decade of the twentieth century. Following Dernberg's policy of "scientific colonization," military and colonial authorities sponsored ethnological studies in the hopes that they would reveal practical information about the psychology and sociology of peoples under German rule. The timing of this emphasis was right for ethnologists, who were just beginning to turn toward ethnographic fieldwork as a superior way to collect data and artifacts. They had long distrusted travelers to bring back accurate information about peoples and ethnographic objects, and voyages to the colonies allowed scientists to gather ethnographic materials for themselves at the source. The first decade of the twentieth century saw the first large-scale fieldwork expeditions, generally funded by local or state governments and run by ethnographic museums. In 1906, a government-funded commission to research Germany's colonies sent Karl Weule, the director of the Leipzig Museum für Völkerkunde, on a six-month research trip to German East Africa.[134] In 1907–09, the German navy funded a major fieldwork expedition to the Bismarck Archipelago, off the coast of New Guinea, in conjunction with the Berlin Museum für Völkerkunde.[135] In 1908–10, city fathers in Hamburg backed a major scientific expedition to the South Pacific staffed by scientists from the Hamburg Museum für Völkerkunde.[136] Museum directors, in competition with one another for ethnographic objects, saw these ventures as a chance to outmaneuver and outshine their counterparts in other cities. Georg Thilenius understood the South Sea expedition, for example, as a means of cornering the market on ethnographic artifacts in that area and boosting the prestige of his institution.[137] But the scientists were also eager to demonstrate the utility of their discipline to colonial officials on the ground as well. Luschan instructed the members of the expedition to the Bismarck Archipelago to aid the colonial effort by researching the customs and habits of previously unknown peoples in the region.[138]

It was less clear whether or not the colonies would present an opportunity to physical anthropologists. Even more so than ethnology, the discipline was still overwhelmingly an "armchair" pursuit, practiced in the safety and comfort of European cities. The concept of fieldwork hardly existed in physical anthropology, and most members of the discipline wanted nothing to do with travel to the colonies because of the hardships and risk of disease. This did not stop them from making the case that their field could be a critical tool in Germany's colonial effort and thus deserved greater institutional support. In 1900 the anthropologist Georg Buschan maintained that anthropology had great potential to aid in German colonialization and thus needed more university professorships. He claimed that physical anthropology could help determine the susceptibility of European peoples to tropical diseases, as well as the vulnerability of the "black races" to illnesses from Europe.[139] Despite such arguments, the immediate colonial utility of physical anthropology, a discipline chiefly devoted to bodily measurement and the determination of physical classifications, remained unclear.

Several members of the youngest generation of anthropologists, how-ever—those born in the 1870s and 1880s and just entering professional life in the decade after 1900—participated in colonial expeditions as a means of furthering their careers. Otto Schlaginhaufen gained his professional experi-ence as a member of the expedition to the Bismarck Archipelago, where he was the only physical anthropologist on the team of scientists. Otto Reche, the resident anthropologist at the Hamburg Museum für Völkerkunde, similarly took part in the South Sea voyage as the lone representative of his discipline on the trip. Both men spent a great deal of their time gathering anthropological materials, chiefly bones and skulls, and measuring live sub-jects. For Reche, the South Sea voyage was the first major anthropological "measuring" project of his career.[140]

Perhaps the most well known example of work by a physical anthropol-ogist in the colonial context was conducted by Eugen Fischer. After laboring in relative obscurity at the anatomical institute in Freiburg for several years, Fischer traveled to German Southwest Africa in 1908 to undertake anthro-pological studies of local populations. His goal was to explore the heredity of "race mixing" by examining the offspring of Boers and Hottentots in the region—the so-called "half-breeds" of Rehobeth. The funding for the project came from the Prussian Academy of Sciences because of the special lobbying and support of Wilhelm Waldeyer, who was then serving as the secretary of that institution. In his justification of the project, Fischer went beyond the traditional scientific arguments to emphasize the "patriotic side" of investigating the colonial peoples of the German empire.[141] He left Germany by steamer in the summer of 1908 and spent several months in German Southwest Africa, taking bodily measurements and recording reams of physiological data about his subjects, all of whom were living under German colonial authority. The work that emerged from Fischer's work in the colonies, *The Rehobeth Bastards and the Bastardization Problem in Humans*, made his professional name, launching a career that would stretch into the 1930s.[142] The colonies, and the colonial power that lay behind them, al-lowed physical anthropologists access to new regions and living subjects under German control. Moreover, anthropologists working in the imperial context could claim that they were working in the service of the nation by studying colonial peoples. Conducting anthropological work could now be "patriotic."

Based on these examples, other young anthropologists began to frame their projects around colonial realities and the opportunities they provided. In 1914 Bernhard Struck, one of Luschan's students in physical anthropol-ogy, applied for a grant to conduct anthropological studies in German East

Africa. Earlier that same year he learned that the second annual German East African Colonial Fair in Daresalam was to include a "exhibition of the various peoples of the colony" and that "all of the ethnic stocks of German East-Africa with perhaps only a few exceptions were to be represented."[143] He immediately generated a proposal to travel to the exhibition and measure the representatives of nearly every ethnic group in the entire colony. The advantages, he explained, were that the subjects would be accessible and gathered in one spot, with disease and deformities already eliminated from the pool, and such measurements would allow him to determine the physical characteristics and relationships of various East African groups, especially the Bantu.[144] Unfortunately, Struck's timing—the summer of 1914—was poor. The Rudolf Virchow Foundation turned down his project just as the war began in August. Earlier that same year, however, it funded Luschan's trip to the South Sea islands, which focused on the German colonies in the region. In the Bismarck Archipelago, Luschan planned to "measure as many indigenous inhabitants as possible."[145] The war, as we shall see, would cut his trip short, but for those willing to travel, the colonies were becoming a kind of laboratory in which political concerns and realities shaped the work that anthropologists undertook.

In addition, physical anthropologists who stayed home sought to link their work to the imperial project in their choice of subjects and topics. When Ferdinand Birkner sent his new anthropological work, *The Races and Peoples of Humanity*, to the Bavarian minister in 1916 along with his rather assertive note, he perhaps hoped that the official would notice an entire section on the "indigenous populations of the German Colonies." In his preface, Birkner explained that his reason for including the section was simple: "In the somatic description of the races, I assumed that above all those peoples who are our countrymen through German colonial policy occupy the interest of the reader; for that reason an independent section is devoted to the population of the German colonies."[146] In a chapter of nearly one hundred pages, the peoples of Cameroon, Togo, German Southwest Africa, and the South Sea islands each received a section containing racial profiles, measurements, and photographs. Birkner admitted that the descriptions remained "subjective" since he was forced to depend on data from colonial officials and missionaries to write the chapter.[147] The peoples colonized by Germany, in other words, received detailed anthropological attention simply because of their political significance, while indigenous groups outside of the German empire played only a minor role in the text. Birkner not only implied that anthropology had a great deal to offer in understanding colonial peoples, but also pointed out that anthropologists needed to do more scientific work in the colonies if the picture of their inhabitants was ever to be more than "subjective." The colonies provided an opportunity not only to demonstrate the utility of anthropology, but also to argue that the discipline thus deserved more attention and support.

Ultimately, however, ethnology was more successful than physical anthropology in associating itself with the colonial effort. Government officials and political pressure groups could quickly grasp the colonial application of a discipline that sought to understand and analyze the customs and psychology of foreign cultures. After 1900, government officials often cited ethnology as the basis of a sound colonial policy. One Prussian official remarked: "It is clear that it is of great importance, yes, a pressing duty, for a state to collect, use, and evaluate ethnographic material as the basis of a healthy colonial policy."[148] Pro-colonial groups outside the government also recognized the practical worth of ethnology. The German Colonial Society demanded more university chairs in *Völkerkunde* by arguing that knowledge of the "customs, practices, habits, modes of thought, and cultural development of peoples with whom we come in contact" was fundamental to the administration of Germany's colonies.[149] No official or private group, on the other hand, argued that the same was true for physical anthropology. The colonial application of a discipline that created physical typologies remained obscure. Moreover, scientific expeditions to the colonies funded by government or military authorities, like the Hamburg South Sea voyage and the naval expedition to the Bismarck Archipelago, remained overwhelmingly ethnographic in nature. Physical anthropologists took part, but the primary function of the voyages in the eyes of the museums was to collect artifacts. In the end, the colonies allowed a few individual anthropologists new opportunities for research, but they did not result in the creation of new university chairs in physical anthropology or an improvement in the institutional condition of the discipline. Insecurity within the field persisted and uncertainty about its future remained the order of the day.

And yet the efforts of individual anthropologists to link themselves to the imperial project, or at least to benefit from it, were significant. They represented the initial steps onto the path toward the political instrumentalization of the discipline. By addressing the colonies through anthropology, several members of the discipline moved toward choosing topics based on political considerations and framing questions around the exercise of colonial power. The problem was that anthropologists found, at best, only mixed success in making their field more attractive and essential in the eyes of government and military authorities by associating themselves with the colonial effort, and in the end, physical anthropology never played a central role in the German imperial project. Anthropologists, particularly those of the youngest generation, continued to seek greater social and political relevance for their discipline. In the face of institutional insecurities, the need to convince the state of anthropology's utility and overall importance was pressing, and anthropologists sought other opportunities to prove the worth of their science to the state and to the nation. The "Great War" would provide one.

TWO

The Meaning of Race: The Liberal Paradigm in Prewar German Anthropology

In October 1902, the Berlin Anthropological Society convened a special meeting to commemorate the life of Rudolf Virchow, the famous pathologist and anthropologist who had died only weeks earlier. The memorial was a lavish affair. The auditorium of the Berlin Museum für Völkerkunde, normally bare and without adornment, had been specially decorated for the event, its stage wrapped in black crepe ribbon and the wall behind the speaker's podium festooned with evergreens. At the middle of the stage stood a freshly sculpted bust of Virchow, surrounded by palm leaves. Invitations had gone out to Virchow's family members, government officials, and members of the society, and the auditorium was full on the night of the memorial. International messages of tribute and condolence were read from anthropologists and scientists in France, England, Italy, Austria-Hungary, Switzerland, and Russia. As the meeting progressed, each of the speakers emphasized the depth of the loss not only for international science, but for German anthropology in particular. Speakers praised Virchow's work in all three anthropological disciplines and celebrated his crucial role in establishing the formal institutions for the study of anthropology. The deceased was referred to as "one of the greatest men of our time," and "the brilliant model for us all."[1] The main speaker, Abraham Lissauer, ended his speech by inviting the members of the audience to lift their eyes to the bust of Virchow, the "spirited image of our unforgettable master," and pledge themselves to "work tirelessly for the science of man" so that his "spirit" would "live on in our society."[2]

The lavishness of the Berlin society's memorial meeting was merely one indication of Virchow's place at the center of German anthropology. Shortly after Virchow's death, the German-born American anthropologist Franz

Boas wrote a tribute to his former teacher in which he maintained that Virchow had been "destined to impress the mark of his personality upon the young science. . . ."[3] The imprint of Virchow's person was particularly deep in German anthropology, mainly because the pathologist and teacher had been the driving force behind the creation of institutions designed to foster anthropological work. Virchow's influence, however, was ideological and methodological as well as organizational. Throughout the late nineteenth century, he and his colleagues Adolf Bastian, Johannes Ranke, and the Swiss anatomist Julius Kollmann championed a liberal and often anti-racist brand of anthropological science. When Virchow died in 1902, this strand of anthropological thought did not simply expire or vanish, but rather continued to influence the discipline in significant ways. In the years following Virchow's death, the rhetorical flourish at the end of Lissauer's 1902 memorial speech resonated in ways that the speaker perhaps did not intend. Virchow's "spirit," or at least the liberal brand of anthropology that he championed, continued to resound in anthropological circles in the decade after his death.

The liberal tradition in German anthropology, which originated with the leading members of the "founding generation" who created anthropological societies in the 1870s and set the tone for the discipline in the decades that followed, had several key elements. Drawing on liberal concepts of universalism, Virchow and his colleagues consistently argued for the "unity of the human species," maintaining that physical and cultural differences among peoples were merely variations on the common of theme of humanity, and that dissimilarities were of minimal importance next to the elements that bound humanity together. Throughout the late nineteenth century, leading anthropologists resisted the construction of racial or biological hierarchies, opposed anti-Semitism, and rejected Nordic racial theories. Moreover, they maintained that the categories of race, nation, and *Volk* (translated roughly as "people" or ethnic group) were distinct and unrelated. Despite frequent contradictions and some equivocation, liberal anthropologists were reluctant to link physical typologies to faculty or ability, and thus maintained that no one race was superior to any other. In addition, Virchow and his followers practiced a science that was characterized by a positivist commitment to inductive empiricism, which held that the central task in anthropology was careful collection of data rather than "speculative theorizing." Anthropologists prized objectivity, and despite drawing inspiration from liberal principles, they argued that their science should avoid entanglement in the politics of the moment, which they saw as antithetical to the work of the serious scientist.

The tight-knit nature of the anthropological community and its leadership make the work of Thomas S. Kuhn on the nature of scientific change useful in analyzing the ideological and intellectual contours of late nineteenth-century German anthropology. Arguing in terms of scientific communities rather than individuals, Kuhn supplied a sociological explanation for how scientific change occurs. He based his model on the elusive and powerful notion of shifting "paradigms," bodies of standards and assumptions accepted by a community of scientists in a particular research tradition.[4] The liberal anthropology practiced by Virchow and his followers clearly constituted a paradigm in the Kuhnian use of the term: an unstated disciplinary "worldview" that shaped the kind of science anthropologists practiced. An unfiltered application of Kuhn's ideas to German anthropology, however, is problematic. It is unclear, for example, whether German anthropologists actually practiced "normal science" in the Kuhnian sense or whether their discipline was in fact "pre-paradigmatic," without a recognizable paradigmatic structure. Moreover, Kuhn himself allowed that his work did not take into account the influence of the "external" conditions in which science is produced.[5] Borrowing from George W. Stocking, it is more useful to conceive of the paradigm as "a resonant metaphor, to be applied flexibly when it seemed to facilitate the understanding of particular historical episodes."[6] Without accepting Kuhn's model of scientific change in its entirety, the paradigm notion can be employed to refer to a theoretical tradition in German anthropology.[7] The liberal paradigm was a research tradition shaped by a liberal set of assumptions and adhered to by the leading members of the German anthropological community.

In the first decade of the twentieth century, elements of the liberal and empirical model gradually fell into disfavor. Members of the next generation in anthropology, who began to take up positions of authority within the discipline after 1900, increasingly embraced Darwinism, explored eugenics, and moved away from empirical induction. The acceptance of Darwinian ideas in German-speaking anthropology undermined loyalty towards liberal concepts of human commonality, replacing them with assumptions of biological inequality among peoples. In addition, a methodological crisis within the field over the worth of craniometry and the assumptions behind anthropological measurement weakened the commitment to empirical induction. Select anthropologists gradually abandoned previous strictures against theorizing and sought out new, illiberal directions for their science in genetics, Nordic race theories, and racial hygiene.

And yet despite these departures, central elements of the liberal tradition persisted after Virchow's death, informing anthropological theory and practice. Leading members of the next generation continued to adhere to key liberal concepts like the division of race, nation, and *Volk*. Moreover, empiricism remained the standard by which scientists conducted anthropological investigations. In the years leading up to 1914, the liberal approach championed by Virchow was far from dead, although it now frequently existed side by side with newer, often contradictory ideas. The first decade of the twentieth century was a period of instability and even confusion within the discipline, but the wholesale turn to an illiberal anthropology had yet to occur. Liberal anthropologists were neither heroes nor free of contradiction, but their continued influence demonstrates that the path toward the biologically deterministic *Rassenkunde* of the 1920s and 1930s was by no means predetermined before 1914. On the eve of the war, the discipline contained multiple strands of thought, only some of which prefigured Nazi race science.

Liberalism and Empiricism in German Anthropology

The influence of liberalism in German anthropology originated with the leading lights of the discipline. In Virchow, anthropologists had a leader who was a major figure in liberal politics for nearly fifty years. His political engagement began early in life and continued until his death. As a young doctor in his twenties, he took to the barricades in Berlin during the revolution of 1848 and agitated for a republican form of government. In the early 1860s he was a founding member of the left-liberal Progressive Party, and he served as a deputy in the Prussian parliament from 1862 to 1902. He also held a seat in the German Reichstag from 1880 to 1893. For most of his adult life, Virchow served as a parliamentarian in one capacity or another. His political career also put him at the center of the events leading up to German unification.

His most active and influential political period was the 1860s. Over the course of that decade, Virchow distinguished himself as a relentless liberal critic of the Prussian government and its minister president, Otto von Bismarck. In 1862 he led the parliamentary resistance to the army reform bill of King Wilhelm I, which sought to expand the military and lengthen the term of military service for recruits. When the bill failed to pass the Prussian Diet, the king precipitated a full-blown constitutional crisis by appointing Bismarck as his minister president, who proceeded to institute the reforms without the consent of parliament. Throughout the stalemate, Virchow insisted that the government must observe the constitution. The tension between Bismarck and Virchow escalated to the point where the

Prussian minister president challenged the pathologist to a duel, claiming that Virchow had called him a liar on the floor on the Prussian parliament.[8] Virchow refused to take up the challenge, but the incident cemented his status as a prominent member of the liberal opposition. When Bismarck orchestrated a successful war against Austria in 1866, thereby laying the foundations for a unified Germany, he split the liberals in Prussia.[9] The newly formed National Liberal Party, anxious for unification at any cost, supported Bismarck's achievements and retroactively approved his extra-parliamentary rule, while the now smaller Progressive Party refused to do so. Virchow remained with the Progressives, continuing to insist on the rule of law. After 1866, he was still a prominent figure in liberal politics, even coining the term "*Kulturkampf*" to describe the government's anti-Catholic campaign in the early 1870s, but his direct engagement in politics gradually declined as his disappointment with the authoritarian direction of the country mounted. Even before German unification, he had decided to turn his energies primarily toward science. "If I must work for the future," he wrote to a friend in 1867, "I would rather do it through science than pseudoparliaments."[10]

For Virchow, that science was increasingly anthropology, and he was in a position to influence the ideological shape of the newly emerging discipline in a liberal direction from the 1870s onward. The leading figures in the field, including Kollmann, Ranke, Bastian, and Boas in the United States, had at one time been Virchow's students and had absorbed the influence of the "old master."[11] In the field of physical anthropology, Virchow joined with Ranke and Kollman to form a powerful trio that championed liberal ideas through their intellectual and institutional influence. Ranke, who served as a de facto second in command to Virchow, held the only full professorship in anthropology in Germany at the University of Munich and worked as the editor of the *Archiv für Anthropologie*, the journal of the national German Anthropological Society. Kollmann, an anatomist and anthropologist at the University of Basel, was on the board of the journal that Ranke edited. Bastian was the leading figure in the institutionalization of German ethnology. This group held the major positions of power in the discipline, controlled the journals, and ran the most important anthropological societies throughout the late nineteenth century.

Liberalism was a heterogeneous ideology in the nineteenth century, a loose ideological "family of ideas and behavioral patterns."[12] Difficult to define, the term has variously been used to describe "an organized political tendency, a cultural allegiance with certain values intrinsic to Western civilization, and the ideology of capitalism."[13] To be "liberal" meant many things to different people, and those meanings changed over time. The roots of liberalism can be traced to the Enlightenment and the French Revolution, but it took shape as a political movement during the reactionary *Vormärz* period that followed the defeat of Napoleon in 1815. In Metternich's Europe, liberals attacked arbitrary government, absolute monarchy, and aristocratic privilege. In the 1820s, to be liberal was "to belong to the party of movement, to oppose tyranny and love liberty, to hate irrationality, and celebrate reason, to fight reaction and advance progress."[14] By the mid- to late nineteenth century, the term encompassed a remarkably diverse set of political and economic viewpoints, including radical republicanism, anti-democratic Whiggish constitutionalism, variations on Benthamite utilitarianism, and the laissez-faire economic theories of classical political economists.[15]

Despite this diversity, liberalism still provided its proponents with elements of a common worldview. A common denominator in liberal thought was the attempt to "safeguard and expand various aspects of individual freedom."[16] In the realm of politics, liberals usually shared a commitment to individual rights, the rule of law, and—to widely varying degrees—representative institutions. Moreover, liberals argued for the equality of all people before the law, because they subscribed to the Enlightenment notion that all individuals were born free. Although they often clashed over exactly what role the population should have in government, liberals generally agreed that sovereignty lay at least to some degree with the people, that constitutional limitations on the power of rulers were necessary, and that civil liberties, such as freedom of speech and of assembly, should be guaranteed. In the realm of economics they believed in the power of the free market, arguing for trade unfettered by government interference and regulation. Another common denominator was the belief in progress. From the Enlightenment, liberals drew an optimistic faith in reason and science as the twin engines of improvement. Suzanne Marchand and David Lindenfeld have pointed out that in the Germany at the fin de siècle, "The term liberal connoted a commitment to rationality in a broad sense, and the middle class took justifiable pride in the accomplishment of German science and scholarship."[17]

Beyond these political and economic positions, however, liberals also shared a common set of assumptions about humanity. Liberalism was based on the belief that, at root, human nature was the same everywhere, and that everyone had the potential to become a rational, autonomous individual. All people, in other words, were united on a fundamental level by their similarities and had the capacity for intellectual improvement.[18] As an ideology, liberalism was dependent on the notion that individuals shared more commonalities than differences. As Thomas Metcalf has pointed out, "At its heart, liberalism . . . can be seen as informed by a radical universalism."[19] While most liberals accepted a hierarchical view of politics and society by, for example, maintaining that certain groups such as women and colonial subjects were as yet incapable of self-rule, they also argued that liberal political and social values—such as freedom, progress, rationality—applied to everyone, regardless of culture or background, because all humans were at base essentially the same. All individuals and societies could be transformed for the better through education, free trade, and the rule of law, and fundamental commonalities between peoples meant that legal and educational reform could unleash the potential of even the most "backward" society. In the process, of course, liberals upheld European cultural values as the standard to which all peoples should aspire, and as believers in progress they readily assumed that some cultures were more advanced than others.

Within the German anthropological community, the term "liberal" encompassed a variety of political viewpoints. Even Virchow's liberalism did not remain static. He espoused republican views early in life, but later muted his democratic demands in favor of an emphasis on individual rights as he became more involved in parliamentary politics.[20] In other areas, Virchow's political positions—support for the rule of law and the sanctity of constitutions—were those of classical European liberalism. Virchow distinguished himself from liberals in Britain and France by subscribing to a Hegelian strain of European liberalism that saw the nation-state as the critical context for securing liberty.[21] On the issue of German unification, Virchow proved to be a devout liberal nationalist, calling for Prussia to unify Germany on the basis of popular representation. Unlike many other German liberals, however, he was also a pacifist who advocated unification by peaceful means, rather than by use of force. Later, in the 1880s, he objected to Germany's acquisition of colonies.[22] Many of these views, however, stood in stark contrast to those of other members of the anthropological community who could also be considered "liberal" in their anthropology. Luschan, for example, was a fierce supporter of imperialism, a "liberal imperialist" who saw violent clashes between nations as a healthy component of international life.[23] He mocked "peace enthusiasts" as utopian dreamers.[24] Originally from Austria, Luschan was not a pan-German nationalist, but he argued for a militarily strong German *Reich* and lamented that low birth rates would weaken the German nation-state.[25] Liberalism was entirely compatible with these views; support for both imperialism and nationalism were frequently part of the liberal program. The imperial "civilizing mission" appealed to liberals throughout Europe who saw the colonies as a laboratory for social, cultural, and political reforms.[26] An aggressive nationalism, to be sure, could also be a centerpiece of the liberal agenda, as demonstrated by the support among German liberals for unification through Bismarck's use of "blood and iron."

What made Virchow, Luschan, and other leading members of the discipline "liberal" was not a specific set of common political ideals but an approach to science and humanity that drew on liberal concepts. The central influence of liberalism in German anthropology came in the ways in which anthropologists and ethnologists framed their study of human groups around a firm conviction in the basic similarity of humankind. This idea was most clearly reflected in the monogenistic concept of the "unity of the human species," a key conceptual touchstone for the discipline that emerged in debates about the origins of humanity. At mid-century, a major point of disagreement for anthropologists throughout Europe was the question of human origins, and more specifically, human racial groups. Opinion was divided, and scientists fell into two general camps. Polygenism, the belief in the separate origins of races, influenced the anthropological traditions in France and Great Britain but had very few defenders in Germany.[27] Polygenists generally held that races were descended from different species. The majority of German anthropologists firmly adhered to monogenism, the argument that all races had a common origin. This position had long enjoyed many supporters among devout Christians because it ran parallel to the biblical story of creation and sustained the notion that humanity was descended from an original pair.[28] In German-speaking anthropological circles, the trained philologist Theodore Waitz was primarily responsible for establishing monogenism as fundamental to the German anthropological tradition. In his influential six-volume work, *Anthropologie der Naturvölker*, published between 1859 and 1872, Waitz argued that the polygenist position rested on faulty categorizations of humankind and was based on "abstract deductions lacking proper empirical basis."[29]

Waitz's monogenism paved the way for Virchow, Bastian, and members of the next generation to make the "unity of the human species" a central plank in their anthropological project.[30] Despite several notable exceptions, there was a remarkable degree of unanimity on the question of monogenism within the German anthropological community.[31] In 1909, Luschan called the issue "settled," claiming that the "the great majority of all specialists adhere to the unified origin of the human species."[32] The Breslau anthropologist Hermann Klaatsch created a stir when he broke from the disciplinary norm in 1910 by arguing that humans originated from two different branches: an eastern strain descended from the orangutan and a western strain derived from the gorilla.[33] Klaatsch's polygenist ideas won few adherents, however, and the resistance that they engendered confirmed the monogenist consensus.[34]

For the leaders of the discipline, the importance of the "unity of human species" went beyond the debate on the origin of humankind to frame a general approach to the study of humanity that was indebted to liberal universalism. For Virchow and his colleagues, the "unity of humankind" meant that human beings shared more commonalities than differences, despite variations of culture or race. If the unity of humankind held true, then all humans were related to each other. Virchow maintained that, "I have a certain tendency, aside from all experience and analysis, to be enthusiastic for the idea of the unity of the human species. I admit that behind it lies a traditional, even sentimental idea, and that I cannot keep myself from thinking, when I look at the entire history of humankind, that we really are brothers and sisters."[35] Ranke, like Virchow, considered the differences separating mankind minimal compared to what bound them together. At meetings of the German Anthropological Society, he consistently emphasized the "equality of feelings and mental life of all humanity."[36] The idea that the peoples of the world shared fundamental characteristics underwrote a great deal of German anthropology in the era of Virchow. In ethnology, for example, Bastian's search for the "elementary ideas" of humanity was based on his assumption that "human nature is uniform across the globe."[37] Ranke went so far as to remark that, "Bastian, more than any other, is the one who has recognized the psychological (*geistige*) unity of the entire human species," allowing anthropologists to "know and feel as one with all of humanity."[38] Monogenist perspectives influenced physical anthropologists as well. Ranke noted that physical variations, while real and visible, were actually "bound together so completely with each other" so as to make "the totality of physical differences appear like a closed row in which we can make distinctions only through more or less arbitrary dividing lines."[39] Kollman, another monogenist among the leaders of the discipline, noted that while as an anthropologist he sought to classify the physical differences among human beings, "I do not have the slightest intention of letting the similarities in the appearance of the human species out of my sight."[40] For these men, liberal principles of universalism framed the anthropological project.

Another key element of the liberal tradition in German anthropology was a methodological commitment to inductive empiricism. Drawing on a scientific model stretching back to Sir Francis Bacon, empiricists rejected deduction and arguments by analogy, instead upholding specific facts as the foundation on which to build larger conclusions. Induction represented the dominant epistemological mode in nineteenth-century German science, and anthropology was no exception.[41] The drive of the anthropological disciplines was to accumulate as much data as possible and to move very slowly from the specific to the general, rather than to propose unsupported theories. The loyalty to empirical induction meant that anthropologists were extremely hesitant to voice overarching conclusions or construct finalized systems of classification. Colleagues described how Virchow would "push his glasses up on his forehead and investigate the [anthropological] object with raised eyebrows," but that he remained "cool, even ironic, toward every rash conclusion. For him, it was primarily about the researching and securing of facts."[42] Ranke championed a similar position, maintaining that "hypotheses belong only in the laboratory of the researcher," not in the "descriptions of research results."[43]

In the nineteenth century, empiricism and liberalism were often viewed as complementary modes of thought. The advance of both intellectual systems occurred at roughly the same time, and considerable overlap existed between them.[44] From its beginnings, in fact, liberalism claimed a special relationship with science. Liberals maintained that their politics represented the application of reason and scientific thinking to the realm of government and human society. This approach has its roots in the Enlightenment, when *philosophes* like Voltaire took philosophical inspiration from the thinkers of the scientific revolution—particularly Isaac Newton, the veritable personification of scientific empiricism—in their efforts to apply the test of reason to political, social, and religious institutions. In Francis Bacon, liberals found concepts that paralleled their political ideals: claims to universal knowledge on the basis of empirical investigation, an emphasis on the individuality of phenomena that mirrored their own ideal of the individual person, and the belief in progress through the application of reason.[45] Liberals, in other words, understood their task as the construction of political, social, and economic systems that rested on facts and natural laws, such as the freedom of the individual, which they saw as derived from nature itself. A liberalism that promised to provide a rational, "scientific" politics, in contrast to the arbitrary and irrational absolutist systems of rule, appealed to scientists for this very reason. During the 1848 revolution, Virchow argued that "as a natural scientist I can be but a republican. The republic is the only form in which the claims, derived from the laws of nature and the nature of man, can be realized."[46] Like many liberals, Virchow justified his political beliefs on scientific grounds. Adhering to empiricism did not make one a liberal, of course, but in their commitment to empirical induction, anthropologists in the liberal tradition reinforced liberal principles like progress, rationality, and claims to universality. Following empirical tenets, they were firm believers in progress through the individual exercise of reason, seeing themselves as engaged in accumulating scientific knowledge by discovering natural laws. Virchow remarked, "We too have a creed, a faith in the progress of our knowledge of the truth."[47] The principles of empiricism thus neatly paralleled the assumptions of the liberal tradition in German anthropology.

The commitment of leading anthropologists to empirical induction was most evident in their rejection of Darwin's theory of evolution. Darwinian ideas became increasingly influential in German social and intellectual life in the late nineteenth century, thanks to popularizers such as the biologist Ernst Haeckel and the novelist Wilhelm Bölsche.[48] Virchow, Ranke, and Bastian, however, refused to accept evolutionary theory, often derisively referring to it as the "monkey doctrine." For them, the debate about Darwinism was at heart a disagreement about methodology and what constituted good science. Their objection was that evolution was an unproven theory reached through deduction rather than induction. In a review of Darwin's *Descent of Man*, Bastian complained about the "evolution sickness that currently rages" and warned against taking a hypothesis as an "absolute law," when in fact it represented nothing more than a "ephemeral operation of the mind."[49] In contrast to Darwin's theory, Virchow argued that variations within species primarily had pathological causes.[50] Although the dismissal of Darwinism was not entirely uniform within the anthropological community—Hermann Schaffhausen in Bonn was a significant exception—Virchow was more or less able to keep the influence of evolutionary theory at bay throughout much of the late nineteenth century.[51]

For anthropologists, the commitment to empirical induction also involved a determination to keep their science out of the tumult of politics. As empiricists, anthropologists opposed the importation of subjective political considerations into what they considered the realm of inductive objectivity. They apparently saw little contradiction between drawing inspiration in their science from liberal conceptualizations of humanity and progress on the one hand and calling for its absolute separation from politics on the other. Liberal anthropologists clearly did not consider universalist conceptions of humankind and the ideal of human improvement that accompanied them to be expressly "political," despite the association of these ideas with liberalism. They were thus able to argue that their science, its methods, and its questions should not be based on political objectives or considerations.

The principle of apolitical objectivity in anthropology was so central that Ranke emphasized it on the opening page of his influential anthropological textbook, *Der Mensch*:

> Corresponding with the previous tradition of exact anthropology in Germany, the avoidance [in this work] of all overlap between the ground of natural observation and that of politics, philosophy and religion was intentional. The dignity of science, in order for its results and questions to be worthwhile and interesting, must not make piquant side glances into [these] foreign areas. . . . Previously one combined all to often . . . the ever changing hypotheses of natural science with the even more fluctuating political and philosophical opinions of the day.[52]

Anthropology was to be objective, "exact," unsullied by the shifting day-to-day positions of politics if it was to maintain its dignity as a science. After Ranke's death in 1916, his obituary emphasized his "position against tugging anthropological research into the realm of politics until his death, despite many attacks."[53] Claims to be practicing a "political anthropology" were met with scorn and derision by the leaders of the anthropological community. In 1892, Julius Kollmann sarcastically derided scientists who sought to demonstrate the superiority of one European race over another: "Whoever feels the desire to practice anthropology with something of a political flavor has free choice to warm to one or the other race."[54] In anthropological circles, the charge that one was practicing a political brand of anthropology was a negative one.

The Liberal Anthropological Tradition and the Search for Race

The liberal and empirical influences on physical anthropology came together in the discipline's central pursuit: the investigation and classification of race. By the 1890s, the identification and classification of human variations had become a central focus of physical anthropology in Germany. From the outset, the goal of the discipline was the categorization of human forms in an effort to understand, as Wilhelm Waldeyer put it in 1890, the "differences and similarities which occur in the construction of humans across the globe."[55] Through measurement and quantification, late–nineteenth-century anthropologists sought to determine the underlying physical or morphological variations, usually constructed as "racial types," thought to be caused by heredity and present in any given population.[56] The aim was not only to identify racial forms but also to determine how they had originated. In 1892, Waldeyer argued that the central questions in anthropology were, "how were these groups, the races, created, when were they created, and what was the cause that allowed them to come into being?"[57]

To answer questions of classification and difference, anthropologists relied heavily on the techniques of anthropometry, the systematic measurement of human anatomical features across large populations. Using anthropometric instruments, they principally sought the measures of racial difference in the shape of the skull and bones. In particular, anthropologists employed craniometry, the practice of measuring the form and proportions of the human skull, to determine racial types. Using statistical methods on large samples of data, they believed that they could calculate the typical form or "pure type" for each group, which they could then compare with other groups to ascertain the relationships between them. Anthropologists traced the origins of craniometry back to Johann Friedrich Blumenbach, the anatomist and professor at the University of Göttingen who pioneered the study of the human skull as a method of classifying human types in the late eighteenth century.[58] Nineteenth-century craniometry, however, had its roots in the work of the Anders Retzius (1796–1860), the Swedish anatomist who provided the foundational techniques of skull measurement. Anthropologists recognized Retzius's calculation of the "cephalic index," the ratio of a skull's width to its length, as central to their project. The index was used to classify of groups as either "long-skulled" (dolichocephalic) or "short-skulled" (brachycephalic). To this basic model, anthropologists added dozens of other measurements and classificatory schemes in their effort to categorize humankind.[59] Facial angles and hair types of subjects also entered into systems of classifications to varying degrees.[60]

What remained constant throughout these attempts was the conviction, derived from inductive principles, that racial categorization could not be determined by the examination of one individual or even a group of skulls, as in Blumenbach's day, but rather by completing complex statistical calculations on large samples of data. In Virchow's view, the attempt to construct a racial category from a single object could not be "embarrassing enough" and led to "foolish conclusions."[61] Instead, anthropologists launched an enormous effort to collect masses of measurements. For this project to succeed, craniometry depended on the standardization of its research methods, so that every anthropologist would be taking and comparing the same data. At a meeting of the German Anthropological Society in Frankfurt in 1883, Virchow led members of the discipline to an accord on how to take the central measurement in craniometry, the horizontal, a line that ran through the skull from front to back and provided a starting point for other measurements. This "Frankfurt Agreement" gave anthropologists the so-called "German horizontal," a standardized method for locating the line, which was to stretch from the eye socket to the top of the ear hole. The measurement could be taken by amateurs as well as seasoned anthropologists, on both skulls and living subjects.[62] Under Virchow's leadership, anthropologists took steps toward uniting behind a common project and methodology in the search for racial categorization.

Despite efforts at standardization, "race" remained an elusive and shifting concept in late–nineteenth-century anthropology. Virchow and his followers constructed it as a statistical value, an ideal type derived from taking the average of physical measurements from a local population. Their method was to chart an array of individual physical variations—of head form, for example—then calculate the mean for the group. In this formulation, race was an abstract category, a point on a graph, and despite their best efforts, scientists continued to lack any precise biological definition of race as a classification. By casting race as an average of measurements and bodily characteristics, anthropologists throughout Europe had difficulty identifying individuals who actually matched the categories they were constructing.[63] As a result, they often took refuge behind the more flexible and nebulous concept of physical "type." In addition, they disagreed on whether race was a fixed physical feature or whether it was mutable. Throughout his career, Kollmann consistently argued that although environmental factors had influenced the formation of races at one time, racial types had persisted unchanged since the earliest prehistoric periods.[64] Although races could mix and produce hybrids, he contended that no new racial types could form in the present, since racial types were fixed and immutable. Virchow accepted this view for much of his life, but came to admit in his final years that mutability might play a far greater role than he had at first assumed.[65] Anthropologists also disagreed about the origins of racial difference. From his perspective as a medical man and a pathologist, Virchow argued that human variations were created by pathological processes, which caused divergences from the parent type and were subsequently handed down.

Central to liberal anthropology, however, was the consistent assumption that "race" was simply a category of physical, rather than cultural or mental, variation. Anthropologists in the liberal tradition considered themselves engaged in the investigation of different physical morphologies which were caused by heredity, not in the classification of groups that were in any way connected to psychology, religion, linguistics, or culture. They referred to groups with similar physical morphologies as "races," "types," or even "varieties," but all these terms were understood as little more than categories of human variation. In 1896 Virchow wrote, "Theoretically, in my opinion, there can be no doubt that races are nothing more than hereditary variations."[66] Similarly, in his anthropological textbook of 1887, Ranke described the main goal of anthropology as the attempt to "divide humanity into sharply distinguished groups (races or varieties) by their physical characteristics," which had nothing to do with psychological or cultural attributes.[67]

The frequent misuse of "race" as a category and confusion surrounding its meaning caused German anthropologists to be very cautious in their use of the term. They consistently tried to limit the concept to refer to categories of physical variation. In his lecture course at the University of Berlin in 1889, Luschan counseled circumspection in the use of the term: "You see already . . . how variable [*schwankend*] the concept of race is even today and how suitable it would be for us to avoid the word altogether; if, however, we do not want to do without it, it is because it affords us a simple expression for the concept of a group of similar human types."[68] Virchow, in a similar vein, expressed caution about the meaning of race, remarking in 1896 that "the term race, which has always had something indeterminate about it, has become more uncertain in recent times."[69] Despite disagreements over systems of racial classification and the origins or racial difference, anthropologists generally agreed that races only referred to categories of human variation.

Following this principle, a central characteristic of liberal anthropology under Virchow was the hesitation, or even refusal, to link the concept of race with human faculty. If race was nothing more than a category of human physical variation, then it could not be connected to mental ability or levels of cultural achievement. Here the influence of liberalism was clear: as firm believers in the universal capacity for reason and progress, liberal anthropologists were reluctant to argue that an individual's capability for improvement was constrained by biology. In Virchow's view, race did not indicate superiority or inferiority. After Virchow's death, Franz Boas put particular emphasis on this aspect of his former teacher's career and work, hailing the importance of Virchow's argument that the "[theromorphic variations of the human body] cannot be considered as proof of a low organization of the races. . . . There is no proof that such forms are connected with a low stage of culture of the people among whom they are found."[70] Virchow argued throughout his career that physical characteristics that were supposedly an indicator of the "lower" races could be found in all human groups: "The question whether characteristics could be found only in certain, namely lower, human races was already decided by earlier observers in the negative sense. My investigations also prove the claim that these characteristics can be found occasionally in all possible races."[71] Even in the years just before his death, Virchow continued to maintain that particular physical characteristics did not indicate superiority or inferiority. In 1901, for example, he argued that small skull size could not be considered a marker of lower, inferior races. "I want to especially emphasize this . . . that in my view no conclusion may be drawn about the lowness of the race from the smallness of the skull."[72]

Other leading voices in anthropology followed Virchow's lead by avoiding judgments on racial groups as inferior or superior. In 1892, Kollmann dismissed anthropologists who argued that either long-headed or short-headed types in Europe had achieved a higher cultural level: "I believe that on the basis of the knowledge of craniometry one must therefore counter every theory of the superiority of any one of the European races."[73] Kollmann, like other liberals, accepted the idea of lower and higher levels of cultural development, but assumed that this had nothing to do with race. After Kollmann's death in 1919, a colleague noted his belief that, "Every ethnic group is . . . the product of mixing among many races, and even if [that group] stands at a lower cultural level, one may not speak of inferior races in the physical sense."[74] Similarly, Ranke argued that the supposed physical markers of inferiority were often present in every individual. In 1897 he contended that in the course of development, every skull possessed elements of "prognathy"—a measure of the degree to which the jaw jutted out from the skull that was usually subscribed to the "lower races." With age, Ranke maintained, every skull developed the very forms "which are typical for those often named representatives of the black and so-called lower races."[75] For Ranke, like Virchow, the "lower races" were indeed "so-called," and he resisted the labeling of one race or another as lower or inferior.

Following this logic, anthropologists in the liberal vein generally avoided the construction of hierarchies based on race. Without the link between race and faculty, the construction of racial hierarchies was not possible, since no one group could be ranked qualitatively higher or lower than any other. On empirical grounds, Virchow rejected the notion that one could place peoples in hierarchical rankings based on race: "In the ethnological research of physical anthropology in the past . . . one has begun with the expectation almost without exception, that one will find a climbing row of lower to higher ethnic stocks (*Volksstämme*) . . . As undoubtedly tempting as this theory is, its factual underpinnings are also unsure."[76] In the same vein, Virchow's lifelong opposition to Darwin's theory of evolution also involved the rejection of hierarchical schemes that placed Africans or other peoples at a lower station on an evolutionary scale, often as the "missing link" between apes and humans. He flatly rejected the notion that the pygmies of Central Africa were more closely related to apes.[77] Similarly, Ranke maintained that Africans did not represent an intermediary step between humans and other primates.[78]

Cultural hierarchy, however, was accepted as a given by liberal anthropologists. As believers in progress, they assumed that certain peoples were more advanced than others. This belief was embedded in the terminology of the discipline in the late nineteenth century. German anthropologists commonly divided humanity into two groups: "cultured peoples" (*Kulturvölker*), literate groups with a written history, and "natural peoples" (*Naturvölker*), those without a recorded past. Both ethnologists and physical anthropologists readily assumed that the "natural peoples" were simpler and less culturally developed than "cultured peoples," whose number included Europeans and Chinese. Anthropologists readily assumed that the Australian Aborigines, for example, had achieved only a low level of culture in comparison to Europeans.[79] This did not mean, however, that "natural peoples" lacked history or culture. According to Bastian, the traces of their past could be found in their material culture, which in turn formed the main object of ethnological study.[80] And perhaps most important, a group's status as a "natural" or "cultured" people was not determined by race.

Conceiving of race as nothing more than a category of physical variation meant that liberal anthropologists were also reluctant to link the concept to language or culture. In a variety of scientific and popular circles, groups defined by language, history or culture, such as the Slavs, Germans, Jews, Anglo-Saxons, Celts, and English, were frequently referred to as races. In fields like archeology and linguistics, the conflation of race with cultural and linguistic groupings was common.[81] German anthropologists in the liberal vein, however, sought to avoid any such overlap by insisting that they were only engaged in investigating physical varieties, not in exploring classifications corresponding to political boundaries or linguistic families. In their view, groups that shared a common tongue or set of customs did not necessarily share a common physical type, and therefore race, language, and culture were not congruent. These distinctions were accepted as veritable givens by many of the leading members within the German anthropological community in the 1880s and 1890s. Virchow, for example, argued that physical anthropology had "nothing to do with culture."[82] After the death of his former teacher, Boas noted that "Virchow always maintained that limits of human types do not coincide with the dividing lines of cultures and languages."[83]

The refusal to link race with language or culture can best be seen in a set of distinctions that lay at the heart of liberal brand of anthropology: the division between the concepts of race, nation, and *Volk*. German anthropologists insisted on the incongruence of these terms because they wanted to distinguish race from language and culture. They argued that nations, which were determined by factors such as politics, customs, language, history and geography, were in no way related to categories of physical variation. At the annual conference of German anthropologists in 1899, Virchow said, "Anthropology really cannot address the question of nationality that is continually raised."[84] He maintained that nationality was a "constructed phenomenon"[85] and pointed out that Russians, for example, were members of a political entity, not a cohesive somatic or ethnological group.[86] Elsewhere, Virchow complained that the rise of "nativism" had led to a situation in which "every nation, even the smallest, wants to represent a particular race."[87]

Likewise, the term *Volk* possessed a wide variety of meanings in nineteenth-century Germany,[88] but in anthropological circles it referred to a particular linguistic or ethnic group, a category that was unrelated to physical makeup. Because anthropologists claimed that race was incongruent with language and culture, they also argued that physical morphologies did not coincide with peoples or ethnicities, which usually contained many physical types. In describing the peoples of Europe, for example, Kollmann explained that, "Peoples [*Völker*] are always constructed from many varieties. Nations may be large, united entities, joined by customs, language, by political structures and historical development, like Italians, French, and Germans, or may represent smaller . . . groups, like the Finns, Hungarians, Bavarians: they are created from many different races."[89] In fact, the very boundaries between the anthropological disciplines themselves depended on the distinction between race and *Volk*. The Austrian ethnologist Friedrich Müller argued that the morphological concept *Rasse* had no place in the cultural inquiries of ethnology, just as the culturally determined *Volk* had no place in the physical studies of physical anthropology.[90]

These distinctions influenced the views of liberal anthropologists on the peoples of Europe. Virchow considered Europeans to be a mixture of racial elements or varieties. In his famous study of the skin, hair, and eye color of German schoolchildren in the 1870s, he posited the existence of two basic European "types": a blond, long-skulled variety and the brunette, short-skulled sort. Admittedly, as John Efron, Andrew Zimmerman, and others have pointed out, the methodology of the studies of schoolchildren was based on assumptions of Jewish and German difference, demonstrating the persistent popular view of the Jews as a "group apart."[91] During the studies, Jewish schoolchildren were separated from German, and the hair and eye color of each group was recorded. In his analysis of the survey results, Virchow also referred to the "strong differences between the races" in his discussion of the characteristics of the Jewish and German schoolchildren. The fact remains, however, that Virchow concluded on the basis of the studies that the national population of Germany was a racial mixture. Virchow not only argued that a mere thirty-two percent of Germans were of the blond type, but also maintained that eleven percent of Jews belonged in the same category.[92] Virchow's study made it clear that his two European "types" transcended national and cultural boundaries.

In other words, Virchow's system of classification did not allow clear-cut physical distinctions to be drawn between European peoples, and he continually maintained that Europeans were interrelated. Virchow's conclusions were based on the assumption that race was not related to *Volk* or nation. Boas summed up Virchow's position this way: "People who belong to the same type may speak different languages and possess different forms of culture; and on the other hand—as is the case in Germany—different types of man may be combined to form one nation."[93] Although Ranke used Virchow's study of schoolchildren to argue that the blond type was more prominent in Germany than in the rest of central Europe, and even maintained that northern Germany was "the land of the blondes," he also affirmed that Poles, Finns, Slavs, and other peoples of Eastern Europe exhibited the characteristics of the blond, long-headed type.[94] Elsewhere, he emphasized the disjunctures between linguistic groupings and physical makeup: "The bodily proportions of the representatives of European peoples [*Völker*] are extraordinarily similar, one may say identical, whether they are linguistically counted as belonging to the Romans or Germans or Slavs, to the Aryans, Finno-Hungarians, or Semitics."[95] Thus, physical type did not correspond directly to linguistic or cultural categories.

The distinctions between race, nation, and *Volk*, however, did not immunize anthropologists from contradictions or prevent them from adopting a hierarchical view of physical development. At times, deep-seated assumptions of cultural hierarchy crossed into physical and racial characterizations. Some anthropologists used terms like "*Kulturrasse*" or "cultured race" in their academic discourse. The Hamburg ethnologist Paul Hambruch, for example, referred to "*Kulturrassen*" in his courses.[96] Virchow himself was not immune. He argued that the skulls of Australians, whom he considered at the "lowest level of culture," exhibited features in the forehead that were generally absent from those of "the carriers of the highest cultures."[97] In the same article, however, he affirmed that characteristics of "lower peoples" actually occurred in all peoples.[98] In general, physical anthropologists avoided any linkage between race and culture, relying on Virchow's dictum that culture was a matter for ethnologists to explore and had no place in physical anthropology.

A further characteristic of liberal anthropology under Virchow was the rejection of "Aryan," "Teutonic" and "Germanic" racial doctrines that were increasingly taking shape in the 1880s and 1890s. In one way or another, these theories all belonged under the rubric of *völkisch* thought, a diffuse and unsystematic set of ideas loosely united by extreme nationalism, social Darwinism, anti-Semitism, and a Germanic brand of racism.[99] Often motivated by what they saw as the ills of modernity and the fragmentation of modern German culture in an age of industrialization, Germanic ideologues drew on a disparate group of sources to create a radical nationalist ideology frequently based on notions of racial superiority and inferiority.[100] One of these sources was the field of linguistics, where philologists had inferred the supposed existence of a prehistoric "Aryan" people from the common roots of Indo-European languages.[101] Linguists and other writers subsequently imbued this concept with racial meaning. Chief among these was French theorist Arthur de Gobineau, whose *Essay on the Inequality of Human Races* popularized a glorified notion of a superior "Aryan" race and claimed that racial difference determined culture.[102] Although published a half-century earlier, Gobineau only began to have popular resonance in Germany in the 1890s. In an era of increasing nationalism, Gobineau's theories were attractive because they appeared to give traditional religious and cultural anti-Semitism a more "modern" and scientific foundation.[103]

Another influential racial theorist was Houston Stewart Chamberlain, an Englishman who adopted Germany as his home and propagated an anti-Semitic and pro-German racial ideology. In comparison with professional anthropologists, Chamberlain regularly conflated the categories of race, nation, and *Volk* in his writings and argued that races differed in mental and moral faculty as well as physical makeup.[104] His best known work, *Foundations of the Nineteenth Century*, published in 1899, argued that the "Germanic" or "Teutonic" race was the driving force behind European civilization. By the turn of the century, the ideas of racial theorists like Gobineau and Chamberlain had taken root in ultranationalist organizations like the Pan German League, whose members readily accepted the notion that race was the central causative force in human history, that biological makeup determined culture, and that Aryans stood at the top of the racial ladder.[105] Despite the unsystematic and diffuse nature of *völkisch* ideologies, a common characteristic of much of Germanic or Teutonic racial thought was the assumption of a congruence between race, culture, and language.

Leading German anthropologists, however, generally rejected *völkisch*, Aryan, and Germanic racial doctrines on the basis that racial, linguistic and cultural groupings did not coincide. Initially, anthropologists entertained theories about Aryan language roots, hoping to discover the prehistoric origins and relationships of European peoples through linguistics. While the Aryan idea was still generally new, members of the anthropological community guardedly accepted the notion of an Aryan language group and even referred to an "Aryan race" at points.[106] Skepticism about Aryan linguistic theories soon set in, however, and anthropologists increasingly avoided any link between the Aryan concept and race. Virchow, for example, expressed doubt about the linguistic evidence upon which the notion of an Aryan language group was based. Reviewing the work of philologists on the subject, Virchow commented that the entire theory was like "an ingenious and artistic building, in which as soon one of the supports is taken away, the result is a strong rocking and shaking of the entire structure."[107] In his anthropological compendium of 1887, Ranke extensively quoted Virchow's doubts about the congruence of the Aryan language group with a blond haired and blue-eyed physical type.[108] Luschan also maintained that although the Aryan language group may have corresponded to race at some point in the distant past, this was no longer the case: "Certainly there is an indo-Germanic language family, but there is no more Aryan race; the peoples that speak indo-Germanic languages today belong to different races that have among them few physical characteristics in common. . . . Whoever simply wants to look around immediately grasps that linguistic unity cannot fully correspond with the physical, as one usually assumed earlier."[109] The dismissal of the Aryan race idea was widespread in the anthropological community by the late nineteenth century.

For similar reasons, anthropologists also generally avoided references to a "Germanic" race. In the 1870s and 1880s, German anthropologists hoped to assemble an anthropological profile of a "Germanic type" and undertook a series of craniological studies to that end.[110] Virchow's study of schoolchildren, however, made it clear that Germans were a mixture of several physical varieties. Anthropologists increasingly abandoned the attempt to construct a "Germanic type" as they became more sensitive about their use of the term in the face of rising Germanic racism. By the turn of the century, Virchow became very cautious about referring to a Germanic "type" or identifying bones and skulls as "Germanic." Near the end of his life, for example, he argued that he could not tell any difference between a Germanic and a Slavic skull and also maintained that there were no clear physical boundaries between Celtic and Germanic peoples.[111] In his view, there was "no positive characteristic of the Germanic skull," which meant that a German skull was indistinguishable from those of other ethnic groups.[112] In other words, national or ethnic categories did not correspond to a set of physical characteristics.[113] In the same vein Kollmann attacked the notion of a "Germanic race" in 1900 by asserting that race and nation as categories did not influence each other.[114]

German anthropologists in the liberal tradition were also generally opposed to anti-Semitism and were hesitant to construct Jews as a distinct race. This hesitation was based not only on liberal ideological grounds, but also on a desire to maintain the distinctions between race, language and culture. As a liberal who supported equal rights before the law, Virchow was ideologically opposed to anti-Semitism throughout his public life. In 1880 he defeated the notorious court preacher and leader of the anti-Semitic Christian Socialist Party, Adolf Stöcker (1835–1909), in an election for a seat in the German parliament. In an era in which anti-Semitic political movements were on the rise,[115] he spoke out publicly against anti-Semitism, particularly in the German university system, and identified himself as an opponent of anti-Jewish sentiment.[116] Virchow's anthropological view of Jews was often contradictory, but also demonstrated the influence of his opposition to anti-Semitism. Although he made references to a "Jewish race" at several points in his career, he became increasingly cautious about constructing Jews as a race by the 1890s. His study of German schoolchildren in the 1880s demonstrated, for example, that Jews in Germany did not possess a uniform physical type. Later, in 1896, he similarly claimed that no one had been able to prove that a specifically Jewish skull type existed.[117] Virchow thus frequently upheld the notion that Jews, like other ethnic groups in Europe, exhibited many different physical types, rather than a uniform morphology that could be construed as a "race." Similarly, Luschan directly challenged the popular conception that Jews were a racially distinct group by emphasizing the difference between race and language. He claimed that Jews, like other European peoples, represented a racial mixture. More importantly, he maintained that it was a grave mistake to refer to Jews as inferior, and he lauded Jewish cultural accomplishments. Ancient Palestine, he argued, had supplied Western civilization with writing, poetry, religion, and architecture.[118]

These views did not prevent anthropologists from subscribing to a variety of negative stereotypes about Jews, however—many of which were typical of the period. Both Luschan and Virchow made remarks at various points about the "Jewish nose," and consistently assumed that Jews were a distinct group apart from Germans.[119] Later in his life, Luschan remarked privately on the "purely Jewish appearance" of several Austrian Jews whom he had known in Vienna.[120] And yet, despite these contradictions, German anthropologists set themselves apart from Germanic and *völkisch* racial theorists by generally opposing anti-Semitism and avoiding the construction of Jews as a distinct race. Moreover, as Benoit Massin has pointed out, German anthropologists remained relatively uninterested in Jews as subjects of anthropological inquiry during this period. Among the thousands of articles that appeared in the major German anthropological journals from 1890 to 1914, only six dealt specifically with Jews.[121]

On a broader level, anthropologists in the liberal tradition opposed the importation of *völkisch* and radical nationalist politics into what they considered the objective realm of science. Teutonic and Germanic racial theorists often claimed to be practicing a brand of "political anthropology" that they maintained was simply an application of biological dictates to social and civic life.[122] Benoit Massin has argued that the major racial theorists in the Germanic and *völkisch* vein had little or no place within the German anthropological community in the late nineteenth century.[123] The leading figures in the liberal tradition—Virchow, Ranke, and Kollmann—prevented *völkisch* theorists from publishing in anthropological journals or promoting their work in anthropological circles. Houston Stewart Chamberlain, for example, neither belonged to a German anthropological society nor published in anthropological journals. Moreover, anthropologists rarely mentioned him in print, treating his theories with a deafening silence. The same was generally true of Gobineau's work, which received almost no mention at all in anthropological circles during the late nineteenth century. Ludwig Schemann (1852–1938), the major popularizer of Gobineau's writings in Germany, remained outside of the anthropological community and did not appear in anthropological journals. Ludwig Woltmann, a major proponent of "political anthropology" and adherent of Gobineau's Aryan racial theories, also did not publish articles in German anthropological organs.

Several men who could be considered Germanic theorists did have a place in German anthropological circles, but they were less than central figures. The most prominent was Otto Ammon, a physician and former newspaper man who adhered to a form of "social anthropology" that sought to find connections between race and class. Inspired by the French anthropologist Gustav de Lapouge, Ammon championed the notion of a superior Nordic race and argued for the construction of a social order built on Darwinist principles of competition and biological selection.[124] Furthermore, he conducted a series of influential anthropological surveys of military conscripts in Baden and concluded that urban social elites were of the long-headed type, while those belonging to the rural areas were round-headed. Yet Ammon remained a marginal figure in the anthropological community throughout the 1890s. He refused to participate in the activities of the German Anthropological Society after funding for one of his projects was refused in 1889, and when he began publishing increasingly Nordic and social Darwinist tracts in the 1890s, Virchow banned him from speaking at the Berlin Anthropological Society.[125] Another Germanic theorist was Ludwig Wilser, an amateur anthropologist, archeologist, and active member of the German Anthropological Society throughout the late nineteenth century. His work was not taken very seriously by other members of the anthropological community, however, and his influence was minimal. The Breslau anthropologist Hermann Klaatsch said that Wilser's work "degraded the dignity of science," declaring it "such a store of errors" that no correction was possible. Klaatsch utterly dismissed Wilser's brand of anthropology: "I am sorry to have to say this, but I see it as my duty to state that we cannot consent to such a kind of anthropology."[126] During the late nineteenth century, Germanic theorists like Wilser and Ammon played a role in the anthropological community, but in comparison to the leading members of the discipline like Virchow, Ranke, or Kollmann, their place was marginal at best.

Departures from the Liberal Tradition, 1900–1914

The first decade of the twentieth century saw the dominance of the liberal model in German anthropology erode. In the decade after 1900, a number of anthropologists departed from liberal assumptions, casting the liberal tradition into a period of uncertainty. It was a tumultuous time for members of the discipline, characterized by competing discourses on race and debates over the direction their science. Virchow died in 1902 and Bastian in 1905, depriving the discipline of its leading liberal champions. In their place, a fresh cohort of anthropologists secured positions of power: members of the "second" generation, including Luschan as professor of anthropology in Berlin (1908), Georg Thilenius as director of the ethnographic museum in Hamburg (1904), and Klaatsch as director of a new anthropological institute in Breslau (1907). These men accepted imperialism and the aggressive tenor of Wilhelmine nationalism as a matter of course. More importantly, anthropology was beset by methodological crises and ideological disagreements that brought the foundations of liberal anthropology into question. Extended debates over the worth of craniometry and the value of Darwinism spurred many anthropologists to question both induction as a methodology and liberal assumptions about humankind. These factors, combined with a rising tide of nationalism within the discipline, led some anthropologists away from the basic assumptions of the liberal tradition and toward eugenics and *völkisch* racial theories.

A major blow to the liberal and inductive consensus in German anthropology was the increasing acceptance of Darwinian evolution. Virchow and his colleagues managed to keep Darwinism at the margins of the anthropological community for much of the late nineteenth century, but by 1900 more anthropologists proved open to Darwinian ideas. A major factor in this turnaround was a series of fossil discoveries that provided more evidence for biological evolution. The Dutch anatomist Eugene DuBois unearthed the *pithecanthropus* in Java in 1891, and finds of new skulls continued at Heidelberg in 1907 and Combe Lachapelle in 1909. In light of these discoveries, resistance to Darwinism appeared harder to justify. The sole champion of Darwinism in German-speaking anthropological circles for much of the late nineteenth century had been Hermann Schaffhausen at Bonn, but in the late 1890s he was joined by Klaatsch in Breslau and Gustav Schwalbe in Strasbourg, who became increasingly influential in the discipline after Virchow's death. Perhaps the most prominent convert to Darwinian evolution was Luschan, the occupant of the full chair in anthropology at the University of Berlin by 1908, who advocated the "struggle for life and existence" as a natural law in political and social life.[127] By the end of the first decade of the twentieth century, Darwinism was widely accepted within the German anthropological community.[128] Even at Virchow's memorial service in 1902, the main speaker portrayed the old man's objections to Darwinism as outmoded and even quaint.[129] The recognition of Darwinian theory ended the monopoly of inductive empiricism within the anthropological establishment, effectively opening it to other, noninductive directions.

The acceptance of Darwinism also meant that illiberal positions on the subject of race became more common. For many, the theory of evolution seemed to justify the assumption of inequality among peoples. The mechanism of natural selection itself was based on struggle and the creation of biological inequality. Even though Darwin himself did not include any notion of progress in his *Origin of Species*, scientists the world over found in

Darwin a justification for labeling certain peoples and cultures backward and inferior.[130] Pro-Darwin anthropologists did the same, assuming in the process a connection between physical characteristics and mental and cultural faculty. Schwalbe was among this group, directly proclaiming a link between the categories of race and psychological characteristics soon after Virchow's death.[131] So too was Reche, the young anthropologist in residence at the Hamburg Museum für Völkerkunde, who by 1909 had accepted the notion of higher and lower races on the basis of a Darwinian perspective.[132]

As the inductive consensus surrounding Darwinism began to fracture, so too did opinions on craniometry. The fin de siècle saw a general revolt against positivism in the social sciences.[133] In anthropology, that trend manifested itself as a growing skepticism toward Virchow's inductively inspired craniometric methods. Even after several decades of cautious data collection on the inductive model, craniometry had yet to achieve firm conclusions about race by the 1890s. In that decade, several prominent anthropologists began to question whether the practice was leading the discipline in a productive direction. In 1891 Abraham Lissauer noted that the "search for new methods and measurements" was natural when researchers considered "how long craniology has been active" and "how few results [it] has produced."[134] The Hungarian anthropologist Aurel von Török created a controversy in the 1890s when he took over 5,000 measurements of a single skull and concluded that the craniometric method did not allow firm conclusions.[135] He questioned not only the cephalic index, but also the very epistemological assumptions behind anthropometric measurement, arguing that the search for "pure types" was doomed to failure. Török subsequently engaged in a lengthy debate with Kollmann over the value of craniometric methods and data. Anthropologists began to wonder whether they should "measure further or not."[136]

Virchow and Ranke led an initial charge to retain the Frankfurt agreement and the German horizontal in the 1890s, and various efforts to reform craniometric systems ensued that stretched into the twentieth century.[137] The issue was not settled in the years leading up to the war, and anthropological journals commonly included articles in which anthropologists rejected the cephalic index only to propose other measurements schemes still in the craniometric mold.[138] In 1911, Boas muddied the waters still further with a study of immigrants in the United States, in which he suggested that head forms actually varied over generations.[139] Meanwhile, Ranke continued to argue that "nothing would more erroneous" than the idea that "all representatives of craniometry must simply give up the practice: certainly not."[140]

In his view, further data collection on the inductive model would eventually solve the problem. Yet despite such entreaties, the debate over the worth of skull measurement fatefully damaged the tradition of empirical induction within the discipline. The inductive resistance to drawing conclusions seemed to delay a reckoning with the flaws of craniometry. By the turn of the century, many anthropologists were searching for new directions.

The rediscovery of Mendel's laws of inheritance by the scientific community around 1900 seemed to offer anthropologists a way out of their methodological problems. On the basis of his work with pea plants in the 1860s, Gregor Mendel posited a theory of how traits were inherited. His work was generally ignored until the turn of the century, but its revival led to a wave of excitement in many fields about the potential of genetics. Anthropologists were not immune. Many younger members of the discipline saw genetic approaches as an alternative to the endless data collection of Virchow's morphological anthropology. Mendel's laws were attractive because they appeared to allow the application of human genetics to the question of physical and even mental difference. Klaatsch was among those who argued that the craniometric method in anthropology had to be revised in light of new discoveries in genetics.[141] Luschan, while remaining committed to craniometry, also expressed interest in exploring the effects of "race mixing."[142]

Anthropological work in the area of genetics was just beginning in the first decade of the twentieth century. Eugen Fischer was one of the first to employ Mendelian principles of inheritance to anthropology in his landmark study of "race mixing" between Dutch settlers and native Hottentots in German Southwest Africa, which he presented to the anthropological community in 1908 and published in 1913.[143] Fischer concluded that certain racial characteristics operated as heritable recessive and dominant traits on the Mendelian model. He maintained that darker skin, hair, and eyes, for example, were dominant genetic characteristics, since these traits appeared more regularly in "mixed race" groups.[144] Specialists took his work as proof that Mendelian genetic principles applied to human populations. In the years leading up to the outbreak of war, articles on the attempts to apply Mendelian laws to the inheritance of human physical characteristics became increasingly common.[145] The shared assumption of this approach was not only that morphological features were permanent and heritable traits, but also that psychological characteristics were passed down. In the genetic conception, both physical and mental traits distinguished races from one another. This view represented a major step away from the liberal conception of races as categories defined by physical characteristics alone.

A further challenge to the liberal tradition came in the form of Nordic racial theories, which increasingly gained acceptance within the international and German anthropological communities around the turn of the century. The increased influence of Nordic racial ideas was largely due to Virchow's absence after 1902 and their greater international currency. Around 1900, several new works from abroad suggested a revised system of racial classification for Europe that centered on the notion of a Northern European or "Nordic" race. Writers such as the American sociologist William Z. Ripley (1867–1941) and the French anthropologist Joseph Deniker (1852–1918) argued for the existence of three and even six races in Europe, contrasting a blond and long-skulled Nordic type with the so-called Mediterranean, Alpine, and Dinaric varieties.[146] In addition, several established and up-and-coming German anthropologists declared their adherence to Nordic racial ideas as the decade progressed. Gustav Schwalbe led the way by calling for a national anthropological survey of Germans on the model of Ammon's study of Baden at the annual meeting of the German Anthropological Society in 1903, one year after Virchow's death. Citing Ripley and Deniker, Schwalbe accepted the existence of the Nordic race and, more importantly, supported the notion that races had different psychological profiles.[147] He also maintained that "Gobineau and Chamberlain's historical [and] philosophical views certainly conceal a healthy core."[148] With this speech, Schwalbe crossed into the realm of Germanic racial theory. Eugen Fischer likewise maintained in 1910 that the Nordic race had been the driving force behind the greatest cultural achievements in European history: "The race that has completed the highest and most intensive cultural achievement in Europe is the Nordic, characterized by physically by tall growth, long skull, blond hair, light eyes and skin."[149] Drawing on anthroposociological notions, he further claimed that the upper classes had the greatest degree of Nordic blood and expressly declared his sympathy the work of Ammon, Chamberlain, and de Lapouge.[150]

While Schwalbe and Fischer increasingly professed and practiced whole-heartedly acceptance of Nordic and Germanic racial theories, there were varying responses among other members of the anthropological community. Some supporters adopted the new Nordic typologies and sought to ascribe nonphysical qualities to the Nordic race on the basis of anthropological method. In 1911, Otto Reche produced an anthropological study of the prehistoric peoples of Silesia and Bohemia in which he concluded that the prehistoric Nordic race had been "warlike" and "powerful."[151] For others, however, the new typologies remained hypothetical or in doubt. Even while accepting the new system of racial classification for Europe, individual anthropologists often referred, for example, to the "so-called Alpine race."[152] In 1907, the Munich anthropologist Ernst Frizzi emphasized that the Alpine type was "a human category which has up until now hardly been looked at scientifically" and that "we are on a very hypothetical ground with [this] topic."[153] Others argued that the "a priori" three-race typology associated with the Nordic race should not be applied to eastern Europe, where the peoples were a complex mixture.[154]

More importantly, even the staunchest advocates of Nordic race theory were hesitant to cross certain boundaries set by the liberal tradition. Those who had begun to break with the liberal paradigm were hesitant to equate race directly with nation or *Volk*. Schwalbe, for example, continued to emphasize that race was not related to the political category of nation or the linguistically determined classification of *Volk*.[155] Even Fischer, a staunch supporter of Nordic race typologies, was reluctant to apply the new racial breakdown to the peoples of Europe. In 1910 he warned against "wanting to connect these anthropological types [Nordic, Alpine, Mediterranean, and Dinaric] with peoples [*Völker*]. I consider the attempt to glean exact relationships to Finns, Slavs, Scythians, etc. premature."[156] Fischer's use of the term "premature" indicated that the time to connect Nordic typologies with specific *Völker* might be coming, but that the new categorizations were still uncertain. The hesitation of these men demonstrates the continued influence of the liberal paradigm, even on those who had begun to move away from liberal assumptions. Nordic racial concepts often existed side-by-side with contradictory assumptions drawn from the liberal tradition.

Equally threatening to the liberal paradigm after the turn of the century, however, was the increased support for eugenics, or "racial hygiene," in anthropological circles. Originating with the ideas of Francis Galton in Britain, academic interest in the selective breeding of human beings had been on the rise since the late nineteenth century, driven in part by the fear of population decline in Germany and other European countries.[157] The central argument in eugenic thought was that the interest of the nation would be served by "improving" the quality of the population. Encouraging the reproduction of the "best" in society and preventing the procreation of those with genetically undesirable traits, the argument ran, would solve a variety of social problems and increase national strength. Combining social Darwinism with powerful new notions of heredity, eugenicists argued for the social control of reproduction in order to limit the numbers of the "unfit"—such as alcoholics, criminals, the insane—and to increase the numbers of the "fit." Advocates of eugenics argued that Germany was suffering from a form of "racial degeneration" caused by medical care for the "weak" and the higher reproduction rate of the "unfit."[158] When combined with concepts of race, eugenics presented a challenge to the liberal tradition by maintaining that certain racial elements, however vaguely defined, were more "fit" and desirable than others. Eugenic ideas were far removed from liberal declarations about the commonalities of humankind.

First articulated in Germany by Wilhelm Schallmeyer (1857–1919) and Alfred Ploetz (1860–1940) in the 1890s, the eugenic position in Germany had begun to take on a scientific and academic sheen by the turn of the century.[159] Ploetz and other enthusiasts worked to institutionalize racial hygiene as an academic science by founding a journal, holding conferences, and lobbying for the foundation of a national institute.[160] The burgeoning field received a further organizational focus in 1905, when Ploetz and supporters founded the German Society for Racial Hygiene (*Deutsche Gesellschaft für Rassenhygiene*). The society remained small in its first few years, but its members were recruited from fields like medicine, social science, and biology, further adding to the aura of respectability surrounding the new field. Presenting their young discipline as a positivistic method for solving social problems, advocates like Ploetz and Schallmeyer attempted to stake out a middle ground between Aryan racial enthusiasts on the one hand and biologists and public health promoters on the other.[161] Their method was to deemphasize the role of race in the eugenic program. Sheila Faith Weiss has pointed out that the initial impulse behind German eugenics on the part of its founders often had little to do with race. Wilhelm Schallmeyer, for example, argued for eugenics from a technocratic standpoint, maintaining that the rational administration of reproduction would improve "national efficiency" and increase national strength.[162] Within the Society for Racial Hygiene and the German eugenics movement in general, this technocratic impulse competed with the arguments of pan-Germanists and other Aryan racial enthusiasts, who argued for racial hygiene as a means of combating racial mixing and racial "degeneration."

Many distinguished anthropologists were attracted to eugenics around the turn of the century. Luschan joined the Society for Racial Hygiene in 1905 and retained close ties with Ploetz. Other prominent members drawn from anthropological circles included Rudolf Virchow's son Hans, an anatomist and anthropologist in his own right, and the ethnologist Richard Thurnwald. Even Johannes Ranke showed an interest by joining a Munich branch of the society.[163] Ploetz also established particularly close ties with Eugen Fischer, who tried to found a local branch of the Society for Racial Hygiene in Freiburg in 1908 at Ploetz's urging.[164] Ploetz himself joined the Berlin Anthropological Society in 1903. In addition to these institutional connections, the university lectures of prominent anthropologists began to include eugenic themes. Luschan first taught a course with an explicit eugenic focus in 1910 and continued to offer the class in the years that followed.[165] After a visit from Ploetz in 1908, Fischer began to lecture frequently on the importance of improving the quality of the population. In 1910, before his appointment as head of the Museum für Völkerkunde in Hamburg, Thilenius expressed interest in lecturing on eugenics in his classes at the University of Breslau.[166]

Eugenics appeared to offer anthropologists new missions with direct social and political relevance. As with colonialism at around the same time, here was another opportunity to apply their expertise in the physical makeup of populations to broader social issues and thus prove the usefulness of their discipline to the state. Anthropological surveys of the population, they argued, could be used to determine the health of the social body and the methods needed to improve the well-being of society as a whole. By adopting the eugenic approach, some anthropologists maintained, their discipline could help protect society from the problems of low birth rates, alcoholism, disease, and weak military recruiting pools.[167] Anthropology could aid, in other words, in gathering information on the populace and identifying the "unfit." Already experts in surveying populations, many anthropologists found it relatively easy to incorporate eugenic thinking into their disciplinary repertoire. The appeal was the applicability and apparent usefulness of the eugenic approach, which anthropologists hoped would bolster the stature and prestige of their discipline and lead to greater institutional security. In a clear attempt to incorporate eugenics directly into their discipline, anthropologists often referred to eugenics as "social" or "applied" anthropology. In public appeals for support of eugenics or "social anthropology," anthropologists like Luschan emphasized the small number of university chairs and institutes in anthropology as whole, thereby indicating that supporters hoped eugenics would generate more interest and funding for anthropology in general.[168]

At the turn of the century, however, eugenics encompassed a wide variety of political tendencies and discourses on race. Many Nordic racial enthusiasts were attracted to eugenics, but "racial hygiene" also had a wide appeal among progressive and liberal circles in Wilhelmine Germany because it appeared to offer a modern and scientific solution to humanitarian and social problems. Despite the potential contradictions and inhumane elements of eugenics, socially conscious German progressives like Getrud Bäumer were attracted to it as a means of fusing humanism with science.[169] In a similar vein, anthropologists in the liberal tradition argued for a liberal form of eugenics: a brand of so-called "progressive" social engineering. These liberal anthropologists often argued that eugenics had little or nothing to do with race.

As the most prominent member of the generation following Virchow and the founders of the discipline, Luschan embodied this transitional moment in German anthropology. On the one hand he adopted Darwinism and eugenics, while on the other hand rejecting the notion of a superior Nordic race and maintaining a liberal stance when it came to mixing categories of race, nation, and *Volk*.[170] Luschan subscribed to a form of eugenics that emphasized national efficiency and the rational management of populations. He often avoided the term "racial hygiene" since, he maintained, the theory behind it was unrelated to racial classifications. He based this particular assertion on the distinction between race, nation, and *Volk*. Commenting on the work of Ploetz and the racial hygiene movement, Luschan cautioned:

> Certainly many of the works and views set down there are only to be enjoyed with caution and tested with stern critique, especially because of the one-sidedness with which many colleagues allow race to step into the foreground and hygiene into the background. I would like to take this opportunity to make it understood at the outset that for my part I put very little weight in all of these questions on *race* and very great weight on health. *Physical, mental* [*geistig*], *and moral* health—that's what it's about, that's *almost only* what it's about. In any case, it is entirely immaterial in reference to the health of the individual and the *NATION* whether the individual has blue or brown eyes, light or dark hair, a broad or a long skull.[171]

Even while arguing for a eugenicist notion of improved health for the social or national body, Luschan struggled to keep race out of the equation. He also rejected and even fought attempts by Aryan racial theorists to insert their German racial ideologies into the field of racial hygiene.[172] By distancing himself from the racial theorists in eugenic circles and trying to maintain clear lines between notions of race and nation, Luschan sought to retain his liberal assumptions even while subscribing to eugenic notions. And yet the overall eugenic project, with its focus on the overall health of the social body and its identification of individuals as "fit" and "unfit," represented a clear departure from the universalism of Virchow and Bastian.

Taken as a whole, the various departures from the liberal tradition also reflected a rising tide of nationalism within German anthropology. In 1909, Luschan argued for support of eugenics or "social anthropology" by calling it a matter of "national security, and even our national existence." In military and economic "fights between nations," he claimed, those who were "healthier in body and spirit" emerged victorious.[173] Nationalist themes also surfaced elsewhere in the discipline as well. Schwalbe's first declaration in support of Nordic race theory came in a public call for a nationwide anthropological survey. Touting the usefulness of such an idea for "politicians and statesmen," Schwalbe argued that the German anthropological society had a duty to "undertake the investigation of our fatherland."[174] Schwalbe soon headed up an "anthropological commission" to push the project, appealing to both the public and the state and arguing that the project was necessary because other European countries like Austria-Hungary and Great Britain had plans to undertake similar studies. The massive sums necessary for the nationwide survey were never forthcoming from the government, and the idea soon stalled. The nationalist impulses behind the proposal remained, however, and would find their way to the surface again during the war.

In the years leading up to World War I, the liberal tradition entered a period of uncertainty. The increasing acceptance of Nordic racial theories, Darwinian ideas, and notions associated with racial hygiene indicated that a more complicated period in German anthropology had begun, in which the dominant disciplinary paradigm was by no means clear. It is important to note, for example, that anthropologists did not constitute themselves into clearly competing liberal and anti-liberal camps during this period. Instead, the boundaries between liberal and anti-liberal became less sharply delineated, so that proponents of the liberal tradition like Luschan subscribed to eugenics while Nordic race theorists like Fischer hesitated to confuse the categories of race, nation, and *Volk*. This situation meant that despite the encroachment of essentially antiliberal ideas within the German anthropological community, the assumptions at the center of the liberal tradition were by no means completely displaced or swept aside.

The Persistence of the Liberal Tradition before 1914

Despite the circulation of antiliberal ideas within the anthropological establishment in the first decade of the nineteenth century, central elements of the liberal paradigm continued to exert a great deal of influence. Chief among these was the notion that race as a category was nothing more than a physical variation, unrelated to culture, psychology, or ability. German anthropology was in the process of an ideological reorientation in the first decade of the twentieth century, but the ideological framework on which the discipline had originally been built by Virchow and others was not quickly demolished or even dismantled. It continued to provide the structure on which many anthropologists built their work.

The persistence of the liberal paradigm can clearly be seen in the continued insistence on the part of prominent anthropologists that race was nothing more than a physical variation. Despite the attempts of Schwalbe and others to imbue race with cultural and psychological import, prominent anthropologists continued to view their task as the investigation of physical morphologies, not the classification of groups that were in any way connected to psychology, religion, linguistics, or culture. The 1914 publication of Rudolf Martin's influential anthropological textbook, the *Lehrbuch der Anthropologie*, confirmed that this fundamentally liberal idea still formed the basis for much anthropological work. Martin earned his degree and taught in Zurich before returning to fill the Munich chair in anthropology after Ranke's death in 1916. His *Lehrbuch* became the equivalent of Gray's *Anatomy* for anthropologists soon after its publication, remaining a standard work of enormous influence for many decades.[175] Martin maintained that the task and purpose of anthropology was simply to investigate the physical variations of humankind: "The goal of anthropology is to distinguish, to characterize and to investigate all recent and extinct hominid forms in relation to their physical characteristics and with respect to their geographical distribution, irrespective of whether it deals with forms, sub-forms, varieties, or types."[176]

Martin's emphasis on the investigation of varying morphologies indicated that the goal of anthropology was not the linkage of physical and psychological characteristics. Remaining cautious in his use of the word "race," he made it clear that the term simply referred to a category of physical variation: "We understand the different forms of *Homo sapiens* more correctly in the zoological sense as 'varieties' or 'races.'"[177] By taking this position, Martin upheld one of the central assumptions of the liberal tradition in a work that was hugely influential within the field. Despite his pursuit of eugenics and Darwinian positions, Luschan also continued to adhere to the precept that races were simply physical variations. In 1916 he maintained that race could only refer to "a more or less sharply defined group that is characterized by a number of anatomical and physiological elements."[178] Given the uncertainties and political connotations surrounding race as a category, anthropologists like Martin and Luschan sought to limit the meaning of race rather than expand it.

In much the same vein, anthropologists also continued to follow the liberal paradigm by maintaining the distinction between race, *Volk*, and nation. In the opening pages of his anthropological textbook, Martin force-fully argued that race, nation, and *Volk* were unrelated concepts:

> The ethnological word *"Volk"* is to be sharply distinguished from the zoo-logical and anthropological term "variety" or "race." Whole units of smaller or larger groupings (tribe, clan, *Volk*, nation) are racial aggregates or racial pluralities that have fused into ethnic unions. The deciding factor [in these cases] is not, as with race, morphological agreement, blood relationship, or common ancestry. Rather, what binds the members of a *Volk* (people) to-gether is a common language and culture, a national feeling developed over time, a common government, political boundaries, etc. In anthropology, the term *Volk* has no place.[179]

In no uncertain terms, Martin admonished against investing categories like nation and *Volk* with racial meaning. Echoing the arguments of the founding generation, he maintained that the investigation of peoples, (*Völker*) was the job of ethnology, not physical anthropology, which focused only on physical morphologies. Ferdinand Birkner's 1913 anthropological com-pendium opened with similar statements insisting on clear distinctions between race, nation, and *Volk*.[180] Prominent liberal anthropologists also made similar claims outside scientific circles. A newspaper article commem-orating Luschan's sixtieth birthday in August of 1914, for example, noted that the distinction between race, nation, and *Volk* was central to the scien-tist's understanding of anthropology. "To him," the article read, "races are groups by physical characteristics, peoples [*Völker*] are socially, politically, religiously, linguistically as well as spiritually related human groups."[181]

Furthermore, many leading anthropologists continued to reject Teu-tonic or Aryan racial theories. Chief among them was Luschan, who consis-tently repudiated and even publicly ridiculed Germanic racial theories. Just months before the outbreak of the war, he proposed that Germanic theories stemmed from the hopeless confusion of linguistic, cultural, and racial categories. "The more unclear the terms are," he argued, "the more one intoxicates himself with big words like Aryan or Teutonic, Germanics and Slavs, Indogermanics and Celts, and defines them . . . by national, political, geographic, or linguistic characteristics. In so doing, one mixes up terms like races and peoples [*Völker*], language or nation, and becomes entangled in an inextricable net of inconsistencies."[182] Birkner advanced a similar position in 1913, arguing that it was totally false to speak of a Germanic, Celtic, or Indo-Germanic race.[183] Anthropologists also continued to reject Aryanism and the ideas of Gobineau by emphasizing distinctions between anthropological categories. In the years leading up to the war, Luschan repeatedly drew on a comment originally made by Max Müller to argue that just as one could not speak of an Aryan skull, one could also not speak of an Aryan physical "type."[184] In a more polemical vein, Rudolf Martin made the same point in 1916, again basing his argument on the distinction between race, *Volk*, and nation and the inability to equate language and skull. He wrote that "Germans, Celts, and Slavs are linguistic terms, and therefore it is as laughable to speak of a Germanic or Celtic race as it would be to refer to a long-skulled language."[185] Johannes Ranke continued to be a lifelong opponent of the Germanic racial theories and rejected the concept of a Teutonic race until his death in 1916.[186] After Ranke passed away, Birkner wrote in his obituary that he had been a lifelong opponent of "modern racial theorists, at whose pinnacle stands the Frenchmen Gobineau and the Englishman Chamberlain."[187]

The advance of Nordic race typologies within the discipline presents a more complicated picture, but also demonstrates the often contradictory process by which liberal assumptions continued to exert an influence in the field. As championed by Schwalbe, Fischer, and others, Nordic race theory made explicit links between race and psychological traits or cultural capacity. Anthropologists in the liberal vein, however, often accepted the new Nordic categorizations without linking them to psychological or cultural characteristics. In his textbook, Martin included Deniker's breakdown of Europe into six races, including the Nordic, Mediterranean, and Dinaric types alongside other systems of racial classification, but he made no statements connecting Deniker's categories to anything other than physical morphologies.[188] Similarly, Felix von Luschan began to accept Nordic racial typologies in the years before the war, but he too was careful to point out that the new categories were not related to national, cultural, or psychological characteristics. The Nordic or even "Germanic" type, he explained in 1914, was "a purely anthropological formulation" with "neither linguistic nor historical nor political meaning."[189] Anthropologists in the liberal tradition often acknowledged or even accepted Nordic racial typologies without fully accepting the ideological and antiliberal elements of Nordic racial theory. In this way they attempted to remain true to their core liberal assumptions, particularly the incongruence of racial, cultural, and linguistic categories.

It is especially telling that despite the growing acceptance of Nordic racial categories within the discipline, major figures in the field continued to take a consistently liberal view of race within the European context. Virchow, for example, had always refused to posit clear-cut distinctions between European peoples because of his liberal political and scientific convictions, and in consequence had consistently maintained that all European peoples were interrelated. In the decade or so after his death, liberal figures in the field continued to advance the very same view, arguing that Germans were racially indistinct from other Europeans. As late as the eve of the war, they maintained that European populations did not possess essentialized racial identities linked to national categories. In the summer of 1914, Luschan publicly championed the view that "among the peoples of Europe, there are extreme types and in-between forms, but nowhere firm boundaries."[190] Even the state of Prussia, he argued, was a racial mixture, adding that only "romantics and fanatics dream of physical unity as the single foundation of the highest cultural development."[191] Luschan went so far as to mobilize Virchow's name and authority to maintain that Europeans were interrelated: ". . . Rudolf Virchow, the undisputed old master of anthropology in Germany, was undoubtedly right when he claimed to see no difference between Slavic and Germanic types."[192]

These views persisted in anthropological circles even after the outbreak of war. Johannes Ranke maintained in 1915 that the idea of racial hatred between the "Germanic" Germans and the "Celtic" English was ridiculous, since the Germans and the English were closely related.[193] In 1915, Rudolf Martin advanced a similar position: "To talk about racial hatred on European soil is . . . nonsense, a thoughtless act." Analyzing the peoples of Europe from the French in the west to the Russians in the east, he concluded once again that they were interrelated:

> From this examination of the prehistoric and historic relationships in Europe, the indisputable conclusion arises that despite regional variations all the peoples of western and central Europe are racially related to the highest degree as a result of their fusion and mixture stretching back thousands of years. In every one of us rolls the blood of innumerable ancestors; we are carriers of a manifold hereditary construction, and what we are, we are by virtue of this constant mixture and renewal of our blood.[194]

Instead of emphasizing the differences among Europeans, Martin argued that the peoples of Europe—his "we"—were not physically or racially distinct, but rather part of a common hereditary group among whom intermingling was a mark of progress. Despite the circulation of new Nordic racial typologies, Martin, Luschan, and Ranke treated "European" as a category that possessed conceptual unity. Even after the outbreak of war in 1914, they adhered to the liberal tradition of separating race, nation, and *Volk*. The insistence on the interrelated nature of European peoples was indicative of an abiding spirit of internationalism in German anthropological circles. Even while nationalism mounted within the discipline, the tradition of liberal universalism continued to persist. This tradition, embodied in the liberal belief in the unity of the human species, was also expressed in the view of Europeans as being closely related. By adhering to a coherent notion of "Europeanness," anthropologists like Martin, Ranke, and others provided a powerful countervailing trend to nationalist chauvinism. Intolerant and even racist forms of nationalism may have made inroads by the turn of the century, but internationalism was also still a palpable presence within the field.

The persistence of the liberal tradition in German anthropology was also evident in the first major museum exhibit devoted to the discipline of physical anthropology, which opened its doors in Munich in 1912. The Munich anthropological exhibit provides the historian with a compelling view of German anthropological science just before World War I. For many years, the anthropological institute at the University of Munich had possessed an enormous anthropological collection, but the materials had never before been exhibited to a wider audience. The opening was a proud moment for the aging Ranke, who had worked for several years to open the collection to nonspecialists. Visitors to the anthropological collection strolled through two main rooms. The first was devoted to prehistoric humans and their culture. Upon entering, visitors encountered a display portraying the development of human forms from the Paleolithic era to the end of the prehistoric period, with plaster molds of Neanderthal and Cro-Magnon skulls featured prominently.[195] In a large display case, a collection of skulls from various prehistoric periods, ranging from the Stone Age and Bronze Age to the Hallstatt period, continued the story of, as Ranke put it, the "development of the skull form from the Ice Age to the migration of peoples."[196] Local Bavarian forms were featured prominently, since the majority of the skulls and skeletal remains in the display had been found in the region. Prehistoric burial methods were also displayed, as well as stone and bone tools from the Paleolithic period and cultural artifacts from Stone Age Egypt.[197]

The second and larger room of the exhibit was devoted to physical anthropology. According to Ranke, this space included the skulls and skeletons from the anthropological collection "insofar as [they] have meaning in the assessment of the modern races." At the very center of the room was a display of skulls from the Bavarian region, which Ranke believed gave a "clear picture of the skull forms now occurring in Bavaria." Also at the center of the space, next to the Bavarian display, was a collection of other "European and Germanic skulls (Württemburger, Slavic, Hungarian, Tirolian, and Parisian)."[198] To the side of the European collection, physically separated from it, was a large case containing non-European skulls, including examples from Peru, China, and Africa. A collection of ape skulls also occupied a large section of this second room. Finally, a display depicting the development of the human skull from the embryo stage to early childhood rounded out the room.

The Munich exhibit of 1912 reveals the persistence of the liberal brand of anthropology in the years leading up the war. By its arrangement, the exhibit not only suggested that European peoples were interrelated, but also adhered to the liberal separation of racial, national, and linguistic categories. The skulls in the cases were apparently labeled to indicate the region from which they originated rather than the ethnic or national group to which they corresponded. Thus the exhibit featured skulls and skeletal remains from the Tirol, Hungary, Württemburg, and Paris rather than skulls that were clearly arranged in national or ethnic categories like French, Italian, or German. In planning the exhibit in 1908, Ranke argued that the purpose of the show was to demonstrate the "current somatic relationships of the Bavarian line [*Stämme*], as well as the older and oldest inhabitants of Bavaria. . . ."[199] Bavarian skull forms thus served as the centerpiece of the exhibit, indicating that varieties of regional forms, rather than national or linguistic categories, constituted the basis of selection and the focus of the exhibit.

Most important, it was entirely unclear from the display how these skulls from different regions actually related to racial categories. The descriptions and commentaries on the exhibit suggest that the skulls and skeletal remains were not arranged into racial classifications at all. According to Ranke, the skulls were chosen on the basis of their worth in representing various racial forms, but race as a category did not play an overriding role in arrangement. A reporter from a local newspaper, for example, interpreted the Neanderthal and Cro-Magnon forms in the prehistoric section as "human races," but did not even mention race in his description of the somatic section of the exhibit.[200] The Munich exhibit also contained no hierarchical breakdown of human racial classifications or mentions of the "Germanic" or "Aryan" race. Instead, judging by the arrangement of the display cases, the central distinction in the exhibit was between European and non-European skulls. The case containing the skulls from Africa, Peru, and China was physically separate from the European case. And while the division between the non-European and European skulls was clear, it did not necessarily reflect a hierarchy. Ranke's exhibit conveyed a series of sometimes conflicting messages that were typical of liberal anthropology. On the one hand, it made clear distinctions between Europeans and non-Europeans, and the presence of ape skulls in the exhibit suggests that Darwinism was increasingly a major influence on the discipline. On the other hand, the exhibit reflected the abiding liberal tendency to maintain that nation had nothing to do with race and that there were no inferior or superior races.

Despite the challenges to the liberal tradition after Virchow's death, the assumptions at the core of the liberal paradigm remained a powerful and potent force within the discipline, informing the work and the writings of the most influential figures in the field. Even in a period in which antiliberal ideas made inroads into the discipline, liberal concepts retained their appeal and their adherents. It is incorrect to maintain that racial or *völkisch* nationalism already dominated German anthropology in the years before World War I. The discipline was in a period of change in the first decade of the twentieth century, but the path ahead was by no means decided or determined. On the one hand, nationalism had entered the discipline in the form of racial hygiene and Nordic race theory. The influence of Darwinism made the assumption of inequality and evolutionary hierarchy much easier for some anthropologists. Many of them desired to make their science useful to the state and nation, as evidenced by the attention to eugenics. On the other hand, the liberal impulse toward an anti-Germanic and antiracist position also still existed within the field. The liberal paradigm, which made it difficult to glorify or even argue for a "German" race, persisted in palpable ways, championed by leading figures who held positions of influence and university chairs. In this atmosphere of contradictory disciplinary paradigms and institutional uncertainty, the war broke out. In the years ahead, World War I would facilitate a further ideological reorientation of German anthropology.

THREE

Nationalism and Mobilization in Wartime Anthropology, 1914–18

Just days after the outbreak of war in August 1914, Felix von Luschan arrived in Australia, a country that had become Germany's enemy during his steam-ship journey from Europe. As a prominent professor of anthropology at the University of Berlin, he planned to attend the international conference of the British Association for the Advancement of Sciences as an honored guest, and his stay in Australia was to be the first stop on a larger anthro-pological research trip to New Zealand, India, and Indonesia.[1] Several of his colleagues, including the geographer Albrecht Penck and the ethnologist Fritz Gräbner, were also due to attend the same conference. For an anthro-pologist like Luschan it was a major event; leading figures in the British field such as W. H. R. Rivers were scheduled to present papers.[2] A future star of British anthropology, Bronislaw Malinowski, was also in attendance, although he was still almost a complete unknown in 1914. The confer-ence proceeded normally at first, despite what Luschan called the "frighten-ing" rumors of German defeat in the press and the "patriotic" mood of the populace. In the first few days, the attitude toward the German participants was open and friendly. The various speakers, including the president of the British Association, emphasized the international character of all science, even during wartime, and praised German contributions to learning.[3] In Adalaide, Luschan was even awarded an honorary doctorate, after which he "was cheered as never before in my life."[4]

This friendly mood did not last long, however. Luschan complained of having to stand and remove his hat for the national anthems of England, France, Russia, and Belgium several times a day during the conference.[5] "If those people had had the Serbian and Montenegran anthems, they would have served those four or five times daily too."[6] Official friendliness also abruptly ceased. Luschan was not allowed to travel to New Zealand, and an initial offer for him to conduct scientific work in Australian museums was rescinded. Luschan had photographic equipment with him, but he refrained from taking any photographs in order to avoid suspicion of espionage.[7] Eventually, the authorities became more interested in the scientists. One of the German academics, Fritz Gräbner, was arrested and imprisoned on the charge of smuggling documents.[8] Albrecht Penck was similarly taken into custody and shipped to London, where he spent the first several months of the war under a loose form of house arrest.[9] Luschan and his wife managed to escape on an American steamer bound for Honolulu, where they spent several weeks before finally traveling to San Francisco and then to New York. Over the next ten months, Luschan struggled unsuccessfully to find passage back to Germany.[10]

Under the influence of war, the initially open and international tone of the British conference in Australia rapidly deteriorated. The experiences of Luschan, Penck, and Gräbner in Australia illustrate the direct and immediate impact of World War I on the wider scientific community, and more specifically, on the discipline of anthropology in Germany. In Luschan's case, the outbreak of war disrupted his plans for anthropological research abroad, poisoned the atmosphere of national cooperation at an international conference, and put him under suspicion as a spy. German-speaking anthropologists were not alone in this regard. As a Polish subject of the Austrian Empire who had lived for four years in Great Britain, Bronislaw Malinowski remained in Australia as an "enemy alien" after the British Association Conference. In 1915 he was briefly arrested when he failed to report to the local authorities in Melbourne.[11] (Despite his status, Malinowski managed to conduct his groundbreaking fieldwork in Papua and the Trobriand Islands.)

As the mood of the conference turned sour in the fall of 1914, the atmosphere of extreme nationalism that Luschan noted in Australia was also peaking in European countries as a surge of national feeling swept across nations like Germany. While not all members of the general populace subscribed to the wild enthusiasm associated with the "spirit of 1914," the ideal of classless patriotism had a huge impact in intellectual circles like the one in which Luschan and his colleagues operated. As Luschan fled Australia, German academics back home were rallying to the German flag with an intense fervor, mobilizing themselves and their disciplines for the war effort.[12] Beginning in the fall of 1914, German science, including Luschan's discipline of anthropology, now operated in a new context, defined by the realities of war and framed by nationalistic mentalities.

The influence of the war on German anthropology was immediate and far-reaching. Anthropological institutions suffered from shortages and limited funds; museums and societies curtailed their operations as resources became scarce. As the limitations on anthropological work increased, so to did the atmosphere of aggressive nationalism within the discipline. Foreign connections and relations with scientists abroad disintegrated. Constrained by the war and determined to do their part, German anthropologists sought ways to support the national effort through their writings and rhetoric. As younger members of the discipline left for the front, older anthropologists propagandized for the war effort, giving talks on war-related topics, defending Germany's honor in public venues, and commenting favorably on wartime activities through their popular scientific writings. But these efforts were only the beginning: over the course of the war, anthropologists used the very content of their discipline to support the war effort. They condemned the Allied use of colonial troops, analyzed the racial makeup of the enemy, and conducted physical studies of German schoolchildren to show the adverse effects of the blockade.

The rush toward "useful," applied science occurred in most scientific fields during the war. Public funds flowed freely as state, industry, and science forged new cooperative relationships under the pressure of the conflict. The imperial government founded a Kaiser Wilhelm Institute for Iron Research in 1917, for example, and another institute for coal research in 1918.[13] Support for engineering was crucial in developing and refining new kinds of weaponry and machines for use in the war, from the torpedo to the tank. Chemistry received increased state subsidies as scientists developed new kinds of poison gas, synthetic fibers for use in munitions, and methods of fixing nitrogen from the air for use in the soil.[14] Likewise, in the field of medicine, many German doctors saw the war as a chance to encourage medical knowledge and rally support for the fields of bacteriology and hygiene.[15] For many scientists the war brought opportunity as well as hardship.

After 1914, German anthropologists fully mobilized their discipline for war, fashioning it into a political instrument. The impetus for this shift originated not with the state but with the scientists themselves, who in the context of war became increasingly eager to define their professional roles and the aims of their scientific work in political and nationalist terms. Several immediate factors facilitated this development. First, the anthropologists were motivated by feelings of institutional insecurity, present since the turn of the century and now sharpened under the pressure of the war. As wartime hardships limited their institutional circumstances and ability to work, they sought new missions related to the conflict that, they hoped, would attract the attention of the state and provide professional opportunities. Second, the war dealt a fatal blow to the spirit of internationalism within the discipline as relations between German anthropologists and their colleagues abroad broke down. This was a significant because internationalism in science meant more than a desire for collegiality with researchers abroad. It signified not only a commitment to the universality of scientific knowledge, but also loyalty to the ideal of scientific work as the pursuit of truth in a realm unsullied by politics.[16] As scientific internationalism fell out of favor, the transition to a more expressly political wartime anthropology was easier to achieve. The full mobilization of anthropology during wartime signaled the final demise of the apolitical stance of Virchow's era, when anthropologists had prided themselves on empiricist notions of objectivity and generally refrained from entering the political fray. Third, the war opened the door to a wave of resurgent and intolerant nationalism which already had been building before the war but now swept the field, influencing nearly all anthropological endeavors. While professional anthropologists criticized the wartime writings of Germanic racial theorists and *völkisch* ideologues, many now also allowed distinctly *völkisch* themes into their wartime anthropology. Anthropologists pushed into uncharted areas where nationalism and anthropology intersected: some sought to highlight racial differences between Germans and their enemies, while others portrayed the connections between Germany and its allies as based on blood. In their zeal to support Germany's war effort, German anthropologists took steps toward an anthropological science mobilized in the service of the nation and moved away from the precepts of the liberal tradition.

Hardships in Wartime Anthropology

The outbreak of war quickly changed the financial and practical landscape in which the institutions of German anthropology operated. From the outset, the European conflict imposed hardships on the main sites where anthropological work took place, particularly anthropological societies, ethnographic museums, and German universities. The chief problems involved shortages of money and personnel, the very resources necessary to keep these institutions in operation. Moreover, the worldwide nature of the conflict also had an effect on the discipline, as international contacts and the ability to travel deteriorated. In the years following the declaration of war, opportunities for anthropological work both at home and abroad were severely limited by wartime realities, causing some anthropologists to seek new avenues of activity. In a variety of ways, the war's influence penetrated nearly every aspect of wartime anthropology.

Anthropological societies and institutions did not simply shut down; most were determined to continue anthropological work in spite of the conflict. Even as the war engulfed Europe, many anthropological societies throughout Germany pledged to keep working. In a meeting of the Munich Anthropological Society on August 17, 1914, for example, the society's president was roundly applauded by the membership for suggesting that the society continue its work during the war.[17] Smaller anthropological societies, like the one in Cologne, made similar pledges.[18] These displays of determination were by no means naïve, however, and members of anthropological societies recognized from the outset that the war would severely affect their normal operations. After the declaration of hostilities in August, the Berlin Anthropological Society did not meet until October, and when it did, its president Eduard Seler (1849–1922) frankly admitted that the war was already having a negative effect on the institution. He opened the meeting with sober words: "In a difficult time, we take up our meetings again. The dreadful war that rages around us and reaches deep into all relationships has of course also affected our society."[19] Seler recognized the nature of total war at the outset: nothing on the home front would remain unaffected, not even anthropological science.

The nature of the war's impact on anthropological societies took several forms, most of which involved memberships and money. The most immediate effects were the departure of younger members for the front and gradually decreasing membership rolls. Sixteen members of the Berlin society were called up for service in the war's first month, and their names were duly read aloud at the first wartime meeting.[20] Other members canceled their memberships because they could no longer pay their dues under the financial pressure of war. Beginning in 1915, the number of members in the Berlin society steadily decreased until the end of the war.[21] Some of the losses were offset with new memberships, and the overall decrease in numbers did not appear severe: the society maintained more than eight hundred members. But the leaders of the Berlin society remained concerned about dropping membership rates, and announced them at the end of every year. Still more serious was that many members still listed as active were not able to pay their dues. This was especially true of foreign members, with whom contact was now largely impossible. The president of the society summarized these problems in a request for a government subsidy in September 1915. He wrote, "In this new year the number of members has fallen off dramatically because of deaths, departures (as a result of diminished ability to work), and the small number of new applications. And above all, the war has interrupted our connections to our foreign members, especially those overseas, so that a good third of our membership dues were not collected. The society finds itself in serious financial distress."[22] The German Anthropological Society, the national umbrella organization for regional and local societies, reported similar financial woes for the same reason: the influx of dues had slackened or ceased altogether.[23]

The grim financial state of anthropological societies enforced limitations on their normal activities. The number of meetings dropped considerably. The German Anthropological Society did not hold a single yearly congress during the war. The Berlin society at first managed to uphold its self-imposed requirement to convene ten meetings per year, but in 1917 the group violated its own statutes by only holding nine.[24] Moreover, the meetings of specialized fields within the Berlin society (anthropology, ethnology, and prehistory) that were common before the war did not take place for the duration of the conflict. Several Berlin society meetings were canceled at the last minute because the space in which they were to take place had no heat.[25] Financial limitations and paper shortages also affected the journals and publications of the societies, which were radically reduced in size. The internationally known flagship journal of the Berlin society, the *Zeitschrift für Ethnologie*, was cut nearly in half for much of the war because of financial limitations.[26] Perhaps even more significant was the lack of funding for anthropological research. A chief source of backing before the war had been the Rudolf Virchow Foundation, an endowment connected to the Berlin society that was designed to support research, especially involving travel, in all the subfields of anthropology.[27] The foundation provided money for Luschan's aborted research trip to Australia and New Zealand. During the war, its activities nearly came to a complete stop; it only provided small sums for limited research, usually for archeological digs in Germany and other accessible parts of Europe.[28]

The war limited plans for foreign travel and opportunities for anthropological research abroad in other ways as well. In the years leading up the war, many ethnologists were beginning to view ethnographic fieldwork as an important source of their data, but this relatively new emphasis was cut short for the war's duration. The outbreak of hostilities between Germany and other European powers trapped most ethnologists in Europe, and several research trips were canceled as a result. Leo Frobenius, an influential private anthropologist who repeatedly called for more ethnographic fieldwork in anthropology, was immediately forced to postpone a privately funded research trip to Africa when the war broke out in August of 1914.[29] Like

Luschan in Australia, other anthropologists who were already in the field also did not escape the war's influence. Richard Thurnwald, an Austrian ethnologist who had been conducting fieldwork in New Guinea since before the outbreak of hostilities, found his research disrupted by foreign troops. In 1916 he wrote to the Berlin society that Australian troops had plundered his camp, forcing him to flee. Afterward he was able to retrieve fifty-two boxes of ethnographic objects from the English authorities and indigenous peoples before sailing to San Francisco.[30] With some difficulty he eventually made his way back to Germany, but his research in New Guinea was over. The war similarly disrupted other ethnologists and anthropologists in their research. While on a trip to Bolivia, the ship that Rudolf Hermann was aboard was forced to take refuge in a foreign port after being attacked.[31] Similarly, Alfred Schachtzabel, an assistant at the Berlin ethnographic museum, could not return to Germany from Portuguese West Africa, where he had been conducting research. Physical anthropologists were also affected. Rudolf Martin, one of the leading figures in the field, was conducting research in Paris when the war broke out. He fled the city as quickly as possible, abandoning his personal library in his haste to leave.[32] The war's global nature prevented anthropologists from undertaking research abroad, even if they were already in the field.

The other major institutions upon which anthropology and ethnology depended were also disrupted by the war. Ethnographic museums, for example, faced a severe scarcity of resources that limited their day-to-day operations. The ethnographic museum in Berlin suffered throughout the war from shortages of paper, coal, and petroleum.[33] It remained open, but only for a few hours a day.[34] In Hamburg the situation was more dire: the opening of a newly constructed and freshly outfitted ethnographic museum was planned for 1914, but the outbreak of war meant that the building remained closed.[35] Many of the museum's personnel, including the heads of three departments, were called to service in that year. As director, George Thilenius was forced to rethink his timetable for opening the collections to the public.[36] With a skeleton crew, including one anthropologist who had returned wounded from the front, he managed to prepare and open one section of the museum, the "Oceanic exhibit," in 1916. Several other sections, most of which remained incomplete, were opened to the public by 1918. Thilenius remained unsatisfied with the quality and organization of the collections, and emphasized the work that needed to be done once the war was over.[37] The celebration that had been planned at the museum's official opening did not take place during the war. Despite its problems, however, the museum in Hamburg fared better than the anatomical institute in

Freiburg, where Eugen Fischer conducted his anthropological work. In 1917 that institute and its collection were bombed and destroyed by English and French planes.[38]

Anthropological institutions were hard hit by the limitations and shortages of life on the home front. The chief problems were financial, but the lack of personnel and active scientists also took their toll. Societies and museums were forced to curtail their normal activities significantly. Foreign travel was now out of the question, eliminating the possibility for anthropological research abroad. This is not to say that the business of anthropology came to a stop from 1914 to 1918. A quick look through any wartime anthropological journal indicates that anthropologists continued to write, publish, and lecture on highly specialized anthropological topics, many of which were not related to the European conflict. The hardships that the discipline faced could not be ignored, however, and the limitations of wartime academic life permeated the activities of anthropological institutions. From 1914 onward, the war was a palpable presence within German anthropology. Wartime hardships framed all work within the field and contributed to a wartime atmosphere within anthropological institutions that was highly nationalistic.

Nationalism and Internationalism in Wartime Anthropology

The impact of the war went far beyond institutional hardships, however, to impinge on the very ideological and methodological frameworks in which scientists conducted their work. A major conceptual touchstone in the European scientific community before 1914 was the ideal of scientific internationalism. Reaching back to the seventeenth-century notion of a "republic of science," scientists assumed that they were engaged in the objective pursuit of truth using common standards and methods, an activity that transcended national boundaries.[39] The central element of the internationalist ideal was the universality of scientific knowledge, the proposition that something was true only if researchers anywhere could obtain the same results using the same methods. A further assumption was that scientific work should remain an activity separate from the sordid machinations of politics. According to Daniel Kevles, "Truth knew no national boundaries, those who pursued it liked to say, and before 1914 scientists everywhere considered themselves members of an international community whose activities were unaffected by the divagations of politics."[40] Indeed, European scientists in the late nineteenth century created institutions—research centers, prizes, and conferences—that encouraged a sense of community and cooperation. International contacts and exchange were considered critical to good science.

The same international structures, of course, also allowed for competition between scientists of different nations. With this in mind, Paul Forman has suggested that scientific internationalism also allowed for the expression of nationalist impulses. International networks validated scientific achievements as legitimate and raised the status of the individual scientist, but success in scientific endeavor also brought national prestige. In times of peace, scientists were not forced to choose between serving the interests of science or the interests of the nation; internationalism and nationalism could coexist without apparent contradiction. In wartime, however, this balance was more difficult to maintain, as scientists often felt compelled to apply their science to practical problems in the service of the country at the very same moment that international prestige and standards suddenly mattered less to individual scientists. Forman theorizes that during wartime, scientists often still publicly supported scientific internationalism as a means of keeping their self-image intact, even while they ignored it in practice.[41] A similar process occurred in the German anthropological community during World War I.

In the years leading up to the war, nationalism and internationalism existed side-by-side in German academic and intellectual circles. German professors, both as civil servants and as "carriers of culture" (*Kulturträger*), were almost uniquely wedded to the goals of the German state, and patriotism ran extremely high in German academic life. On the other hand, international contact between scholars of different nations increased dramatically in nearly all fields of knowledge over the same period.[42] Scholarly organizations, international conferences, and faster modes of communication and transportation aided in the establishment of academic relationships across national borders. The war unleashed a tide of national feeling in German academic circles, but the tension between internationalism and nationalism also remained palpable in many fields of intellectual endeavor. This was particularly true in the natural sciences, where international ties were strong.[43] While humanist scholars like historians and theologians aggressively denounced Germany's enemies, those in the natural sciences often cautiously protected their links to academics in other countries. Anthropology, which considered itself a natural science, was also faced with a tension between its international associations and the patriotism of its members during World War I.

Under the influence of Virchow the anthropology of the founding generation had been characterized by a profound internationalism, and that tradition continued after 1900. As empiricists, they understood themselves as being engaged in an objective pursuit, separate from politics, that produced universally verifiable scientific knowledge. Expressions of scientific internationalism, however, usually took the form of international exchange and cooperation. Members of the discipline frequently declared their understanding of anthropology as a science with a profoundly international character. Wilhelm Waldeyer's 1909 comment before the German anthropological society upon his return from the fifty-year celebration of the French Anthropological Society in 1909 was typical: "The celebration fully carried the character of an international brotherhood. A science, like anthropology, that wants to be of use to humanity, must be international by necessity."[44] Luschan publicly praised Virchow's efforts to "cultivate international connections and . . . in the realm of science to push political jealousy into the background."[45] Members of the German anthropological community developed close ties with anthropologists throughout western and central Europe, as demonstrated by the high numbers of international "corresponding members" on the membership rolls of the Berlin Anthropological Society. German anthropologists also received training abroad. Luschan, for example, was an Austrian who studied under Paul Broca in Paris and then made his career in Berlin.

International contacts had increased in the first decade of the twentieth century, but aggressive nationalism had been on the rise within anthropology as well. German anthropologists attended international conferences and increased their contacts abroad, but they also almost overwhelmingly supported German colonialism, an endeavor laced with nationalist visions of a greater Germany. Luschan provides a good example of the complex dynamic between internationalism and nationalism in anthropology. Over the course of his career he attended numerous international conferences, and was traveling to exactly such an event in Australia as the war broke out. In 1911 he served as vice president of the First Universal Races conference in London, a meeting that brought together white and "colored" intellectuals from all over the world who shared a distinctly antiracist perspective. At that very conference he affirmed liberal notions of the unity of the human species, questioned the notion of "savage" peoples, and maintained that no one physical type was superior to any other, but he also argued against pacifism and claimed that national struggle was necessary. Without national competition, he argued, "mankind would remain like a herd of sheep, if we were to lose our national ambition and cease to look with pride and delight, not only on our industries and science, but also on our splendid soldiers and glorious ironclads."[46] The tone of nationalist and militarist threat in this statement was palpable. Before 1914, the coexistence of international connections and nationalism in anthropology was not necessarily contradictory, but once the war broke out, the need to resolve the tension between the two presented itself in earnest.

During the war, some voices in German anthropology continued to insist on the international character of science while also supporting the need for connections with scholars abroad. Waldeyer noted the loss of all international scientific contact during the war and argued that such contact was crucial. "International scientific enterprises . . . have given up their contact for the duration of the war. International scientific congresses and learned societies have not met since the outbreak of the war. It is clear that the common work of all countries must and will be initiated again, because it is a necessity."[47] Other anthropologists were still more direct. Rudolf Martin, the author of the standard textbook for anthropology, argued in 1914 that science was inherently international. In response to wartime calls to cultivate a uniquely "German science," he wrote, "There is no real national and therefore also no German science . . . . The question, 'national or international science' is superfluous. All science is by nature international."[48] It is also important to note that Martin did not use the term *Naturwissenschaft*, or natural science, in this context, but rather the more general term *Wissenschaft*, a word that connotes any organized body of knowledge. All fields of inquiry, in his view, were international undertakings.

Several actions within anthropological institutions also suggest that internationalism was a presence in the discipline during the war. At the outbreak of the conflict, the Berlin Anthropological Society simply tabled the membership requests of several British anthropologists with the expectation that they would be taken up after the war had ended.[49] Moreover, international connections with neutral countries continued to flourish. Thilenius, head of the Hamburg ethnographic museum, traveled to Switzerland in 1918 to examine the ethnological collections in four cities there.[50] The leading American anthropologist Alfred L. Kroeber, of the University of California at Berkeley, traveled to Germany in 1915 and gave a lecture to the members of the Berlin Anthropological Society in October of that year.[51] When the leading German anthropologist Johannes Ranke died in 1916, Franz Boas, then a professor at Columbia University in New York, was initially the leading candidate to fill Ranke's open position at the University of Munich.[52] Even as international connections between Germany and their European enemies were severed, anthropologists maintained contact with scholars in other countries as best they could. In these limited ways the spark of internationalism remained alive.

A wartime incident involving Otto Hauser, an archaeologist and member of the Berlin Anthropological Society, also underlined the caution of some society members in denouncing the actions of other nations. Hauser, a *völkisch* racial theorist and archaeologist who had been living in France and conducting a dig there, claimed that the French authorities had plundered his house and his primary archaeological site at the outbreak of war, ruining his scientific work in the process. German newspapers were filled with condemnations of the French actions and sympathy for Hauser.[53] When pressed to take a stand on the issue, however, the president of the Berlin Anthropological Society announced that the institution would not condemn the French, because, he claimed, Hauser's story was full of errors and exaggerations.[54] Hauser had never been a friend of the anthropological establishment because of his *völkisch* views, and the rejection of his version of events by Berlin anthropologists may have reflected this adversarial relationship. But even so, when presented with a unique opportunity to vilify an enemy nation, the Berlin society reacted with caution and demurred.

These strains of internationalism within the discipline, however, were countered and eventually overwhelmed by the growing nationalist feeling in anthropological circles. This process began immediately in September 1914, when a prominent anthropologist became embroiled in a famous controversy between German academics and their counterparts in Britain and France. Late in that month, British and French scholars launched a public attack on German intellectuals for condoning the "barbarous" actions of the German army in Belgium and supporting Prussian militarism. A collection of ninety-three German professors and intellectuals responded in October of that year with the *"Aufruf an die Kulturwelt!"* ("Appeal to the World of Culture!")—a document that asserted that Germany had not started the war, and which denied that the German army had committed atrocities in Belgium. Perhaps more significantly, the manifesto claimed that Prussian militarism was the primary defender of German culture against the invasion of Russian hordes, and it condemned the British and French for using colonial troops. It also maintained that "the German army and the German people are one."[55] This manifesto and a series of others that followed were the beginning of a concerted effort on the part of German academics to portray the worldwide conflict as a cultural war, one that pitted German culture against British materialism and French rationalism.[56] These declarations represented the first shots in the "war of intellectuals," during which German academics mobilized themselves, their disciplines, and their pens in support of German war aims and actions. The *Aufruf* also represented a fateful step away from internationalism in the German academy. It created a huge rift between German academics and their foreign colleagues, and discredited German science and scholarship in the eyes of intellectuals abroad.[57]

One of the ninety-three academics to sign the document was Waldeyer, who, as the secretary of the physical-mathematical section of the Prussian Academy of Science, was an extremely visible member of the anthropological community. Waldeyer's actions in the first years of the war demonstrated the complicated tension between internationalism and patriotism in German science and German anthropology. In September of 1914 he signed the *Aufruf* and publicly aligned himself with a vigorous brand of wartime nationalism. As we have seen, however, he also argued publicly in 1916 for internationalism in science, even after he had signed a manifesto that drove a wedge between German academics and their counterparts abroad. In November 1914, soon after adding his name to the *Aufruf*, Waldeyer also published an article in which he warned against "hatred between peoples."[58] Moreover, two years later he publicly associated himself with Max Planck's attempt to play down the *Aufruf* as being not necessarily representative of the opinion of the German intelligentsia.[59] And yet despite these examples of ambivalence and tendencies toward internationalism, Waldeyer remained decidedly nationalistic. In his postwar memoirs, he defended his signature on the *Aufruf* by claiming that the declaration had not been an attack on the Allies, but rather a defense against the "slanders and diatribes, which our enemies heaped on the Germans at the beginning of the war."[60] Perhaps more significantly, Waldeyer served as president of the ad hoc propagandistic organization that grew out of the *Aufruf*, the *Kulturbund deutscher Künstler und Gelehrter* (Cultural Asssociation of German Artists and Professors). Through connections with colleagues and friends in neutral countries, this organization sought to "combat the systematic lies and incitements spread by our enemies."[61] As a group of professors with high national profiles, the members of the *Kulturbund* intended to defend Germany's honor and war aims by spreading the German perspective in neutral countries.[62] By signing the *Aufruf* and working concertedly for the German propaganda effort, Waldeyer took an active part in the "war of intellectuals." As we shall see in a later section of this chapter, Waldeyer's patriotism also seeped into the content of his anthropology.

Waldeyer was perhaps the most visible academic associated with anthropology to take a nationalist line during wartime, but other members of the wider anthropological community publicly did so as well. Along with Ernst Haeckel and other German scholars, Gustav Schwalbe, the professor of anthropology at the University of Strausburg, signed the "Statement of

German Professors" in September of 1914 and formally renounced, along with the other signees, the English academic honors that he had received during his lifetime. The document to which Schwalbe added his name aggressively claimed the Entente powers were responsible for the war: "Out of despicable greed for Germany's economic success, England, related to us by blood and ancestry, has incited peoples against us for years and in particular allied with Russia and France in order to destroy our power in the world and to shake our culture."[63] Manifestos like this one repeated a common theme among German academics: the greed and jealousy of the Allies were the root cause of the conflict. The implication that the English had betrayed the Germans because of their blood relationship was also present in the document. It was perhaps unsurprising that Schwalbe signed the document, since he had already converted to *völkisch* racism and had displayed the nationalist motivations behind his science before the war. But as well-known anthropologists like Waldeyer and Schwalbe publicly adhered to nationalist themes, the same thing also occurred at the lower levels of the German anthropological community.

Patriotic rhetoric that matched the nationalist line of the German academy also surfaced within anthropological institutions. Here, too, the Entente powers were blamed for the conflict. This theme emerged at the first wartime meeting of the Berlin Anthropological Society in October of 1914 in statements that demonstrated a tension between internationalism and nationalism. In his remarks on the outbreak of war, the president of the society, Eduard Seler, combined regret for the loss of international contacts with a denunciation of Germany's enemies:

> Our scientific relations with both neutral and enemy countries and the contact with our members living there has been massively disturbed and directly interrupted. We hope and wish, however, that this war, forced on us in a dastardly manner through the hatred and jealousy of our enemies, will lead to an end as happily as it began, to a lasting and honorable peace. Then, we hope, the deep chasm that has opened up between peoples . . . will gradually fill in again. And our science, above all others, will be called first to effect this work of peace.[64]

In practically the same breath, Seler blamed the Entente powers for the war and portrayed anthropology as the discipline to create understanding between peoples. He also implied that the beginning of the war was a happy event, something that Germans wanted. In these few remarks, he simultaneously exhibited a desire to take up international contacts again and mounted a patriotic defense of the fatherland. During the conflict, internationalism in anthropology may have been mourned or missed, as Seler seemed to do here, but everyone understood that it could not be unequivocally defended in the nationalistic atmosphere of the first months of the war. Seler thus tempered his internationalist views with patriotic statements.

Other common themes in wartime rhetoric included portrayals of German troops as nationalist heroes and statements of supreme confidence in German victory. In his report on the destruction of the Freiburg anatomical collection by British and French planes, Eugen Fischer employed both of these motifs. He wrote that the "heroic courage of our brave troops" had protected universities in Freiburg and Strasbourg at the beginning of the war, but that the "brave watch" in the Vosges mountains could not have prevented the attack from the air that destroyed the Freiburg institute. Looking to the future, Fischer wrote that the damage caused by the "common enemy" would be repaired, so that work could again be undertaken "when our students with our victorious army turn homeward and again take up their studies."[65] For German academics, public declarations of confidence in victory were understood to be their wartime duty, a part of their role in keeping up morale on the home front.[66] Examples of wartime rhetoric in German anthropological institutions and publications such as these kept up the steady nationalist drumbeat that was heard throughout German academic circles: the greed and jealously of the Entente powers were responsible for the war, people in the opposing countries were unreasonable if not insane, and a German victory was sure to come.

Underneath the public displays of rhetoric in German anthropological circles swirled still deeper currents of nationalist feeling and patriotic paranoia. In the context of war, the compulsion to stand by the flag and support the fatherland was intense, and some members of the German anthropological community questioned the loyalties of other members. Internationalism within the discipline suffered a further blow as members whispered rumors about one another, and the pressure to be patriotic within anthropological circles increased. At the center of the controversy was Luschan, who in early 1915 was still stranded in New York, unsuccessfully seeking passage to Germany and giving guest lectures throughout the United States to support himself and his wife. Albrecht Penck, who had returned to Germany after several months of house arrest in London, wrote to Luschan in 1915 about rumors that were circulating in Berlin's scientific circles, particularly in the anthropological society. Penck wrote, "Here in Berlin, mind you, in some places people think differently than I about the extension of your stay in New York and are pointedly surprised that you still have not returned."[67]

The whispers went far beyond Luschan's long stay in America, however. At the core of the controversy were the actions of Penck and Luschan in Australia in 1914. Citing a letter from a "young friend," Penck revealed that their chief accuser was August Brauer (1863–1917), the professor of zoology in Berlin and member of the Berlin Anthropological Society. Penck's "young friend" reported on a conversation with Brauer:

> I spoke with Professor Brauer about the hard fate that had befallen you [Penck]. He maintained that one could not have pure sympathy, because what was said about you made it appropriate to harbor great doubts about your patriotic convictions. While Professor Walther traveled home on a Dutch ship immediately after the declaration of war, you and above all Professor Luschan remained enamored with the English nation. When I asked where that [idea] originated, he said that you both remained guests of an enemy nation, you didn't pull back from national rallies, and yes, that you stood up from your seats for the national anthem. After the beginning of the war, you [also] accepted an honorary doctorate from an enemy state.[68]

The heart of Brauer's charge was that Luschan and Penck had maintained relations with their hosts in Australia even after the war had started. Gestures of internationalism at the Australian conference in the first weeks of the war were now enough to bring the patriotism of both men into question. Penck's friend also reported that some professors in Berlin saw the affair as a "national scandal." Upon his return to Germany, Penck immediately addressed the gossip in the first meeting of the Geographic Society, calling the rumors "cowardly slander." He warned Luschan, however, to be aware that there were individuals in the anthropological society who were whispering the same sorts of things about him: "I also ask you to take my naming of Brauer as something secret, because he is undoubtedly not the only one who is responsible for the spreading of the rumors: they have definitely found other representatives in the committees of the anthropological society."[69] This incident demonstrates that beneath the public pronouncements of German academics, there also existed great personal pressure to be patriotic and to display nationalist sentiment in anthropological circles. International connections were grounds for suspicion.

Upon his return to Germany in 1915, Luschan wasted no time in staking out his nationalist credentials. As a native of the Austrian empire, he may have felt an even greater need to do so. He quickly and publicly took up themes that were central to wartime nationalist rhetoric. One of the allied charges that particularly riled German academics, for example, was the claim that Prussian militarism was the defining characteristic of the German state.[70] Luschan addressed this issue in a wartime speech, claiming that militarism and imperialism were ideal forms on which to build a strong state. The allied nations were simply jealous:

> Imperialism and militarism—these are the same catchwords that for a year and a half now are always put before us daily in all columns, especially in the American and English press. . . . To me the definition of militarism that Fritz Mauther recently gave in an open letter to Anatole France appears to be the right one. "Militarism," he said, "is any excellent military organization that one does not have oneself." And so I would like to label what our enemies call imperialism as any ideal form of state that they wish in their hearts they had themselves. I recall an English colleague, to whom I showed and explained something from our museum and research institute in Dahlem just before the war. "Yes," he said, "your Kaiser! If we only had a Kaiser. We would gladly trade you for our king."[71]

According to a reporter, the popular audience at the talk greeted this particular passage with "stormy applause and mirth."[72] By defending militarism and the German monarchy, Luschan publicly demonstrated his nationalist fervor. And in a further rejection of internationalism, he also mocked his English colleague, depicting the man as a jealous of German power.

The international spirit in the anthropological community was further eroded by the actions of anthropologists abroad. A particular wartime incident involving a prominent British anthropologist opened the rift between German scientists and their British counterparts still further in the months following the outbreak of war. In January of 1915, Arthur Keith, the president of the Royal Anthropological Institute of Great Britain and Ireland, gave an address on "The Bronze Age Invaders of Britain," in which he claimed that Germans and British were descended from two different and competing racial stocks. In comparison to the predominantly "long-headed" population of Britain (a physical characteristic that he claimed was indicative of naval prowess), Keith claimed that the modern inhabitants of Prussia, southern Germany, and Austria were primarily "round-headed" because they had assumed the Russian or Slavic head form. He ended his talk by warning that the long-headed stock of Europe was threatened with extinction by the round-headed. Ultimately, however, the long-headed peoples would emerge victorious, because "sea power is a also a potent factor in anthropology, and so far much power in Europe had been in the hands of the long-headed stocks."[73] Keith had been a consistent British nationalist before the war, and he now adjusted the content of his anthropology to match wartime political alignments. Glossing over the history of the Anglo-Saxons in Britain, he turned to the Bronze Age in order to portray Germans as racially "other," as an ethnic group corrupted by mixture with a Slavic strain. In a popular publication after the talk, Keith went even further, providing photographs of the German General Paul von Hindenburg alongside an English politician as evidence that the Germans and the English were of two distinct racial stocks.[74] He sought to distance the British from the Germans, their continental cousins and current enemies, and employed anthropology to differentiate the two nations physically and racially. If ever there was a way to sever international ties between German and British anthropologists, this was it, especially because the talk did not emanate from a crank on the fringes of the British anthropological establishment, but from the president of the Royal Anthropological Institute in his yearly presidential address. Such views were rare in the British anthropological establishment, and some members objected, but Keith gained a very public hearing for his views and used the institute as the platform for his ideas.[75]

Anthropologists in Germany and Austria reacted to Keith's argument in strong terms. Luschan told the students in his lecture courses at the University of Berlin that Keith seemed to be a fine colleague before the war, but that his irrational arguments proved that he had clearly fallen victim to "pure war psychosis."[76] The president of the Austrian Anthropological Society in Vienna, Carl Toldt, addressed the issue at the society's annual meeting in 1915, admitting that he had considered Keith a friend and colleague before the war, but that the arguments of the British anthropologist were "naive" and an example of "wartime partiality." Toldt pointed out the overwhelmingly political nature of the popular article and tried to refute its claims in several ways: Keith's statements were unanthropological, the Germans were not short-skulled, and head shape had nothing to do with naval dominance.[77] In commenting on Keith and his arguments, both Luschan and Toldt mentioned that they had considered him a colleague before the war. After Keith's talk and his article, they clearly felt otherwise.

An incident within the French scientific world also damaged internationalism within the wider anthropological community. In 1916, Louis Capitan, a professor of prehistoric anthropology at the Ecole d'Anthropologie in Paris and a corresponding member of both the Viennese and Berlin anthropological societies, made a series of negative statements about Germans in the French press. He asserted that Germans were suffering from degeneration in both civilian and military life, claiming that alcoholism, criminality, and foolishness were the rule in the German population.[78] Perhaps even more damaging, the French Society for Prehistory supported a motion from Capitan to strike all Germans, Austrians, and Hungarians from its membership list. Carl Toldt condemned both Capitan and his statements in a meeting of the Viennese Anthropological Society, complaining vehemently that the worst thing about the statements was that they emanated from someone who was supposed to be a man of science. Toldt again blamed war psychosis as the root of the problem: "[Such outbursts] can find their explanation, but by no means their excuse, only in a mental state altered by war psychosis."[79] Here was another example of the breakdown of internationalism among European anthropological communities as wartime nationalism took hold.

Taken as a whole, these examples demonstrate that nationalism surged in the anthropological community in the first few years of the war, overwhelming the currents of internationalism that had existed before 1914. Some scientists tried to maintain contact between anthropologists in neutral countries and continued to support internationalism in science, but these voices were frequently drowned out as international contacts disintegrated and patriotism ran high. Several anthropologists mobilized for the "war of intellectuals" by signing nationalist manifestos and heaping blame and scorn on the countries arrayed against them. Rumors also circulated about the national loyalty of members of the anthropological community, indicating that the atmosphere within the discipline from 1914 onward was intensely nationalistic. The attempts to denigrate and racialize Germans in anthropological circles abroad contributed further to the decline of international feeling in German anthropology. Moreover, incidents like those involving Keith in England and Capitan in France provided the German community with examples of professional anthropologists who used their science and their scientific authority to further their nationalist agendas. This idea was not unique to the British and French, however. Anthropologists in Germany also took up their science as a tool in the war effort.

Mobilizing the Content of Anthropology

During the war, anthropologists and ethnologists did much more than sign manifestos and spout nationalist rhetoric; they also mobilized the content of their discipline for the war. By involving the categories and concepts of anthropology in their commentaries on the war and their statements about the participant nations, anthropologists used their scientific authority and, more significantly, their science itself as an instrument in the war effort. In the process, they moved further away from the apolitical stance of

Virchow's day. The late-nineteenth-century claim of a non-political science, based on a dedication to empirical induction, was now cast aside in favor an anthropology defined strictly by national goals. By mobilizing the content of their discipline with the express purpose of propagandizing for the state and supporting national ends, anthropologists abandoned the objections to "political" anthropology that had characterized the liberal tradition. In the process, many of them also abandoned the cohesive notion of the European that had distinguished liberal anthropology. In many cases, the process of mobilizing anthropology for the war effort also involved a blurring of the distinctions between race, nation, and *Volk*, the categories at the heart of the liberal tradition.

It is useful to consider forms of anthropological mobilization along a spectrum according to the use of race. At one end were Germanic racial theorists and anthropologists influenced by *völkisch* thought. These men, many of them at the very fringes of the anthropological establishment, interpreted the war in strictly racial terms. At the center of the spectrum were mainstream members of the discipline, many of whom belonged in the liberal tradition. Professional anthropologists generally rejected the *völkisch* interpretation of the war as a racial conflict, but they too mobilized racial concepts in their own commentaries on the war. They described the enemy in racial terms, emphasized blood relationships between Germany's allies, and painted negative ethnic portraits of Germany's opponents. At the other end of the spectrum were attempts to mobilize anthropology behind the war effort that did not directly involve the concept of race. Here too, however, anthropologists and ethnologists used their discipline to support the state and nation by condemning the use of colonial troops by the Allies and demonstrating the negative physical effects of the blockade on German schoolchildren. The common element at all points along the spectrum was that the aims of anthropological science were defined in political and nationalist terms.

From the outset of the war, Germanic and *völkisch* theorists, most of whom were not professional anthropologists, turned their energies toward a racial interpretation of the conflict. The point on which most of these men could agree was that the war had racial roots. Ludwig Wilser, the amateur scientist who was a member of the German Anthropological Society and enjoyed a degree of acceptance within the discipline, was perhaps the member of this group most directly connected to the anthropological establishment. He proclaimed in 1915 that the war "in the end [was] nothing more than the attack of inferior peoples on the best developed types of human beings, represented predominantly in the German Empire, the accepted leader of all Germans."[80] In an article in a popular German science magazine on the racial makeup of the warring nations, Wilser took this argument further:

> . . . the current struggle for world domination on a scale never seen before is a striking [piece of] evidence, an instructional example for the correctness of the opinion I have always held that "all migrations, troop movements, wars, conquests, indignations and radical changes are nothing more than isolated occurrences of the racial drive for expansion and the struggle for survival . . ."[81]

Inspired by the father of Aryan racial thought, Arthur de Gobineau, Wilser considered race the motive force behind all human history and maintained that the world war in its true form could be explained using racial terms.

Other racial theorists outside professional anthropological circles took similar stances. Karl Felix Wolff, a pan-German archeologist and regular contributor to the racialist and Germanic journal *Politisch-Anthropologisches Revue*, argued in 1915 that current conflict was an "unconscious racial war" between the "middle and east European races" and the "blond Aryans, who have their organization in the two [German] monarchies."[82] In radical right wing newspapers, authors claimed that the war represented a later stage in the ancient conflict between the Germans and the peoples they had conquered in the prehistoric era.[83] Some pointed to the Slavs as the ancient enemy,[84] while others located the Celts as the chief opponent.[85] Josef Stolzing, a disciple of Gobineau, interpreted the war as a conflict between "the three great Indogermanic races, Slavs, Celts, and Germans."[86] The radically nationalist Pan-German League also took up a similar interpretation, arguing in its newspaper, the *Alldeutsche Blätter*, that the racially superior Germans were now surrounded by inferior racial groups, such as the Russians, who were defined by "Mongolian blood," the Belgians, who possessed a "blood mixture of the most colorful and worst kind," and the French, whose once proud racial makeup had recently taken on "inferior" elements.[87]

Despite differences in emphasis, several elements united these radical right-wing and *völkisch* views. The first was the notion that the great war was actually a conflict between races in the larger Darwinian struggle for survival. Beneath the superficial level of national antagonism, ancient racial groups were locked in mortal combat. The second was the core belief that Germans were a distinct and superior racial group, different from other Europeans. Wilser admitted that Germans were no longer "pure" representatives of the Nordic or Aryan race, but still argued that the "noble blood of the German fighters" was more "valuable" than that of Germany's enemies.[88] Wolff also argued the peoples of Europe were racial mixtures, but that race still operated as the permanent guiding force beneath the shifting linguistic and political categories of *Volk* and nation. The German people were descendants of the "North European" or Aryan race which had its origin in northern Germany and Scandinavia.[89] Mixed or not, the Germanic (or Nordic) peoples were a racial group distinct from other Europeans.

The chief problem with the *völkisch* explanation of the war, however, was the place of the English within its interpretive framework. If the conflict was a racial war, then why were the English, a Germanic people, allied with the Entente powers rather than Germany? Germanic theorists used a number of different tactics to circumvent this problem. The chief strategy was to claim that the blood of Germanic English had been hopelessly diluted by their mixture with the Celts. Stolzing maintained that Germans, Celts, and Slavs were all descendants of the Aryans, but that the Germans had remained pure while the other two groups mixed with other races and became diluted.[90] He argued that "the German has kept his blood pure, while the Englishman, with the exception of the Scot and the Irishman, is a thoroughly mixed human being." This fact, he claimed, was visible in the "makeup of the [English] social classes . . . ."[91] Wolff argued that the "mass of the English people was just as ungermanic as the English language" and that the English had mixed with the "smaller, brunette breed still very visible in the lower classes."[92] He also maintained that the English had mingled with Semitic blood and thus gained shorter skulls and darker hair.[93] Wilser admitted that the English were indeed Germanic but maintained that there was often conflict for survival within peoples and races. Moreover, he emphasized English materialism in his claim that the English soul had been hopelessly warped by commerce.[94]

Wilser and other racial theorists similarly racialized Germany's other European enemies. Wilser explained that the "French race" carried the "hallmarks of an unfavorable blood mixing" and was suffering from a "degeneration that is clear to see in the reduction of population growth."[95] The Russians were portrayed as mixtures of Slavic and Asiatic strains, as a people whose Germanic blood had been combined with Mongolian. Fritz Lenz, one of Germany's chief proponents of racial hygiene in the 1920s, wrote an article during the war in which he argued that the Nordic element in the Slavic peoples of Eastern Europe was under threat from the "Turanic" or Asiatic racial element from the East. His chief example was the "unfavorable" mixture of the Nordic and Asiatic elements in the peoples of the Russian empire.[96]

These often illogical and contradictory racial interpretations of the war shared a common perspective: the nation and its companion concept, the *Volk*, were concepts irrevocably linked to race. In the mental world of Germanic theorists, the boundaries between these categories were blurred if not completely invisible. Wilser and Wolff claimed that race and *Volk* were two separate concepts, but the details of their writing contradicted this assertion. Germanic racial theorists cast the enemy in racial terms because they understood the German *Volk* to be a category defined by race. In so doing, they infused the idea of Germanness with racial meaning, glorified the role of race in the history of the world, and displayed a virulent and racialist form of German nationalism.

At the middle of the spectrum, many professional anthropologists sought to distance themselves from the *völkisch* interpretation of the war that originated at the fringes of the discipline. As experts in their field, the leading figures in German anthropology had a stake in discrediting the opinions of theorists outside the discipline as unscientific and unsubstantiated. By doing so, they sought to maintain their scientific credibility and emphasize their status as professionals. Leading figures in anthropology avoided and often outright rejected the racial interpretation of the war. Following the liberal tradition, many leading German anthropologists repeatedly insisted on strict, non-national definitions of the term "race," and in the process rejected the idea of a Germanic or Aryan race. Martin, for example, dismissed the idea of racial antagonism in Europe during the war as groundless. In an article clearly designed to debunk racial explanations of the war, he expressed his disgust at the discussion of wartime racial and ethnic hatred in the popular press.[97] Ranke, the professor of anthropology in Munich until his death in 1916, took a similar view early in the war years. He maintained that the idea of "instinctive racial hatred between the 'Germanic' Germans and the 'Celtic' English" was "obvious nonsense" since the Germans and the English were related by blood and had also allied with one another to defeat Napoleon early in the nineteenth century.[98] Professional anthropologists also attacked the idea of a Germanic or Aryan race that often lay at the heart of racial interpretations of the war. Martin harshly ridiculed the concept of a Teutonic race, pointing out that the original description of the Germans in Tacitus's *Germania* was a purely artistic creation of the Roman writer, who had never actually seen the Germanic tribes.[99] Similarly, Luschan repeated during the war that "anthropologists do not recognize an Aryan race," and maintained that Wolff's theories about the makeup and origin of the Aryans "sound almost like a joke." In fact, he flatly dismissed Wolff as an amateur:

". . . it is sad to see how dilettantes continue to surface in anthropology again and again."[100]

But even as anthropologists refuted Germanic racial theorists, many were also involved in their own efforts to mobilize the content of anthropology for war. As experts on the various cultures and peoples of the world, they were uniquely situated to comment on the belligerent nations and relations between the warring parties. In these commentaries they often employed anthropological categories and interpretations. Furthermore, their interpretations of the war and analyses of the peoples involved often featured race as the centerpiece of analysis. In his writings on Germanic racial theorists, Martin condemned those who sought to give nations a biological foundation, or who sought to strengthen national ties and deepen national antipathies by relating them "back to blood."[101] But several anthropologists in German academic circles were often involved in that very activity during the war.

In these instances, references to "blood" relationships served as a way for anthropologists to refer to racial makeup without violating the strictures in the discipline against using race as a national category. By referring to blood, anthropologists confused the category of race and even skirted the boundaries of *völkisch* ideology, which underscored the mystical blood bond among members of a national community as a central theme. For anthropologists who had already converted to a *völkisch* perspective, such as Fischer, this was an easy task. In 1914 Fischer wrote an article for a popular science magazine about the ancestry of the South African Boers. In his view, the pressure of the war made ancestral relationships to Germans worth investigating: "Precisely at this moment it is perhaps worthwhile to examine how close the Boers stand to us in their ancestry."[102] Fischer concluded that they were much more German than Dutch in their descent, and that this connection had relevance in the current conflict: "So we want to consider, that when our magnificent 'Southwestern' [colonial troops] fight shoulder to shoulder with the Boers, that 'German' blood stands against 'English'— and hopefully soon German victory against English defeat!"[103] Here Fischer made a clear distinction between the blood of the Germans and the English, portraying them as two separate groups with two separate ancestries. The implication was the English and the Germans had different racial makeups as well.

More liberal anthropologists also argued for "blood" connections between Germany and its allies. Even the generally liberal Luschan, for example, used the same terminology toward the same end, but in this case the ally in question was the Ottoman Empire. As an expert on the peoples and cultures of Asia Minor, Luschan was often invited to speak on that region at anthropological societies and other venues.[104] In 1916 he gave a similar lecture on the Turks at a meeting of the Württemberg anthropological society, a professional rather than popular venue. In his talk he claimed that the Germans and the Turks were related "not only by the brotherhood of arms, but also by a blood relationship."[105] He asserted that blond northern Europeans had migrated east and south in the pre-historical period and that, as a result, blond and blue-eyed Kurds who spoke a European language could still be found in areas where they had remained "pure and unmixed."[106] (The Kurds were a minority in the Ottoman Empire, but well represented in the Ottoman military during the war.)[107] Luschan also claimed that evidence of blond and blue-eyed peoples had been found during excavations of medieval sites in Asia Minor. In short, he was anxious to show a biological relationship between Germany and the peoples of the Ottoman Empire, and in the process he evoked several physical characteristics that were considered the hallmarks of race, such as eye color and hair color. He did not directly mention a racial relationship between Turks and Germans, but his mention of blood and his discussion of physical characteristics certainly implied it. In the highly nationalistic context of war, even Luschan confused liberal distinctions between race, nation, and *Volk*.

Luschan's argument did not end with his presentation in Württemberg; he also took his ideas about the Turks and the blue-eyed Kurds into his classroom at the Berlin School of Commerce (*Handelshochschule*]). In addition to his normal duties at the University of Berlin, he taught several courses every year at the commerce school. In 1916, for the first time in his career, he offered a course called "The Ethnology of Turkey." The description of the course in the lecture catalog included a statement about the ancestry of the Turks and Kurds: "Originally unified, the extreme short-headed original population came around 4000 BC out of northern Europe, as preserved for us today in the blond Kurds. The great majority of today's Turks, Greeks, and Armenians belong to a pre-Semitic original population. From this [group] the members of the alpine race of western Europe also originated."[108] Judging by this description, Luschan emphasized the ancient racial relationship between the Turks and western Europeans in his class. He also offered a course on the "Anthropology of the Near East" at the University of Berlin for the first time in 1917.[109] As he wrote in an unpublished wartime text, "There was a time, and not too long ago, when the Near East interested us very little. That has now changed and the relationship to our brothers in arms now stands in the middle of public interest throughout Germany."[110] It was no coincidence that Luschan suddenly started offering courses on the Near East and Turkey during the war. Through his talks and courses he not only used anthropology to fill the new interest in that region, but also used it to show a biological and racial relationship between Germans and their Turkish allies. Presumably, Germans would feel more closely linked to the Turks if their biological ties were emphasized.

While anthropologists commented on both allies and enemies during the war, there was also an increased focus on the racial makeup of Germans. In 1914, the German Anthropological Society announced a contest for the best "photographic images of the racial elements and stocks that make up the German *Volk*."[111] J.F. Lehmann Verlag, a publishing house that would later become the chief outlet for works in *Rassenkunde* and racial hygiene in the 1920s, provided the money for the competition. The judges—Fischer, Rudolf Virchow's son Hans Virchow, and Fritz Lenz—were drawn from professional anthropological circles. The competition aimed to find images of racial elements in the German *Volk*, including the so-called Nordic, Alpine, Dinaric, Mongoloid, Mediterranean, and Armenoid types, all of which were then to be contrasted with pictures of other "stocks" (*Stämme*) such as the Poles, Czechs, Hungarians, Finns, and Jews.[112] The competition had been conceived before the war, but in the context of the world conflict it took on new meanings. As it was presented to the public, the competition amounted to an attempt to distinguish Germans racially from other peoples in Europe. A newspaper article announcing the contest implied that the armies of the Central Powers contained the "best types." "Right now," its author noted, "the best types of the different stocks inhabiting Germany and Austria are gathered together on the different war fronts."[113]

Two much more visible examples of mobilizing anthropology for war occurred in 1915. Midway through that year, both Waldeyer and Luschan agreed to participate in a lecture series entitled "German Speeches in Hard Times" (*Deutsche Reden in schwerer Zeit*), patriotic and popular talks given by professors at the University of Berlin. Waldeyer and Luschan were the last two to talk in the series, and the list of those who participated before them reads as a veritable who's who of the German academy, including the historian Friedrich Meinecke, the theologian Rheinhold Seeberg, the military historian Hans Delbrück, the historian of religion Adolf von Harnack, and the theologian and sociologist Ernst Troeltsch. The purpose of the talks, as the organizer explained to Luschan, was to "have an explanatory effect on the war, but also to strengthen and maintain the confident mood of the people."[114] Entry to the talks was free, and to ensure that the message reached a larger audience, the lectures were also published in 1915. Waldeyer, who cowrote the preface to the three published volumes, described the purpose of the talks in a similar vein: "Today there need be no gatherings to awaken and maintain the confidence in our people that victory must be on our side at the end. Despite difficult sacrifices, which no one has been spared, the trust and the will to hold out is firmly and securely rooted. In this direction, however, lay the intention of the undertaking, and in this regard the speeches completed their task."[115] The lecture series was designed to maintain the morale of the German populace and contribute to popular confidence in victory. As such, the talks were an important site in the "war of intellectuals." Through their lectures, Luschan and Waldeyer engaged anthropology in that struggle.

Waldeyer's talk, given in October 1915, represented an instance in which an anthropologist used the tools of his discipline to present a racialized portrait of the enemy. In the process, Waldeyer dealt a series of blows both to the unified concept of the European that was characteristic of liberal anthropology and to the tradition of internationalism within the discipline. The title of the speech, "The Peoples of the World War in Anthropological Perspective," made the intentions of his lecture clear: the application of anthropological analysis to Germany's enemies and allies. Because Waldeyer's professional identity was chiefly linked to the field of anatomy, his choice to speak on anthropology is significant. Since anthropology concerned itself with the makeup and characteristics of the world's peoples, it was presumably easier to mobilize for a patriotic enterprise than anatomy would be. Echoing a common theme of wartime propaganda, Waldeyer began his talk by pointing out that Germany and its two allies were "at war with half the inhabited planet" and that "from all parts of the world, from all races and peoples, enemies are intruding on us." The diversity of the peoples arrayed against Germany made anthropological analysis of them necessary. "Therefore," he argued, "it is certainly worth the effort to consider more carefully the physical and psychological characteristics of our enemies and compare them with our own and those of our allies; in short to examine ourselves and our enemies from an anthropological perspective."[116] Here, anthropology was presented as a tool that could reveal something new about the character of Germany's enemies, who were drawn from all peoples and races.

Waldeyer drew a sharp distinction between race and *Volk* at the outset of his talk and rejected the notion of a Germanic or Slavic race, but at the same time he maintained that race was a category defined by both physical *and psychological* characteristics, a claim that departed from the insistence of liberal anthropologists that they were not in the business of investigating mental qualities.[117] Armed with this definition, he could then discuss the physical and mental makeup of Germany's enemies. In another crucial departure, he argued at the beginning of the talk that the purpose of anthropology was to investigate the "classification of humanity into races, peoples, and states [*Rassen, Völker, und Staaten*] and the origins of that classification." Here was another sharp break from the liberal tradition, since this statement implied that the physical and psychological makeup of "states" or nations was a focus of anthropological inquiry.

Indeed, Waldeyer organized his talk around national groups and explored the racial makeup of each. He maintained at the outset of the lecture that only three races existed: the Asiatic-Polynesian, the European-Westasian, and the "Negro." Waldeyer classed all the participants in the European conflict as belonging to the "European-Westasian" category and confirmed the close ancestral relationship between the Germans and the English. But there was another level of description and analysis for each group as well. Waldeyer described and analyzed the *physical* makeup of each group, as if each were distinct in its racial and bodily constitution. Each people received such a description, and comments ranged from the "outstanding physical development of the English, Scots, and Irish" to the "tiny, dainty bodies and physical agility" of the Italians and French, which "reminds one of the Japanese."[118] By singling out each people and explaining its physical characteristics and specific racial mixture, he created the impression that each group did indeed possess a distinct racial composition. Moreover, Waldeyer's comments on each group combined physical descriptions with stereotypes of character and psychological qualities. His description of the Serbs was typical:

> By race, they belong to the European-Westasian, are light-skinned but mostly dark-haired, very short-skulled, high in growth, a powerful lineage. Mentally they are on average well equipped . . . Long and in part bitter wars with the Goths, Huns, and Turks . . . steeled this people, but also awoke the frequent violence and unscrupulousness that gave rise to the current World War.[119]

Here, Waldeyer described a distinct physical type which appeared racial in many respects. Making no secret of his pro-German sentiments, he also used the opportunity to degrade the Serbs and blame them for the war. The conclusion of his talk, in which he praised the peoples arrayed against Germany as her "equal in physical ability, bravery, courage," struck a more moderate tone. In fact, in anthropological circles, Waldeyer's talk was considered the direct opposite of Arthur Keith's lecture, and the German anthropologist was lauded as striking the correct tone of objectivity and moderation, unlike his English counterpart.[120] While the talk was by no means a racist or *völkisch*

diatribe, it represented a case in which nationalist politics influenced a supposedly objective scientific presentation. Waldeyer presented the audience
with a subtle racialization of the enemy.

Luschan's lecture in the same series represented a similar example of mobilizing anthropology for the war effort, but Luschan focused on eugenics,
or what he called "applied" or "social" anthropology. The organizer of the
lecture series had encouraged him to develop a thematic talk that had a
"loose connection to the war," and suggested the topic of "the necessity of
Germany's colonies."[121] Luschan rejected this suggestion and prepared a talk
called "Races and Peoples" (*Rassen und Völker*), a lecture on the necessity of
eugenics. He had been interested in racial hygiene or "social" anthropology
since the turn of the century and had served a member of the German racial
hygiene society from its inception in 1903 to 1912. As we saw in the previous chapter, he claimed in various venues that the term "racial hygiene"
was confusing, since the idea primarily concerned the health and quality
of national populations and had little to do with race.[122] In his wartime
speech, however, Luschan mobilized eugenic concepts to present a nationalist vision of a fitter, more competitive German population well suited to
expansion. He also inserted race into his presentation at a key moment. In
the process, he made a number of statements that represented departures
from the liberal tradition.

Like Waldeyer, Luschan carefully defined the anthropological terms in
his talk according to the liberal tradition, particularly race and *Volk*. He argued from the beginning of the lecture that race was a term that could only
mean a collection of physical characteristics in the zoological sense, not
to be confused with concepts like *Volk* or nation. He also maintained that
there were no inherently inferior or superior race and ridiculed the concept
of an "Aryan" race.[123] Sticking to the liberal conception of the interrelation
of Europeans, he claimed that the Germans, French, and English were made
up of a mixture of racial elements and that the diversity within each population was actually a positive quality. He did not discuss the racial makeup
of the peoples in the world war, or try to racially distinguish Germany from
its enemies.

Instead, Luschan examined a topic timely in wartime: the reasons behind
the rise and fall of the great empires and peoples throughout history: "So
therefore races, peoples, states, and nations arise. But from the becoming
follows sooner or later also a passing away. Even great and firmly established
states fall."[124] The question was why. Luschan quickly claimed that war was
not the reason for the fall of great empires like Rome. Rather, the cause was
a form of degeneration that weakened the population. In his view European

countries, particularly France, were now suffering from similar problems under the influence of "modern culture." The quantity and quality of Germany's population was also being degraded by mental illness, alcoholism, urban life, and criminality. These were typical eugenic arguments, but with several important wartime variations. First, Luschan stuck to the goals of the lecture series by portraying the war as a positive development. Struggle developed national strength, he argued. The war would not cause degeneration, because both wounded and unwounded among the "war heroes" would still be able to have children when they returned: "Therefore I don't believe that degeneration is a necessary result of this war. . . . A war like the one now so deceitfully forced upon us causes deep wounds; many of us will not recover from them. But already the next generation will hardly suffer any more under these wounds."[125] Luschan refused to portray the war in a negative light, or to cast doubt on its essential correctness for Germany.

Despite his rejection of Germanic racial theory, Luschan's statements about degeneration and the war also included themes that represented small but significant departures from the liberal tradition. In discussing degeneration and the war, he asked, "What will be the effect of the war on our race, our people [*Volk*]?"[126] Here the two categories appeared to be related, or perhaps even to intersect. It is unlikely in this context that "our race" referred to the French, Russians, or English. Luschan also used "social" or "applied anthropology" to present a visions of a strong and expansionist Germanic nation. He painted colorful images of a powerful and "fit" Germany that would overpower the rest of the world: "Yes, it depends on good customs, not on good laws. . . . Our youth must think so themselves; they must grow up with Tacitus's ideal of a young and manly nation ready to conquer the world. Eugenic thinking must become a part of our beliefs."[127] The emphasis on expansion and the mention of Tacitus evoked the expansionist dreams and Germanic mythology, themes that were central to the *völkisch* movement and to Germanic racial theorists. Luschan ended his talk by urging the German people to conquer both "today's enemies" on the battlefield and the enemy of degeneration within.[128] Choosing eugenics as a theme allowed him to emphasize national competition, the importance of victory, and the positive function of war. Despite his rejection of Germanic racial theory and insistence on racial liberalism at the beginning of the talk, Luschan departed from key elements of the liberal tradition elsewhere in the lecture by blurring the line between race and *Volk* in at least one instance and nearly crossing the line into Germanic-style mythology in another. Taken as a whole, the lecture represented an attempt to mobilize anthropology for the war effort and the nation.

At the other end of the spectrum, the war saw a number of efforts to mobilize anthropology and ethnology that did not directly employ race but still used science to rally support for the nation and emphasize the themes of wartime propaganda. Like anthropologists, ethnologists often involved themselves in Germany's war efforts and propagandized for the Central Powers. Perhaps the best example was Leo Frobenius, the freelance explorer and ethnographer known for his privately funded journeys to Africa. Frobenius was a controversial figure in the German anthropological community who did not possess a professional position in the field, but as one of the founders of *Kulturkreis* theory his work was important.[129] During the war he used his position as an ethnologist to condemn the use of colonial troops by the Allied powers and to refute negative images of Africans, even while he suggested that Germany might make a superior imperial master for the colonized peoples of the world. He visited African soldiers in various POW camps throughout Germany and gave public lectures denouncing the colonial policies of the Entente powers. At a public lecture about African POWs in Berlin in 1917, he condemned popular stereotypes of Africans and denounced those European powers who would use colonials as cannon fodder: "The outrage about the 'black dogs' is completely unjustified and must be turned against those who would use the colored population only as cannon fodder, rather than cultivating their worthy qualities."[130] Frobenius cleverly combined a condemnation of the Entente powers with an alternative—and equally paternalistic—imperial vision that focused on "cultivating" and aiding colonials. Germany was the nation to take up this task, since it was clearly the "most able" to solve the problems of middle Africa.[131] Frobenius's voice was shriller still in a 1916 popular publication on the use of colonial troops in the war, provocatively entitled *Our Enemies' Circus of Peoples* (Der Völkerzirkus unserer Feinde). The book, which included photos of colonial troops, amounted to a blistering denunciation of the British, whom he accused of acting like a veritable circus trainers and treating Africans and other colonials as wild animals. Germany, he argued, had always been the last line of defense against the imperial abuses of the British.[132]

Another example of the mobilization of physical anthropology for the German war effort, however, came from the Munich Anthropological Institute and Rudolf Martin. After the death of Ranke in 1916, Martin was named full professor at the Ludwig Maximilian University in Munich. Immediately upon his arrival in September of 1917, he organized a new anthropological project: the measurement study of German schoolchildren designed to determine the effect of the Allied blockade on their nutritional levels and bodies. Later, in the early 1920s, the assistant at the institute, Ferdinand Birkner described Martin's motives and the project's genesis:

> On September 1, 1917, Martin was appointed as Ranke's successor for the chair of anthropology at our university. The conditions of the time led him to place his outstanding technical measuring knowledge and his talent for organization at the service of the German *Volk*. It was necessary to supply the basis for the American meals for children and to produce exact proof of in what measure the health of German children had been harmed by the hunger blockade of the enemy powers. For this purpose, he erected in the anthropological institute of our university a laboratory for physical measurements. . . .[133]

From the outset, Martin's goal was to put his discipline and his skills as an anthropologist at the service of the German nation and people. But the state was also on his mind. In the early 1920s he argued that the data from the project would be of great interest to the government.[134] During the war, the project to measure German schoolchildren became the overriding aim of the entire anthropological institute in Munich. New facilities like the laboratory were created, and assistants were assigned to the project.

The Munich studies of schoolchildren had nothing to do with race. When his conclusions were finally released in the early 1920s, Martin argued that German schoolchildren were significantly smaller in size than those of other countries like the United States.[135] He rejected race as an explanation for the differences, since both groups were of "Anglo-Saxon descent."[136] The differences in stature, he maintained, were the result of bad nutrition during and after the war. While he refrained from overtly political statements, the underlying message of the studies was clear: the actions of the Entente powers during the war had caused German children to suffer, permanently affecting them physically. Here was anthropology mobilized for national ends. For Martin, this kind of politically motivated anthropological project was something new. Before the war he had strictly limited himself to the supposedly "apolitical" morphological work of the liberal tradition, as evidenced by his monumental *Lehrbuch* of 1914. The pressure of the war, however, convinced him to turn his science to more politically salient matters.

The mobilization of anthropology for war took various forms across a wide spectrum. The most common was the rhetorical support for Germany and the war effort that occurred in nearly every corner of German intellectual life. Trading on their prestige as scientists and experts on the "peoples of the world," anthropologists took part in the "war of intellectuals" by signing manifestos and repeating the nationalist themes emanating from the German academy during the war. More significant, however, was the mobilization of the context of anthropology itself, the fashioning of the science as a political instrument to be wielded in the service of the nation and the state. Martin's studies of schoolchildren demonstrated that not all of these efforts involved concepts of race, but most did. In a disciplinary atmosphere defined by institutional hardship and surging nationalism, anthropologists framed their professional roles and even the goals of their science in nationalist terms. In the process they moved away from the approach of the founding generation of the late nineteenth century, who had championed racial liberalism, attempted to keep political influences at arm's length, and valued the international nature of their science. Wartime anthropologists may not have realized it at the time, but they were in fact preparing the way for the anthropology of the 1920s.

FOUR

"Among Foreign Peoples": Racial Studies of POWs during World War I

In the first six months of World War I, 625,000 prisoners of war streamed into holding camps in the German empire.[1] Anthropologists in Germany took special note of this development, because among the long columns of men marching into German POW camps were thousands of soldiers from the colonial armies of the French and British. Troops from Africa and Asia were of great scientific interest to German anthropologists who recognized in them the rare opportunity to study non-Europeans on European soil. With growing excitement, they regarded the camps as a "very rich observational area for anthropologists"[2]—an "opportunity for scientific research never present before and never to return."[3] Anthropologists were exultant: "Our enemies have collected such a colorful mixture of peoples around their flags that almost all the races of the world are represented."[4] For the specialist, they argued, "a visit to some of these camps [is] as worthwhile as a trip around the world."[5] To some, the POW camps represented the ultimate manifestation of the nineteenth-century *Völkerschauen*, the popular exhibitions of non-European "exotics" that had toured Europe in the 1880s and 1890s. As one anthropologist put it, the POW camps simply were "a *Völkerschau* without comparison!"[6] As the title of a popular wartime ethnographic volume on the POWs suggested, anthropologists in the camps considered themselves "among foreign peoples."[7]

The overwhelming enthusiasm about the non-European populations in the camps notwithstanding, once the project to study the POWs was underway, it focused as much on Europeans as it did on peoples from Africa, India, and Asia. As the project progressed, it was especially the physical anthropologists who became increasingly interested in European peoples.[8] In the process, the question of race among Europeans became a major focus of inquiry. Exploring how and why the POW projects developed into a study of European racial identity sheds light not only on the construction of race in the European context, but also on the effect of war on physical anthropology.

The story of the POW projects suggests another way in which war played a critical role in the transformation of German anthropology by creating new contexts in which the science could be pursued. In particular, practicing anthropology in the camps helped to reorient German anthropologists toward European subjects in ways that contributed significantly to the erosion of the categories at the heart of the liberal tradition. Since Virchow's heyday, liberal anthropologists had maintained that the categories of race, nation, and *Volk* were distinct and unrelated. They sought to identify different physical morphologies or racial types, but argued that these classifications were in no way linked to cultural identities or national groupings, which were determined by language, customs, geography, and politics rather than by physical characteristics. Before the war, the leaders of the German anthropological community had used this principle to emphasize the interrelated nature of the peoples on the European continent, arguing that Germans, Slavs and other groups were not physically or racially distinct. In the camps, leading members of the youngest generation of anthropologists began to conflate the concepts of nation and race in their research on the POW population. Working in the camps, they investigated and portrayed the European enemies of the Central Powers as racial "others," assigning distinct racial and biological identities to European peoples and nations in the process.

The stories of three principal scientists working in the camps—Otto Reche, Egon von Eickstedt, and Rudolf Pöch—illustrate three different ways by which anthropologists arrived at the construction of the European enemy as a racial "other." In each of these cases, this process was driven by two central factors. The first was some form of heightened patriotism which encouraged the anthropologists to view the POWs in national terms and to imbue the category of nation with biological meaning. The high tide of nationalism that enveloped the discipline during the conflict that drove anthropologists to mobilize their discipline for the war effort also influenced anthropological practice on the ground in the camps. The second was the particular context in which the studies took place—or, more accurately, the series of contexts, which circumscribed the process of racial investigation. A critical combination of ideology and circumstances, in other words, came together in the camps. On the one hand, the war intensified the participants' nationalism, thereby creating a dichotomy between allies and enemies; on the other hand, it provided the specific setting in which the studies took place: the POW camp. The camp milieu was a major influence on all three anthropologists. It served to collapse the distinction between European and non-European groups, replacing it with a dynamic that highlighted the differences between captors and prisoners—a situation that encouraged these anthropologists to link nation and race and facilitated the unproblematic refashioning of their national rivals into racial "others."

The story of POW studies thus suggests that the larger shift in German anthropology was not simply a matter of a generation of racist nationalists suddenly emerging fully formed in the 1920s. Instead, the turn toward *völkisch* modes of thought and the conflation of race and nation was contingent on the political, personal, and environmental contexts in which the anthropologists did their work during the war—a set of contexts in which the proteges of a liberal anthropologist like Felix von Luschan felt free to link nation and race. In this regard, the camp projects demonstrate the ways in which experience influenced anthropological discourse and practice reshaped theory. The wartime circumstances in which anthropologists worked significantly affected the directions they would take in the postwar period, accelerating certain nationalistic tendencies and leading them away from the tradition of liberal anthropology.

Setting up the Studies

The POW project was an enormous undertaking that involved the military, a variety of government ministries, and representatives from various academic disciplines. Among the physical anthropologists, the plan to conduct studies in the camps also involved the scholarly communities of two countries, Germany and Austria-Hungary. In both the scope of the undertaking and the degree of government involvement, the POW studies were a significant departure from past patterns of state support for anthropology. Before the war, physical anthropologists felt a great deal of uncertainty about the place of their discipline in the wider world of German science, and they bemoaned its lack of a secure institutional home. During the war, however, anthropologists suddenly found themselves involved in a state-sponsored project that necessitated close cooperation not only with government ministries but also with the German military. The POW projects represented a potential first step in a larger process that German anthropologists had long hoped would occur: an increasing alliance between their discipline and the German governmental-military complex. The close connection between the scientists, the state, and the military that was necessary to carry out the studies undoubtedly contributed to the patriotic and nationalist impulses with which the project was eventually imbued.

The original impetus for the studies in POW camps came from several sources; chief among them was the anthropological community in the Austro-Hungarian Empire. In the summer of 1915, Carl Toldt (1875–1961), the president of the Viennese Anthropological Society, raised the idea of studying the large numbers of captured Russian soldiers streaming into the POW camps of the Habsburg Empire.[9] He argued that the society would be "downright guilty of an unjustified omission" if it did not "exploit this opportunity as well and as thoroughly as . . . possible."[10] Toldt's suggestion included a note of urgency, since it was unclear how long the war—and the scientific opportunities it created—would last. Stressing the singular opportunity that the camps presented to scholars, the anthropological society sought and quickly received approval of the Austro-Hungarian Imperial War Ministry to carry out studies in June of 1915.[11] Toldt chose Rudolf Pöch, the professor of anthropology at the University of Vienna, to lead the Austrian POW project, and by the early summer of 1915 Pöch prepared a team for visits to camps in Bohemia. From the outset, the Austrian project received support from the state and the military. The Royal Academy of Science in Vienna provided the bulk of the money for the studies, and the military worked with Pöch to determine which camps he should visit. Military authorities circulated a questionnaire to the POW camps, for example, asking camp commandants to provide lists of the ethnic makeup of their camp populations.[12]

At the same time, anthropologists and ethnologists in Germany broached the possibility of scientific work in the German camps. The independent cultural anthropologist Georg Buschan, a writer of popular works in ethnology who nevertheless did not have an academic position at a German university, recognized the scientific utility of the camps in the spring of 1915. During his Easter vacation in that year, Buschan traveled independently to a POW camp near Stettin and undertook anthropological investigations of seventy-five prisoners. He received approval for his studies in advance from the general command of Stettin and proceeded to examine captured soldiers from the Caucasus, Lithuania, Estonia, Latvia, England, and even Korea. Soon afterward, he published a short article in a well-known scientific journal calling the attention of his colleagues to the camps and summoning them to do scientific work there.[13] Other anthropologists, such as Fischer from Freiburg and Fritz Lang from Munich, also undertook individual trips to POW camps in 1915 to investigate POWs.[14] But these excursions were independent and unsystematic, unconnected to any larger coordinated effort.

The first official step toward organized work in the camps was taken by the psychologist Carl Stumpf (1848–1936), a professor at the University of

Berlin, who organized support for a "phonographic commission" designed to record the languages and songs of the POWs. Stumpf's idea found an early champion in Wilhelm Doegen (1877–1967), a *Gymnasium* teacher in Berlin with connections in the government and an interest in languages, who soon became the driving force behind the project.[15] Professors at the University of Berlin such as Alois Brandl, Heinrich Lüders, and other scholars involved in the Oriental Seminar at the University were intrigued by the project and lent their weight to the plan. Scholars in Hamburg, including the linguist Carl Meinhof (1857–1944) and the ethnologist Paul Hambruch (1882–1933), also expressed interest in joining the project. Under the aegis of the Oriental Seminar in Berlin and the Prussian Cultural Ministry, the Royal Prussian Phonographic Commission was created in 1915.[16] Stumpf was put in charge of the commission, but Doegen, who organized the phonographic recordings and arranged the visits to the camps, became the project's central figure.

Although the commission originated around the study of language, it also included a section for physical anthropology, headed by Luschan. Luschan's group was to conduct measurement-based studies of bodily characteristics, a project that presented a research opportunity for his students. Luschan quickly chose Egon von Eickstedt, a young anthropologist in search of a dissertation topic, as a central participant. Serving as a doctor in a mobile X-ray unit on the western front, Eickstedt was particularly anxious to secure leave and pursue his scientific interests. Months before the phonographic commission was formally organized, Luschan had suggested that Eickstedt find a "few hundred prisoners to measure (head and body)" and that the project could become a "useful work" that Luschan would gladly take on as a dissertation.[17] Once the commission was organizing in earnest, Luschan quickly chose Eickstedt as a participant, who was able to gain temporary leave time from his unit. Presented with the chance to participate, Eickstedt was relieved that no end to the war appeared in sight, remarking enthusiastically that "a speedy end to the war [was] not likely" and that "an unpleasant surprise from the . . . angel of peace is scarcely to be feared."[18] Otto Reche, the resident physical anthropologist at the ethnographic museum in Hamburg, also joined the project in 1917 after returning from the front with an illness that made continued military service impossible.[19] Thus, as the project took shape, many of the scientists who undertook the work of physical anthropology on the ground in the camps were younger scholars in the very early stages of professionalization.

Like the Austrian project, the German plan to conduct studies in the camps received a great deal of support from the state. In the case of the phonographic and anthropological commission, state support came chiefly from the Prussian authorities. The Prussian Cultural Ministry oversaw the project and retained ownership of the phonographic recordings made in the camps, confirming the influence of the office on the projects.[20] Perhaps most important, a great portion of money for the POW studies came from the highest levels of the German government. Wilhelm II, the German Kaiser, personally approved the project and provided large sums for it from his own personal dispensation fund.[21] It is difficult to determine how much money the Kaiser actually gave to the project, but Stumpf wrote to Luschan in 1916 that "a further contribution of 30,000 marks" had been made available, suggesting that the sums were indeed large.[22] In conducting the POW studies, anthropologists enjoyed a new level of government support and cooperation. With their work in the camps, the discipline began to enter into a new relationship with the state, effectively becoming a part of the governmental-military complex for the duration of the war.

The anthropologists on the project also came to enjoy the cooperation of the German military. The approval and support of military authorities was by no means assured at the outset. Despite the early success of Georg Buschan in receiving permission from local authorities to enter conduct studies early in 1915, independent efforts of several other academics to gain access to POW camps for scientific purposes failed. Meinhof, the Hamburg linguist and ethnologist who eventually joined Doegen's phonographic commission, suggested the idea of phonetic studies in the camps in 1915, but the Ministry of War rejected it. Meinhof even tried to use high-ranking officials in the Colonial Ministry to convince military functionaries otherwise, but to no avail.[23] In initially rejecting the entry of some individual academics into the camps, the Ministry of War argued that "in general it appears urgently desirable to keep the prisoner-of-war camps free of visitors."[24] Perhaps fearing negative reaction about the conditions of the internees, military authorities initially adhered to a policy of keeping civilians away from them.

The members of the phonographic and anthropological commission, however, were able to circumvent this policy. Doegen managed to secure permission to conduct the studies from General Friedrich, the military head of POW affairs.[25] The importance of military approval was confirmed by a popular ethnographic volume that resulted from the POW studies, published in 1925, which included a lavish posed photograph of Doegen eagerly spreading out papers and plans before Major von Wrzodek of the War Ministry.[26] Even after army officials had given their approval, they remained cautious about the studies, a feeling that was reflected in an initial order from the War Ministry to keep the POW studies confidential. General

Friedrich instructed his underlings at the War Ministry that "the entire plan [was] to be handled as 'secret'" and that no one but the designated scientists were to take phonographic recordings of the prisoners.[27] Eventually, however, anthropologists overcame the hesitations of military officials. Camp authorities worked closely with the scientists, helping to set up facilities for the studies and making the prisoners available for investigation. Also, judging by the photographs and information that reached the public from the camp studies during the war, the strictures on secrecy were also lifted. Through their work in the camps, anthropologists forged a partnership with the military in order to conduct their work. The close association with the military and the state during the studies helps to explain not only the willingness of anthropologists to repeat the official line on the conditions in the camps and the treatment of prisoners, but also the spirit of patriotism with which many of the anthropologists approached the project.

The significance of the POW studies for German anthropology was evident in the desire of other scientists to participate. As the projects gradually took shape, news of them spread throughout the scientific community, attracting the notice of other members of the discipline. Another of Luschan's students, Bernard Struck, wrote repeatedly from his post on the eastern front expressing his deep regret that he could not participate in the POW undertaking and complaining about the lack of scientific opportunities where he was stationed.[28] Theodor Mollison, an up-and-coming young anthropologist who later assumed a professorship at Munich in the 1920s, also expressed interest in the studies but was limited to Heidelberg, where he was stationed.[29] George Thilenius, the head of the Hamburg Ethnological Museum, pushed hard to have scientists from his museum involved in the studies, mainly because he did not want professors from Berlin to dominate the project.[30] Stressing the competition between anthropologists in Hamburg and Berlin, Thilenius argued to his city's authorities that Hamburg's participation in the projects was essential: "It is urgently desired that our museum take part in these studies as much as possible, because the commission always falls back on Berlin scholars first and foremost, and only turns to outsiders if it does not have an expert at its disposal."[31] Aside from Reche, who joined the anthropological section of the commission, several other anthropologists and linguists from Hamburg were eventually included in the linguistic portion of the studies, including the linguist Meinhof and Hambruch, an anthropologist and ethnologist who had been added to the Doegen team because of his expertise in South Sea languages.[32] The high degree of organization and the widespread desire to participate signaled that the POW project was the most prominent anthropological endeavor of the war years.

Luschan, who had been born and raised near Vienna and retained close ties to anthropologists there, was eager to collaborate with the Austrians. He agreed with Pöch's suggestion that the German and Austrian POW projects adopt standardized methods of measuring prisoners and recording data.[33] The two men resolved to work together closely throughout the war to coordinate the German and Austrian efforts. It was determined that both teams would seek to investigate the physical and racial makeup of prisoners in order to determine the original racial elements that had combined to form the groups under study.[34] In practice, this goal meant that anthropologists investigated a host of physical characteristics by taking measurements of heads and bodies and conducting observations of bodily features ranging from hair color to eye shape. These methods were no different from those of Virchow's generation, but the interpretations that emerged from the camps diverged considerably from the liberal tradition. The shift was fueled not only by wartime nationalism, but also by the surroundings in which the anthropologists conducted their work.

Encounters in the Camps

Unlike previous anthropological undertakings, the study of POWs took place within a peculiar context in the history of the discipline. The project was defined not only by the realities of a major world war, but also by a specific wartime milieu: the POW camp. The conditions at these sites had a direct impact both on the studies as scientific practice and on the conclusions drawn from them. As locations for anthropological inquiry, the camps placed Europeans into subject positions that were almost identical to those of many non-Europeans in similar camps created during earlier colonial wars. Indeed, in this prison environment the distinction between Europeans and non-Europeans quickly collapsed, replaced by a new constellation that sharply contrasted a variety of national and ethnic groups with their captors. Housed together as enemies of the German or Austrian empire, the prisoners were already political "others" by virtue of their affiliations in the European conflict—a division that was further underscored by the difficult physical conditions and military discipline of the camps. Within this world, German anthropologists held positions of significant power and authority, often equaling or even exceeding the dominance they had enjoyed in colonial situations. In the camps, anthropologists gained unprecedented access to the bodies of prisoners, non-Europeans and Europeans alike, compelling them to take part in anthropological investigations. The physical circumstances and lopsided power relationships drastically altered the sub-

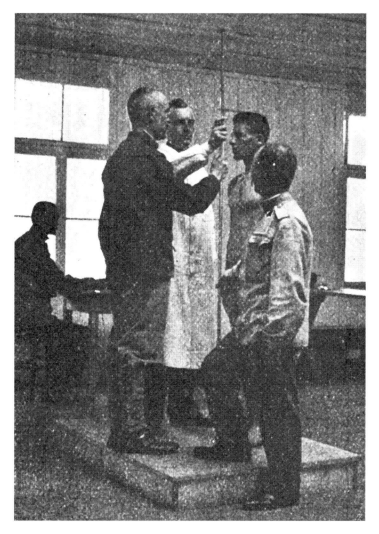

1. Rudolf Pöch's team at work taking measurements in the camps during World War I. Subjects were forced to stand naked in fixed positions. Reproduced from Rudolf Pöch, "III. Bericht über die von der Wiener Anthropologischen Gesellschaft in den k. u. k. Kriegsgefangenenlagern veranlaßten Studien," *MAGW* 47 (1917): 84.

ject position of the European prisoners, highlighting their difference from Germans and thereby allowing new categorizations to emerge.

For the scientists, the POW camps were ideal for anthropological work. The concentration of so many different peoples in one place rendered them veritable laboratories for the study of race. In addition, anthropologists like

Pöch were pleased that the camps contained a population in which bodily deformities and abnormalities had been eliminated, as the men had been selected for fitness and health by their respective armies. As he noted, "all the preparations for finding and bringing in those to be measured fall away: the people are there and at our disposal. The [human] material doesn't need to be sifted through first; through the requirements of fitness for service, less useful elements for the study of racial characteristics are shut out."[35] Perhaps most important, the camps also allowed immediate comparisons of the POWs from diverse racial backgrounds, an undertaking that was normally impossible even in the colonial context. Pöch wrote that "the prisoner-of-war camps offer a rare opportunity for comparative observations; never before have representatives of the most different human groups been [available] to observe alongside each other under such similar conditions!"[36] In the camps, the European prisoner stood alongside the non-European, both inviting anthropological comparison as racial "others"—different, in other words, from Germans.

One potential drawback to the camps was that the population was entirely male. No women were included in the sample. Anthropologists acknowledged this issue, but waved away any potential objections. Pöch argued that the racial characteristics of any given group occurred in both the male and the female sex, making the measurement of women unnecessary.[37] When it came to race, he claimed, the sex of the subject was unimportant. Rudolf Martin, commenting on the potential of the camps for anthropological study, acknowledged the lack of women but argued that the sample of men was just too good to ignore. He wrote, "The female sex is indeed missing, but the men present are in the most healthy age and their backgrounds are exactly known."[38] By glossing over the absence of women, the POW studies fit into a long tradition of sexism in anthropology and the sciences in general that took the male form as the model of humanity.[39] The racial "types" and statistical characterizations that emerged from the camps were implicitly gendered, since they created a male version of each racial categorization. Pöch and the other anthropologists did not give this problem a second thought, however, since the nearly exclusive use of males in creating "types" had been the practice in the discipline throughout the nineteenth century.

On a daily basis, the spaces in which the anthropologists lived and moved distinguished them from the prison population. Indeed, the conditions in the camps highlighted the distinction between inmates and captors at the same time as they broke down divisions between European and non-European prisoners. From the very beginning of the war, the German military housed all imprisoned soldiers together. Despite the protests of the Allied powers, inmates were not separated or sorted according to nationality or ethnicity.[40] This policy meant that POWs from Russia, Britain, Belgium, Serbia, and France shared living space not only with each other but also with colonial soldiers from Africa, India, and other parts of the globe. As a result of this arrangement, the primary institutional distinction in the camps was not between groups of inmates, but between the staff and the peoples under their control. Moreover, physical conditions in the compounds further served to demarcate the camp personnel from the imprisoned soldiers. Because of the enormous influx of prisoners in the first few months of the war, the camps were often overcrowded and ill-equipped.[41] While prisoners were housed in cramped barracks, the anthropologists resided in separate military quarters that, while by no means luxurious, were certainly more spacious. The scientists also ate with the camp officers and doctors, separate from the inmates.[42]

The military discipline of the camps further distanced the internees from their captors. The POWs were under the martial law of the German army and subject to a battery of rules, ranging from regulations about the washing of clothes to restrictions against smoking in the barracks.[43] Although the general level of discipline within the camps varied widely and depended heavily on the camp commander,[44] the prisoners' movements and behavior were always supervised and monitored: a camp schedule determined the prisoners' daily routine, mail was censored, escape attempts were punished. All aspects of life were conducted in a common space under the singular authority of the German army. Erving Goffman has noted that in institutions controlling the time and space of inmates, a fundamental split occurs between the prisoners and the staff.[45] The organizational dynamic of such a situation creates social distance between the two groups, limiting the flow of information and social interaction across the divide. The arrangement of life in these camps similarly accentuated the distance between the prisoners and the staff, further demarcating the anthropologists from the POWs they were to study.

In many ways, the camp dynamic replicated and even heightened the dominance that anthropologists enjoyed over their subjects in many colonial contexts. A comparison between the POW projects during World War I and the well-known German South Sea expedition of 1908–10 is particularly useful in this regard, especially because several anthropologists, including Hambruch and Reche, participated in both enterprises. On the South Sea voyage, ethnological and anthropological study took place in a militarized atmosphere in which scientists often used weapons and threats

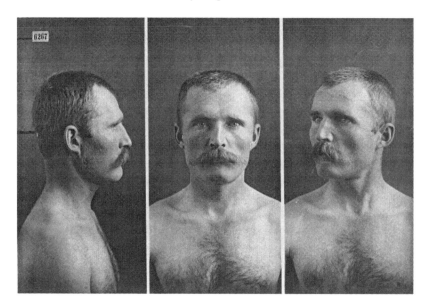

2. Photograph of a Ukrainian soldier taken by Pöch's team in the standard anthropological format of profile, frontal, and three-quarter views, 1917. Reproduced from Pöch, "III. Bericht über die von der Wiener Anthropologischen Gesellschaft in den k. u. k. Kriegsgefangenenlagern veranlaßten Studien," *MAGW* 47 (1917): Tafel 1.

of violence to force their subjects to hand over cultural artifacts or participate in measurements.[46] And to this end, scholars often arrived at indigenous villages backed by armed escorts. The situation in the camps was similar. The wartime prison milieu was militarized, and the anthropologists clearly had the backing of the German army to conduct their studies.

But in several respects, the power of the scientists in POW camps even exceeded that of most colonial undertakings. During the South Sea expedition, for example, Reche complained that it was difficult to measure or photograph the indigenous peoples, since they were "afraid of every instrument and [ran] away."[47] In the camps, by contrast, the prisoners could not escape; they were at the disposal of the anthropologists. Martin commented in 1915 that the military discipline of the camps made the prisoners more available: "The people are not busy (or only partly), and because they stand under military guard, [they] are more accessible for bodily measurements than they would be in their homeland."[48] Moreover, in the POW camps the anthropologists felt no danger from their subjects. During the South Sea expedition, groups of antagonized islanders had attacked the anthropologists on several occasions, both on land and on water.[49] In the POW

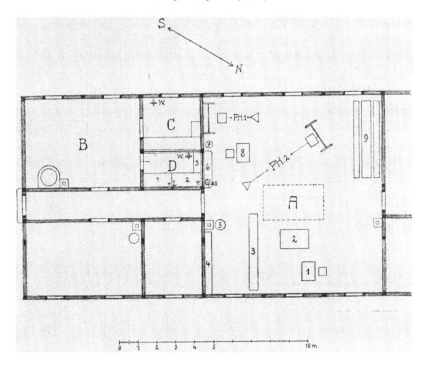

3. Pöch's plan for setting up a barracks for anthropological investigations, 1917.
The space included a podium for anthropological measurements (2), a table and benches
for recording geographical data (9), areas for photography (PH. 1 and 2), and a room
for making plaster casts (B). Reproduced from Pöch, "III. Bericht über die von der
Wiener Anthropologischen Gesellschaft in den k. u. k. Kriegsgefangenenlagern
veranlaßten Studien," *MAGW* 47 (1917): 91.

camps, by contrast, the presence of the military rendered the encounter
with the inmates a nonthreatening venture. Anthropologists like Pöch felt
safe, and therefore claimed that the camps allowed for a more objective anthropological science: "The investigation can take place in the best possible
outer conditions . . . All hindrances from prejudices fall away, all possible
thoughts or fear of the unknown."[50] For the same reason, he described the
study of POWs as "work in a laboratory, compared to that of the research
trip outside."[51] The lopsided power relations in the camps confirmed the
position of the prisoners as subjects of anthropological and racial inquiry,
as "others" fundamentally unlike their captors. In this "laboratory," anthropologists could study both Europeans and non-Europeans alike.

In the camps, anthropologists constructed the spaces in which they conducted the investigations to resemble laboratories, areas defined primarily
by the control of the scientist over the process and the subjects. Pöch, the

standardizer of the studies, provided a detailed model for how the investigations were to proceed. Before physical investigations could take place, anthropologists sought to determine the ethnic and regional background of the subject. In a room that had been carefully arranged for anthropological work, subjects were first to seat themselves on a bench, pick out their own home geographical region on a large map, and explain their ethnic backgrounds. This verbal interaction took place with the aid of an interpreter, when one was available. Subjects were then instructed to undress and stand on a small podium, where various anthropometric measurements were made under the observation and supervision of several assistants.[52] Other measurements followed in other parts of the room. In all, Pöch's team recorded some forty-four physical measurements for each prisoner, each meticulously noted on individual cards.[53] The assistants also took notations on skin color, hair color, body hair, eye shape, eye color, nose form, and lip shape. Within the space of these anthropological "laboratories," the dominant position of the scientist vis-à-vis the prisoners was readily apparent.

The resistance of both Europeans and non-Europeans to this procedure and the studies in general further confirmed the common subject position of the prisoners. Officially, Pöch proclaimed that the participants in his studies were volunteers who enjoyed the investigations as an escape from the crushing boredom of imprisonment.[54] In reality, however, many of the prisoners sought to avoid or even undermine the studies by disrupting or resisting the process of taking bodily measurements, photographs, or plaster moldings. When working in a POW camp near Berlin, for example, Pöch had to rely on the camp commander for help in overcoming prisoners' hesitations regarding the plaster casting process. The commander allowed a molding of his own head to be taken in an attempt to surmount, as Pöch put it, the "persistent shyness of the people toward this procedure."[55] Many prisoners clearly did not wish to undergo the process. Eickstedt, for his part, complained to Luschan about the unwillingness of some prisoners to participate: "I have begun to measure the Russian Jews. Most of these find little pleasure in anthropology and seek . . . to get out of my nice [nett] measurements in every way possible."[56] Eickstedt's "nice measurements" were clearly unpleasant for these POWs, who were hardly volunteers. Eickstedt also complained that some of the prisoners, such as the Algerians, purposefully tried to "shirk" the studies by misleading him about their ethnic backgrounds and home regions.[57] The French were particularly untrustworthy, he claimed, because they made false statements about their origins; the Tartars, in contrast, were "nice people and don't do this."[58] As subjects of anthropological inquiry, the French thus came to occupy the same category as Algerians or Tartars. Located opposite Germans in a difficult and tense power relationship, the researchers put these Europeans in the same colonial position as Africans and Asians: disciplined by outside control, their racial background defined by those with power over them.

Nationalism, Race, and the European Enemy

In their work with the POW population, each the three principal anthropologists in the camps—Eickstedt, Reche, and Pöch—came to conflate the categories of nation and race, thereby departing from the tenets of Virchow's liberal anthropology. In so doing, they also implicitly crafted a new definition of the "European" modeled on the peoples of the Central Powers. There were several different avenues that led to the investigation and portrayal of national enemies as racial "others," as each anthropologist made decisions that, while governed by his ideological convictions, were nevertheless channeled, shaped, and in many ways made possible by conditions and experiences within the camps. Of the three men, Eickstedt was most influenced by the camp milieu, investigating Europeans on the basis of national citizenship only after several months on the project. Motivated by a brand of expansionist nationalism, Reche in turn was more interested in establishing racial connections between Germans and the peoples they might rule over as a result of the war. Pöch, for his part, was influenced by his position as a subject of Austria-Hungary. In his work he avoided the racial investigation of ethnic groups that were part of the Dual Monarchy, assigning non-European racial identities to the Eastern opponents of the Central Powers instead. The common element in each case was the combination of wartime nationalism and the scientific practice of camp studies. In and of themselves, neither the camps nor the nationalist ideologies were enough to cause the conflation of nation and race; but in combination they greatly facilitated the efforts of these three anthropologists to move away from the sharp distinctions of liberal anthropology.

Eickstedt's gradual path to the conflation of race and nation demonstrates the dual effects of the camp experience and wartime nationalism. At the outset of his project, he had been thoroughly uninterested in European prisoners as objects of anthropological inquiry. Following Luschan's advice, he had initially sought to investigate the physical characteristics "of an anthropologically interesting group: Indians, Turks, or inner Asians."[59] Eventually settling on the racial characteristics of the Sikhs as the topic for his dissertation,[60] Eickstedt at first considered camps that contained large concentrations of peoples from western or eastern Europe a disappointment. On one of his first visits to a camp near Gross-Brusen, he reported to Luschan that Armenians, Georgians, and Tartars were available for study there, but added with a hint of frustration that "otherwise there are only known Europeans."[61] After several months, however, his view changed. His correspondence with Luschan reveals a growing sense that certain European groups did warrant racial investigation; and when faced with a shortage of "foreign" (i.e., non-European) peoples in June of 1916, he asked permission to expand his focus: "Under these conditions allow me to ask . . . if it would not be appropriate to take on the investigation of peoples like the Scots, Irish, English, Ukrainians, Poles, ethnic Russians, etc."[62] Eickstedt's delay in identifying European peoples as anthropologically interesting suggests that his shift in focus was motivated by more than pure contingency or a shortage of "exotics." Only after he had spent several months in the camps, and worked in an atmosphere that helped break down the distinctions between Europeans and non-Europeans, did he begin to place Europeans into the new position of anthropological object.

This gradual development of new categorizations was also fueled by Eickstedt's nationalist perspective. He came to consider certain Europeans as racial "others" because of their status as enemies. His letters reveal that he subscribed to a brand of wartime nationalism that imagined Germany as being surrounded by hostile opponents. He referred to the allied blockade, for example, as a "boa constrictor set upon us by our enemies." More importantly, he associated the Allies with non-European peoples, speculating that their possible victory would unleash a new "yellow danger" on Europe and signal cultural domination by east Asia.[63] In the milieu of the camps it was a short step from a nationalism that coded Germany's enemies as non-European to a view of Europeans as racial others. As overtly nationalist considerations began to drive his selection of subjects, he, for example, wrote to Luschan that he had located a number of Jews, but wanted to change his focus to the "enemy peoples" of Russia: "I would like to ask . . . if I can finish with this group so that I can turn to the generally harder to reach enemy Russian peoples."[64] His use of the term "enemy" suggests that he considered the peoples of Russia anthropologically interesting not only because they were harder to reach, but also because they were Germany's opponents in the Great War.

In a process of contingent negotiation shaped by the conditions in the camps and his own nationalism, Eickstedt fully abandoned the liberal distinction between nation and race, beginning to select and investigate his subjects on the basis of national citizenship. The organization of his data provided evidence for this process. Before the war, anthropologists usually had organized their data according to ethnic group, region, or physical type; but Eickstedt listed the peoples he examined according to national citizenship. A summary of the individuals he examined in 1916 revealed that he had measured hundreds of subjects from Russia and western Europe, including 743 "Russian citizens," ranging from "Jews from Russia" to "peoples of the Caucasus." And while Eickstedt made a distinction between "colored" soldiers and those of "European descent" in his list of 353 "French citizens," he nonetheless organized sub-Saharan Africans, Moroccans, Corsicans, Basques, and "Southern French" under one overall heading. In other words, he considered the French soldiers as a coherent racial "other," classing them in a grouping that included troops from Africa and the Near East. He also listed 104 "Serbians and British"—an odd category that unified only Scots, Serbian Gypsies, and Irish.[65]

Equally telling, however, were the groups Eickstedt did not select. For example, he apparently never measured any English POWs, even though he had mentioned them as possible objects of study. Nor did he examine any soldiers from northern France, a region whose inhabitants were considered to be closely related to Germans. Most important, however, he did not examine Russian POWs of German descent, despite the presence of Volga Germans in the camps.[66] All these groups were linked, however tangentially, to "Germanness"—a fact that precluded their investigation as racial "others." Thus, Eickstedt's implicit category of "European" included the English, northern French, and, at the center, Germans, suggesting that a notion of Germanness functioned as the standard against which racial otherness was judged. By selecting anthropological subjects on the basis of national citizenship, Eickstedt filled the concept of nation with racial meaning. At the same time he narrowed the category of European, casting many groups as worthy of anthropological attention because of their hypostatized difference from an unstated German norm.

While Eickstedt created new categories of Europeanness based largely on his experience in the POW camps, Reche brought a fully formed nationalist perspective to the project from the very beginning. Before the war, he had already signaled his adherence to a brand of Nordic racialism with a 1909 article on the prehistoric peoples of the Stone Age that characterized the Nordic race as "warlike" and "robust."[67] And if anything, Reche's wartime experiences strengthened his nationalist convictions even further. He joined the POW project in 1917 after being injured at the front, where he had served as an infantry officer for three years. Later, during the 1930s, his admirers pointed out that his service during the Great War had been crucial in shaping his nationalist convictions as well as his politically driven anthropology. In 1939, for example, Günther Spannus wrote that Reche had "found his way to the *völkisch* movement and with it to political anthropology as a old frontline soldier and nationalist . . . ."[68]

In addition to his overtly nationalist motivations, the camp milieu also had an effect on Reche, who did not immediately begin his investigations with the study of Europeans. Luschan initially recommended that he focus on an ethnic group from central Asia, and Reche briefly examined Tartars and other Asian groups when he began work on the project.[69] After some weeks, however, his nationalist motivations came to the fore as he shifted his attention to Germany's western European enemies: "I have occupied myself less with the Eastern theater of war—Pöch already has [made a] pleasant series there—and more with our Western enemies, especially those which until now have been the least measured."[70] This process of selection was motivated by more than a shortage of "exotic" subjects, however, as Reche eventually also turned to the investigation of groups from the eastern front, such as the peoples of the Baltics.

Motivated by an expansionist vision of the German empire, Reche selected those Europeans for study who might fall under German dominion in the wake of the Great War. In other words, he was primarily interested in determining the racial makeup of the peoples who might be permanently incorporated into the German empire. Reche readily admitted that political considerations drove his selection of subjects. In 1918, his report to his superiors in Hamburg read:

> I devoted my work to the representatives of smaller peoples that until now have been less accessible to anthropology or were completely uninvestigated, and in particular those that *as a result of the war may come into a tighter political connection with us and therefore deserve our special attention.* Therefore I measured Lithuanians, Latvians, Estonians and especially Flemish, as well as Rumanians, Southern French, Bretons, Irish, Scots and English from a general anthropological point of view and for purposes of comparison.[71]

Writing in a period when German victory still seemed possible, Reche thus paid particular attention to the peoples who lived in territories already occupied by Germany. In 1918, when Reche conducted his investigations, the German empire did indeed control the Baltic, which it was fashioning into a veritable German colony.[72] Likewise, Germany controlled large stretches of Belgium, where the Flemish were a major part of the population. In another report, Reche stated that he also investigated POWs from northern France, where Germany had a foothold as well.[73]

Reche's conclusions represented an attempt to legitimize the extension of the German empire on racial terms. Not surprisingly, the peoples he envisioned as part of a future Germany were of predominantly northern European extraction. To these groups he assigned primary racial characteristics that emphasized their connection to northern European—that is, Germanic—stock. He reported that "in Estonians, Latvians, and Lithuanians, one finds a quite extraordinarily strong element of northern-European blood." Similarly, he argued that "the Flemish were certainly to be characterized anthropologically as Germans," implying not only that Germans possessed a singular anthropological profile, but that the Flemish matched it.[74] Reche maintained that the Rumanians, under German control when he studied them in 1917, were primarily of Mongolian and Mediterranean extraction; those from the Carpathian mountains, however, demonstrated a strong strain of Nordic blood and often possessed blond hair and blue eyes.[75] In contrast, the Irish and Bretons, opponents whose eventual inclusion in the German empire was unlikely, demonstrated elements of a "long extinct old European type," ostensibly unrelated to the Nordic race. Conflating race, nation, and *Volk*, such judgments served to assign racial types to the peoples under consideration at the same time as they identified Germans as possessing a unified anthropological makeup associated with the Nordic race. While Eickstedt cast a selection of Germany's enemies as racial others, Reche in effect sought to accomplish the inverse: he portrayed certain European groups as racially related to Germans as a means of legitimizing political expansion and national aggrandizement.

Much like Eickstedt, the Austrian team under Pöch concentrated its energies on creating anthropological definitions of the Central Powers' chief opponents. In doing so, however, they avoided national groups represented both in the POW population and in the Austro-Hungarian Empire. In the process, Pöch and his assistants primarily focused on the racial identities of Russians and other enemies on the eastern front. For those living in wartime Austria-Hungary, the complicated issue of Austrian identity was extremely divisive and potentially damaging to wartime unity.[76] In the multiethnic context of the Habsburg monarchy, rife with nationalist struggles, the association of the enemy with non-European racial elements was an effective means of creating difference between Austria-Hungary and its opponents while maintaining the precarious image of a unified empire. Thus, Pöch's conflation of nation and race was motivated by pro-imperial patriotism, reflected in the path he took to arrive at his position.

Pöch's patriotic politics combined with his experience in the camps to determine the selection and characterization of his subjects. Like Eickstedt (and to a lesser extent Reche), Pöch and his team found their way to the racial characterization of Austria-Hungary's enemies only after some time in the camps. Initially they privileged the "exotic," officially targeting peoples from central Asia as their primary interest. In his first report on the studies, Pöch claimed that his team aimed at investigating "the smaller, anthropologically less well-known peoples of the Russian Empire . . . such as the peoples of the Caucasus, Siberia, and the Mongolian tribes in the southeast of European Russia."[77] Elsewhere he claimed that he anticipated data that would help determine the answer to the "Berber question" of how the peoples of northern Africa were related.[78] But despite these official goals, Pöch and his assistants quickly came to focus most of their attention on peoples from the western parts of the Russian Empire. Pöch's choices demonstrated the dual influence of the camp milieu and his political considerations. Depending on the particular camp, Pöch investigated ethnic Russians, Ukrainians, Bulgarians, Serbs, and others—most of whom were hardly part of a "smaller, less anthropologically known group." In fact, ethnic Russians, Ukrainians, and Serbs made up the bulk of the individuals he investigated.[79] Italians also played a role in the studies as subjects.[80] The German press, which reported on Pöch's project, noted that the initial focus in the first camp had been primarily on "Mohammedans," while the work at subsequent sites included all the peoples of Russia.[81]

In part, this focus reflected the proportions of peoples actually present, as there were few "exotics" from central Asia in most Austrian camps, but more important were political considerations. Pöch's inclusion of the Serbs and the Italians, for example, indicated that his project went beyond the boundaries of the Russian Empire to encompass all of Austria-Hungary's principal enemies. In the same vein, although he measured some twelve Poles at a camp in 1917, Pöch generally avoided the investigation of other ethnic groups that were part of Austria-Hungary, even though many of them were represented in the Russian army. As in Eickstedt's case, it is also significant that Russian POWs of German descent never turned up in the lists of subjects. In short, aside from the Serbs and Italians, Pöch implicitly refused to consider the peoples of the Austro-Hungarian Empire as racial "others." His choices suggested that he had the tenuous multinational configuration of the Dual Monarchy in mind when he conducted his studies. Rather than make physical distinctions among the peoples living within the empire, he sought to emphasize its unity through the characterization of its principal enemies as racially different. The Serbs and Italians, aligned against

Austria-Hungary and thus beyond the pale, were cast as racial others,while the remaining ethnic groups within the Dual Monarchy were ignored in an attempt to highlight the unity of the empire's other peoples.

Pöch's blending of race and nation can best be seen in his characterization of the peoples of Russia. Despite examining a huge assortment of ethnic groups from a variety of regions and backgrounds, he produced a portrayal that suggested a unified racial identity associated with Asia rather than Europe. Specifically, he set out to determine the degree of Mongolian influence on the peoples of the Russian Empire; and he spent a great deal of time scrutinizing his subjects' eyes, because they "were the carrier of characteristics that easily gave away a mixture of Mongolian blood."[82] Pöch judged each specific characteristic of each individual eye by the extent that it deviated from the eye features of the "Mongolian race." In his account of the work in a camp near the town of Eger, he described how he and his assistants used the "Mongolian" characteristics as the standard: "In order to make a quick orientation possible, usually two characteristics are placed in a pattern next to one another, for which that which is characteristic of the Mongolian race is provided with a plus sign, the other, that is distant from the Mongolian type, is provided with a minus sign."[83] By using this "yes or no" schema, Pöch indicated that he was interested not in all types of eyes, but only in eyes in which Mongolian influence could be seen. His emphasis on Mongolian features in the studies of Russian POWs was documented in an article for a popular science journal in 1916, in which he provided a montage of eyes designed to demonstrate the degrees of Mongolian influence in the peoples of the Russian Empire.[84] Despite his overall claim that those peoples were a racial mixture, he sought to cast his subjects, albeit to widely varying degrees, as Mongolian. Considering the political situation in Europe during World War I, it is hardly surprising that Pöch characterized Russians through racial characteristics traditionally viewed as alien to Central Europe. While he never discussed the history of the Mongols in Europe and avoided popular stereotypes of invading Mongol hordes, his emphasis on the Mongolian makeup of Russians cast Austria-Hungary's eastern enemy as a non-European racial "other." Operating within the multiethnic context of Austria-Hungary, Pöch deemphasized the potentially divisive notion of Germanness; instead, he implicitly contrasted Central Europeans to "Asian" Russians—a characterization that rendered the categories of nation and race fluid and ascribed a racial identity to the enemy.

A similar mode of operation characterized the work of Pöch's chief assistant in the camps, Joseph Weninger. In a lecture before the Viennese anthropological society on the POW studies, Weninger argued that Serbs and

Albanians exhibited "Near Eastern" racial characteristics. In this case, the Serbs—a principal antagonist of Austria-Hungary on the eastern front and the group blamed for the outbreak of the war—received a distinctly non-European racial identity:

> In the middle of the [Balkan] peninsula as well as in the north with the Serbs and in the west with the Albanians the [physical] elements classify themselves as closely related to the Near Eastern. Yes indeed, these racial elements contribute a great deal to the makeup of the physical characteristics of the peoples who oppose us there today.[85]

The message was clear: the enemies of the Central Powers on the eastern front, particularly the Serbs, were not of European origin. Moreover, by linking the Serbs to the Near East, Weninger implicitly associated them with the Turks, the quintessential racial and cultural "other" in the history of the Austrian Empire. Like Pöch and Eickstedt, he used anthropology to narrow the category of "European" by tying the enemies of the Central Powers to regions and peoples outside of Europe.

The path to the conflation of liberal categories and the particular form it took depended on the personal perspective of the scientist and the particular context in which he worked. The German anthropologists Eickstedt and Reche produced racial portrayals that mobilized Germanness as an implicit standard. The Austrians, in contrast, assigned non-European racial identities to the enemies of the Habsburg monarchy in an effort to fortify the distinction between Austria-Hungary and its eastern opponents. In each case, some form of nationalism or patriotism drove the process, but always did so in combination with the practical experience in the camps. The camp milieu was crucial to the conflation of nation and race because it collapsed earlier distinctions between "exotic" and "non-exotic" subjects and facilitated the racial study of national enemies. Thus, the experience of camp anthropology enlivened a discourse on race that in many ways anticipated the directions anthropologists would take in the postwar period; it was a path that took them further afield from the tradition of liberal anthropology.

The story of the POW studies indicates the degree to which German anthropology was influenced by the war being fought around it from 1914 to 1918. The European conflict not only created the initial opportunity to examine captured soldiers, but also increasingly informed the goals and results of anthropological research. During the war, the anthropologists who worked on the POW projects developed a new political outlook that reoriented their approach to the European context of race. Deep-seated wartime nationalism combined with the unique conditions in the camps to shape a view of the European enemies as racial "others." In the process, the liberal view of Europeans as interrelated and physically indistinguishable was replaced by a nationalist perspective that defined peoples according to their racial character. Opposing the position articulated by Virchow and his followers in the late nineteenth century, camp anthropologists began to conflate the categories of race, nation, and *Volk*, thereby helping to prepare the intellectual atmosphere that was to produce the virulently racist *Rassenkunde* of the 1920s and 1930s.

FIVE

Capturing Race: Anthropology and Photography in POW Camps during World War I

In July of 1915, Rudolf Pöch visited his first prisoner-of-war camp near Eger, a town two hours northeast of Budapest by train. Pöch and his five assistants arrived carrying anthropometric instruments, equipment to make plaster molds, and several cameras. The men were assigned to an empty medical barracks, which they proceeded to arrange for anthropological investigations, measurements, and photography.[1] After several months of planning, Pöch was eager to begin conducting anthropological studies of the prisoners at Eger and other POW camps. As he and his team set up their equipment and cameras, they prepared for an element of their future work that particularly excited them: the prospect of creating "racial types" through photography. Pöch's efforts with the camera marked the beginning of a larger wartime project in German anthropology: photography of POWs, an enterprise that promised intriguing new data for the discipline. In the context of total war, however, this supposedly objective undertaking was not simply a "scientific" endeavor; from the outset, racial photographs of the enemy became political as well as public documents. As Pöch and his team set up their cameras at Eger, they took the first step, perhaps unwittingly, in a process of communicating wartime messages about the enemy, the camps, and the Central Powers to a wider public through photographic images.

In early-twentieth-century anthropology, photographs were considered essential to recording the riddles of racial definition, and every anthropologist working in the camps included photography as a central part of his methodology. Like others in their discipline, camp anthropologists were primarily interested in classifying human forms, but because race remained an abstract and ambiguous category without a precise biological definition, they often used the term "type" to categorize different physical morphologies. The creation and definition of "racial types" was at the center of prewar

anthropology and naturally played a major role in the methodology of anthropologists in the camps. Photography, a technology that "captured" the
physical characteristics of the subject, was regarded as an essential mechanism in this enterprise. Along with measurements and other quantifiable
data, anthropologists saw photographs not only as a method of recording
what they found in the camps for later analysis, but also as a tool in the creation and formulation of the racial categories they sought to determine.

Photographs make up a large portion of the sources that remain from the
POW studies and provide the historian with a means of investigating how
anthropologists constructed the racial and colonial "other" in the context
of war. Rather then taking an ethnographic approach to the images in an
effort to determine what they tell us about day-to-day life in the camps,[2]
an examination of the photographs and an analysis of their uses reveals
the changing contours of the discipline during the conflict. By placing the
POWs in the format of the anthropological photograph, anthropologists
"racialized" the enemy, both European and non-European. In the context of
the world conflict, the "mug-shot" images of the POWs represented foreign
and colonial soldiers as racial strangers, menacing enemies in need of control and confinement. The photographs allowed Germans and their allies to
see the face of the foe and identify him as someone physically different from
themselves. The images thus assisted the Central Powers in their attempts
to foster a sense of unity against a clearly differentiated enemy. Furthermore, many of the anthropologists working in the German Empire went a
step further to aid in creating a vision of "Germanness" based on race. By
racially representing the enemy and in turn defining whom Germans were
not, many of the characterizations from the camps implied that a unity of
German physical characteristics also existed. By capturing the race of the
POWs on film, the anthropologists in the camps implicitly constructed a
wartime identity, often cast in racial terms, that emphasized the characteristics considered crucial to victory: power and unity.

The photography in the POW camps revealed another instance in which
the conceptual boundaries of the liberal tradition weakened and even collapsed. The racialized images of the enemy that emerged from the camps
represented national enemies as racial "others," allowing the categories of
race, *Volk*, and nation to bleed into one another. Moreover, as in the practice
of camp anthropology, Europeans were placed in new subject positions in
the photographs, defined and disciplined by an anthropological format that
had traditionally been reserved for non-Europeans. Portrayed as menacing
others alongside non-European soldiers, European prisoners were portrayed
as physically different from the peoples of the Central Powers. The photo-

graphs from the camps indicate the degree to which the liberal conception of Europeans as interrelated and racially indistinct fell away during the war. Finally, many of the images reached the public in venues that were clearly designed to lend support to the war effort of the Central Powers. Here was another instance in which anthropologists fashioned their science into a political implement in support of the state and the nation, thereby altering the contours of their discipline in the process.

Creating "Types": The Anthropological Format and the POW

Since the invention of the daguerreotype, students of natural science and human biology had been excited by the potential of photography.[3] Scientists in a variety of fields in the late nineteenth century saw the camera as a positivist tool that recorded the natural world with high degree of accuracy. Throughout the Victorian age, the emerging technology of photography seemed to promise a new brand of scientific objectivity that would replace the frailties and errors of human observation with the ever-vigilant and self-disciplined workings of a machine. The camera seemed to guarantee "images that were certified free of human interference," an ideal that in turn reflected nineteenth-century bourgeois notions of self-command and restraint.[4] The idea that nature could "speak for itself" through the lens of a camera was powerfully attractive to scientists in all fields that upheld positivism as an ideal.

Like their colleagues in other emerging disciplines, early anthropologists embraced this idea and turned to photography as a means to improve the quality and quantity of their data on humankind.[5] Initial efforts to achieve this goal produced mixed results, however. In the late 1860s, British anthropologists such as Thomas Henry Huxley and J. H. Lamprey developed systems to take exact scientific measurements directly from photographs, but these endeavors ended in failure.[6] In Germany, anthropologists in Berlin in the 1870s and 1880s also had high hopes that the "mechanical" objectivity of photography would provide an antidote to the subjective nature of artistic representations. These hopes, as Andrew Zimmerman has shown, did not mean that German anthropologists were naive realists when it came to photography. In fact, in their search for more precise data, they often favored precise geometric drawing techniques over the perspectival distortions of the camera.[7] By the turn of the century, anthropologists recognized that photographs did not reproduce an exact "parallel projection" of reality, but they still considered the camera an objective technology and placed it at the center of anthropological methodology. Even after 1900, leading anthropologists continued to maintain that by following strict methods and calculations of proportion, photographs could be used as devices for anthropological measurement.[8] In the early twentieth century, the camera was considered a powerful scientific instrument to be used for purposes of comparison and illustration.

The German anthropologists involved in the POW studies saw the camera as an objective tool for their work in the camps. Pöch, for example, encouraged the strict standardization of photographic techniques among his colleagues working with POWs in order to ensure the "scientific comparability" of the images.[9] He referred to the images as "scientific portrait photographs" and gave rigorous instructions as to the position of the subject and camera in order to secure comparable images of exactly the same size. With the same aims in mind, Pöch was also extremely concerned that the images of the POWs be reductions to exactly one-fifth the natural size of the subject.[10] Although the anthropologists in the camps also relied on plaster casts and anthropometric techniques for precise measurements, they considered the camera an objective technology that, if used correctly, represented reality with a great degree of accuracy.[11] This view was common elsewhere in Europe during the war, where military uses of photography encouraged the notion that photography represented the world "as it is." Aerial photography, for example, was understood to be an exact reflection of the tactical situation on the battlefield.[12]

Since the nineteenth century, the most common form of photographic data in anthropology had been a form of portraiture called the "type." As Elizabeth Edwards has pointed out, the type photo could be many things, from the *carte de visite* to the scientific portrait, but the basic format of profile and frontal views was considered a key to classifying the races.[13] Because race was essentially a visual phenomenon, the "type" photograph was crucial both to "seeing" racial differences and confirming the notion that racial types existed. Early twentieth-century anthropologists sought to identify the mixture of hereditary characteristics in each population, and believed that by doing so they could reconstruct the various racial elements within a group or people. The "type" photograph was a central tool in this process of classification, used to identify and record the racial components thought to be present in a population. Using this method, the face or body of a "type" was understood to represent a generality, an entire group of people, rather than an individual. Combined with a positivist view of photography, the image of the "racial type" turned the abstract notion of race into something real and concrete—that is, into a classification that could be seen and thus verified. Anthropological photography and "type" portraiture also belonged within the larger popular discourse of physiognomy, a nineteenth-century practice of reading the character of an individual in the face and body.[14] Under the physiognomic gaze, the body was a legible text that could be read for signs of criminality and immorality, qualities that were thought to express themselves in physical deviations from the classical standard of beauty.[15] Although professional anthropologists generally avoided physiognomy, the anthropological format that they used not only invited the viewer to identify race, but also to locate character in the bodily traits of the subject.

Anthropologists in the POW camps sought to identify racial types, and they turned to photography to do it. In his efforts to standardize the methods for the POW studies, Pöch insisted that anthropologists use the traditional "type" format, which included profile and frontal views of the subject, as well as the three-quarter-angle shot.[16] All of Pöch's photographs of faces included these three perspectives, and he also took full-body photographs from three similar viewpoints: front, profile, and back. The subject was to be photographed naked, and the background was to be blank.[17] By placing the subject against a blank setting, the format presented the individual in a scientific isolation meant to emphasize bodily characteristics, so that racial markers could be more easily read in the body of the subject.[18] For example, in the photograph of a prisoner of war from New Caledonia taken against a blank background and later published by the Doegen group, the "type" format removes the individuality of the subject and invites the viewer to examine the physical characteristics that make the subject typical of a certain group (figure 4). The caption of this photo—"A New Caledonian in measurement photograph"—not only emphasizes the individual anonymity of the subject by labeling him as a typical New Caledonian, but also underscores the objective authority and scientific accuracy of the camera by referring to the image as a document suitable for measurement.[19] The standard method for the anthropologists in the camps was to take photographs of individuals such as these, then designate them as "types" upon publication, usually in a caption. Egon von Eickstedt proudly sent a photograph of a Sudanese African to his mentor Felix von Luschan as an example of the successful "type" photographs that he and his assistant had taken in a camp near Darmstadt (figure 5).[20] Later, in 1922, Eickstedt used the photo for an article in a popular German scientific periodical with the caption: "Black race: Sudanese Negro."[21] Type photographs such as these allowed the anthropologist to label the subject as the representative face of a sweeping racial category, thereby confirming for the viewer the existence of racial classifications.

How did the anthropologists decide who was typical and who was not? Despite claims of scientific objectivity, the selection process was based on a method of picking representative subjects that was far from empirical. In his explanation of how to choose subjects in the POW camps for study, Pöch argued that "while the final decision on the makeup of a population group certainly belongs at the end of the studies, it is advisable to begin right away with a provisional list of types, because then the main types . . . are easier for an observer to pick out."[22] In short, he maintained that the selection of the "typical" representatives in a population should be based on preexisting categories and the ability of the anthropologist to pick out these classifications. He instructed his colleagues to choose subjects by relying on their previous anthropological experience and "eye" for types. Pöch, Eickstedt, and others usually distinguished between two kinds of subjects to be photographed: those considered most typical and those thought to deviate the most from the norm.[23] Of the group selected for measurement, usually only half would be again selected to be photographed. These subjects were always either

4. "New Caledonian in Measurement Photograph." Unknown photographer, Wilhelm Doegen's project, c. 1915–16. Reproduced from *Unter Fremden Völkern*, ed. Wilhelm Doegen, 1925.

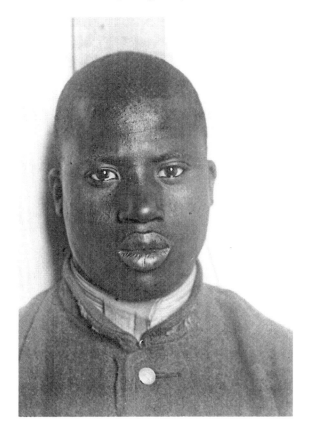

5. "Black Race: Sudanese Negro." Unknown photographer, Egon von
Eickstedt's project, 1916. Berlin, Staatsbibliothek zu Berlin,
Preußischer Kulturbesitz, Handschriftenabteilung.

considered typical or a curious departure from the norm. Eickstedt, for his
part, only sent photos to Luschan that he considered "typical" in some way.
By their choices, the anthropologists in effect created the categories of "typical" for each group.

Although scientists generally regarded photography as a more objective,
"truthful" medium, the photographic enterprise in the camps was nevertheless influenced by graphic art. This trend can best be seen in Luschan's 1917
volume, *Prisoners of War*. The book included a short essay for a popular
audience on basic questions in anthropology, but was primarily a collection of illustrations that included not only anthropological photographs
from the camps and elsewhere, but also 100 charcoal drawings of POWs
by the artist Hermann Struck (1876–1944). Although the captions beneath

the drawings included the names of the subjects, the portraits represented the prisoners in the traditional anthropological format of profile and frontal views (figure 6). In his preface, Luschan acknowledged that the drawings were works of art, but then argued that they also possessed scientific value. He wrote, "Of course these pictures are works of art first and should be judged as such, but beyond their artistic worth they undoubtedly also have scientific [*wissenschaftlich*] meaning."[24] In his view, the sketches could be a source of factual data for anthropologists to use in making judgments about racial typologies. German anthropologists had long maintained a contradictory stance on the scientific worth of artistic images. They considered the painstaking drawings made exactly to scale using the "geographic" method to be scientific documents, but often questioned the value of images created by the "artistic hand."[25] Struck's drawings were clearly the freehand sketches of a graphic artist, not the exacting diagrams of a geographic procedure.

Luschan glossed over such complexities, however, by arguing that the POW camps were so scientifically rich that the anthropologist should greet "every graphic representation and every kind of scientific work" from the camps with enthusiasm.[26] While he did not deny the artistic nature of the portraits, he chose in his introduction to emphasize their scientific potential. Moreover, by pairing a popular introduction to anthropology with Struck's drawings, Luschan suggested that the images were to be accepted as accurate and factual representations of race, rather than strictly as works of art. In this instance, art and science overlapped.

The inclusion of photographs in the same volume further underscored the parallels that the viewer was to draw between the photographs and the sketches as scientific documents. In Luschan's view, the photographic illustrations of non-European peoples and POWs lent further factual weight to the collection. Upon closer examination, however, it becomes clear that the subjective quality of the photographic and hand-drawn images, rather than their empirical and objective nature, is what unites them. Both sets of images were selected and constructed to match stereotypes and preconceived notions about race. Several of the photographs, such as the portrait of an Algerian taken by Eickstedt in a Darmstadt camp, are prime examples of the subjective construction of racial types through photography (figure 7). In a letter to Luschan, Eickstedt described his reasons for selecting this particular subject to sit in front of the camera. "I photographed the Algerian as a type, as a typical representative. These kinds of noses, and also slight small ones, are often represented, though mostly with a longer face and not seldom combined with a longer skull, deformed by head bindings."[27]

6. Hermann Struck, "Mahmadon Gregoire (Christian), Negro from
Ouida," c. 1915. Reproduced from *Kriegsgefangene, ein Beitrag zur
Völkerkunde im Weltkriege: Einführung in die Grundzüge der Anthropologie*.
Berlin: Dietrich Reimer, Ernst Vohsen, 1917.

Eickstedt included no statistical data or scientific reasoning—his arguments for inclusion were purely subjective, based on his personal "eye" for
types. Luschan apparently agreed with his assessment, because he included
the photo in *Kriegsgefangene*, with a caption that read, "'Arab' from Algeria. . . .
The face is pure Near Eastern. Similar types are occasionally detected in the
middle empire of Egypt and today are also found in small percentages from
North Africa to the Canary Islands."[28] Luschan's commentary fixes the face
of the Algerian as typical for an entire region and racial type, but the crite-
rion by which Eickstedt originally picked the subject was based on a lone
physical characteristic: the nose. By placing photographs such as these in a

7. Type photograph of Algerian POW. Unknown photographer,
Egon van Eickstedt's project, 1916. Berlin, Staatsbibliothek zu
Berlin, Preußischer Kulturbesitz, Handschriftenabteilung.

volume with the drawings, the two forms were essentially equated as having scientific worth—but both were primarily subjective, rather than positivistic, documents.

The correspondence between Luschan and Struck about the drawings further demonstrates the blurred boundary between the subjective and the empirical in Luschan's mind. The evidence suggests that Struck altered the drawings to match Luschan's preconceptions about race. In a response to Luschan, Struck wrote:

> Your remarks in relation to the Negro-Type were thoroughly correct, and I immediately did his hair. He now has received the very pretty, frizzy Negro hair, and I believe that he will please you. In addition, on the Russian that you already eliminated some time ago, I have enlarged the skull and ear. I will present these new prints to you after your return, and then bow very happily to your dictum.[29]

This passage makes it clear that Struck often took orders from Luschan on how to draw features like the hair of the "Negro-Type" and that Luschan also rejected certain drawings, like that of the Russian, which he felt were somehow inappropriate or inaccurate. Luschan implied that these drawings had scientific value as objective documents, yet he had them altered to suit his own mental images of racial characteristics.

The assumption of equivalence between Struck's drawings and the photographs of POWs persisted into the postwar period. After the war, Eickstedt planned an anthropological work based on the POW studies and asked Luschan for permission to use Struck's drawings in his study. Eickstedt decided to write on the racial characteristics of the Sikhs, a group that Struck had sketched while visiting the camps. His correspondence suggests that he viewed Struck's drawings, like his own photographs, as objective documents useful for purposes of comparison. In a letter to Luschan, he described how he had judged the quality of his photographs of Sikh "racial types" by comparing them to Struck's charcoal sketches. He wrote, "I photographed about 15 Sikhs. I presume that I captured the average type, and it appears to deviate only slightly from Struck's drawings. . . . Could a few of his beautiful heads appear in my work?"[30] Here the drawings and the photographs are easily comparable forms, used to judge the accuracy of a type. The notion that the drawings and the photographs confirmed one another persisted in Eickstedt's publication on the POW studies. When Eickstedt's article was published in 1921, Struck's drawings appeared alongside photographs to illustrate the various racial elements present in the Sikh population.[31] The drawings, like the photographs, were labeled with captions identifying the four kinds of racial types that Eickstedt identified among the Sikhs. Both kinds of images were included as scientific documents, as hard evidence of anthropological fact, but it was their subjective qualities that united them. Like the anthropological drawings of the POWs, the photographs were created on the basis of subjective judgments of what was "typical" for various peoples and racial "types." In the case of the POW images—both the photographs and drawings—the artistic and the scientific collided and merged.

Anthropological Photography and German Power

Despite claims of objectivity from the anthropologists, the POW photographs also functioned as a means of conveying a sense of German power. While the photographs of POWs may have been threatening to Germans unused to seeing supposedly "savage" colonial soldiers on German soil, the images were also potentially reassuring because they depicted the enemy soldier not only in the controlled environment of the camps, but also in the disciplining format of the type photograph. By the early twentieth century, photography had long been an instrument of repressive power and social control. Alan Sekula has argued that by defining the typology of criminal deviance in the nineteenth century, the criminal "mug shot" pioneered by Alphonse Bertillon operated according to a repressive logic.[32] Many criminals violently resisted the "policing eye of photography" (and the possession of their face by anyone other than themselves), often to the point where policemen had to force their bodies into the correct "mug shot" position. The photograph functioned as an instrument designed not only to identify and apprehend criminals, but also as a tool to define what criminality looked like in general. In criminal photography, the image was the first step in the identification of the criminal as outsider by the state, and the camera functioned as a tool of state power.[33]

There were several similar levels of control and power at work in the POW photographs. First, on a physical level, the anthropological format of profile and frontal views forced the body of the prisoner into a prearranged position, thus taking away agency from the subject. In fact, anthropologists borrowed the very methods of criminal photographers like Bertillon and applied them to the POW projects. Pöch followed Bertillon's instructions for photographing individuals and even employed a "Bertillon chair" that forced the photographic subject to hold his back straight.[34] His photographic equipment was also directly connected to criminal photography. He began his studies using a "Bertillon camera," which he later replaced with a "police-anthropological camera" designed for travel.[35] Moreover, the subjects' status as prisoners regularly appeared in the photographs. In the photograph of a Siberian Jew taken by Eickstedt's assistant, for example, the subject wears a prisoner's number on his chest (figure 8). This photograph depicted a captured enemy who was under control, objectified by the format, and clearly detained in a prison camp. For the viewer, images such as these confirmed that this particular soldier was in custody and no longer a threat.

Photographs from the camps that included anthropologists also emphasized the power of the scientist over the subject. In a photograph of Eickstedt at work measuring a Nepalese man, the anthropologist is depicted in the white coat of scientific authority, subjecting the naked body of the prisoner to investigation (figure 9). The unclothed colonial subject, his body open to examination by the probing fingers of the anthropologist, is subjugated and objectified. The nakedness of the prisoner underscores not only his vulnerability and powerlessness, but also emphasizes the position of the scientist as the person in control. A photograph of Paul Hambruch with a

8. POW photograph of Siberian Jew. Unknown photographer,
Egon von Eickstedt's project, 1916. Berlin, Staatsbibliothek
zu Berlin, Preußischer Kulturbesitz, Handschriftenabteilung.

group of men from Madagascar depicts a similar power relationship (figure 10). Hambruch stands wearing a fedora at the center of the crowd, holding a piece of paper, clearly in charge. The caption reads, "Paul Hambruch and Malagasy of the three main types."[36] The caption not only reminds the viewer that three "types" are present in this crowd, but it also identifies Hambruch as the only individual among them. This photograph was published in 1925, during a period in which a weakened Germany often sought reminders of its previous power. In the context of the postwar era, in which Germany was struggling economically and black French colonial troops occupied the Rhineland, this photograph may have served as a reminder of Germany's earlier power and a confirmation of the "correct" relationship between the races before the arrival of black troops as occupiers. In short, the photographs of POWs, both in and out of the standard anthropological "type" format, underscored the authority of the anthropologists, and by extension, the power of Germans over their enemies.

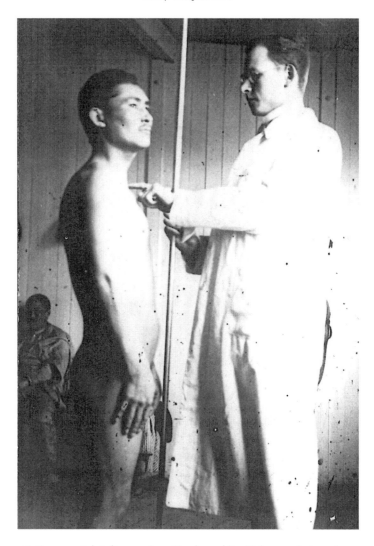

9. Egon von Eickstedt measuring a Nepalese soldier. Unknown photographer,
Egon von Eickstedt's project, 1916. Berlin, Staatsbibliothek zu Berlin,
Preußischer Kulturbesitz, Handschriftenabteilung.

The struggle for dominance and the dynamic of power was also evident
in the subtle resistance of many prisoners to anthropological photography.
To photograph and measure the prisoners the anthropologists needed access to their bodies, and the interactions in the camps suggest that the scientists used a mixture of coercion and persuasion to achieve it. Eickstedt

often tried to become friendly with his subjects, even though his attempts remained strained and false.[37] When referring to the prisoners with whom he remained on good terms, Eickstedt used the term "befriended" in quotation marks, indicating his view of the relationship's obvious inauthenticity and pure instrumentality. A group portrait of Algerian troops taken by Eickstedt's assistant in a Darmstadt camp illustrates the dynamic of control and resistance (figure 11). Despite its unusual framing as a group portrait, Eickstedt wanted to use the photograph as an anthropological document. The subjects, however, resisted his attempts to discipline them in small but significant ways. In a letter to Luschan, Eickstedt wrote:

> Of the sitting ones, the three to the left are [Berbers], and I assume this also of the man creeping in from the left. I had bad luck with the body photographs—the people wouldn't stand still! It was also very shortsighted of me not to have told the people in the group portrait that they should put my cigarettes in their mouths only after the picture.[38]

The cigarettes with which Eickstedt bribed the POWs to sit for the photograph were part of his attempt to "befriend" his subjects, but the soldiers

10. "Paul Hambruch and Malagasy of the three main types." Unknown photographer, Wilhelm Doegen's project, c. 1915–16. Reproduced from *Unter Fremden Völkern*, ed. Wilhelm Doegen, 1925.

11. Group portrait of Algerian troops. Unknown photographer, Egon von Eickstedt's project, 1916. Berlin, Staatsbibliothek zu Berlin, Preußischer Kulturbesitz, Handschriftenabteilung.

put the cigarettes in their mouths too early and nearly blocked his attempts to analyze the faces. Moreover, the Algerians in the photograph refused to "stand still," thereby disobeying his instructions. With tiny acts of disobedience such as these, the subjects resisted Eickstedt's attempts to discipline and photograph them. Still, despite attempts to resist, most prisoners had no final choice but to participate, allowing anthropologists access to their bodies and faces. The process of measuring and photographing the POWs suggests that German anthropologists enjoyed a high degree of control over the POWs, which contributed to the messages of power that emanated from the images.

The German government was sensitive about which images from the camps reached the public, but allowed the anthropologists a great deal of leeway. At first, government and military officials sought to place limits on the photographs that could be taken in the camps. In 1914 the War Ministry maintained that, in general, permission to take photographs in the camps would not be granted.[39] A major exception to this rule was made in the case of the anthropologists, who had permission to photograph camp populations. Even in the case of the scientists, however, the state remained cautious. The main concern of government officials was that the photos would reveal the conditions of camp life. They approved the photography of POWs as long as the "pictures only represented people," and they sought to limit images that depicted the POWs undertaking specific kinds of work in the camps.[40] Furthermore, the War Ministry recommended that group images of POWs that included German soldiers with sidearms visible not be taken. Soldiers should remain at a distance, if they must be included in the photographs at all. Thus, depiction of direct oppression by soldiers or camp personnel was not permissible, but the overall messages of power and control were. "Type" photographs from the camps were clearly allowable, since they focused on race and did not reveal the conditions in which they were taken. Military authorities instructed photographers, including the anthropologists, to reduce the visual references in their images to the realities of prison camp life. As long as the anthropologists complied with this basic rule, the other images they took were permitted.

The photographs also demonstrated German power in the larger realm of knowledge; they confirmed that it was German and Austrian scientists who had the authority to recognize, define, and label racial groups from all over the world. Just as the state had the authority to define the criminal type in Bertillon's criminological photography, here the peoples of the Central Powers (both the anthropologists and the viewers of the photographs) possessed the power to define the racial makeup of the enemy. In addition, the POW studies were often described at the time as evidence of energetic mood of German science during wartime, and as proof of the strength of Germany and Austria-Hungary. In an article on the POW studies for a popular science journal in 1916, Pöch emphasized the larger meaning of the POW studies, as he saw it:

> It is to be hoped that these different scientific investigations will not only be a worthwhile enrichment of our knowledge, but also will lay down evidence of the unconquerable strength of the Central Powers. While the homeland is threatened on all sides by enemies, and battles rage on all fronts, science is in a position to perceive the unique opportunity offered by the war and complete its work during the [conflict], just as during peace![41]

In this passage, Pöch portrays the POW project not simply as a scientific undertaking, but as a patriotic enterprise that proved both the power of the Central Powers and the indefatigable spirit of the German-speaking scientific community. The refusal of German and Austrian scientists to discontinue research, even during wartime, was a source of pride. Pöch saw the POW studies as a scientific endeavor that had international meaning, a project that attested to the might of Germany and Austria-Hungary.

Nearly all the elements of the POW photographs—the format, the setting, the process, and the overall enterprise—reinforced a notion of German power. In the context of total war, an unfailing belief in the strength of the Central Powers was crucial to morale and victory. The POW studies and the photographs that emerged from them not only transmitted an image of Germans and their allies as confident and powerful, but also represented the enemies of the Central Powers as disciplined and under control.

Racializing the Enemy

On still another level, the images of POWs from the camps functioned as racial portraits of the enemy. In the photographs and the commentary on them, anthropologists implicitly represented the wartime enemy as a racial stranger, not only different from Germans, but also redolent with savagery and menace. Just as the photographers' preexisting racial categories often crept into the images, so too did the context in which the photographs were taken. In spite of Pöch's strict instructions to eliminate the context, to keep the background blank and the subject naked, the war became a presence in the images and influenced their interpretation. In other words, the status of the subjects as foreign soldiers appeared in the photographs, and the remarks accompanying the images often identified the prisoners as opponents of the Central Powers. The result was a highly racialized view of the enemy, both European and non-European, and a further departure from the tradition of liberal anthropology.

It is important to note that the racialized images of the POWs, which signified difference and even threat, were published primarily in the mass media. Although several participants like Pöch and Eickstedt published scholarly pieces based on the POW project, a large number of popular publications by anthropologists also appeared on the subject. Luschan's *Prisoners of War* (1917) was a popular work, and articles on the POW studies appeared in a leading popular science journal, *Die Umschau*. After the war, Eickstedt used photographs taken in the camps for popular articles on race and anthropology.[42] During the war, Doegen gave public ethnographic lectures on the population in the camps.[43] The anthropological and ethnological work of the Doegen team did not appear in print until after the war, but was also intended for a lay audience. In 1925 the anthropologists and ethnologists connected to Doegen's Phonographic Commission published

Among Foreign Peoples, a collection of ethnological treatises on the variety of ethnic groups in the POW camps. The volume was amply illustrated with anthropological photographs. The writings on the POW studies—and the photographs that accompanied them—were far from limited to the scientific community alone. The public was exposed to racialized images of POWs both during and after the war that originated with the anthropologists working on the POW project.

The anthropological images from the scientists in the camps, however, must be understood in the wider context of images in the popular press, where other representations of colonial POWs, frequently posed in the anthropological format, appeared during the war. These images, often taken by those unconnected to the anthropological studies, helped to create an atmosphere in which the representation of the POWs as a menacing racial enemy was relatively common. The representation of the prisoners as threatening and physically "other" paralleled the view in newspapers and popular journals that colonial troops, particularly those from Africa, were wild savages turned loose on civilized Germans.[44] In popular publications, stereotypes about colonial POWs, which were often replete with military threat and racial difference, made up the bulk of the substance. Wartime articles in popular illustrated journals, such as A. Korbitz's "Types from the German Prisoner-of-War Camps," combined galleries of POW photographs in the classic anthropological style of profile and frontal views with textual descriptions of colonial troops. The author of this particular article reported that "wild" Senegalese Africans had been transported to the front "fully naked, wearing only loincloths, and many with rings in their noses. . . ."[45] He also described the tactic of Nepalese and Indian troops of "creeping through the German trenches like tigers, with broad, crooked knives between their teeth, cutting off the heads of those they overran."[46] Most importantly, the author connected these descriptions with the images of the POWs by inviting the viewer to "read" the photographs in the physiognomic vein. The look of a Belgian solider was described as "brutal," while the head of a Nepalese soldier expressed a "massiveness and brutality" typical of the "yellow soldier people."[47] Viewers of these photographs were enmeshed in a context in which colonial soldiers were often considered savage and inferior, and physiognomic readings of photographs were normal. Non-academic writers like Korbitz openly employed physiognomic assumptions that went unstated in the anthropological publications, both popular and scholarly.

The German government also sponsored popular propaganda that used references to anthropology and anthropological photographs from the camps to circulate negative stereotypes about colonial troops and condemn the Entente powers that employed them. A prime example of this phenomenon was a collection of photographs from the POW camps, *The POWs in Germany*, published in 1915. The author of the commentary that accompanied the images was Alexander Backhaus (1865–1927), a professor of agriculture employed by the War Ministry during the war. Both Backhaus's connection to the military administration and the content of the volume, which included a vigorous defense of Germany's treatment of POWs, suggest that this book was pure propaganda, aimed at refuting the charges of "barbarism" leveled against Germany by the Allies. In a section entitled "Types of Peoples" (*Völkertypen*), Backhaus hailed the opportunities for anthropological study in the camps and proceeded to analyze several anthropological photographs. Although he had no connection to anthropology as a field of study and the anthropologists in the camps did not take his photographs, he made references to the discipline in order to lend scientific weight to his discussion of the images. His commentary consistently emphasized the physical—and implicitly racial—differences between Germans and their enemies. Describing a group of Russian prisoners, Backhaus wrote, "A typical [group] of Russians is visible in next photograph, in part handsome men with intelligent faces, in part vastly inferior to German soldiers physically, with dull facial expressions. The Mongolian type is clearly expressed in an entire series of Russians."[48] Using physiognomic assumptions, the Russian troops are described as slow-witted people of inferior Mongolian stock, a group more associated with Asia than Europe and fundamentally different from Germans. Backhaus also used quasi-anthropological portrait photographs of Africans and POWs to ridicule the Entente powers and further racialize the enemy. Mobilizing all the racial stereotypes and physiognomic assumptions at his disposal, Backhaus described a gallery of African and Middle Eastern POWs as follows:

> The fourteen individual pictures [of African and Middle Eastern POWs] . . . demonstrate . . . the kind of riff-raff that Germany must fight with and what the "Champions of Freedom and Civilization" [the Entente Powers] lead into the field against the "German barbarians." With bitterness and anger we must meet the thought that many hopeful and highly educated German brothers found their ends through the bullets and knives of these hordes. . . . if it had been up to [England and France], such journeymen would have raided flourishing German regions and turned back European history one thousand years . . .[49]

Using the photographs as his central evidence, Backhaus portrayed the colonial troops as dangerous masses who were without civilization or culture and who stood in stark contrast to Germans. These statements are all
the more significant because Backhaus expected the faces of the POWs to
provide concrete proof of savagery and barbarism. In a context in which
physiognomic assumptions and racial inferiority were taken for granted
by members of the public, he clearly believed that the photographs would
speak for themselves.

Unlike more popular writers like Backhaus and Korbitz, anthropologists
cautiously avoided crude stereotypes and the explicit use of physiognomy,
but the photographs of POWs that emerged from the anthropological studies still played on prejudices and depicted a racially strange and menacing enemy to the public. Photographs from the anthropological studies of
POWs, for example, such as two profile and frontal views of soldiers from
Sierra Leone and the Mossi tribe, represented a threatening enemy to viewers (figure 12). The filed teeth of the man in the two lower photographs,
in combination with the battered uniforms of both subjects, combined to
create an impression of threat and racial strangeness. The commentary in
the caption highlighted the "otherness" of the POWs by drawing attention
to the "artificially filed teeth," the "peppercorn hair," and the "tribal marks
of the Mossi: three cuts on the cheek and chin" on the face of the lower
subject.[50] During and after the war, many Germans often expected to find
savagery, brutality, and menace inscribed in the faces and expressions of
colonial soldiers, and in anthropological photographs such as this one, the
caption guided them in where to look for physical "oddities" and evidence
of "savagery." The anthropologists in the camps were careful never directly
to ascribe these qualities to the faces of the POWs, but their photographs, by
drawing attention to physical differences, certainly fit into a physiognomic
tradition that did.

In addition, the anthropological photographs from the camps racialized
the enemy by allowing the status of the subjects as soldiers to enter the images in fundamental ways. The dress and bearing of the POWs, for example,
combined with the racial connotations of the anthropological format to produce racialized images of the national foe. In many of the photographs of
colonial POWs, the subjects wore foreign uniforms, which underscored not
only the military context in which they were taken but also clearly identified
them as enemy soldiers. This was true of a collage of four Nepalese "types"
published by Doegen in the mid 1920s (figure 13).[51] The headgear of several
of the subjects is part of a foreign uniform, and the text that accompanied
these pictures identifies the subjects as colonial soldiers by emphasizing

12. Racial portraits of African POWs. The original caption reads, "Above: Negro from Sierra Leone. Below: Mosi Negro with the peppercorn hair and the tribal marks of the Mosi: three cuts on the cheeks and chin. A Baule-Negro with artificially filed teeth." Unknown photographer, Wilhelm Doegen's project, c. 1915–16. Reproduced from *Unter Fremden Völkern*, ed. Wilhelm Doegen, 1925.

13. "Gurkhas." Unknown photographer, Wilhelm Doegen's project, c. 1915–16.
Reproduced from *Unter Fremden Völkern*, ed. Wilhelm Doegen, 1925.

their military ability and affirming their affiliation with English forces: "What makes the [Nepalese] such a valuable soldier for the Englishman is his physical condition. The [Nepalese] are the best material available to the Indian Army. Small, but powerful and muscular, they are superior to the weak and frail Hindus in their ability to endure hardships."[52]

The photographs, in combination with the text, designate the subjects as enemies who are strong, powerful, and tough. It is also significant that the collection of articles from the camps included representations of the "powerful and muscular" Nepalese but contained no images of the supposedly "weak and frail" Hindus, even though the volume included an article on Hinduism. The peoples arrayed against the Central Powers that deserved the most attention were those that appeared the most threatening. Images such as these of colonial POWs in uniform depicted the POWs as threatening enemies, as soldiers who were not only fighting against Germany and its allies, but also, because they were pictured in the "type" format, were racially different.

Non-European colonial soldiers, of course, were not the only subjects of anthropological photography in the camps. Europeans became one of the most frequent targets of the camera during the studies. Pöch, Eickstedt, and members of the Doegen group took photographs of European POWs from all regions and populations, including Scots, English, Irish, French, Lithuanians, Russians, and others. In so doing, they placed the European prisoners in the same anthropological format as the non-European colonial subject, and in the process designated European peoples as racially different from the peoples of the Central Powers, and from Germans in particular. As discussed in the previous chapter, the milieu of the camps and the nationalism of the participants in the studies facilitated the placement of Europeans in new subject positions. In a surprising reversal of roles, European POWs now occupied the place of racial outsider in these anthropological images, a position usually reserved for colonial peoples. By using a technology—photography—to measure and objectify enemy bodies from a distant and hidden perspective, the anthropologists in the camps placed European POWs in the line of what James R. Ryan has called "colonial vision."[53] In this sense, they treated the European prisoners like "exotic" colonials and implicitly classified them as racially distinct from Germans. By pitting the Central Powers in a defining struggle against other Europeans, the war created a context in which the European enemy could be more easily seen as physically, even racially, distinct from Germans.

In the process of defining European POWs as racially "other," the anthropologists implied that a unity of German physical characteristics must also exist. Photographs of the European soldiers in the Doegen volume *Unter Fremden Völkern* racialized the subjects, setting them in a group apart from those viewing the photograph. Here the liberal categories of race, nation, and *Volk* blurred and overlapped. The volume featured type photographs of soldiers from Russia and the Ukraine in the classic anthropological format that invited the viewer to see racial difference. The article on Russia was accompanied by anthropological portraits of four separate Russian POWs, each wearing a uniform and framed in the anthropological format.[54] The caption for one pair of photographs read, "Russian types of peoples [*Volkstypen*]: Russian from the province of Tambow, Russian from the province of Woronicek." This caption clearly spelled out the nationality of the soldiers, and indicated that the viewer was to look for the racial character by indicating that these were "types" without indicating what kind. Thus, the national and ethnic category of "the Russians," the enemy on the eastern front, was also given a racial character through type photographs in the collection. In addition, even though the camp populations included Russian POWs of German descent, such as Volga Germans, anthropologists on Doegen's team neither examined nor photographed them.[55] Likewise, the only French solider pictured in the anthropological format in the volume was a Basque from southwestern France. Anthropological portraits of groups traditionally considered closely related to Germans, such as the northern French, the English, and the Flemish, were not included, although each of these groups garnered an article in the volume devoted to linguistics. In the case of the anthropologists and ethnologists working under the auspices of Doegen's Phonographic Commission, Germanness was often the implicit standard by which the anthropologists judged the "otherness" of the POW population and produced anthropological images of the enemy.

Anthropologists on Doegen's Phonographic Commission also took photographs of Jews and Gypsies in the POW camps using the anthropological style (figure 14). These photographs defined both groups as members of a separate race, as people who were physically different from Germans. The chapter on Jews in Doegen's volume, from which these images are taken, is the only section in the entire collection to include captions beneath the photographs that identify the profession of each subject. Following clockwise from the top left, the subjects are identified as "teacher and prayer leader," "lawyer," "teacher," and "merchant." Captions for other groups in the collection, such as the Russians or Nepalese, did not mention occupation. These vocational designations not only highlighted the religious difference of the Jews ("prayer leader") but emphasized their presence in intellectual and professional life (the two "teachers," the bespectacled "lawyer") and

14. Racial portraits of Jewish prisoners. The original caption reads, "Jewish ethnic types.
Above: Teacher and prayer-leader from Volhynia (left), lawyer from Moscow, leader of the
Jewish theater in the Cassel prisoner-of-war camp, Niederzwehren (right). Below: Trader from
Podolia (left), teacher from Lithuania (right)." Unknown photographer, Wilhelm Doegen's
project, c. 1915–16. Reproduced from *Unter Fremden Völkern*, ed. Wilhelm Doegen, 1925.

commerce ("merchant"). In this way, the captions reinforced stereotypes about Jews and Jewish vocations while the photographs simultaneously marked Jews as physically and racially different. Liberal anthropologists in the late nineteenth century did not consider them a distinct race and paid them little attention in anthropological publications, but the images from the camps reflected a changing atmosphere within the discipline regarding Jews, who were by the 1920s increasingly regarded as racial "others" in comparison to a vague standard of "Germanness."

The photographic images that appeared in *Among Foreign Peoples* also served a larger political purpose. Doegen, the organizer of the Phonographic Commission and the postwar volume, saw the collection's role as propagandistic from the outset. After the war he wrote that his original intention was to collect ethnographic data as a concrete means of demonstrating that the entire world was attacking Germany and its allies. His intention was to produce, through the commission, a portrait of a nation unfairly outnumbered and under attack by practically all the known peoples of the earth. He wrote:

> It was originally my intention to organize in an overview the countless peoples of the prisoner-of-war camps and present them in a cultural volume at home and in foreign countries in order to show what kinds of people fought against Germany, what kinds of ethnic stocks were called up to destroy Germany! Germany did not fight against a world of gentlemen, as is always said, but against a world of peoples.[56]

By undertaking the ethnographic and anthropological project in the camps, Doegen wanted to project an image of Germany as a victim, as a nation unjustly overwhelmed by "ungentlemanly" and thus uncivilized peoples of the world. The racialized images of Germany's enemies served his goal well by portraying Germany's opponents as fundamentally unlike Germans, as foreign and "other."

In fact, *Among Foreign Peoples* was actually the second volume in a series sponsored by the postwar German government and designed to defend Germany's treatment of POWs during the war. Doegen, naturally, was in charge of this effort. In 1920, the new German administration named him the "study commissioner of the war minister on POW matters" (*Studiencommissar des Reichwehrministers in Gefangenensachen*), a position that involved what he called "propaganda work" and included duties such as defending Germany against attacks in the press on the issue of POW treatment.[57] Soon after his appointment, Doegen organized a committee charged with the difficult mission of setting the record straight on the treatment of POWs in Germany during the war. The list of committee members reads like a who's who of the late imperial and early Weimar period: Friederich Ebert, Gustav Noske, Adolf von Harnack, and others. The political and social prominence of the participants and the high level of government interest indicate that this was a significant undertaking.[58] The committee's original purpose was to raise money to distribute the first volume in a series, which Doegen wrote expressly to defend the treatment of the POWs in Germany. Thousands of free copies of this book, entitled *Prisoner-of-War Peoples* (*Kriegsgefangene Völker*]) were to be distributed to "troops and authorities."[59] Doegen claimed that "through the work, the German people should be given the opportunity to cleanse themselves and protect the national honor and the national consciousness of future generations against the accusation of cruelty and inhumanity."[60] The ethnographic collection, *Unter Fremden Völkern*, was the second volume in this undertaking. Thus the ethnographic and anthropological work of the Phonographic Commission was published as part of a highly political series which sought to "relay the truth" about Germany's treatment of POWs. *Unter Fremden Völkern* was the kind of collection that Doegen had set out to produce from the beginning: a volume that profiled the various ethnic groups aligned against Germany and demonstrated that the Central Powers had been besieged not by "gentlemen" but by a "world of peoples." The racialized views of both non-European and European prisoners found in the collection served Doegen's goal by representing Germany's enemies as not only threatening and foreign, but physically unlike Germans.

Even a liberal anthropologist like Luschan put his name on a wartime publication that implicitly cast the European enemy as racially different. Of the 100 published drawings of POWs by Hermann Struck in Luschan's *Kriegsgefangene*, there were 35 charcoal representations of European POWs. In the anthropological format, Struck drew French, English, Russian, Irish, Flemish, and Scottish soldiers. In a drawing of a Scottish soldier, the shoulder epaulet reading "Gordon" and plaid cap clearly identified the subject as a Scottish member of the Gordon Highlanders, while also placing him in an anthropological profile meant to highlight race (figure 15). Again, the presence of the uniform in this and other images indicated that these prisoners were enemies of the Central Powers, while the anthropological format also implied that they were racially different than the peoples of Germany and Austria-Hungary. Luschan's insistence in his introduction that the drawing had "scientific worth" further lent them legitimacy as racial portraits. The effect was a subtle racialization of the enemies of Germany and Austria-

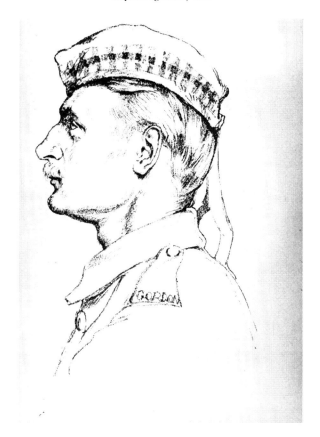

15. "I. Anderson, Scot." Hermann Struck, c. 1915. Reproduced from
Kriegsgefangene, ein Beitrag zur Völkerkunde im Weltkriege:
Einführung in die Grundzüge der Anthropologie. Berlin: Dietrich Reimer,
Ernst Vohsen, 1917.

Hungary. In 1918, one journalist cited Luschan's book and essay as proof that "every single race is represented in the support troops of the Entente. . . . There is no other race on the planet that wouldn't stand against us in the service of England."[61] It is hard to imagine that Luschan was unaware that these representations portrayed Germany's opponents in the Great War—both European and non-European—in racial terms.

The photographs that emerged from Pöch's studies also racialized the European enemy, but the process of creating the racial "other" differed slightly in the multiethnic context of the Austro-Hungarian empire. Pöch's racialized images provided an implicit contrast not just with Germans, but with the peoples of the Dual Monarchy. As in the practice of the studies, he was careful not to publish or display anthropological images of certain ethnic groups who were represented in the POW population but were also part of the Habsburg Empire, such as Poles. Instead, he concentrated on the chief enemies of Austria-Hungary. The photographs from his studies presented a particularly racialized view of Russians, for example. Images such as his collection of Russian eyes, published in 1916, not only disembodied and thus dehumanized the subjects, but also pointed to the supposed markers of racial difference (figure 16). The caption beneath the photographs read, "Different grades of expression of Mongolian character in the eyelids of the peoples of European and Asiatic Russia."[62] It implied that nearly all the peoples of the Russian Empire had some degree of Mongolian character in their physical makeup, and furthermore that those groups belonged to a markedly different racial category from the peoples of the Central Powers.

Pöch's racial photographs of the Habsburg Empire's European enemies reached the public through a variety of avenues. One of the more unorthodox was the popular "war exhibit" in Vienna. Conceived by the Austrian War Ministry, it aimed at supplying the home front with a patriotic vision of events in other theaters of war. Very popular with the public, the show provided a demoralized citizenry not only with wartime entertainment, but with further arguments for sacrifice.[63] Pöch and his group were eager to participate. In the first year of the exhibition, the War Ministry asked them to provide objects for a special section of the exhibit on prisoners-of-war. The anthropologists chose ten plaster casts of heads that were representative of racial "types" found in the camps, with the eyes and faces of the moulds painted in the correct colors for added effect, as well as twelve life-sized photographs of physical "types" hung in full view of the spectators.[64] The following year, Pöch and the Anthropological Society contributed forty-eight life-sized photographs to the POW section of exhibit. The members of the Viennese Anthropological Society were clearly proud of their participation, and organized a large group visit to the exhibit in 1917.[65]

The enormous, life-sized images that Pöch and the society contributed to the war exhibit in 1916 and 1917 were nothing less than racial portraits of Austria-Hungary's European enemies. As the meeting minutes of the Anthropological Society of Vienna noted, the images "represented twenty racial types of POWs from the Russian Empire, Italy, and Serbia," the three chief enemies of the Austro-Hungarian Empire.[66] Images of "exotic" peoples from Africa or elsewhere, whom Pöch had also investigated in the POW camps, played no role in the display, which focused only on the European enemies of the Central Powers. There were also no photographs of ethnic or national groups who were present in the POW population but also lived in the

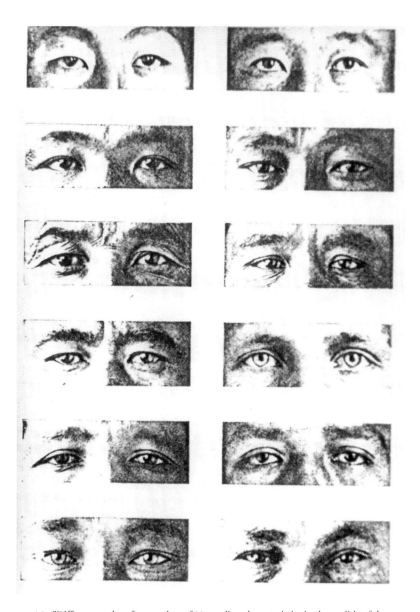

16. "Different grades of expression of Mongolian characteristics in the eyelids of the peoples of European and Asiatic Russia." Unknown photographer, Rudolf Pöch's project, c. 1915–16. Reproduced from "Anthropologische Studien an Kriegsgefangenen," *Die Umschau* 20 (1916), 990.

Austro-Hungarian empire, such as Poles or Volga Germans. The two central exceptions to this rule reflected political considerations. Both Italians and Serbian prisoners were included—two groups who, as central enemies of the Dual Monarchy during the conflict, apparently warranted racialization. The effect of Pöch's photographs at the "war exhibit" was to present a highly racialized view of the enemy for public consumption that stood in contrast to the peoples of the Austro-Hungarian empire. Here was the antagonist, literally life-sized, and the message was that he differed fundamentally from the person viewing the exhibit.

The photographs from the anthropological studies of POWs during World War I demonstrate a blurring of the boundaries between race and nation in the context of war. The format and the context of the photographs placed the POWs—and by extension entire populations—into racial categories that were understood to be other than that of the peoples of the Central Powers, and Germans in particular. The process was slightly different in the case of Pöch, but he too created racial contrasts between the peoples of the Dual Monarchy and their national enemies in the great war. As Sander Gilman has pointed out in his work on the Jewish body, the physical make-up of Jews was always understood in contrast to an idealized "Christian" body, and later in comparison to an idealized and secularized "German," "English" or other national corpus.[67] A similar process took place in the POW studies as anthropologists sought to categorize their subjects by physical characteristics, but always implicitly in contrast to themselves. By defining their enemies racially, anthropologists necessarily defined a racial identity of their own. Clearly, Jews were not part of that identity, and Russians, Italians, Serbians and others were considered different as well. In a great number of the characterizations from the camps, some notion of "Germanness" lurked at the center of that category. The POW photographs ran parallel to a larger political process at work within certain sectors of German society in the late nineteenth and early twentieth century: the infusion of "Germanness" with racial meaning. By racializing the enemy through the photography of POWs, many of the anthropologists who worked in the camps took a step into the territory of the *völkisch* movement.

In the end, the anthropological portraits of POWs taken during World War I reveal more about the people behind the camera than about the people in the photographs. The anthropologists at work in the camps considered the camera a technology that reflected reality accurately. They believed that the photograph functioned as a reasonably objective recorder and indicator of racial types, categories that lay at the heart of their discipline and their science. A close examination of the POW studies, however, demonstrates that the creation of racial typologies was anything but an objective enterprise. Pöch, Eickstedt, Luschan, Hambruch, and members of the Doegen project often fashioned racial groupings and types by depending on their "anthropological eye" and subjective evaluations. German anthropologists allowed the background of the war to influence images that were supposed to be free of context and without outside accompaniment. In the process, they helped create and disseminate a vision of the enemy based on race. The inverse of that image, however, proved even more potent. The POW photographs had the potential to serve the Central Powers in their attempt to represent themselves as powerful allies united against a common, racialized enemy. Moreover, the images aided the efforts of many Germans to define themselves as a racially unified people in their drive to establish themselves as a dominant military and political power. In 1916 and 1917, strength and unity were considered imperative to a German victory in the Great War. The photographs from the POW camps were an attempt to convey those very messages about Germans and the Central Powers.

The photography from the camps thus represented a further stride away from the traditions of late-nineteenth-century liberal anthropology. By creating and disseminating racial portraits of national and ethnic groups opposed to Germany and Austria-Hungary, anthropologists abandoned the firm distinctions between race, nation, and *Volk* that had been upheld in the old days by liberal stalwarts like Rudolf Virchow. Those same images also dealt a blow to the liberal conception of Europeans as interrelated and racially indistinct. The photographs of European POWs reflected the exact opposite perspective: that the national enemies of Germany and Austria-Hungary from Russia and elsewhere were racial "others" in the same subject positions as the Africans and Asians found in the camps. Finally, by participating in events like the war exhibit in Vienna and Doegen's propaganda project, many camp anthropologists signaled that they had abandoned the old liberal injunction against allowing political motives and concerns to enter into their work. In the context of war the rules of the game had clearly changed, and in the aftermath of the war those changes would become even more apparent.

SIX

Anthropology in the Aftermath: *Rassenkunde*, Racial Hygiene, and the End of the Liberal Tradition

The fiftieth-anniversary celebration of the Berlin Anthropological Society in 1919 was a muted, mournful affair. That date marked a half-century since the society was founded, but it was also the first year after Germany's defeat in World War I, a period characterized by economic dislocation, political chaos, and a feeling of national humiliation. Some society members, such as Luschan, felt that any celebration during a period of such hardship was "highly inappropriate and thoroughly misplaced."[1] But despite these and perhaps other unarticulated misgivings, the gathering went forward anyway. Members of the society assembled in the lecture hall of the Berlin Museum für Völkerkunde on a November afternoon to hear tributes and speeches in commemoration of the society's founding. The tenor of the celebration reflected the events that had occurred outside of the hall over the last several years. Carl Schuchardt, the president of the society, opened the gathering on a mournful note: "Such a celebration cannot be observed today without melancholy. From the lush, blooming garden of the last human lifetime we have been cast out into the barren heath of the present, where one is happy to be able to roast potatoes on a sparse fire. . . ."[2] It was impossible for Schuchardt to ignore the new postwar context in which society members found themselves, or to neglect the memories of the war that had just ended, a conflict that he called a "heroic fight like no other."[3]

In fact, taken as a whole, the celebration was "essentially an act of melancholy remembrance," as one historian put it.[4] Looking back at the year 1869 and the founding of the Berlin society from the vantage point of 1919, members were filled with nostalgia for a bygone era. Schuchardt called the period of the society's creation some fifty years earlier a "time of the happiest expectation," and he dubbed the prewar period in general a "golden age" in which Germans had been the "first scientific people of the world. . . ."[5]

He lauded the achievements of the society's two principal founders, Rudolf Virchow and Adolf Bastian, as well as the efforts that had led to the heroic creation of the Museum für Völkerkunde. Schuchhardt's speech, like all nostalgia, represented a form of selective remembrance, since he neglected to mention the unending difficulties in establishing the anthropological disciplines as viable fields of scientific inquiry during those same years. The nostalgic tone of the celebration suggested, however, that the "days of happy expectation" were long past and that a new period in the history of the society and the discipline had begun. Anthropologists now found themselves on the "barren heath of the present," wondering what the future would bring.

That present was fundamentally shaped, of course, by the worldwide conflict that had just ended. Anthropology in the immediate postwar period was influenced not only by internal forces, such as specialization and the increased importance of genetics, but also by the continued impact of the war itself. The triple upheaval of defeat, revolution, and inflation—all outgrowths of the war—touched nearly every aspect of postwar life, including the sciences. On the most basic level, the war's impact continued to influence the conditions in which anthropologists did their work. In the initial years after the defeat, they labored in difficult material and financial circumstances, struggling to keep anthropological institutions operating with scarce resources and a devalued currency. It is little wonder that in 1919 Schuchhardt looked back wistfully upon the late nineteenth century as a period of expansion in the anthropological sciences, because the immediate future did not appear to promise anything other than dogged attempts to keep anthropology and its institutions afloat. There was also the matter of a new national government to cultivate for financial support and institutional aid. These postwar conditions were particularly daunting for physical anthropologists. During the war these men had fully mobilized their discipline in the service of the state and nation, motivated by their feeling of institutional insecurity and powerful sense of nationalism, only to find themselves facing a new government and a period of economic dislocation once the conflict ended. In the postwar context, the institutional uncertainty that physical anthropologists felt before 1914 was heightened, and the need to make their discipline relevant to the state and nation now seemed all the more pressing.

Even more significant, however, were the ways in which wartime anthropology helped set the tone for the anthropology of the Weimar period. It was after World War I that the discipline began to transform itself into *Rassenkunde*, the overtly racist brand of racial science that dominated German anthropological circles in the 1920s. At the heart of this transformation was the abandonment of the liberal definitions of race, nation, and *Volk*, the same categories that had been eroded and blurred in the practice of wartime anthropology. Armed with a genetic conception of race, adherents of *Rassenkunde* sought to link physical, cultural, and psychological attributes—the very characteristics that had remained separate in the conceptual and terminological world of the prewar liberal tradition. The remaining liberal stalwarts of the prewar world now faded from the scene, replaced by members of the "third" anthropological generation who were intent on abandoning what they saw as the overly restrictive distinctions of the prewar years. This new group, members who had professionalized immediately before and also during the war, sought to cross disciplinary boundaries and advance into the realm of *Völkerkunde* in order to determine the relationships between race and culture. The emergence of *Rassenkunde* as the dominant paradigm in Germany anthropology marked the demise of the liberal tradition.

The shift toward *Rassenkunde* was the umbrella that encompassed several other developments influenced by wartime anthropology. The racialization of the European enemy that took place during World War I accelerated a change in the focus of anthropological inquiry in Germany, as anthropologists became increasingly concerned with the racial categorization of Europeans. Rejecting the liberal notion of Europeans as intimately related and racially indistinct, they became deeply engaged in determining the racial makeup of Germans and their relationship to other peoples within Europe. Moreover, the rise of *Rassenkunde* encouraged greater acceptance of *völkisch* racial thought, since the new paradigm was influenced by the precepts of Gobineau and other *völkisch* racial thinkers. The war played a role here as well, since the increasing approval of *völkisch* thought was related to the surge in pro-German nationalism within the discipline during and after the conflict. Finally, these developments were also linked to the growth in support for racial hygiene and eugenic thinking among anthropologists in the postwar period. After 1918, eugenics seemed more than ever to offer practical solutions to the social problems of a weak and defeated nation. Interest in racial hygiene was nothing new in anthropological circles, but the difference in the postwar period was that race became a centerpiece of the eugenics equation in ways that it had not been before 1914. Here too, the war years had set a precedent: the postwar effort to enlist anthropology in the service of the state and nation simply continued the mobilization of the discipline that had occurred during the crisis of the worldwide conflict.

By the mid 1920s, the discipline of anthropology had changed almost beyond recognition: it was now called "Rassenkunde,"[6] its focus was overwhelmingly linked to a racialist version of racial hygiene, and the liberal concepts that had once been at the core of anthropological practice and theory had been abandoned. In 1914 the liberal tradition had been still alive and well represented, but by 1925 it was essentially dead. At the fiftieth-anniversary celebration in 1919, Schuchhardt and the other members of the Berlin society had only the first inklings of the transformations in store, but their general anticipation of change was accurate: the war had brought a new era, especially for physical anthropology.

Conditions and Institutions in the Immediate Postwar Period

The effects of World War I on German anthropology did not end with the armistice in 1918. The close of the conflict simply marked a new stage of the war's impact as Germany entered a period of political chaos and severe economic dislocation that accompanied the fall of the Second Empire, the revolution of 1918, and the foundation of the Weimar Republic. In the war's immediate aftermath, general social and economic conditions throughout the country remained poor, and the sciences, like all aspects of German life, were directly affected by the upheaval. For disciplines still uncertain about their place within the academy and the larger world of German science, the initial postwar period was a harrowing time. Faced with difficult conditions, a new government, and a severe shortage of financial resources, many anthropologists worried about the future of their institutions and their field.

The wartime erosion of internationalism within the discipline continued after the defeat, despite the desire of some liberal anthropologists to rebuild relationships with academics abroad. German scientists tended to place the blame for poor relations on their foreign colleagues rather than on their own rhetoric or actions during the war, even when they desired renewed contact. In 1919, Luschan remarked in correspondence with the American anthropologist Franz Boas that the "future connections between German academics and colleagues in enemy lands" remained "uncertain. . . . The great majority of Frenchmen will naturally remain crazy for a very long time, and I fear that the English will remain unfriendly for a long period as well."[7] Rudolf Martin maintained that German science could only be revived when the "academic circles abroad move away from their unjustified and unfounded tone of hatred toward German science . . . ."[8] Boas organized emergency funds to aid in the continued publication of German anthropological journals, but in general German anthropologists felt increasingly cut off from their colleagues abroad. The 1920 creation of an International Union of Academics in Paris that excluded members of the Central Powers highlighted this feeling. Martin mentioned the organization to Boas as proof of the unfair exclusion of German scientists from the international community.[9] Internationalism as a methodological and ideological orientation in science depended on such institutions—conferences, associations, research centers, and prizes—for its existence. As these networks suffered, so too did the deeper ideals of scientific internationalism: the universality of scientific knowledge and the principle of keeping science separate from politics. The lack of healthy international networks in the wider anthropological community further cleared the path toward a more politicized and narrowly nationalistic physical anthropology in Germany.

Closer to home, hardships took a number of forms in the initial months and years after the end of the war in November 1918. The institutions in which anthropology was represented continued to function, but not without difficulty. Most *Völkerkunde* museums remained closed or only partially open. Even the work spaces of the Berlin Museum für Völkerkunde, for example, were closed for a period in early 1919 for lack of coal to heat the building.[10] In 1919 a shortage of employees nearly brought the work of the Rudolf Virchow Foundation, the private institution that represented the major source of funding for anthropological research, to a halt.[11] In 1920, new publications in the foundation's library could not be catalogued for lack of heat.[12] In a truly extreme case that same year, British occupying forces commandeered the Prehistorical Museum in Cologne, prompting a desperate letter from the director of the museum, Willy Foy, asking for help.[13] Anthropological societies like the Berlin organization continued to meet, but overall activity remained at a minimum and members conducted scientific work only with great difficulty.[14] In Austria, the Viennese Anthropological Society not only suffered from a severe paper shortage but also reported in 1919 that their finances were in an extremely "unfavorable condition."[15]

Anthropological institutes fared no better. Months before the war was over, Luschan admitted that his ambition of creating an anthropological institute in Berlin would have to be shelved indefinitely. He wrote to Eickstedt in October of 1918 that "as for the anthropological institute, that I could not push through even in the good times, I must now completely do without. With it disappears every possibility to bring a great number of young colleagues into halfway decently paid positions."[16] Even Rudolf Martin's anthropological institute at the University of Munich, perhaps the best supported anthropological institution in Germany, was informed in 1919 that the funding for future assistantships could not be promised "under prevailing conditions."[17] Martin expressed fears that the institute would not survive with only minimal funding from the state, and he described colleagues as having been aged by wartime deprivations.[18] Moreover, the economic and political dislocation of the immediate postwar period also meant that paying positions for scientists were extremely rare. Writing to Franz Boas in the hopes of securing a job in the United States, Eickstedt described the situation this way: "Modern Germany does not want at all men of science. More or less it is a socialistic state, where culture is considered to be perhaps agreeable, but at any rate a very superfluous thing: men of culture are in a certain degree outcasts, are economically uprooted and, as the greater part of the middle classes, left to their fate."[19] Eickstedt clearly thought so little of the new government, not to mention the new cultural context in which he found himself, that he considered leaving Germany for good. Conditions for younger anthropologists just entering the field were grim.

The greatest concern of most anthropological institutions in the immediate aftermath of the war, however, was the falling value of the German currency. The rampant inflation of the initial postwar years cut into nearly every aspect of scientific work in anthropological institutions. The Berlin Anthropological Society provides perhaps the clearest example. During the war, the society had invested a great deal of its money in public bonds, which now proved worthless. As prices rose, the society was hard pressed to make ends meet. The 1920 volume of the society's journal, the *Zeitschrift für Ethnologie*, was radically reduced in size because of rising costs of production, especially the price of paper. Hans Virchow, the son of Rudolf and the president of the society from 1920 to 1922, turned to the Prussian government for help in 1921, asking for an increase in the society's usually meager subvention to cover the "enormous cost increase in publishing the journal."[20] The state responded with the usual subsidy of only 1500 marks, the same amount the society had received before 1914, unadjusted for inflation.[21] In an effort to make up the difference and trim costs, the society raised member dues and combined the journals for 1920 and 1921 into one volume. The executive committee of the society reported in 1922 that "what keeps us above water is the contributions in gold of our outside members and occasional donations of our better-placed members."[22] The hyperinflation of 1923, however, eliminated the last of the society's investments.[23] Perhaps more importantly, the freefall of the German currency liquidated the capital of the Rudolf Virchow Foundation, which no longer had money to grant for anthropological research and essentially existed in name only.[24] The same story was repeated in other anthropological societies as the inflation exacted a heavy toll.[25]

These pressures alone were enough to contribute to institutional insecurity among anthropologists, but uncertainty about the stance of the new government toward the sciences in general and anthropology in particular added to the tension. Would the new republic support the sciences to the same degree that the imperial government had done? Anthropologists and ethnologists fretted that intellectual pursuits would suffer under a representative democracy. In a Berlin society meeting immediately after Germany's defeat in December 1918, Karl Schuchhardt articulated these worries: "We hope that Germany's good nature can overcome this shock to the system and that education [*Bildung*] and intellectual work need not go into a decline under mass rule. Work and do not doubt, that has to be the solution."[26]

Part of the work that had to be done, of course, was to convince the new government that the anthropological disciplines were viable fields of study. Specialists in all three anthropological fields wasted no time in making the case that their disciplines deserved increased attention and, above all, financial support from the state. The natural issue with which to begin the lobbying effort was the place of anthropology, ethnology, and prehistory at German universities, which were part of the state bureaucracy. In 1919 the German Anthropological Society published a public appeal to the new German government, calling for improvement in the representation of all three disciplines at German universities. The time was right, the appeal argued, for a reformation of the university curriculum to include the three anthropological fields, which had "not yet found proper attention in Germany."[27] The executive committee of the German Anthropological Society argued that it was the "duty of German science, which is embodied in the universities, to take the still young scientific disciplines under their protection."[28]

Ethnologists, however, found several reasons to be optimistic about the growth and success of their discipline in the immediate postwar period. After the war, *Völkerkunde* began to experience some moderate success in achieving representation at German universities. The two German universities founded in the immediate aftermath of the war in Hamburg and Frankfurt included full professorships (or *Ordinariaten*) of *Völkerkunde* on their faculties.[29] This brought the number of full professorships devoted strictly to *Völkerkunde* to three, since a full chair of ethnology had been created at Munich's Ludwig-Maximillian University in 1916. In contrast, physical anthropology had one full chair in Munich and one in Berlin, and the second was actually a combination of physical anthropology and *Völkerkunde* under the direction of Luschan. *Völkerkunde* seminars and institutes also proliferated. In 1922, Karl Weule, the director of the Museum für Völkerkunde in Leipzig, noted the institutional growth of *Völkerkunde* with satisfaction:

[*Völkerkunde*] is now considered a part of cultural history, yes, even as a foundation, as fundament. That secures it a growing importance in a time like
the present with its search for connections. Symptomatic for this is the rapid
foundation, one right after the other, of full professorships [*Ordinariaten*]
in Munich, Hamburg, and Frankfurt, of seminars in Leipzig and Hamburg,
of research institutes in Leipzig and Berlin, and the growing tendency of
neighboring fields oriented toward cultural history to evaluate ethnographic
[*völkerkundliche*] things from their standpoint.[30]

Even in a postwar era in which overall conditions for scientific work were
difficult at best, Weule and other ethnologists saw their discipline as enjoy-
ing a period of some growth.[31]

The status of physical anthropology after the war, however, was another
story altogether. Like their colleagues in *Völkerkunde*, anthropologists appealed to the state in 1919 for more professorships and greater support
for their discipline. The German Anthropological Society's public call for
greater representation at German universities included a separate entreaty
by Eugen Fischer asking for more support for physical anthropology. When
comparing his nation's funding for anthropology to that other countries,
Fischer noted "Germany's shameful underdevelopment [*Ruckstand*]" and
argued that, "The state will not be able to evade the duty [to support an-
thropology] in the long term."[32] But unlike *Völkerkunde*, no new professorships in physical anthropology were created immediately after the war.
Moreover, physical anthropologists, unlike ethnologists and ethnographers,
did not have a stable home in ethnographic museums. In addition, one of
the major complaints of anthropologists in 1919 was that nonspecialists,
especially from medical faculties, were teaching physical anthropology at
German universities.[33] The university in Bonn created an associate professorship in anthropology, but then filled it with an anatomist rather than an
anthropologist, to the frustration of Fischer and others.[34] The lack of newly
created positions devoted strictly to physical anthropology meant that this
situation remained unchanged in the years that followed.

In Berlin, Luschan's repeated attempts to convince Prussian authorities
to create an anthropological institute after the war came to naught. The
anthropological collection in Berlin remained part of the Berlin Museum
für Völkerkunde, but the ethnologists in charge of the museum wanted to
see it moved elsewhere to free up the extra space.[35] Luschan complained
that he was forced to work in extremely cramped conditions with only one
assistant to aid him in maintaining the collection, as compared to Martin's
fourteen at the anthropological institute in Munich.[36] Luschan's student

Bernhard Struck reacted privately to the prevailing conditions for anthropological work in Berlin by asking, "Is this supposed to be the answer of the authorities to the public appeal of the German Anthropological Society?"[37] Indeed, it appeared that the call for official support of physical anthropology in 1919 had fallen on deaf ears, at least in Berlin. Luschan became increasingly suspicious of promises of support from the Prussian Ministry of Finance, calling their assurances "pure con tricks."[38] His bitterness also seeped into his public pronouncements. In October 1921 he gave a talk at the Berlin Anthropological in commemoration of Rudolf Virchow's one-hundredth birthday. In a speech that was designed primarily to address Virchow's achievements, Luschan worked in a series of acrid complaints about the current institutional conditions within anthropology: "Since then [the founding years of the discipline] almost a quarter century has passed. Anthropology is no longer a *Universitas Litterarum*, but rather has become a university field with a solid teaching base [*Lehrgebäude*] and fully recognized as a discipline—in theory, at least; in practice it must admittedly still satisfy itself with a miserable Cinderella position [*Aschenbrödelstellung*] and with often pathetic and really disgraceful outward facilities."[39] Concern about the institutional situation in Berlin was not limited to physical anthropologists in that city. Martin also remarked privately that a Berlin "institute" existed only on paper, and wondered why Luschan could not complete the push for the foundation of an institution like his own in Munich.[40] Aside from Luschan's professorship, physical anthropology did not have an institute or a stable institutional home even in Berlin, the capital of Germany.

In this postwar context of increased institutional uncertainty and difficult working conditions, the process of specialization also added to the concern among physical anthropologists. A growing number of specialists in *Völkerkunde* gave voice to the notion that their discipline should be even more radically separated from physical anthropology. Karl Weule supported such a move, in part because of the growing size of each field: "For *Völkerkunde* everything points to a clean division from anthropology, not least its youth and the currently unmined state of the huge field of work connected with it."[41] It was no longer practical to train students in all three, or even two, of the three anthropological disciplines. These fields had simply grown too large for one person to master them all, as might have been possible in the late nineteenth century.

In addition, by the second decade of the twentieth century, many ethnologists viewed the work of physical anthropology as obscure and unrelated to their own work. In 1919, Georg Thilenius noted the gulf between *Völkerkunde* and physical research in the immediate postwar period—there were few connections between the two, he maintained.[42] Years later he wrote of the "isolation" of anthropology vis-à-vis its two sister disciplines during this period, in part because of its reliance on statistical averages and physical descriptions that were too far removed from the lives and behaviors of people, the topics with which *Völkerkunde* was primarily concerned.[43] To many ethnologists, the endless measurements and statistics of physical anthropology seemed irrelevant and boring. Karl Weule cited the work of the late polygenist Hermann Klaatsch as giving a bit of life around the turn of the century to what he called "this by itself somewhat dry science."[44] In an era of increased specialization, the close connection and even overlap between *Völkerkunde* and anthropology of the previous decades was becoming a thing of the past.

The struggle over Luschan's position at the University of Berlin in the early 1920s reflected the growing tension and increased competition between the two disciplines. Luschan, aging and increasingly frail, was due to retire in 1922,[45] and the university began a search for his replacement in advance of that date. When originally created in 1908, Luschan's chair had been defined as encompassing both ethnology and anthropology, although Luschan decidedly favored the latter throughout his academic life. For his part, he wanted the position to remain a combination of the two fields, arguing forcefully to university officials that his replacement should be an anthropologist influenced by *Völkerkunde*.[46] But the chance to put a representative from their own specific fields into Luschan's position raised the competitive hackles of both physical anthropologists and ethnologists. Fischer, for example, wrote that Luschan's position should be devoted solely to physical anthropology, despite the complaints of the ethnologists: "To me, the main issue appears to be that your chair remain granted to physical anthropology. The ethnologists will probably move heaven and earth to make an ethnological chair out of the anthropological position, and that cannot be."[47] Several ethnologists did indeed recommend representatives from their own discipline for the position.[48] And in a further testament to the feelings of uncertainty in physical anthropology, Luschan caught wind of a rumor soon after his retirement that his position was to eliminated altogether by the university administration, prompting panicked letters on his part to prevent any such move.[49]

The institutional pressures in the early 1920s need to be understood against the backdrop of the war that had just ended. During that conflict, anthropologists had mobilized their discipline behind the nation, often putting their science at the service of the state. They had propagandized for the government, analyzed the anthropological makeup of the enemy, and conducted studies to prove that German schoolchildren were undernourished because of the blockade. What was their reward? For a short time, some of them had enjoyed an increased measure of state support through their participation in the wartime POW projects, but in the immediate postwar years it appeared that anthropology once again had some reason to be fearful of its institutional future. The aftereffects of the war, particularly the difficult material and economic conditions of the early 1920s, heightened the atmosphere of uncertainty and spurred the search for new scientific missions that would make anthropology more relevant.

Rassenkunde and the Demise of the Liberal Tradition

In 1925 the young anthropologist Walter Scheidt offered a stinging critique of the development of his discipline over the past several decades. His topic was the relationship of anthropology to its sister disciplines, and his judgment of his own field was harsh:

> For some time now in many circles anthropology can no longer take pleasure in high esteem, because it is often emphasized, more or less correctly, that one must pursue accomplishments with the expectation of useful research in order to justify one's existence. Jokingly, but not without serious reproach, one calls anthropology a science out of which nothing comes, or even a science out of which nothing is allowed to come. Inasmuch as certain directions in anthropology are meant, above all of the last sixty years, one cannot completely deny the justification of such mockery.[50]

Scheidt's annoyance was palpable. Physical anthropology had been the butt of jokes in the past, he claimed, because it could not justify its existence with useful research and, even worse, because the members of the field did not seem to want to produce any. His frustration was directed at the morphological tradition in anthropology of the past sixty years, which sought only to describe and categorize physical forms rather than to draw larger conclusions about the relationships between racial, societal, economic, and cultural patterns.[51] Scheidt's criticism of this older tradition, which in his opinion had led to a methodological dead-end around the turn of the century, also represented a rejection of liberal anthropology. He and many younger anthropologists of his generation, those born between the late 1870s and early 1890s, favored a new kind of "racial science," or *Rassenkunde*, designed to search for links between the racial, the psychological, and the cultural.[52]

The adherents of *Rassenkunde* described it as the triumph of genetic thinking over the morphological and descriptive anthropology of Virchow's day.[53] In the late nineteenth century, anthropologists had measured and quantified the human form, trusting that the creation of averages from the data would allow them to draw conclusions about categories of human variation. Craniometry, the practice of measuring the form and proportions of the human skull, epitomized this morphological approach. Even before 1900, some anthropologists had begun to question whether this practice was a methodological cul-de-sac, leading only to a mass of statistics that pointed in no particular direction. In the first decade of the twentieth century the rediscovery of Mendelian genetics seemed to offer a way out of the dilemma. Anthropologists began to apply genetics to the question of racial inheritance. The pioneer in this field was Fischer, whose 1913 study of "race mixing" between Dutch settlers and native Hottentots in German Southwest Africa applied Mendelian principles of inheritance to anthropology. Supporters of *Rassenkunde* after the war reconceptualized race not as a sum of quantifiable physical attributes, as had been the norm in the morphological vein, but as a "group of genetically selected characteristics."[54] Armed with this genetic conception, they believed that they could now seek out the connections between physical qualities and psychological/cultural traits.

Anthropology based on morphological methods and liberal precepts, best represented by Martin's monumental *Lehrbuch* of 1914, now began to appear outmoded. Despite his departures from prewar anthropology, Martin produced a revised edition that remained remarkably free of Darwinism, hierarchical racial theories, and genetics. He died in 1925, and the new edition was published posthumously in 1928. Fischer had lauded the first edition as "a monument" in 1914, but in his review of the 1928 version he noted the absence of "all racial theory" and added that the work was a "memorial to the teacher who must be seen as the last classic representative of the descriptive direction in this science."[55] Another commentator said of the *Lehrbuch* in the 1920s that it "represented the highpoint of the old anthropology, but at the same time its end."[56]

During the 1920s there was a rapid shift to a biologically and genetically based *Rassenkunde* as the dominant paradigm within German anthropological circles. The first major publication in the new genre was Hans F. K. Günther's *Rassenkunde des deutschen Volkes*, a non-academic work for a popular audience released in 1922. Günther himself was not an anthropologist, but he had editorial help from several specialists, including the racial hygienist Fritz Lenz and Luschan's own student Bernhard Struck.[57] Günther's work marked the beginning of a major publishing wave of new works in *Rassenkunde*. Among the most scholarly was Walter Scheidt's *Allgemeine Rassenkunde*, published in 1925 and designed to become the standard in the new field. Eickstedt was also involved, founding the periodical *Archiv für Rassenbilder* (Journal for Racial Images) in 1925 as a vehicle for the pictorial representation of racial typologies and as a means of addressing questions related to *Rassenkunde*. That same year, Scheidt founded the journal *Volk and Rasse*, a popular periodical also dedicated to *Rassenkunde*. By the mid-1920s, the very terminology of the anthropological fields had changed. Thilenius noted this trend in 1926: "When the [German Anthropological] Society was founded in 1870, its fields were called '*Anthropologie*,' '*Ethnologie*,' and '*Urgeschichte*.' Today one would say '*Rassenkunde*,' '*Völkerkunde*,' and '*Vorgeschichte*.'"[58] It was clear to most members of the discipline that things were changing. In 1925, Hans Virchow declared before the annual meeting of the German Anthropological Society that the introduction of genetic and biological methods meant that the discipline "stood at the end of one era, and at the beginning of another."[59] German anthropology was undergoing a conceptual transformation that was nearly complete by the mid-1920s. In several crucial respects, the ideological changes wrought by World War I were a major force behind this shift.

Race and Volk *in* Rassenkunde

Wartime anthropology probably had its greatest impact in the breakdown of liberal distinctions and definitions. After the war it was apparent that the boundaries between the liberal conceptions of race, nation, and *Volk* had blurred considerably. In 1914 Martin had asserted that, "In anthropology, *Volk* has no place."[60] By the early 1920s, however, anthropologists increasingly began to seek associations between these concepts.

It was still true that no anthropologist in the early 1920s was prepared to proclaim the exact equivalence of race, nation, and *Volk*. Many of the younger anthropologists continued to affirm the distinctions between the categories of the liberal tradition in the years immediately after the war. In 1922 Eickstedt still maintained, ". . . does race = *Volk*? That cannot be."[61] Similarly, Fischer wrote that the racial relationships in southern Europe demonstrated that "in fact *Volk* and race are different concepts."[62] Otto Reche also maintained that "concepts like *Volk*, nation, language group, etc. are purely ethnological-based categories, that in and of themselves are not causally related to purely physical characteristics. In contrast, race is a purely zoological concept. . . ."[63]

Beneath these declarations, however, younger anthropologists began to bend and even abandon the liberal distinctions between these concepts in the postwar period. It was no coincidence that anthropologists who worked in the POW camps, where the categories of race, *Volk*, and nation had often converged, were at the forefront of this effort. Reche, for example, commenced research on the connections between race, language, and culture immediately after the war. In 1921, two years after completing his *Habilitation*, he published an article in the leading journal for physical anthropology, arguing that "language was part of the racial soul."[64] Language, traditionally considered the defining characteristic of peoples or *Völker*, had remained unconnected to race in the liberal anthropological tradition, but Reche was eager to link ethnic and racial characteristics. While he conceded that race and *Volk* were not exactly congruent, he maintained that language indicated to which racial group each people essentially belonged. Discussing the article some eighteen years later during the Nazi era, one of Reche's students noted that "these views were hardly found anywhere in 1921, but today belong to the core of our racial thought!"[65] Reche succeeded Pöch to the prestigious chair of anthropology at the University of Vienna in 1924, and he became professor of anthropology in Leipzig in 1927.[66]

Other anthropologists, particularly those who worked in the POW camps during the war, made similar moves in the same direction. Pöch died in 1921, but before his death he also continued to blur the boundaries between race, nation, and *Volk*. In 1919 he argued, ". . . we anthropologists know that these '*Völker*' are indeed not identical with races, but that every ethnic group [*Völkerschaft*] contains a specific percentage of racial mixture and in this way is very specifically characterized anthropologically."[67] In Pöch's formulation, race and *Volk* were not exactly congruent concepts, but every *Volk* had a specific racial makeup and thus a particular anthropological identity. Despite his affirmation of the distinctions between race, nation, and *Volk*, Eickstedt also revealed a concern for the connections between them in his postwar writings. In 1922 he worried about the effects of racial and demographic mixing on the life of the *Volk*: "we know nothing certain about whether and when such mixtures are favorable or unfavorable for the individual or our public and ethnic [*völkische*] life."[68] In a similar vein, Fischer argued that postwar anthropology could indeed answer "questions about racial change within a *Volk* through cultural influences, and the meaning of these things for the fate of the *Volk*."[69] A younger generation of anthropologists had clearly abandoned the liberal restriction on seeking connections between race and other concepts like language and *Volk*.

In this atmosphere, a central concern of *Rassenkunde* as it developed in the early 1920s was the exploration of the connections between race and *Volk*. The work of Scheidt provides perhaps the best example of the principles of this new racial science. Having served on the eastern front during the war, he brought a nationalist perspective to *Rassenkunde*, which he saw as a eugenic means of countering postwar German weakness and encouraging "Germany's renewal."[70] With the completion of his *Habilitation* under Martin at the University of Munich in 1923, he launched a career based on the assumption that races were genetic, rather than simply morphological, formulations.[71] In 1924 he was hired to succeed Reche as the resident physical anthropologist at the Hamburg Museum für Völkerkunde. Although he continued to insist that *Volk* and race were not exactly congruent concepts, he argued that the exploration of the relationships between them was a central task of *Rassenkunde*. In a 1925 article in a leading anthropological journal, he argued that *Rassenkunde* dealt with two main questions: "1. To what extent does the racial makeup of a *Volk* influence its cultural achievement? 2. To what extent do cultural, economic, and social relationships in turn affect the racial makeup of a *Volk*, and to what extent do they alter the life process of the races concerned?"[72] Likewise, the journal editors at *Volk and Rasse*, the periodical that Scheidt founded in 1925, posited the notion that the "culture of a people [*Volk*] must be dependent on [its] racial character,"[73] and saw their task in the elucidation of their mutual connections. By the early 1920s, Scheidt, a student of Martin, was ignoring his mentor's warning that *Volk* had no place in anthropology.

Since *Volk* in the German ethnological tradition was traditionally considered a cultural category related to the collective psychology of peoples, exploring the connections between this concept and race further opened the door in German anthropology to the assumption that physical and psychological characteristics were linked. In the prewar period, liberal anthropologists like Virchow and his heirs had insisted that physical types and racial categories were unrelated to mental ability or faculty. In the postwar period, adherents of *Rassenkunde* felt that they were no longer limited to the description of physical forms, and the assumption that races had specific psychological attributes became widespread. Postwar anthropologists, for example, frequently used the term "psychological racial characteristics [*seelische Rasseneigenschaften*]" to describe the qualities that *Rassenkunde* sought to investigate. Scheidt argued, for example, that "the study of psychological racial characteristics" could "expand the explanatory possibilities of cultural, economic, and social expressions."[74] Scheidt's journal, *Volk and Rasse*, took the existence of "psychological [*seelische*] racial qualities" for granted.[75] In what was also a clear break from the liberal tradition, it was equally common in the postwar period to describe race as a category that encompassed psychological characteristics. In 1922 Eickstedt described race as "a group of physically and mentally similar humans."[76] In 1921, even while claiming that categories like *Volk* and nation were purely ethnological, Reche defined race as a "a group of humans who differentiate themselves from other human groups through a very specific genetic makeup and through a sum of interconnected morphological, physiological, and psychological characteristics that are always inherited."[77] In this patently racist view, race and psychology were intimately linked—the trick was to determine the connections. By doing so, anthropologists believed they could make judgments on the mental ability and overall faculty of the group under study. In 1926, Thilenius described the advantage of *Rassenkunde* studies in the area around Hamburg in precisely these terms: "The connection between achievement [*Leistungsförderungen*], psychological aptitude, and physical characteristics could also be uncovered."[78]

This biological approach represented by *Rassenkunde* also meant that physical anthropologists believed that they were now able to investigate the elements of culture—a topic of study left to ethnologists in the prewar days. By investigating the links between *Volk* and race, anthropologists often aimed at uncovering the biological foundations of cultural phenomena. Thilenius complained on several occasions that the problem with the old anthropology of the liberal and morphological tradition was that it made no connection to culture: "Above all the old anthropology lacked any connection with the life that happened in the population, and it cannot produce the connection between the physical constitution and the mental [*geistigen*], as it is expressed in the culture and tradition [*Volkstum*]."[79] Scheidt planned his work to address this very problem by conceptualizing it as a form of "cultural morphology" that would combine biological and cultural analysis.[80] Describing a planned volume on *Rassenkunde* in 1923, he claimed that the foundational assumption of the work would be the notion that ". . . all or almost all ethnic manifestations have racially scientific [*rassenkundlich*], or even better, racially determined, meanings . . . ."[81] By assuming that cultural manifestations were an expression of racial makeup, anthropologists now had an opportunity to make judgments on the cultures of European and non-European peoples. And, of course, they were also de facto engaged in the analysis of *Volk* as a concept, which was understood to be a cultural category. Thanks to *Rassenkunde*, anthropology now took the study of culture, as well as the investigation of physical forms, into its range.

Some anthropologists saw this new approach as a means of making forays into the territory of *Völkerkunde*. Analyzing the elements of culture from a racial perspective seemed to offer the golden chance to break anthropology out of its disciplinary isolation, increase its overall viability, and even combat the negative effects of specialization. As an ethnologist trained in physical anthropology, Thilenius was particularly interested in combining the two disciplines within his own Hamburg Museum für Völkerkunde. In 1916 he had argued that anthropology had "not yet developed sufficiently in the direction that it joins together in all circumstances with *Völkerkunde*."[82] After the war he argued that a chasm still existed between the two disciplines, but hoped *Rassenkunde* might be in a position to bridge the gap. In Scheidt, Thilenius seemed to have found an anthropologist who promised to combine the two disciplines. When Reche left the Hamburg Museum für Völkerkunde for Vienna in the early 1920s, Thilenius hired Scheidt with the express hope that the young anthropologist would combine anthropology and *Völkerkunde* through the "modern biological trend" in anthropology.[83] Scheidt did indeed argue that close cooperation between the two disciplines was necessary, and expressly sought to combine the two with his studies in "cultural morphology."[84] In 1923 he wrote, "I consider a 'cultural morphology' in the sense of a real combination of ethnological and racial scientific [*rassenkundlich*] results equally possible and desirable."[85] Members of the discipline considered the long-term success of the attempts to combine the two disciplines to be questionable at best, but the significance lay in the effort itself.[86] Adherents of *Rassenkunde* sought to transform anthropology from what Scheidt called the "discipline out of which nothing comes" into a field with the authority to analyze cultural phenomena on the basis of race. This very pursuit represented an abandonment of the tenets of the liberal tradition.

The first *Rassenkunde* exhibit in Germany, opened at the Hamburg Museum für Völkerkunde in 1928, demonstrated not only the attempt at a new relationship between the disciplines but also the emphasis in *Rassenkunde* on the connections between race and *Volk*. Thilenius claimed that the exhibit had been planned before the war, but it was not until Scheidt arrived at the museum that the project took shape as being expressly dedicated to *Rassenkunde*.[87] Thilenius noted that the exhibit was not only the first of its kind in Germany but also that "until now racially scientific [*rassenkundlich*] exhibits oriented toward *Völkerkunde* did not exist. . . ."[88] Scheidt emphasized the educative function of the event for the public, arguing that the Hamburg exhibit was designed to "communicate knowledge of the basic facts and problems of genetic history" to a wide audience and to provide a "representation of the most important physical markers of race."[89] The organizers also originally planned to present racial profiles of various peoples, or *Völker*, in an effort to connect physical anthropology to *Völkerkunde*: "In content, it is planned that so-called racial images [*Rassenbilder*] of individual peoples should be shown in connection with the ethnological [*völkerkundlichen*] exhibits."[90] The juxtaposition of racial images of peoples, or *Völker*, with ethnographic materials was typical of the ways in which *Rassenkunde* sought to make links between race and culture. When the exhibit opened in 1928, it contained images of facial profiles of the German *Volk* in particular, drawn from the "north German area."[91] In addition, the exhibit contained representative images of specific "racial forms" from around the world.[92] The specific emphasis on racial categories proved how far anthropology had come from earlier anthropological exhibits like Johannes Ranke's display in Munich in 1912. The racial categories in the prewar exhibit had been vague and unclear, but the express purpose of the Hamburg exhibit in the postwar period was to make those classifications manifest to the viewer.[93]

How did the remaining liberal anthropologists react to the blurring of distinctions represented by *Rassenkunde*? Part of the problem in the postwar era was that fewer and fewer liberal stalwarts were still part of the discipline. Ranke had died in 1916, Julius Kollmann in 1918. Martin replaced Ranke at the University of Munich in 1917 and continued to pursue a basically liberal anthropology until his early death in 1925. An obituary for Martin, written by Ferdinand Birkner in 1925, noted that his conception of anthropology remained essentially morphological and descriptive, a far cry from *Rassenkunde*: "He saw anthropology, which is not identical with racial anatomy, as an expansion of descriptive human anatomy, because it had the task not only to uncover the physical differences within the human species, but also to discover the origins of their creation."[94] Martin supported the biological pursuits of his student Scheidt, but he did not make any forays into genetics or *Rassenkunde* himself. When the racist and anti-Semitic J. F. Lehman Press approached him after the war to write what later became Hans Günther's *Rassenkunde des Deutschen Volkes*, he refused, citing insufficient evidence.[95] And yet despite Martin's continued presence in the field during the first few years of the immediate postwar period, his brand of morphological, nongenetic, and liberal anthropology appeared increasingly outmoded by the time of his death in the mid-1920s—even in the eyes of his own students, like Scheidt.[96]

Luschan also faded from the scene, retiring in 1922 and dying in 1924. His departures from the liberal paradigm during the war notwithstanding, he generally upheld liberal principles after the war. His last major work, the

1922 volume *Völker, Rassen, Sprachen*, represented a reaffirmation of liberal distinctions in its very title. The book was aimed at a popular audience, and the publisher saw it as a counter to unscientific polemics on the matter of race.[97] Luschan's list of the book's main theses at the end of the volume read like a reaffirmation of liberal notions: "There are no 'savage' peoples; there are only peoples with a different culture from others. . . . There are no races that are inferior in and of themselves. . . . The difference between the different races is, especially as far as moral qualities and intelligence is concerned, not nearly so great as those between specific individuals of the same race."[98] Luschan also retained a definition of anthropology as the discipline that concentrated on physical forms and races, while ethnology and ethnography took "material and psychological culture" as their objects of study.[99] His voice remained generally liberal in these areas, but it became weak after 1922 as he became increasingly ill.

Wartime anthropology and the subsequent rise of *Rassenkunde* as the dominant paradigm helped prepare an atmosphere within the discipline that allowed for a nearly complete abandonment of liberal terminological distinctions. By 1933 Eugen Fischer was able to affirm directly the connections between race and *Volk*: "While the concepts of race and *Volk* are indeed different, in reality, however, race and *Volk* are not to be divided."[100] This view obviously played well under National Socialism, but the groundwork for such an assertion had been laid years before, during the war and the early 1920s.

Europeans and Germans in Rassenkunde

The influence of wartime anthropology also shaped the direction of *Rassenkunde* in a second major area during the immediate postwar period: the anthropological view of Europeans, and of Germans in particular. During the war, the liberal concept of the European as racially indistinct had broken down as German anthropologists racialized the European peoples arrayed against the Central Powers. By representing the enemy on the eastern front and elsewhere as racially different than the peoples of Central Europe, wartime anthropology essentially narrowed the racial space for Germans in Europe. The wartime collapse of the liberal concept of the European, as well as the decline in the spirit of internationalism to which it was often connected, profoundly affected anthropology in the postwar period. Members of the third generation in anthropology often sought to make distinctions between the racial makeup of the German *Volk* and the rest of Europe. Germanicized and Nordic racial concepts, which had achieved growing acceptance in the prewar period, now became the norm within German anthropological circles. In a marked shift in the focus of inquiry from the prewar period, *Rassenkunde* took the racial classification of Europeans, and especially Germans, as perhaps its central task.

The focus on the racial makeup of Europeans was evident from the very outset of the postwar period. As soon as the war ended, anthropologists issued a series of adamant calls for the anthropological investigation of Germans. In one respect these calls were nothing new. Virchow had studied German schoolchildren in the 1880s, and Gustav Schwalbe had proposed a sweeping anthropological study of Germans in 1903. By the 1920s, however, it had been almost four decades since Virchow's studies, and Schwalbe's proposal had come to naught in the early years of the century, despite the formation of a special committee within the German Anthropological Society to push the idea at the time. The call for the study of Germans was renewed in the postwar period with a new urgency and focus. The German Anthropological Society again took up the cause immediately after the war was over, proposing a wide-ranging anthropological investigation of the German *Volk* and calling it a continuation of Virchow's work.[101] The difference was that while Virchow's investigation in the 1880s had punctured the notion of clear racial divisions among European peoples, the German Anthropological Society's postwar proposal implied that Germans had a particular racial makeup that was being diluted. The society's statement argued that if the anthropological study of Germans continued to be ignored, ". . . we will never learn in the face of increasing internationalism which races make up the German *Volk*. . . ."[102] After World War I, "increasing internationalism" was something to be feared, because it meant that the races within the German population would soon be mixed to the point where they could no longer be determined. Something valuable—a kind of Germanness—was in danger of being lost.

Like the proposal of the German Anthropological Society, most postwar calls for the racial study of Europeans, and especially Germans, originated from a nationalist perspective that was the direct result of the wartime experience. Postwar anthropologists of the youngest generation wanted to study Europeans not simply to determine the physical forms within the German people but also to learn about the strengths and weakness of various national populations. The motivation to study Germans was linked to concern about the future of Germany. In 1922 Eickstedt argued that anthropological investigation of Germans was essential for the future: "Our self is our fate, humans build the fate of nations, the human is the measure of all things. . . . So it appears a bit funny that we are better instructed about the inhabitants of the east African Mosai steppes than about the farmers of Brandenburg."[103] Other anthropologists stressed the military application of anthropological studies of Europeans in general and Germans in particular. Fischer heralded anthropology as the discipline that could not only solve the "problem of the racial makeup of our *Volk*," but also answer questions about "the military capabilities of our *Volk*."[104] Schwalbe had made the same point when he proposed the study of Germans in 1903, but the war gave the argument about military ability new urgency. Scheidt similarly argued in 1925 that racial knowledge about Europeans would aid in avoiding the mistakes that Germany had made in World War I: ". . . I certainly believe that . . . the knowledge of the racial makeup of an army and its success or lack of success in earlier wars could certainly save the knowledge that had to be acquired anew in the war just past."[105] These concerns represented new nationalist motivations to study Europeans, especially Germans, created by the experience of the war and wartime anthropology.

It was no surprise, then, that *Rassenkunde* took the classification of Europeans as one of its central aims in the 1920s. One might ask why a thorough investigation of Germans and Europeans had not already been completed by the postwar period. After all, the growing acceptance of Nordic racial typologies within the discipline in the first decade of the twentieth century had heralded a move toward the detailed categorization of Europeans. And yet despite growing anthropological interest in Europeans before the war, Luschan could note as late as 1922 that ". . . until now no European scholar has dared to write an anthropology of Europe, and the first try came from an American, W. Z. Ripley."[106] Luschan ascribed this to the complexities of the European continent, but he might also have cited the liberal conception of Europeans as being interrelated as an impediment to conducting such a study in the prewar period. The liberal notion that Europeans were closely interrelated and racially indistinct made the investigation of Europeans, as opposed to that of non-Europeans, a second priority at best.

As they broke from the liberal tradition, younger adherents of *Rassenkunde* set out to reverse this trend. They wanted to determine the racial makeup of European peoples, and of Germans in particular. Gunther's bestselling book, *Rassenkunde des deutschen Volkes*, which analyzed the racial makeup of the German people, was the first of its kind, and it inspired similar studies. Scheidt undertook a major project to conduct anthropological investigations and genealogical research on the population in and around Hamburg, studies which he later described as belonging "in the area of communal work on the *rassenkundliche* survey of the German population."[107] Thilenius saw great potential in this new emphasis and made it clear that *Rassenkunde* was primarily focused on the anthropological investigation of Germans, a group previously ignored by the field. "The anthropological map of Europe shows the area of Germany as simply a white fleck," he wrote, but "a new direction of anthropology is being created in Germany . . . that will begin the examination of the population of the German Reich."[108] That new direction, *Rassenkunde*, promised detailed racial profiles of Germany.

The systems of racial classification produced by anthropologists in the early 1920s reflected a subtle effort to set off central Europe racially from other areas of Europe and, by extension, from other European peoples. The most common examples were attempts to distinguish the peoples of eastern Europe from the rest of Europe. Prewar Nordic typologies, which usually included four races (the so-called Nordic, Mediterranean, Alpine, and Dinaric), now gave way to five or six races in Europe as categories were added for eastern Europe.[109] The anthropologists who worked in the camps were at the forefront of this change, and in each case eastern Europeans were associated with Asia. In 1922, two years after he received his doctorate, Eickstedt produced a racial typology that distinguished all of eastern Europe from the rest of the continent by claiming the existence of an "Eastern Race" (*Ostrasse*) that was a "pronounced hybrid" and was "represented above all in Russia."[110] Similarly, Reche proposed the existence of a "*sudetische* race" or "pre-Slavic type" in Bohemia and Poland, and also maintained that "Asian short-heads" could be found in eastern Europe.[111] After the war, even Luschan assumed the existence of a "Slavic race" in eastern Europe, associated with "inner Asia."[112] This position contradicted his prewar statement that ". . . Virchow . . . was undoubtedly right when he claimed to see no difference between Slavic and Germanic types."[113] The racialization of eastern Europeans during the war, and especially their association with Asia, had taken its toll, even on Luschan.

The place of Germans in these systems of racial classification was complex. Postwar anthropologists admitted that Germans represented a mixture of the various European races, but they tended to emphasize the "Nordic" element and continued to define a narrowed racial space for Germans within Europe. Eickstedt argued that Germans, like the French, represented a mixture of Nordic and Alpine elements, and asserted that there was no such thing as an Aryan or German race.[114] Elsewhere, however, he referred to the "Northern European or Teutonic race," thereby linking a notion of "Germanness" to the Nordic racial concept.[115] In his five-part typology of European races, Eickstedt identified nearly all of eastern Europe, including specific regions such as Bosnia and Serbia, as belonging to racial groups that were not found in the German racial mixture.[116] Reche similarly maintained that Germans represented a racial mixture of Nordic, Alpine, and Mediterranean elements, but also claimed that "whiteness" was primarily associated with northern and central Europe, the geographic region in which Germany was the dominant presence. He wrote, "Only the group of humans with 'white' pigment is geographically concentrated; to it belong only the northern Europeans and a part of the population of central Europe, strongly mixed with them. Already the southern Europeans are noticeably darker, often markedly light brown, and hardly differ in their skin color from the inhabitants of Asia Minor, in many ways not even from those of many northern and northeastern Africans."[117] Postwar anthropologists tended to limit the racial space for central Europeans in general and Germans in particular, setting them apart from other European peoples, particularly those in the east and south.

The liberal notion of Europeans as interrelated and racially indistinct was clearly dead by the early postwar period. The experience of wartime anthropology, with its emphasis on finding racial differences between the Central Powers and their enemies, facilitated its demise. Nordic racial theories, which had been on the rise before the war, now assumed center stage in German anthropology as the new discipline of *Rassenkunde* dedicated itself almost exclusively to the investigation of European, and especially German, racial makeup.

Völkisch *Directions*

The ideological changes wrought by the war also affected postwar German anthropology in Germany in one additional and crucial respect: elements of *völkisch* thought now gained wider acceptance within the discipline. Before the conflict, liberal anthropologists like Virchow, Ranke, and later Luschan tried to hold the line against the influence of Germanic racial theorists and *völkisch* writers like Gobineau, Chamberlain, and Lapouge. Aside from the conversion of men like Schwalbe and Fischer to *völkisch* perspectives and the increased acceptance of ideas drawn from so-called anthroposociology, they more or less succeeded. In 1916, for example, Ranke could claim that ". . . for science, the racial theories of [Gobineau and Chamberlain] have been taken care of," and that the "general standpoint of science" was that their theories "fully contradicted the real content of science."[118] During the war, however, an atmosphere of radical and even Germanicized nationalism intensified within the discipline, thereby opening the doors to the acceptance of *völkisch* racial ideas after the conflict was over. *Rassenkunde* was built on a foundation of *völkisch* thought, and its rise as the dominant paradigm marked an embrace of *völkisch* ideas within the discipline, as well another fatal blow to the liberal tradition.

Rassenkunde had its roots in *völkisch* circles. The term *Rassenkunde* first appeared in connection with the "political anthropology" of the racial theorist Ludwig Woltmann, a major proponent and popularizer of Gobineau's Aryan theories around the turn of the century.[119] In the early 1920s, Scheidt conceded privately that the theoretical foundations of *Rassenkunde* had their origins in the racial thought of Gobineau, who had maintained that cultural phenomena had their foundations in racial makeup. Even while Scheidt sought to distance himself from the excesses of Gobineau's most extreme opinions, he accepted the Frenchman's basic viewpoint as the basis for his work in the field of *Rassenkunde*. He wrote:

> My central idea that all or almost all ethnic manifestations have racially scientific [*rassenkundlich*], or even better, racially determined, meanings, could perhaps experience anti-Gobineau objections. That this is an idea from Gobineau is perfectly clear. However, I would like to emphasize from the start, in order to avoid misunderstandings, that I in no way share Gobineau's spleen about the absolute primacy of one particular race . . . I also don't share Gobineau's tendency to squeeze everything, under all circumstances, into a racial viewpoint.[120]

Scheidt's attempt to renounce some of the more illiberal elements of Gobineau's thought was almost beside the point. The fact remained that he freely admitted that the basic assumption of his own work, and by extension *Rassenkunde* in general, was built on a foundation laid down by the premier racist and *völkisch* theorist of the late nineteenth century. Even more importantly, he felt confident enough to express these opinions to Luschan, who had once again publicly repudiated Gobineau's views as "thoroughly unscientific" just a few years earlier.[121]

The sea change in the attitude toward *völkisch* and Aryan racial theorists within the new field of *Rassenkunde* could also be seen in general anthropological works and textbooks of the period, which often included short historical overviews of the field. In works associated with the morphological method and liberal tradition, the names of Germanic and Aryan racial theorists like Gobineau, Lapouge, and others were completely absent in the sections that dealt with the history of the discipline. Martin's monumental textbook of 1914, for example, included a short "historical overview" section designed to "make the reader familiar with the names of the men who had contributed the most to the history of anthropology."[122] The names of *völkisch* thinkers like Gobineau, Lapouge, Chamberlain, Ammon, Woltmann, Schemann, and others did not appear there. By contrast, Scheidt's *Allgemeine Rassenkunde* of 1925 devoted five pages to Gobineau in its historical section, concluding that "One can fully say of Gobineau's theory . . . it understood the goal, but the path that could lead one to that goal was missing in Gobineau."[123] The goal was the racial analysis of culture, and by the 1920s Scheidt and others believed that genetics and biological conceptions of race provided them with the path that Gobineau had lacked. Scheidt also made reference to Lapouge, Schemann, and Ammon in his work.

The acceptance of Günther's work by younger anthropologists also demonstrated the extent to which *völkisch* theories had penetrated the discipline. Bernhard Struck, one of Luschan's students, helped Günther edit the final version of *Rassenkunde des Deutschen Volkes* and contributed a map to the final product. Günther was widely recognized in scientific circles as the heir to racist writers like Chamberlain, Woltmann, and Lapouge. Franz Boas, for example, included him on the list of writers responsible for spreading the "myth" of northern European racial superiority.[124] In letters to Luschan, Struck disavowed the "intuitive aspects" of the work but also said that Günther had "an astonishing quick eye for descriptive characteristics" and maintained that "the book corresponds to a need."[125] He also noted that a variety of figures within the field, including Theodor Mollison, Eugen Fischer, Erwin Baur, and Carl Toldt, had spoken highly of Günther's book. Luschan remained bewildered by his student's opinion and rejected the work utterly: "I again have Günther's book before me and am amazed anew that you defend it. There is nothing, nothing good in the entire book aside from your map sketch."[126] The elderly Luschan's liberal voice, however, increasingly represented a minority opinion within the discipline. Günther's *Rassenkunde* and its *völkisch* elements were taken up by many younger members of the discipline.

As *Rassenkunde* rose to dominance in the 1920s, the stock of Germanic and Aryan racial theorists within the discipline gradually improved while the lingering liberal aversion to *völkisch* racial thought dissipated. Schwalbe had attested to the worth of Gobineau and other Germanic racial theorists as early as 1903, but it was not until the postwar period that the racial theories of *völkisch* thinkers like Gobineau, Chamberlain, Woltmann, and Ludwig Schemann (the founder of the Gobineau Society) attained wide acceptance within the discipline. It was little surprise that Fischer, already committed to a *völkisch* perspective before the war, wrote in 1917 that, "I honor Gobineau and consider his work genius,"[127] but in the postwar period his voice was no longer a minority. By the mid-1920s, the atmosphere within the discipline had changed to the extent that Scheidt felt comfortable claiming in the journal of the German anthropological society that the "core" of *völkisch* racial thought was useful and should be considered by anthropologists.[128] Reche, whose nationalist and *völkisch* tendencies were strengthened by the war, became a major proponent of *völkisch* and Aryan racial theories in the postwar period. He signaled his acceptance of an pro-Gobineau perspective in his anthropological writings of the early 1920s, where he equated the Nordic race with the "Aryan or Indogermanic."[129] Later, in the 1930s, he wrote a laudatory preface and biographical sketch for a re-release of the works of Woltmann, the principal popularizer of Gobineau's thought in Germany.[130] Rather than dismissing *völkisch* racial theorists, as liberal anthropologists had done, a younger generation looked to them for inspiration in the postwar period.[131]

Racial Hygiene and the Continued Mobilization of Anthropology

The ascent of *Rassenkunde* to dominance was accompanied by the rise of another illiberal strand of thought within the anthropological community: a highly racialized version of eugenics. A good number of anthropologists had embraced eugenic thinking before 1914, but these ideas gained a new urgency and currency as a result of the war. The ruinous human cost of the conflict fanned fears of population decline, and the economic and political dislocations after 1918 fostered the sense that German society was in crisis. In racial hygiene, anthropologists found a means of addressing what they saw as a broken and ailing society. It also furnished them with a tool to demonstrate the practical uses of their discipline. Perhaps most important, it provided the opportunity to continue the wartime mobilization of their discipline into the postwar period, maintaining the discipline's place in the service of the state and nation. The crucial difference between the eugenic thinking of the prewar and postwar periods, however, was that the version of racial hygiene favored after the war aggressively incorporated racial ideas.

The war caused widespread public fear of population decline in Germany. It was obvious that the demographic effects of the conflict had been devastating. A total of 2,057,000 Germans died during the war or of wounds after the conflict was over.[132] Of the German men between the ages of nineteen and twenty-two when the war broke out, thirty-five to thirty seven percent were killed.[133] The scope of the losses was so great that population experts became alarmed. During the war, speakers at the Berlin Society for Racial Hygiene, for example, worried that the technological nature of the conflict was defying Darwinian laws of selection by killing off the "fittest." The "long-range shot hits the strong as well as the weak indiscriminately," the argument ran, and therefore Germany's best and brightest were being eliminated.[134] After 1918, as Germans took stock of the demographic devastation caused not only by the fighting but also by disease, hunger, and lack of wartime births, fears of population decline took a central place in the tangle of social and economic concerns facing the postwar generation.

Anthropologists responded to population concerns after 1918 by offering the help of their discipline in general and eugenic solutions in particular. Increased population fears allowed anthropologists to claim that their field was useful, if not indispensable, in the new postwar world. Racial hygiene or "social anthropology" was cast not only as a panacea for Germany's social, economic, and demographic ills, but also as a means for anthropology to escape its disciplinary isolation. In 1919, Fischer argued that the "youngest branch of anthropology, social anthropology [eugenics]," had "won eminent meaning for the state in recent times" because it had "placed itself next to national economics, sociology, and others."[135] Listing a series of issues that anthropology could address, Fischer noted, "Right now population concerns indeed stand in the foreground of interest, [and] the question of population increase and declining births is the life question of the future."[136] Similarly, Luschan took up his prewar battle against the "pest" of the "two-child system" with renewed vigor in view of the postwar demographic situation.[137] To his storehouse of arguments for the foundation of an anthropological institute in Berlin, he now added the theme that eugenics or "social anthropology" would be crucial in fostering the "reconstruction [*Wiederaufbau*] of the German *Volk*."[138] Eickstedt claimed that racial hygiene could address economic problems by improving the quality of the population and therefore increasing national efficiency.[139] According to anthropologists, eugenics was the perfect tool to address the pressing economic, social, and demographic problems of the immediate postwar period.

Enlisting anthropology in the fight against the social and economic problems of the postwar period was a natural progression after the wartime mobilization of the discipline as a political instrument. Anthropologists simply continued on a wartime footing, as it were, after the conflict was over. Now, however, they mobilized their science to address what they saw as a sick society and an ailing nation devastated by defeat. Luschan, in particular, gave voice to the feeling that anthropology had to be mobilized to save the German nation in its hour of crisis. Eugenics or "social anthropology" was to be the central weapon in that fight. Luschan argued that "in this time of the deepest humiliation for our fatherland," Germans had emerged from the war "unconquered but nevertheless destroyed." Therefore it was his duty as the "representative of anthropology at the largest university of the Reich" to use his discipline "in order to promote our physical, mental, and moral recovery."[140] Luschan's sense of urgency was unmistakable, and his nationalist motives were plain. He went on to call for eugenic measures to reduce alcoholism, mental illness, criminality, and high mortality rates in the cities. These proposals were similar to those he had made before the war, but they gained a tone of near desperation after 1918. It is important to note that his eugenic proposals included no mention of race, as befitted his generally liberal standpoint, but the application of anthropological science to the rebirth of the German nation demonstrated the war's impact on German anthropology. Oriented more than ever toward the interests of the nation after the experience of wartime mobilization, it was the nearly sacred duty of anthropology to come to the aid of Germany in its hour of crisis. After the experience of the war, the plodding measurements and cautious morphological calculations of the liberal tradition seemed beside the point, especially in a postwar situation that appeared to demand action.

It is perhaps for this reason that Martin persisted in a wartime mode after the war by continuing his studies of German schoolchildren into the 1920s. During the war, the anthropological investigations of German children had been designed to demonstrate the blockade's negative effects on Germans' health, and Martin continued the project after the armistice, dedicating nearly the entire staff at the anthropological institute in Munich to the effort.[141] Continuity in the studies of schoolchildren was needed, he argued, if the true effects of the war were to be understood. He wrote that "the individual child must be studied during his entire development and the influence of the war years and the postwar period on the physical development of individual class years must be researched."[142] He concluded in 1924 that German schoolchildren were physically smaller than those of other countries like the United States as a result of bad nutrition during and after the war.[143] In the early 1920s, Martin expanded his focus to include measurements of German gymnasts and athletes.[144] All of his studies were designed in one way or another to encourage health and exercise, but he was also motivated by the impression that German society in defeat was undernourished, sick, and in need of treatment. He viewed physical training as a means of strengthening the health of the German *Volk* as a whole. Upon Martin's death in 1925, Ferdinand Birkner noted that "in word and writing, Martin utilized the results of the investigations of schoolchildren and gymnasts in order to make clear the importance of physical exercise for the toughening up [*Ertüchtigung*] of our *Volk* . . . ."[145] In all of these efforts, the desire to mobilize anthropology for the good of the nation and the state was evident. Martin argued that the studies of schoolchildren had meaning "not only for the individual but for the state."[146] The anthropological institute, he maintained, "served not only scientific purposes, but is at the same time a productive state agency."[147]

Martin's studies of schoolchildren were related only indirectly to eugenics—he did not call for selective breeding of populations. The Munich studies also had nothing to do with race. He rejected racial differences as an explanation for the smaller size of German schoolchildren after the war, for example.[148] But his work after 1918 did address eugenic concerns, in particular Germany's population deficit and the overall health of the social body. On the whole, his studies sought to gain "an overview of the bodily development of our youth for the entire Reich."[149] In addition, the anthropological institute in Munich applied his data to the problem of Germany's population decline. Martin noted, for example, that the Reich Public Health Office and several foreign commissions would be interested in the "results of our investigations of already considerable material about easing the need for children [*Kindernot*]."[150]

By 1923, in fact, anthropologists from Martin's Munich institute were taking part directly in eugenic measures. In that year the institute set up a "consultation station for biological and family research," designed to provide free information about the genetic makeup of one's family, ostensibly to be used in decisions about reproduction.[151] An anthropologist from the institute, as well as a doctor, were on call at the center to consult with families about their genetic profile. The consultation station represented a move from eugenic rhetoric to eugenic action. The Munich Anthropological Society followed suit by setting up a new study group for biological and family research, which sought connections with the Society for Racial Hygiene.[152] In addition, the university in Munich was fast becoming a center for racial hygiene in other ways as well. In 1923, the eugenicist Fritz Lenz joined the medical faculty to teach racial hygiene, a position that university officials were very conscious of as the first of its kind in Germany.[153] Lenz, who worked closely with Fischer on a number of publications dedicated to racial hygiene, naturally sought connections to the anthropological institute. The acceptance of eugenics in Munich was part of a larger trend to mobilize anthropology to address population fears and the health of German society in the service of the state and the nation.

Although anthropologists in the liberal vein like Luschan and Martin mobilized the discipline to address population concerns and even eugenic issues after the war, it was primarily the youngest generation of anthropologists that transformed eugenics within German anthropology into a highly racialized pursuit that favored certain races over others. The conceptual building blocks of *Rassenkunde* facilitated the change. The acceptance of a genetic conception of race encouraged the introduction of that very concept into racial hygiene, which aimed at the genetic manipulation of large populations. The more anthropologists accepted a genetic definition of race and its link to psychological characteristics and culture, the shorter the leap was to the idea of selecting the best racial elements to improve the quality of Germany's cultural and social life. In the minds of many anthropologists, *Rassenkunde* was linked to racial hygiene since both were grounded in genetics and biology and both seemed to lead to questions about pathology and health in large populations. As Fischer saw it, the old morphological and descriptive anthropology of Virchow's day had given way to two new areas of inquiry: a "natural science/biological, whose inspiration came from genetic research," and the "social, national economic side, which one speaks of as social anthropology." "Both branches," he argued, "bend narrowly together."[154] *Rassenkunde* and racial hygiene were intimately related, and the rise of the former facilitated the adoption of racial concepts in the latter. One indication of this change was the degree to which postwar writings on racial hygiene among younger German anthropologists tended to favor the cultivation of one particular race. Fischer, in particular, was explicit about this goal: "New races are never created simply through mixture, but can build suitable new combinations before and after through new positive selection. Then the characteristics of the Nordic race would live in the future Europe, perhaps rule! . . . Racial hygiene can help maintain and tend them."[155] Fischer did not hesitate to state that racial hygiene was a tool for preserving and cultivating the Nordic race.

Another indication of the change in the nature of postwar eugenics was the degree to which advocates of racial hygiene made racial mixing one of their central concerns. Unlike its prewar formulation, eugenics or "social anthropology" was increasingly designed to determine the effects of racial mixing on the quality of a particular national population. Eickstedt wrote that the question of racial mixing provided the central field of inquiry for social anthropology: "The study of mixtures, whether it be in South America, Norway, or elsewhere, must finally provide clear knowledge on the question of prejudices or assumptions in relation to the worth of those same [mixtures]. Generally speaking, it appears that mixtures between races that stand far apart from one another are unfavorable, while those between more closely related [races] turn out favorably for the descendants."[156]

Different races reacted differently with the "Asiatic," he added, and there was the possibility of "racial death" from physical degeneration and mixing with inferior forms. In addition, Eickstedt noted that the effects of these forms on the nation had not been investigated and thus were not known.[157] These views amounted to a departure from prewar eugenics in anthropological circles, which had been mainly concerned with improving the quality of the human race in general.

The foundation of the Kaiser Wilhelm Institute for Anthropology, Human Genetics, and Eugenics in 1927 represented the victory of a racialized version of racial hygiene in German anthropological circles. Here was the Berlin institute that Luschan had wanted before his death in 1924, supported by the government and working in the service of the nation—but the new institution was headed by Fischer and was dedicated overwhelmingly to a racist form of eugenics. Fischer's 1926 sketch of his vision for the institute—its focus and concerns—contained all the hallmarks of the postwar version of racial hygiene. The new institute would be based on an anthropology built around a genetic conception of race, and the investigation of the effects of racial mixing, especially in Europe, would be one of its chief aims. Fischer maintained that one of the major questions of anthropology at present was "what are the occurrences in individuals when races mix. Aside from the behavior of hair and eye color, we know next to nothing on an indisputable basis about racial mixing in Europe."[158] In his reports to government officials he claimed that the racial hygiene was not concerned with the cultivation of one race, like the Nordic, over any other.[159] But in other statements to those same officials he clearly included the investigation of the positive and negative qualities of specific races, especially as they related to disease, as a central concern of the new anthropological institution. In a report describing the work of the institute, he wrote:

> Together with genetic teachings, anthropology today also encompasses the investigation of individual genetic lines within a population. Above all, the spread of diseased genetic lines, the continuation of genetic lines burdened by criminals, epileptics, cretins, idiots, and on the other side favorably burdened by special abilities, talents, physically and mentally favorable constitutions, are not followed in detail in our population. We still don't know today, for example, whether tuberculosis and cancer are equally frequent for blond and brown, for the Nordic and Alpine race. We still have no idea whether racial mixture as such, above all parts of the mixture [happening] without hesitation in our big cities, predispose for certain sicknesses or diseased constitutions. . . . Here a giant field for research lies before us.[160]

Fischer's eugenic interests combined notions of health with concepts of race. He was interested in learning which *racial* elements were the healthiest and which not, so that those elements could be manipulated within the population. Of course he was particularly interested in the racial makeup of Germans, arguing that a racial investigation of the German population topped the list of projects that the institute would pursue.[161] Although he repeatedly cautioned that racial hygiene was not about cultivating a particular race, he also noted that it was designed to "create the most favorable relationships for living and reproduction for the racially healthiest within a group . . ."[162] Judging by his other writings, he viewed the Nordic race as the superior, and therefore "racially healthiest," group.

The new institute was understood as benefiting the German state, nation, and people in troubled times. The president of the Kaiser Wilhelm Society, Adolf von Harnack, emphasized its importance in a 1926 letter of support: "I don't even need to explain what meaning the creation of such an institute can have for the German *Volk*."[163] Fischer used similar argumentation in what represented the continuation of a wartime theme: anthropology should be mobilized in the service of national goals and in support of the German *Volk*. Fischer wrote, for example, that solving eugenic questions held the key to future dominance in Europe: "One may dare to maintain that the European people that solves this problem will have the future."[164] The state and the German people in general had, he claimed, an overwhelming self-interest in eugenic questions. He argued that, "The state has the utmost interest, the whole *Volk* really vital interest, in gaining flawless information about the inheritance of healthy and sick, physical and mental structures, about the de- or regeneration of parts of the population with possible racial differences, the meaning of inbreeding, mixture, increase and decrease in children, and all the other questions of social anthropology."[165] This passage implied that eugenics or social anthropology was crucial to the future of Germany, exactly as Luschan and others had argued before the war—but it also incorporated race into the eugenic equation.

The foundation of the Kaiser Wilhelm Institute of Anthropology in 1927 was a watershed for German anthropology in a variety of ways. First, it appeared that anthropologists were beginning to solve, at least in part, the institutional quandaries that had beset them since before the turn of the century. By highlighting and mobilizing the eugenic aspects of their science in the service of the state and the nation, anthropologists seemed to have found a formula for attracting the support of the government and finding a stable institutional home. The institute meant jobs and funding for anthropologists. Upon taking charge, for example, Fischer hired a cohort of younger anthropologists to work at the institute.[166] Second, and equally important, the foundation of the institute marked the acceptance of the racialized version of racial hygiene as the dominant form of eugenics in German anthropological circles. The technocratic, non-racial, and "progressive" eugenics of Luschan, Schallmeyer, and others increasingly faded from the scene in the late 1920s and early 1930s. The creation of the Kaiser Wilhelm Institute was a final indication that the influence of the liberal tradition in German anthropology had run its course.

The ascent of Fischer within German anthropological circles by the late 1920s demonstrated how much the discipline had changed since 1914. In the years from 1925 to 1927, Fischer was not only made the head of the Kaiser Wilhelm Institute but was also named as Luschan's replacement at the University of Berlin. As the occupant of these two prestigious posts he wielded considerable power within the field, enjoyed the respect of his colleagues, and found himself in a position to determine the direction of the discipline in the years to come. The fact that Luschan's chair could be occupied by one of the most illiberal anthropologists of the younger generation indicated the extent to which liberal anthropology no longer held sway within the discipline by the mid- to late 1920s. Fischer, after all, was a proponent of *völkisch* racial theories, a booster of the Nordic race, a believer in the inequality of races, and a supporter of a racist form of eugenics. If anything, these views qualified him for success within the discipline more than they worked against him after the war. The atmosphere of the field had changed radically since the prewar years, when anthropologists in the liberal tradition had rejected the very ideas that Fischer rode to triumph in the 1920s. In the postwar context liberal anthropology, with its emphasis on equality, internationalism, and universalism, was doomed.

CONCLUSION

In 1933, soon after the Nazi seizure of power, the chief anthropologist at the University of Munich made a proposal. Theodor Mollison had been the professor of anthropology at Ludwig Maximillian University since 1926, occupying the chair that had once been held by the liberal anthropologists Ranke and Martin. As the full professor at the university, he was also in charge of the anthropological institute and the extensive anthropological collection connected with it. In March of 1933, several months after Hitler came to power, Mollison proposed that the anthropological collection be organized into a new public exhibit on *Rassenkunde*. The skulls and bones kept at the institute had been restricted to scientific use since 1917, when Martin had closed the anthropological exhibit. Now, Mollison argued, was the time to arrange the collection into a new exhibition for the "instruction and teaching of the public."[1] Several years later he noted that the *Rassenkunde* exhibit was something he had "worked on for many years and already long planned for," but the space for the exhibition was found only after the Nazi seizure of power in 1933.[2]

The exhibit, as conceived by Mollison and his assistants, was an excellent example of Nazi anthropology. Its express purpose was to put anthropology at the ideological service of the National Socialist state. Mollison described the aim simply: "The anthropological exhibit wants to support in the most effective way the endeavor of the government to awaken an understanding of the racial question in the entire people."[3] One of Mollison's assistants at the institute described the exhibit as "taking Adolf Hitler's motto 'blood and soil' [*Blut und Boden*] as its foundation."[4] Munich anthropologists also noted that the exhibit could be arranged for "racial education courses" (*Rassenschulungskurse*) for members of the SS, SA, and Hitler Youth.[5]

Perhaps just as importantly, the Munich exhibit represented a veritable catalog of the illiberal directions anthropology had taken in the 1920s, many of which happened to parallel neatly the racial ideology of the National Socialist state. The principles of *Rassenkunde*, which Mollison called an "indispensable foundation of our world view [*Weltanschauung*]," structured the presentation of the material in the exhibit.[6] The genetic nature of race was emphasized up front, and the second half of the display was devoted to the races of the current age.[7] In keeping with the postwar emphasis on racial distinctions within Europe, the racial makeup of Europeans, and of Germans in particular, received a great deal of attention. The exhibit was to make it clear that individual races had "different worths."[8] Germany was depicted as containing five races (the Nordic, Mediterranean, Alpine, Dinaric, and Eastern Baltic), while the Slavs were described as a "center of infection for Asiatic blood."[9] In addition, the "white race" was in danger of unfavorable racial mixtures by mingling with Jews. In a classic blurring of the liberal categories of race, nation, and *Volk*, the exhibit argued that the task of "the Germanic peoples, and Germans in particular" was to serve as a "racial filter" in Europe, particularly against the Asiatic influences of the east. Eugenics or "racial cultivation" was portrayed as the central weapon in the fight against "racial weakness, the increasing deterioration of genetic worth, and the mixture with foreign races."[10] The proposal for the Munich exhibit was a clear example of an anthropological science that not only had been fully mobilized for the state and nation, but also had fully embraced a racist and *völkisch* perspective.

As the Munich exhibition indicates, the period of National Socialist rule was a profitable one for many of the anthropologists who gained their professional experience and credentials around the time of World War I and adopted *Rassenkunde* as a scientific direction in the early 1920s. Reche, who was named to a professorship in anthropology at the University of Leipzig in 1927, enjoyed a great degree of professional success under National Socialism, working as an anthropologist for the SS Race and Settlement Office (*Rasse und Siedlungsamt*).[11] On the occasion of his sixtieth birthday in 1939, his "students and friends" put together a commemorative Festschrift that included forty-six contributors.[12] Reche continued to argue for close connections between *Volk* and race throughout his career. In 1934, he posited that every "change in the racial makeup of a people (*Volk*) must also result in a corresponding change in its culture."[13] By 1939 his career was seen as an effort to clarify the "racial history of the Nordic race" in order to account for the "racial foundations of our *Volk*."[14] Eickstedt also gained positions of influence. In the late 1920s he was an instructor of anthropology at the

University of Breslau; and in 1933, a few months after the Nazi seizure of power, he was named full professor. Throughout the late 1930s he worked closely with the Nazi Office of Racial Policy, publishing an anthropological series entitled *Race, Volk and Genetic Makeup in Silesia*.[15] During this period he called for an "anthropology of the whole," a brand of anthropological science designed to explore the "psychosomatic configuration [*leibseelische Gestalt*] of man" that took the connection between racial traits and psychological makeup as a given.[16]

Scheidt, like Eickstedt, was named full professor in 1933. That same year, he presided over the renaming of the anthropological section at the Hamburg ethnographic museum as the "Racial biological institute."[17] During the Nazi era he prospered as an *Ordinarius* of "Racial and Cultural Biology," continuing to argue for the connection between race and culture. He never joined the Nazi party, but in 1936 the Rector of Hamburg University assured officials in the Prussian Ministry of Education that "Professor Scheidt is . . . not a party member, but he affirms National Socialism unconditionally as a researcher who for more than ten years has advocated for racial thinking."[18] Fischer became one of the most prominent anthropologists of the Nazi period from his position as professor of anthropology in Berlin and head of the Kaiser Wilhelm Institute for Anthropology, Human Genetics, and Eugenics. Championing the ideas of Gobineau and a distinctly *völkisch* racial biology, he aligned himself with Hitler's government after the Nazi seizure of power and was named rector of the University of Berlin in 1933. Under Fischer's leadership, the institute provided certificates of racial background to paying members of the public during the 1930s.[19] As questions of racial belonging entered the legal system, anthropologists from Fischer's institute served on "racial courts" designed to settle questions of racial standards and history. Fischer himself served on a "genetic health court" that made decisions about sterilizing the so-called genetically flawed. For many members of the youngest generation in German anthropology, the Nazi period was a time of institutional support and professional success.

This book suggests, however, that the racist and *völkisch* directions that anthropology took in the 1920s and 1930s were not necessarily prefigured by the anthropological science of the late nineteenth century. The Munich *Rassenkunde* exhibit of the early 1930s, for example, was not the natural successor of the anthropology that reigned around 1900. At the turn of the century the discipline of anthropology encompassed a variety of different strands of anthropological thought, but chief among them was a liberal variety. The liberal anthropology championed by Virchow and other members of the founding generation took an antiracist stance on a phalanx of key issues. Races, they argued, were nothing more than morphological variations; the category of race was in no way linked to psychological makeup and could not be used to make judgments on mental ability. This formulation, which emphasized liberal notions of universalism and progress, was based on the notion that no race was superior or inferior to any other. Race also had nothing to do with culture, they argued, since it was simply a physical classification. Moreover, liberal anthropologists like Virchow, Martin, and Luschan considered Europeans of different nationalities to be a mixed and intimately interrelated group within which it was difficult to make racial distinctions. Some members of the discipline began to retreat from liberal anthropology by the first decade of the twentieth century, but liberal precepts still maintained a central place within the field. In the very period that anthropologists like Schwalbe and Fischer championed the ideas of Germanic racial theorists and other anthropologists began to pursue a racially based form of eugenics, Martin published his *Lehrbuch* of 1914, reaffirming many of the basic tenets of the liberal and morphological tradition. Despite the challenges of the racist and illiberal strands of thought within the discipline, elements of the liberal tradition persisted within anthropology in the years leading up to World War I.

The dominance of the liberal paradigm in late-nineteenth-century anthropology and its continued influence in the early twentieth century suggest that teleological narratives of the development of racial thought in Germany need to be revised to incorporate the trends that did not necessarily culminate in National Socialism. Claims that Germany developed along a "special path" in the development of racial and anthropological thought leading from the late nineteenth century to the Nazi period oversimplify the history of German-speaking anthropology.[20] Likewise, efforts to find the roots of later Nazi race science in the work of Virchow and his followers downplay the liberal and pluralistic elements of their science.[21] The liberal tradition eventually died out, but its ascendancy before 1900 must be acknowledged in order to construct a more nuanced picture of how anthropology developed in Germany and in the world. In fact, Matti Bunzl and Glenn Penny have noted that the incorporation of German anthropology into the wider history of anthropology as a discipline challenges the traditional narrative of the field's development, which is usually written as a progression from evolutionary and hierarchical understandings of humankind in the nineteenth century to more tolerant and pluralistic approach in the twentieth.[22] This story, however, is based primarily on the Anglo-American experience. The history of German anthropology reverses that periodization, with the discipline moving from a liberal and cosmopolitan science to a virulently racist and nationalist endeavor by the 1920s. Casting aside teleology reveals a more complex, and potentially more perplexing, constellation of trends in late-nineteenth-century anthropology.

How then, was the liberal paradigm virtually extinguished in German anthropological circles, and replaced by a racist and *völkisch* form of anthropological science epitomized by *Rassenkunde* and racial hygiene? World War I was crucial in facilitating the shift. This is not to say that there were no critical developments within the field that helped to determine the shape of anthropological science in the 1920s. The internal world of the discipline itself was indeed a central context in which anthropologists worked. The embrace of genetics within the field, for example, was underway in the first decade of the twentieth century. Appearing in 1913, Fischer's study of the so-called "Rehobeth bastards" of east Africa marked a shift toward genetic approaches in the discipline. Equally important was the increased acceptance after 1900 of Darwinian evolution as a means of explaining human origins and development. Darwinian perspectives, which often brought with them notions of inequality associated with the "survival of the fittest," achieved a growing consensus after the passing of Virchow, who had opposed evolutionary ideas until his death in 1902.

These developments alone, however, cannot fully explain the shift in direction within German anthropology. Rather, historians must also incorporate a wider set of contexts. In particular, political contexts and scientists' reactions to them played a critical role in altering the discipline's trajectory. Historians of science have long been interested in this issue, but as Michael Gordin, Walter Grunden, Mark Walker and Zuoyue Wang point out, "Scholars have generally assumed that a political environment can influence science, but relatively little is known about how this functioned in particular circumstances."[23] The story of anthropology at war suggests that change within a scientific field—in fact, the utter transformation of a scientific discipline—can be driven by efforts at political accommodation, by scientists altering their focus and aims to match the ideological and political concerns of the moment. World War I, Europe's first "total war," required the full mobilization of each nation's economic, social, and political resources in order to fight. In Germany the war created a highly charged nationalist satmosphere, and no sector of its society and culture remained untouched by the pressures of the conflict. In this context, German anthropologists fashioned their science to meet what they saw as the needs and interests of the moment. The result was the creation of a wartime version of "ideologically correct science," a phenomenon usually associated with science during the cold war or under totalitarian regimes.[24]

Unlike in those contexts, however, the process in wartime anthropology was not driven by the state, which had little interest in anthropology as a discipline. Rather, the scientists themselves transformed their science into a political tool and wielded it to support the war effort. The process of political instrumentalization began in the decade before the war as anthropologists tried to capitalize, with minimal success, upon the opportunity represented by Germany's colonies—but it culminated after 1914. The change was not always deliberate. Anthropologists during World War I did not suddenly and resolutely set out to transform the overall character of their discipline. Instead, the process occurred as a gradual accumulation of alterations and adjustments in focus. Scientists moved away from elements of the liberal tradition, which had become unfashionable in the context of war, and toward nationalist projects and political themes that had gained in importance as a result of the conflict. These small changes added up to a major transformation. Members of the discipline were active agents in this process, making decisions and reacting to the world around them, but they did not always have the big picture in view or fully realize the consequences of those decisions. Disciplinary change can occur, in other words, through the creeping accretion of small, politically motivated adjustments. Over time, the repeated shifting of a trajectory by a degree, and then by another and another, can dramatically alter a course.

A combination of factors drove these adjustments, all of them related to the contexts in which anthropologists worked. Institutional circumstances in physical anthropology played a critical role. Before the war, members of the discipline were nagged by a feeling of institutional insecurity and frustrated by what they saw as a lack of government support for their discipline. In particular, they wanted greater representation within the university system—the mark of true disciplinary success in imperial Germany. In the years leading up to the war, these sentiments were amplified by disciplinary specialization, which had increased the distance between anthropology and ethnology. The latter discipline maintained a secure institutional home in ethnographic museums and was becoming increasingly important to the German colonial effort. The war appeared to offer anthropologists an opportunity to catch up. By making their science more useful, more instrumental, and more attuned to the needs of the nation, they hoped for greater political relevance and greater state support. At the same time, the war altered the ideological context of their work by encouraging a wave of nationalism within anthropological circles. Although nationalism had already been on the rise in their discipline before the war, the conflict encouraged anthropologists to define their roles and the aims of their work in strictly nationalist terms. The countervailing trend—internationalism, which held that scientists were engaged in the universalist pursuit of knowledge separate from the realm of politics and based on transnational networks—crumbled under the pressures of total war as the relationships between German anthropologists and their colleagues abroad broke down, paving the way for a more overtly political, instrumentalized science.

The war also provided a series of concrete new settings in which to conduct anthropological studies. Among these were the POW camps, which filled with thousands of foreign soldiers in the initial months of the war. In the atmosphere of the camps, anthropologists entered into new relationships with their subjects, largely defined by their status as enemies of the Central Powers. The camp setting served to collapse the distinction between European and non-European prisoners, thereby facilitating a refashioning of the enemies of the Central Powers as being racially different. Similarly, the aftermath of the war provided new political and ideological contexts for anthropological work. After 1918, members of the discipline toiled in an atmosphere of national weakness and economic crisis. More than ever, they sought to make their discipline relevant to the state and national interests.

Within these new ideological and environmental contexts, many anthropologists, particularly the youngest, abandoned the central precepts of the liberal tradition. Chief among these precepts were the distinctions between race, nation, and *Volk* that had underpinned the anthropology of Virchow and his circle. In the writings, photographs, and conceptions that emerged from the POW camps, anthropologists produced a highly racialized view of the enemy, often conflating or blurring the distinctions between race and nation, race and *Volk*. The liberal notion of the European as a racially indistinct group also eroded as members of the discipline produced a view of particular European groups as racial "others," fundamentally different from the peoples of central Europe, especially Germans. These conceptual shifts, combined with aggressive wartime nationalism, opened the way to greater acceptance of *völkisch* and Germanic racial theories which took the centrality and superiority of the so-called Nordic race for granted. In addition, the wartime mobilization of anthropology in support of the nation pushed the discipline further in the direction of eugenics or "racial hygiene," which increasingly took on racial meanings. All of these ideas had been present, to various degrees, before the war, but the new ideological and environmental contexts created by the worldwide conflict facilitated their embrace by anthropologists. In the context of war and its aftermath, the liberal precepts that Virchow and his circle had championed around the turn of the century appeared increasingly irrelevant.

The 1920s thus saw the rise of *Rassenkunde* as the dominant paradigm—a virulently racist brand of anthropology based on the acceptance of *völkisch* racial theories and the exploration of the connections between race, nation, and *Volk*. The ideological and conceptual shifts of the war years aided in creating an intellectual atmosphere in which liberal distinctions no longer held sway. The youngest generation in German anthropology now felt freer to determine the links between physical makeup and cultural or psychological qualities. They also focused obsessively on the racial makeup of Germans, especially in relation to other European groups. In this atmosphere, a racialized version of eugenics now became the norm within anthropological circles. By the mid- to late 1920s the conceptual remnants of the liberal tradition had all but disappeared.

In German anthropology, as in so many other areas of German life, the Great War proved to be a critical turning point. The story of the discipline's engagement with World War I and its transformation in the aftermath can be read as a cautionary tale about the relationship between science and politics, and the dangers embedded there. In wartime the temptation to yield to ideological fashion was great. By doing so, German anthropologists imperiled their intellectual independence, departed from international standards of scientific work, and abandoned a humanistic and cosmopolitan approach to humanity. This was a bargain that signaled the end of one tradition in German anthropology and the beginning of another that would culminate in the Nazi anthropology of the 1930s.

NOTES

INTRODUCTION

1. "Charakterköpfe aud dem Gefangenlager in Ohrdruf," *Die Gartenlaube* (1915): 469; Albrecht Wirth, "Das Völkergemisch unserer Feinde," *Die Gartenlaube* (1915): 72–76.
2. Felix von Luschan, *Kriegsgefangene, ein Beitrag zur Völkerkunde im Weltkriege: Einführung in die Grundzüge der Anthropologie* (Berlin: Dietrich Reimer [Ernst Vohsen], 1917), 6.
3. Felix von Luschan, *Kriegsgefangene*, 2.
4. The terms *Ethnologie* and *Völkerkunde* were often used interchangeably, but there were differences between them. *Völkerkunde* usually described the study of peoples without written culture, while *Ethnologie* encompassed the study of literate peoples as well. For a concise discussion of terminology in German-speaking anthropology, see H. Glenn Penny, "Traditions in the German Language," in *A New History of Anthropology*, ed. Henrika Kuklick (Oxford: Blackwell, 2008), 80.
5. See Margit Berner, "Forschungs-'Material' Kriegsgefangene: Die Massenuntersuchungen der Wiener Anthropologen an gefangenen Soldaten, 1915–1918," in *Vorreiter der Vernichtung? Eugenik, Rassenhygiene, und Euthanasie in der österreichischen Diskussion vor 1938*, eds. Heinz Eberhard Gabriel and Wolfgang Neugebauer (Wien: Böhlau Verlag, 2005), 167–98; Margit Berner, "Die 'rassenkundlichen' Untersuchungen der Wiener Anthropologen in Kriegsgefangenenlagern 1915–1918," *Zeitgeschichte* 30 (2003): 124–36; Britta Lange, "Ein Archiv von Stimmen: Kriegsgefangene unter ethnographischer Beobachtung," in *Original/Ton: Zur Mediengeschichte des O-Tons*, eds. Harun Maye, Cornelius Reiber, and Nikolaus Wegmann (Constance: UVK, 2007), 317–42.
6. See, for example, George L. Mosse, *Towards the Final Solution: A History of European Racism* (Madison: University of Wisconsin Press, 1978). Initially, intellectual historians sought to trace the rise of racial thought from certain foundational figures like Count Arthur de Gobineau or Paul de Lagarde to the anti-Semitic and racist movements of the twentieth century. The classic accounts are Fritz Stern, *The Politics of Cultural Despair: A Study in the Rise of the Germanic Ideology* (Berkeley: University of California Press, 1961) and Goerge L. Mosse, *The Crisis of German Ideology: Intellectual Origins of the Third Reich* (New York: Grosset and Dunlap, 1964). Other studies located the origin of the racial ideas of the 1930s and 1940s in the growth of Aryan

racial thought or the social Darwinism of German biologist Ernst Haeckel. See Léon Poliakov, *The Aryan Myth: A History of Racist and Nationalist Ideas in Europe*, trans. Edward Howard (New York: Basic Books, 1974); Daniel Gasman, *The Scientific Origins of National Socialism: Social Darwinism in Ernst Haeckel and the German Monist League* (New York: American Elsevier Publishing Company, 1971).

7. Michael Burleigh and Wolfgang Wippermann, *The Racial State: Germany, 1933–1945* (Cambridge: Cambridge University Press, 1991), 23–28.

8. Gretchen E. Schafft, *From Racism to Genocide: Anthropology in the Third Reich* (Urbana: University of Illinois Press, 2004).

9. Wilhelm E. Mühlmann, *Geschichte der Anthropologie* (Frankfurt am Main: Athenaum Verlag, 1968). On Mühlmann and Nazism, see Andre Gingrich, "The German Speaking Countries: Ruptures, Schools, and Non-Traditions: Reassessing the History of Sociocultural Anthropology in Germany," in *One Discipline, Four Ways: British, German, French, and American Anthropology* (Chicago: University of Chicago Press, 2005), 131–34.

10. Hans-Ulrich Wehler, *The German Empire, 1871–1918* (Leamington Spa: Berg, 1985).

11. David Blackbourne and Geoff Eley, *The Particularities of German History: Bourgeois Society and Politics in Nineteenth-Century Germany* (Oxford: Oxford University Press, 1984), 22.

12. For a general discussion, see Robert A. Nye, "The Rise and Fall of the Eugenics Empire," *The Historical Journal* 36 (1993): 687. Also see Daniel Pick, *Faces of Degeneration: A European Disorder, 1848–1918* (Cambridge: Cambridge University Press, 1989); Richard Soloway, *Demography and Degeneration: Eugenics and the Declining Birth Rate in Twentieth-Century Britain* (Chapel Hill: University of North Carolina Press, 1990).

13. The History of Anthropology series, edited by George Stocking and published by the University of Wisconsin Press since 1983, is perhaps the best example of this phenomenon. See, among others, George W. Stocking, ed., *Functionalism Historicized: Essays on British Social Anthropology* (Madison: University of Wisconsin Press, 1984); George W. Stocking, ed., *Bones, Bodies, Behavior: Essays on Biological Anthropology* (Madison: University of Wisconsin Press, 1988); George W. Stocking, ed., *Colonial Situations: Essays on the Contextualization of Ethnographic Knowledge* (Madison: University of Wisconsin Press, 1991).

14. See Hans Fischer, *Die Hamburger Südsee-Expedition: Über Ethnographie und Kolonialismus* (Frankfurt am Main: Syndikat, 1981); Manfred Gothsch, *Die deutsche Völkerkunde und ihr Verhältnis zum Kolonialismus: Ein Beitrag zur kolonialideologischen und kolonialpraktischen Bedeutung der deutschen Völkerkunde in der Zeit von 1870 bis 1945* (Hamburg: Institute Institut für Internationale Angelegenheiten der Universität Hamburg, 1983); Hans Fischer, *Völkerkunde in Nationalsozialismus: Aspekte der Anpassung, Affinität, und Behauptung einer wissenschaftlichen Disziplin* (Berlin: Reimer Verlag, 1990); on German anthropology and colonialism, also see Pascal Grosse, "Turning Native? Anthropology, German Colonialism and the Paradoxes of the Acclimitization Question, 1885–1914," in *Worldly Provincialism: German Anthropology in the Age of Empire* (Ann Arbor: University of Michigan Press, 2003), 179–97; Rainer Buschmann, "Colonizing Anthropology: Albert Hahl and the Ethnographic Frontier in German New Guinea," in *Worldly Provincialism*, 230–55.

15. George W. Stocking, Jr., *Race, Culture, and Evolution: Essays in the History of Anthropology* (Chicago: University of Chicago Press, 1968); Matti Bunzl, "Franz Boas and the Humboldtian Tradition," in *Volksgeist as Method and Ethic: Essays on Boasian Eth-*

nography and the German Anthropological Tradition, ed. George Stocking, Jr. (Madison: University of Wisconsin Press, 1996); Douglas Cole, *Franz Boas: the Early Years, 1858–1906* (Seattle: University of Washington Press, 1999).

16. Andrew Zimmerman, *Anthropology and Anti-Humanism in Imperial Germany* (Chicago: University of Chicago Press, 2001).

17. Uwe Hoßfeld, *Geschichte der biologischen Anthropologie in Deutschland* (Stuttgart: Franz Steiner Verlag, 2005).

18. Woodruff Smith, *Politics and the Sciences of Culture in Germany, 1840–1920* (New York: Oxford University Press, 1991); Benoit Massin, "From Virchow to Fischer: Physical Anthropology and Modern Race Theories in Wilhelmine Germany," in *Volksgeist as Method and Ethic: Essays on Boasian Ethnography and the German Anthropological Tradition*, ed. George Stocking, Jr. (Madison: University of Wisconsin Press, 1996), 79–154; Robert Proctor, "From Anthropologie to Rassenkunde in the German Anthropological Tradition," in *Bones, Bodies, Behavior: Essays on Biological Anthropology*, ed. George Stocking, (Madison: University of Wisconsin Press, 1988), 138–79; H. Glenn Penny, *Objects of Culture: Ethnology and Ethnographic Museums in Imperial Germany* (Chapel Hill: University of North Carolina Press, 2003); H. Glenn Penny and Matti Bunzl, "Introduction: Rethinking German Anthropology, Colonialism, and Race," in *Worldly Provincialism: German Anthropology in the Age of Empire* (Ann Arbor: University of Michigan Press, 2003).

19. Robert Proctor, "From Anthropologie to Rassenkunde," 148–52.

20. For descriptions of the growing consensus on the shift from liberal to illiberal anthropology, see Andre Gingrich, "Liberalism in Imperial Anthropology: Notes on an Implicit Paradigm in Continental European Anthropology before World War I," *Ab Imperio: Studies of New Imperial History and Nationalism in the Post-Soviet Space* 8 (1/2007): 224–39; H. Glenn Penny and Matti Bunzl, introduction to *Worldly Provincialism: German Anthropology in the Age of Empire* (Ann Arbor: University of Michigan Press, 2003), 17–22.

21. Benoit Massin, "From Virchow to Fischer," in *Volksgeist*, 79–154.

22. Robert Proctor, "From Anthropologie to Rassenkunde," 138–79.

23. Woodruff Smith, *Politics and the Sciences of Culture*.

24. H. Glenn Penny, "Bastian's Museum: On the Limits of Empiricism and the Transformation of German Ethnology," in *Worldly Provincialism: German Anthropology in the Age of Empire* (Ann Arbor: University of Michigan Press, 2003), 86–126; H. Glenn Penny, *Objects of Culture: Ethnology and Ethnographic Museums in Imperial Germany* (Chapel Hill: University of North Carolina Press, 2003).

25. H. Glenn Penny and Matti Bunzl, introduction to *Worldly Provincialism*, 20, f. 43.

26. Mark Walker, introduction to *Science and Ideology: A Comparative History*, ed. Mark Walker (New York: Routledge, 2003), 1–4.

27. Carola Sachse and Mark Walker, "Introduction: A Comparative Perspective," in *Osiris Politics and Science in Wartime: Comparative International Perspectives on the Kaiser Wilhelm Institute* 20 (2005), 18.

28. Mitchell G. Ash, "Wissenschaft und Politik als Ressourcen für einander," in *Wissenschaften und Wissenschaftspolitik: Bestandaufnahmen zur Formationen, Brüchen und Kontinuitäten im Deutschland des 20. Jahrhunderts*, eds. Rüdiger vom Bruch und Brigitte Kaderas (Stuttgart: Franz Steiner Verlag, 2002), 32–51.

29. Roy M. MacLeod, introduction to *Science and the Pacific War: Science and Survival in the Pacific, 1939–1945*, ed. Roy M. MacLeod (Dordrecht: Kluwer Academic Publishers, 2000), 2.

30. See, for example, the articles collected in Carol Sachse and Mark Walker, eds., *Osiris Politics and Science in Wartime: Comparative International Perspectives on the Kaiser Wilhelm Institute* 20 (2005).

31. Quoted in Lynn Nyhart, *Biology Takes Form: Animal Morphology and the German Universities, 1800–1900* (Chicago: University of Chicago Press, 1995), 12.

32. Wolfgang Mommsen, "German Artists, Writers, and Intellectuals and the Meaning of War," in *State, Society, and Mobilization in Europe during the First World War,* ed. John Horne (Cambridge: Cambridge University Press, 1997), 28–29; Peter Jelavich, "German Culture in the Great War," in *European Culture in the Great War: The Arts, Entertainment, and Propaganda, 1914–1918,* ed. Aviel Roshwald and Richard Stites (Cambridge: Cambridge University Press, 1999), 42–47.

33. Nyhart, *Biology Takes Form,* 20–28.

34. Ibid., 20.

35. Andre Gingrich, "Liberalism in Imperial Anthropology," 237–38.

36. Henrika Kuklick, "Continuity and Change in British Anthropology, 1914–1919," in *Doing Anthropology in Wartime and War Zones: World War I and the Cultural Sciences in Europe,* eds. Monique Scheer, Reinhard Johler, and Christian Marchetti (Bielefeld: Transcript Verlag, 2010).

37. Henrika Kuklick, "The British Tradition," in *A New History of Anthropology,* ed. Henrika Kuklick (Oxford: Blackwell, 2008), 63–65.

38. Henrika Kuklick, "Continuity and Change in British Anthropology, 1914–1919."

39. Andre Gingrich, "After the Great War: National Reconfigurations of Anthropology in Late Colonial Times," in *Doing Anthropology in Wartime and War Zones: World War I and the Cultural Sciences in Europe,* eds. Monique Scheer, Reinhard Johler, and Christian Marchetti (Bielefeld: Transcript Verlag, 2010).

40. Emmanuelle Sibeud, "The Metamorphosis of Ethnology in France, 1839–1930," in *A New History of Anthropology,* ed. Henrika Kuklick (Oxford: Blackwell, 2008), 100–103.

41. Robert Parkin, "The French-Speaking Countries," in *One Discipline, Four Ways: British, German, French, and American Anthropology* (Chicago: University of Chicago Press, 2005), 186.

42. Andre Gingrich, "After the Great War: National Reconfigurations of Anthropology in Late Colonial Times," in *Doing Anthropology in Wartime and War Zones.*

43. Matti Bunzl, "Franz Boas and the Humboldtian Tradition"; Douglas Cole, *Franz Boas: the Early Years.*

44. George Stocking, *Race, Culture, and Evolution,* 270–307.

45. Sydel Silverman, "The United States," in *One Discipline, Four Ways: British, German, French, and American Anthropology* (Chicago: University of Chicago Press, 2005), 264–73.

46. Marina Mogilner, "Doing Anthropology in a Russian Military Uniform," in *Doing Anthropology in Wartime and War Zones: World War I and the Cultural Sciences in Europe,* eds. Monique Scheer, Reinhard Johler, and Christian Marchetti (Bielefeld: Transcript Verlag, 2010).

47. Marina Mogilner, "Doing Anthropology in a Russian Military Uniform" in *Doing Anthropology in Wartime and War Zones.*

48. Andre Gingrich, "After the Great War: National Reconfigurations of Anthropology in Late Colonial Times," in *Doing Anthropology in Wartime and War Zones.*

49. Douglas A. Lorimer, "Race, Science, and Culture: Historical Continuities and Discontinuities, 1850–1914," in *The Victorians and Race,* ed. Shearer West (Aldershot: Scolar Press, 1996), 12–14.

50. Nancy Stepan, *The Idea of Race in Science: Great Britain, 1800–1960* (Hamden: Archon Book, 1982), xvii.
51. Shearer West, introduction to *The Victorians and Race*, ed. Shearer West (Aldershot: Scolar Press, 1996), 3.
52. Walter Scheidt, "Die Stellung der Anthropologie zur Völkerkunde, Geschichte, und Urgeschichte" *AA* 20 (1925): 138.

CHAPTER ONE

1. Birkner makes these intentions clear in his "Vorwort." See Ferdinand Birkner, *Die Rassen und Völker der Menschheit* (Berlin: Allgemeine Verlag, 1913).
2. Birkner to Haller, Staatsminister, Nov. 22, 1916, BHSTA, MK 18087.
3. Haller to F. Birkner, Nov. 25, 1916, BHSTA, MK 18087.
4. Wilhelm Waldeyer, "Eröffnungsrede," *CBDAG* 21 (1890): 79.
5. The best representative is Joseph Ben-David, *The Scientist's Role in Society: A Comparative Study* (Englewood Cliffs: Prentice Hall, 1971). See also Charles E. McClelland, *State, Society, and University in Germany, 1700–1914* (Cambridge: Cambridge University Press, 1980), 139–68. For critical appraisals of the traditional narrative of the "rise of German science," see Alan Beyerchen, "On the Stimulation of Excellence in Wilhelmian Science," in *Another Germany: A Reconsideration of the Imperial Era*, ed. Jack R. Dukes and Joachim Remak (Boulder, London: Westview Press: 1988). Also see Arleen Marcia Tuchman, "Institutions and Disciplines: Recent Work in the History of German Science," *Journal of Modern History* 69 (1997): 298–319.
6. Margit Szöllösi-Janze, "Science and Social Space: Transformations in the Institutions of Wissenschaft from the Wilhelmine Empire to the Weimar Republic," *Minerva* 43 (2005): 339–60, here 347.
7. Fritz Stern, *Einstein's German World* (Princeton, NJ: Princeton University Press, 1999), 16, 85–86.
8. Ibid., 15.
9. Rüdiger von Bruch, "The Academic Disciplines and Social Thought," in *Imperial Germany: A Historiographical Companion*, ed. Roger Chickering (Westport: Greenwood Press, 1996), 344.
10. Ben-David, 129.
11. Fritz Ringer, *The Decline of the German Mandarins: The German Academic Community, 1890–1933* (Cambridge, MA: Harvard University Press, 1969), 51.
12. Szöllösi-Janze, 343.
13. The classic work on the conservatism of the German professoriate is Fritz Ringer, *The Decline of the German Mandarins*.
14. Ben-David, 131.
15. The Prussian cultural ministry, for example, compelled universities to accept biochemistry and physical chemistry as new fields. See Szöllösi-Janze, 345.
16. Bruch, 347.
17. Charles E. McClelland, *The German Experience of Professionalization* (Cambridge: Cambridge University Press, 1991), 135–48.
18. Woodruff D. Smith, *Politics and the Sciences of Culture in Germany, 1840–1920* (New York: Oxford University Press, 1991), 28 and 58.
19. James Ryding maintains that the anthropogeography of Carl Ritter and the cultural history of Gustav Klemm were possible alternative models to the natural scientific ethnology that was eventually institutionalized under Adolf Bastian. See James N.

Ryding, "Alternatives in Nineteenth-Century Ethnology: A Case Study in the Sociology of Science," *Sociologus* 25 (1975): 1–28.

20. See the explanation in Rudolf Martin *Lehrbuch der Anthropologie in systematischer Darstellung* (Jena: Gustav Fischer, 1914), 1.

21. Wilhelm Waldyer, "Eröffnungsrede," *CBDAG* 21 (1890): 79–83, here 79.

22. The Munich anthropologist Johannes Ranke credited the Göttingen scholar with laying the "foundations of modern anthropology" as a natural science through his "practical craniology." Johannes Ranke, "Anthropologie, Urgeschichte, und Ethnologie," in *Die Deutschen Universitäten, für die Universitätsausstellung in Chicago, 1893*, ed. Wilhelm Lexis (Berlin: Asher, 1893), 113.

23. Johann Friederich Blumenbach, *The Anthropological Treatises of Johann Friedrich Blumenbach* (London: Longman, 1865).

24. See H. Querner, "Zur Geschichte der Anthropologie," *Anthropologische Anzeiger* 44 (1986): 281–97, especially 281–82.

25. "Ausserordentliche Sitzung von 13. October, 1902: Gedächtniss-Feier für Rudolf Virchow," *ZfE* 34 (1902): 322.

26. For a concise discussion, see Robert Proctor, "From Anthropologie to Rassekunde in the German Anthropological Tradition," in *Bones, Bodies, Behavior: Essays on Biological Anthropology*, ed. George Stocking (Madison: University of Wisconsin Press, 1988), 140–42.

27. Felix von Luschan, handwritten lecture notes, NL Luschan, Allgemeine Phys. Anthropologie, File: "Erledigte Vorlesungen, Phys. Anthrop."

28. Adolf Bastian, *Der Mensch in der Geschichte: Zur Begründung einer psychologischen Weltanschauung* (Osnabruck: Biblioverlag, 1860).

29. H. Glenn Penny, "Traditions in the German Language," in *A New History of Anthropology*, ed. Henrika Kuklick (Oxford: Blackwell, 2008), 85.

30. For a particularly lucid discussion of the motivations behind the ethnographic project, see H. Glenn Penny, *Objects of Culture*, 19–49.

31. See H. Glenn Penny, *Objects of Culture*, 18–23. See also Klaus-Peter Koepping, *Adolf Bastian and the Psychic Unity of Mankind: The Foundations of Anthropology in Nineteenth-Century Germany* (St. Lucia: University of Queensland Press, 1983); Annemarie Fiedermutz-Laun, *Der Kulturhistorische Gedanke bei Adolf Bastian: Systematisierung und Darstellung der Theorie und Methode mit dem Versuch einer Bewertung des Kulturhistorischen Gehaltes auf dieser Grundlage* (Wiesbaden: Franz Steiner Verlag, 1970).

32. Brent Maner, *The Search for a Buried Nation: Archaeology in Central Europe, 1750 to the Present* (Ph.D. dissertation, University of Illinois at Champaign-Urbana, 2001), 67–129.

33. See John Reader, *Missing Links: The Hunt for Earliest Man* (Boston: Little, Brown, 1981), 20–36. Also see Donald Johanson and Maitland A. Edey, *Lucy: The Beginnings of Humankind* (New York: Simon and Schuster, 1981), 27–29.

34. Maner, 133–36.

35. Wilhelm Waldyer, "Eröffnungsrede," *CBDAG* 21 (1890): 79–83, here 79.

36. Rudolf Virchow, Gutachten, Nov. 10, 1892, BAL, R49.01/1403, Bl. 10.

37. Ibid., Bl. 12.

38. Penny, *Objects of Culture*, 26.

39. Zimmerman, *Anthropology and Antihumanism*, 126.

40. Adolf Bastian, "Das natürliche System in der Ethnologie," *ZfE* 1 (1869): 1–45, here 1–2.

41. Martin, *Lehrbuch*, 1–2.

42. Benoit Massin, "From Virchow to Fischer," 83.

43. Andreas Daum, *Wissenschaftspopularisierung im 19. Jahrhundert: Bürgerliche Kultur, naturwissenschaftliche Bildung, und die deutsche Öffentlichkeit, 1848–1914* (München: R. Oldenbourg, 1998), 83–95.

44. Christian Andree, "Geschichte der Berliner Gesellschaft für Anthropologie, Ethnologie und Urgeschichte, 1869–1969," in *Festschrift zum Hundertjährigen Bestehen der Berliner Gesellschaft für Anthropologie, Ethnologie und Urgeschichte*, eds. Hermann Pohle and Gustav Mahr (Berlin: Verlag Bruno Hessling, 1969), 10.

45. Zimmerman, "Anthropology and the Place of Knowledge in Imperial Berlin," (Ph.D. dissertation, University of California, San Diego, 1998), 30–31.

46. *Statuten der Münchener Gesellschaft für Anthropologie, Ethnologie und Urgeschichte* (München: Akademische Buchdruckerei von F. Straub, 1870), BHSTA, MK 40497.

47. Massin, 83.

48. Smith, *Politics and the Sciences of Culture*, 100–101.

49. Penny, "Traditions in the German Language," 80.

50. P.W. Schmidt, "Die moderne Ethnologie," *Anthropos* 1 (1906): 134–63, here 150.

51. Wolfgang J. Smolka, *Völkerkunde in München: Voraussetzungen, Möglichkeiten, und Entwicklungslinien ihrer Institutionalisierung, ca. 1850–1933* (Berlin: Duncker and Humboldt, 1994), 120–21.

52. Zimmerman, *Anthropology and Antihumanism in Imperial Germany*, 124–30.

53. *Das 25 jährige Jubiläum der Münchener Gesellschaft für Anthropologie am 16. März 1895*, (K. Hof und Universitätsdruckerei Dr. C. Wolf und Sohn, [1895]), 4.

54. Massin, 83.

55. Andree, 20.

56. "Verhandlungen der Berliner Gesellschaft für Anthropologie, Ethnologie und Urgeschichte," *ZfE* 32 (1900): 4–7.

57. Massin, 83.

58. Bernhard von Brocke, "Wissenschaft und Militarismus: Der Aufruf der 93 'An die Kulturwelt!' und der Zussammenbruch der internationalen Gelehrtenrepublik im Ersten Weltkrieg," in *Wilamowitz nach 50 Jahren*, eds. William M. Calder III, Hellmut Flashar, and Theodor Lindken, (Darmstadt: Wissenschaftliche Buchgesellschaft, 1985), 658.

59. "Verhandlungen der Berliner Gesellschaft für Anthropologie, Ethnologie und Urgeschichte," *ZfE* 22 (1890): 593.

60. "Verhandlungen der Berliner Gesellschaft für Anthropologie, Ethnologie und Urgeschichte," *ZfE* 39 (1907): 977.

61. Vorsitzende der Berliner Gesellschaft to Minister der geistlichen, Unterrichts- und Medizinal-Angelegenheiten, 1908–1919, GstA PK, I HA, Rep 76 Vc, Sekt. 1, Tit. 11, Teil I, Nr 4 Band 4, Bl. 13–104.

62. Annette Lewerentz, "Forschungsprojekte und staatliche Förderung: Die Berliner Gesellschaft für Anthropologie, Ethnologie, und Urgeschichte und die preußischen Ministerien biz zum Ersten Weltkrieg," *Mitteilungen der Berliner Gesellschaft für Anthropologie, Ethnologie, und Urgeschichte* 20 (1999): 59.

63. Vorsitzende der Berliner Gesellschaft to Minister der geistlichen, Unterrichts- und Medizinal-Angelegenheiten, 1908–1919, GStA PK, I HA, Rep 76 Vc, Sekt. 1, Tit. 11, Teil I, Nr 4 Band 4, Bl. 10–11.

64. Annette Lewerentz, "Die Rudolf Virchow Stiftung der Berliner Gesellschaft für Anthropologie, Ethnologie, und Urgeschichte: Ein Einblick in einige ihrer Forschungsprojekte," *Mitteilungen der Berliner Gesellschaft für Anthropologie, Ethnologie, und Urgeschichte* 21 (2000): 93–110.

65. Vorsitzende der Berliner Gesellschaft to Minister der geistlichen, Unterrichts- und Medizinal-Angelegenheiten, 1908–1919, GStA PK, I HA, Rep 76 Vc, Sekt. 1, Tit. 11, Teil I, Nr 4, Band 4, Bl. 67.

66. "Verhandlungen der Berliner Gesellschaft für Anthropologie, Ethnologie und Urgeschichte," *ZfE* 5 (1873): 186.

67. Lewerentz, "Forschungsprojekte und staatliche Förderung," 51.

68. Rudolf Virchow, "Gesammtbericht über die Statistik der Farbe der Augen, der Haare und der Haut der Schulkinder in Deutschland," *CBDAG* 16 (1885): 89.

69. Rudolf Virchow, "Gesammtbericht über die von der deutschen anthropologischen Gesellschaft veranlassten Erhebungen über die Farbe der Haut, der Haare und der Augen der Schulkinder in Deutschland," *AA* 16 (1886): 277.

70. Ibid., 280.

71. Ibid., 279.

72. Gustav Schwalbe, "Ueber eine umfassende Untersuchung der physisch-anthropologischen Beschaffenheit der jetzigen Bevölkerung des Deutschen Reiches," *CBDAG* 34 (1903): 73–84.

73. See Zimmerman, "Anthropology and the Place of Knowledge in Imperial Berlin," 48–49. See also Massin, 84–86.

74. "Verhandlungen der Berliner Gesellschaft für Anthropologie, Ethnologie und Urgeschichte," *ZfE* 22 (1890): 3–15.

75. The title "Professor" did not always indicate that a person taught at a university, however. It was often given as a reward for various kinds of service. See Zimmerman, "Anthropology and the Place of Knowledge in Imperial Berlin," 49.

76. "Verhandlungen der Berliner Gesellschaft für Anthropologie, Ethnologie und Urgeschichte," *ZfE* 22 (1890): 3–15.

77. P. W. Schmidt, "Die Moderne Ethnologie," *Anthropos* 1 (1906): 134–63, here 150.

78. H. Glenn Penny, "The Civic Uses of Science: Ethnology and Civil Society in Imperial Germany," *Osiris* 17 (2002): 228–52; Glenn Penny, "Fashioning Local Identities in an Age of Nation-Building: Museums, Cosmopolitan Visions, and Intra-German Competition," *German History* 17 (1999): 489–505. See also Penny, "Cosmopolitan Visions and Municipal Displays," 62–81.

79. H. Glenn Penny, "Bastian's Museum: On the Limits of Empiricism and the Transformation of German Ethnology," in *Worldly Provincialism: German Anthropology in the Age of Empire*, eds. H. Glenn Penny and Matti Bunzl (Ann Arbor: University of Michigan Press, 2003), 86–126.

80. Penny, "Bastian's Museum," 101.

81. Georg Thilenius, "Die Museen für Völkerkunde," in *Die Kunstmuseen und das Deutsche Volk*, hrgs. vom Deutschen Museumsbund (Munich: Kurt Wolf Verlag, 1919), 187.

82. Annette Lewerentz, "Die Berliner Gesellschaft für Anthropologie, Ethnologie, und Urgeschichte und ihre Bedeutung für die Berliner Museen," *Mitteilungen der Berliner Gesellschaft für Anthropologie, Ethnologie, und Urgeschichte* 22 (2000): 114.

83. The 1892 guidebook for the museum promised: "A special anthropological section will later be supplementally added, in order to illustrate not only the development of the human species, especially our ancestors in their conduct and ability from the lowest levels forward, but also the physical differences of the stocks [*Stämme*] and races in comparative perspective . . . ." Despite these promises, no such section was added in the coming years. See Königliche Museen zu Berlin, *Führer durch das Museum für Völkerkunde*, 5th ed. (Berlin: W. Spemann, 1892), 8.

84. Königliche Museen zu Berlin, *Führer durch das Museum für Völkerkunde*, 14th ed. (Berlin: Georg Reimer, 1908).

85. Felix von Luschan to Minister der geistlichen und Unterrichts-Angelegenheiten, Feb. 9, 1914, BAL, R49.01/1403, Bl. 23–25. After the war, the director of museums in Berlin wrote that enough space had been found for the anthropological collection, which had been "stored until now." Wilhelm v. Bode, Generaldirektor der Staatlichen Museen, to Minister für Wissenschaft, Kunst und Volksbildung, Konrad Haenisch, June 11, 1919, MfVB, I/MfV 67, Ic, Band 15. 580/19.

86. Floor plan of Museum [Kunstgewerbe Museum] with indication of collections in each room. MfVB, [Jan. 1922] I/MfV 68, Ic, Band 16. 1342/21.

87. Rudolf Virchow, Gutachten, Nov. 10, 1892, BAL, R49.01/1403, Bl. 12–13.

88. Quoted in Massin, 84.

89. Felix von Luschan to Ministerium der geistlichen, Unterrichts- und Medizinal-Angelegenheiten, Nov. 23, 1891, BAL, R49.01/1403, Bl. 2–3.

90. "Verhandlungen des Hauses der Abgeordneten, Sitzung 2. Mai 1914," Bl. 5942, BAL, R49.01/1403, Bl. 31.

91. Georg Thilenius, "Die Museen für Völkerkunde," 190.

92. The museum's holdings were fundamentally ethnographic, organized around the famous Siebold collection of Japanese ethnographic materials and an assortment of artworks from China that belonged to Ludwig I. See Smolka, *Völkerkunde in München*, 87, 119.

93. Hermann Dannheimer, "90 Jahre Prähistorische Staatssammlung München," *Bayerische Vorgeschichtsblätter* 40 (1975): 1–33, here 19.

94. McClelland, *State, Society and University*, 281.

95. Ibid., 280–83.

96. Massin, 86.

97. Niels Lösch, *Rasse als Konstrukt: Leben und Werk Eugen Fischers* (Frankfurt amMain: Peter Lang, 1997), 36–51.

98. Lothar Schott, "Zur Geschichte der Anthropologie an der Berliner Universität," *Wissenschaftliche Zeitschrift der Humboldt Universität Berlin*, Math.-Naturwissenschaftliche Reihe, 10 (1961): 57–65, here 62.

99. Cited in Zimmerman, *Anthropology and Antihumanism*, 45.

100. *Verzeichnis der Vorlesungen an der Königlichen Friedrich-Wilhelms-Universität zu Berlin* (Berlin: Universitäts-Buchdruckerei), 1914–19.

101. Zimmerman, *Anthropology and Antihumanism*, 45.

102. Felix von Luschan to Ministerium der geistlichen, Unterrichts- und Medizinal-Angelegenheiten, Nov. 23, 1891, BAL, R49.01/1403, Bl. 2–3.

103. Lothar Schott, "Zur Geschichte der Anthropologie an der Berliner Universität," 62.

104. Felix von Luschan to Wilhelm v. Bode, Generaldirektor der Staatlichen Museen, Oct. 10, 1906, NL Bode, File Luschan, 2910.

105. In 1920, Bode continued to argue that Luschan's plans for an institute had only a loose connection with the goals and duties of Berlin's museums. He said that the Museum für Völkerkunde was ready to give up the anthropological collection at the first instance, and implied that the university should take possession. Wilhelm von Bode, Generaldirektor d. Staatlichen Museen, to Minister für Wissenschaft, Kunst und Volksbildung, Sept. 4, 1920, MfVB, I/MfV 67, Ic, Band 15, 820/20.

106. Luschan's marginal notations on a letter from Karl Weule, the director of the Museum für Völkerkunde zu Leipzig. Karl Weule to Minsterialrat Prof. Dr. Richter, Nov. 15, 1922, HU, Phil. Fak. 1472, Bl. 419–23.

107. Massin, 85.

108. Ilse Schwidetzky, "Die institutionelle Entwicklung der Anthropologie," *Maus und Schlange: Untersuchungen zur Lage der deutschen Anthropologie*, eds. Ina Spiegal-Rosing and Ilse Schwidetzky (München : R. Oldenburg, 1982), 88.

109. Karl Weule to Prof. Dr. Richter, Nov. 15, 1922, HU, Phil. Fak. 1472, Bl. 419.

110. A. Jacobi to Felix von Luschan, Dec. 21, 1912, File Jacobi, NL Luschan.

111. Felix von Luschan to Ernst Frizzi, July 24, 1912, File Frizzi, NL Luschan.

112. Massin, 85.

113. Smolka, *Völkerkunde in München*, 303–4.

114. Some caution is necessary when approaching the membership rolls for concrete numbers of anthropological professionals. A large number of members are simply listed as "professor" without any indication of their specific field. Moreover, the number of *Privatdozenten*, or lecturers, in the wider field of anthropology is difficult to determine. Another difficulty is that many of the full members of the society were foreigners living outside of Germany. Moreover, the German membership of the Berlin society was not limited to the Berlin area; the organization had members in Leipzig, Freiburg, Hamburg, and many other German cities. The data are useful in several ways, however. Every member who worked at an ethnographic museum is listed, for example, along with their specific position, and several members are also specifically listed as professors of anthropology. By counting only those members within Germany who worked at ethnographic museums or were specifically listed as professors of anthropology, it is possible to get a sense of the changing numbers of anthropological professionals from 1880 to 1910. See "Verhandlungen der Berliner Gesellschaft für Anthropologie, Ethnologie und Urgeschichte," *ZfE* 12 (1880): 3–9; *ZfE* 22 (1890): 3–15; *ZfE* 32 (1900): 3–15; *ZfE* 42 (1910): 3–15.

115. "Verhandlungen der Berliner Gesellschaft für Anthropologie, Ethnologie und Urgeschichte," *ZfE* 12 (1880), 3–9, here 5.

116. "Verhandlungen der Berliner Gesellschaft für Anthropologie, Ethnologie und Urgeschichte," *ZfE* 22 (1890), 3–15.

117. "Verhandlungen der Berliner Gesellschaft für Anthropologie, Ethnologie und Urgeschichte," *ZfE* 32 (1900), 3–15.

118. "Verhandlungen der Berliner Gesellschaft für Anthropologie, Ethnologie und Urgeschichte," *ZfE* 42 (1910), 3–15.

119. Rudolf Martin was also listed, but his position was in Zürich.

120. Ursula Schlenther, "Zur Geschichte der Völkerkunde an der Berliner Universität von 1810-1945," *Wissenschaftliche Zeitschrift der Humboldt Universität Berlin* 9 (1959/60): 67–79, here 70–71.

121. Felix von Luschan, "Die Wichtigkeit des Zusammenarbeitens der Ethnographie und der somatischen Anthropologie mit der Prähistorie," *CBDAG* 43 (1912): 52–56, here 53.

122. Kazimierz Stolyhwo, "Die Anthropologie und ihre Einteilung," *CBDAG* 47 (1917): 56–61, here 58.

123. "Verhandlungen der Berliner Gesellschaft für Anthropologie, Ethnologie und Urgeschichte," *ZfE* 49 (1917): 52–53.

124. For a general account, see Woodruff D. Smith, *The German Colonial Empire* (Chapel Hill: University of North Carolina Press, 1978); also see Woodruff D. Smith, *European Imperialism in the 19th and 20th Centuries* (Chicago: Nelson Hall, 1982), 103–9.

125. Zimmerman, *Anthropology and Antihumanism in Imperial Germany*, 220.

126. Woodruff D. Smith, "Colonialism and Colonial Empire," in *Imperial Germany: A Historiographical Companion*, ed. Roger Chickering (Westport: Greenwood Press, 1996), 430–53. See also Woodruff D. Smith, *The German Colonial Empire* (Chapel Hill: University of North Carolina Press, 1978).

127. Ackerknecht, *Rudolf Virchow: Doctor, Statesman, Anthropologist* (Madison, University of Wisconsin Press, 1953), 184.

128. By the turn of the century, as Sierra Bruckner has shown, scientists gradually became contemptuous of *Völkerschauen*, which became increasingly associated with entertainment instead of edification. See Sierra Bruckner, "Spectacles of (Human) Nature: Commercial Ethnography between Leisure, Learning, and *Schaulust*," in *Worldly Provincialism: German Anthropology in the Age of Empire* (Ann Arbor: University of Michigan Press, 2003), 127–55; Hilke Thode-Arora, *Für fünfzig Pfennig um die Welt: Die Hagenbeckschen Völkerschauen* (New York: Campus, 1989); Bernth Lindfors, ed., *Africans on Stage: Studies in Ethnological Show Business* (Bloomington: Indiana University Press, 1999); Zimmerman, *Anthropology and Antihumanism in Imperial Germany*, 15–37.

129. Penny, *Traditions in the German Language*, 89.

130. Massin, *From Virchow to Fischer*, 104.

131. R. Andree, "Eröffnungsrede: Über den Wert der Ethnologie für die anderen Wissenschaften," *CBDAG* 39 (1908): 65–71, especially 70.

132. Königliches Museum für Völkerkunde in Berlin, *Anleitung für ethnographische Beobachtungen und Sammlungen in Afrika und Oceanien* (Berlin: Unger, 1904), 6.

133. "Verzeichnis Kolonial-Wissenschaftlichen Vorlesungen in Berlin," 1909, GStA PK, I HA, Rep 76 Vc Sekt. 2, Tit. 23G, Nr. 14, Bd. 1, Bl. 12–16.

134. Hans Meyer, Vorsitzende der Landeskundlichen Kommision des Kolonialrates to the BGAEU, Jan. 26, 1906, BGAEU-ADE-73. The expedition resulted in a major publication that received international attention: Karl Weule, *Negerleben in Ostafrica: Ergebnisse einer ethnologischen Forschungsreise* (Leipzig: Brockhaus, 1908); H. H. Johnston, "Dr. Weule's Expedition to German East Africa," *Journal of the Royal African Society* 8 (1909): 383–86.

135. Zimmerman, *Anthropology and Antihumanism*, 217–38.

136. Hans Fischer, *Die Hamburger Südsee-Expedition: über Ethnographie und Kolonialismus* (Frankfurt am.Main: Syndikat, 1981).

137. Penny, *Objects of Culture*, 93.

138. Zimmerman, *Anthropology and Antihumanism*, 221.

139. Georg Buschan, "Die Notwendigkeit von Lehrstühlen für eine 'Lehre vom Menschen' aud deutschen Hochschulen," *CBDAG* 5 (1900), 71.

140. Hans Fischer, *Die Hamburger Südsee-Expedition*, 70; Katja Geisenhainer, *'Rasse ist Schicksal': Otto Reche, ein Leben als Anthropologe und Völkerkundler* (Leipzig: Evangelische Verlagsanstalt, 2002), 60–80.

141. Niels Lösch, *Rasse als Konstrukt*, 57–60.

142. Eugen Fischer, *Die Rehobother Bastards und das Bastardierungsproblem beim Menschen* (Jena: Fischer, 1913).

143. Letter from Bernhard Stuck to Hans Virchow, June 24, 1914. BGAEU-RVS-66, Bl. 70.

144. Struck to Hans Virchow, June 24, 1914. BGAEU-RVS-66, 74–75.

145. Luschan to Curatorium of the Rudolf Virchow Stiftung, Dec. 9, 1913. BGAEU-RVS-65, Bl. 74.

146. Ferdinand Birkner, *Die Rassen und Völker der Menschheit* (Berlin: Allgemeine Verlag, 1913), viii.

147. Ibid.
148. Minister der geistlichen, Unterrichts- und Medizinal-Angelegenheiten to Reichskanzler, Reichsamt des Innern, Jan. 2, 1907, GStA PK, I HA, Rep 76-Vc, Sekt. 1, Tit. 11, Teil I, Nr 4 Band 4, Bl. 5–8.
149. Präsident der deutsche Kolonialgesellschaft to K. Bayer. Minister des Innern, Feb. 1, 1900, Bay. HSTA, MK 11018, [no Blatt numbers].

CHAPTER TWO

1. "Ausserordentliche Sitzung von 13. October, 1902: Gedächtniss-Feier für Rudolf Virchow," *ZfE* 34 (1902): 311–30, especially 315, 318.
2. Ibid.: 327.
3. Franz Boas, "Rudolf Virchow's Anthropological Work," in *The Shaping of American Anthropology, 1883–1911: A Franz Boas Reader*, ed. George W. Stocking, Jr. (New York: Basic Books, 1974), 39–40.
4. Thomas S. Kuhn, *The Structure of Scientific Revolutions*, 3rd ed. (Chicago: University of Chicago Press, 1996), 10–19.
5. Kuhn, xi–xii.
6. George W. Stocking, *Ethnographer's Magic and Other Essays in the History of Anthropology* (Madison: University of Wisconsin Press, 1992), 344.
7. Woodruff Smith follows a similar model in his work on the German cultural sciences. He uses the term "theoretical patterns" to describe research traditions in the German cultural sciences. See Woodruff D. Smith, *Politics and the Sciences of Culture in Germany*, 8–9.
8. Byron A. Boyd, *Rudolf Virchow:Tthe Scientist as Citizen* (New York: Garland, 1991), especially 103–4.
9. A standard account of these events, with some attention to Virchow's role in them, is Otto Pflanze, *Bismarck and the Development of Germany*, vol. 1, *The Period of Unification, 1815–1871* (Princeton, NJ: Princeton University Press, 1990).
10. Christian Andree, *Rudolf Virchow als Prähistoriker*, vol. 1 (Cologne: Böhlau-Verlag, 1976), 53.
11. Erwin Ackerknecht *Rudolf Virchow: Doctor, Statesman, Anthropologist* (Madison: University of Wisconsin Press, 1953), 232. On Boas, see Douglas Cole, *Franz Boas: the Early Years, 1858–1906*, 276–77.
12. James J. Sheehan, *German Liberalism in the Nineteenth Century* (Chicago: University of Chicago Press, 1978), 5–6.
13. Richard Bellamy, ed. *Victorian Liberalism: Nineteenth-Century Political Thought and Practice* (New York: Routledge, 1990), 1.
14. James J. Sheehan, *German History, 1770–1866* (Oxford: Oxford University Press, 1989), 448.
15. Guido de Ruggiero, *The History of European Liberalism*, trans. R. G. Collinwood (London: Oxford University Press, 1927).
16. Richard Bellamy, *Victorian Liberalism*, 1.
17. Suzanne Marchand and David F. Lindenfeld, eds. *Germany at the Fin de Siécle: Culture, Politics, Ideas* (Baton Rouge: Louisiana State University Press, 2004), 11.
18. Woodruff D. Smith, *Politics and the Sciences of Culture in Germany*, 103.
19. Thomas R. Metcalf, *Ideologies of the Raj* (Cambridge: Cambridge University Press, 1995), 28–65, here 34.
20. Byron A. Boyd, *Rudolf Virchow: Scientist as Citizen*, 51.

21. On this tradition in liberal thought, see Edmund Neil, "Political Ideologies: Liberalism, Conservatism, Socialism," in *A Companion to Nineteenth-Century Europe*, ed. Stefan Berger (Malden, MA: Blackwell, 2006), 214.
22. Ackerknecht, *Rudolf Virchow: Doctor, Statesman, Anthropologist*, 183–84.
23. H. Glenn Penny, "Traditions in the German Language," 91. On Luschan's views on nationalist competition, see Felix von Luschan, "Anthropological View of Race," in *Papers on Inter-racial Problems, communicated to the First Universal Races Congress* (London: P. S. King, 1911), 13–24.
24. Massin, "From Virchow to Fischer," 105.
25. "44. Hauptversammlung der deutschen Anthropologischen Gesellschaft," *Fränkischer Kurier*. Aug. 4, 1913.
26. Thomas R. Metcalf, *Ideologies of the Raj*, 28–65.
27. For the French case, see William B. Cohen, *The French Encounter with Africans: White Responses to Blacks, 1530–1880* (Bloomington: Indiana University Press, 1980), 232–34. For the British case, see Nancy Stepan, *The Idea of Race in Science: Great Britain, 1800–1960* (Hamden, CT: Archon Books, 1982), 35–44, 48–49.
28. Stephen Jay Gould, *The Mismeasure of Man* (New York: Norton, 1981), 71–74.
29. Quoted in Bunzl, "Franz Boas and the Humboldtian Tradition," 44–45.
30. Andre Gingrich, "The German Speaking Countries: Ruptures, Schools, and Non-Traditions: Reassessing the History of Sociocultural Anthropology in Germany," in *One Discipline, Four Ways: British, German, French, and American Anthropology*, Fredrik Barth et al. (Chicago: University of Chicago Press, 2005), 80.
31. In 1910, the Breslau anthropologist Hermann Klaatsch broke from the consensus in the discipline by arguing that the human species originated from two different branches, an eastern and a western. See Massin, 88.
32. Felix von Luschan, "Die gegenwärtigen Aufgaben der Anthropologie" *Verhandlung der Gesellschaft deutscher Naturforscher und Ärtze* 2 (1910): 201–8, here 201–2.
33. Hermann Klaatsch, "Menschenrassen und Menschenaffen," *CBDAG* 41 (1910): 91–100.
34. Massin, 88.
35. Cited in Johannes Ranke, *Der Mensch*, vol. 2 (Leipzig: Verlag des Bibliographischen Institutes, 1887), 233.
36. Quoted in Massin, 87.
37. Cited in Penny, *Objects of Culture*, 22.
38. Johannes Ranke, "Wissenschaftliche Bericht des Generalsecretärs," in *CBDAG* 27 (1896), 91.
39. Ranke, *Der Mensch*, vol. 2 (1887), 231.
40. Ibid., 231.
41. Douglas Cole, *Franz Boas: The Early Years, 1858–1906*, 128.
42. "Gedächtniss-Feier für Rudolf Virchow," *ZfE* 34 (1902): 327.
43. Ranke, *Der Mensch*, vol. 1 (1886), v.
44. Anthony Arblaster, *The Rise and Decline of Western Liberalism* (Oxford: Basil Blackwell, 1984), 25–27, 82.
45. Arblaster, 130–32.
46. Ackerknecht, 16.
47. Fritz Stern, *Einstein's German World*, 16.
48. Alfred Kelly, *The Descent of Darwin: The Popularization of Darwinism in Germany, 1860–1914* (Chapel Hill: University of North Carolina Press, 1981).

49. Adolf Bastian, review of *Descent of Man* by Charles Darwin in *ZfE* 2 (1871): 133–43, here 133, 136.

50. Taking inspiration from Lamarckian thought, Virchow accepted the notion that acquired characteristics could be inherited and passed down to the next generation. Frederick B. Churchill, "Rudolf Virchow and the Pathologist's Criteria for the Inheritance of Acquired Characteristics," *Journal of the History of Medicine and Applied Sciences* 31 (1976): 133.

51. See Massin, 114–18. For a description of Virchow's debate with Schaffhausen over the remains of the so-called Neanderthal man, see John Reader, *Missing Links: The Hunt for Earliest Man* (London: Penguin, 1981), 12–13.

52. Ranke, *Der Mensch*, vol. 1 (1886), vi.

53. F. Birkner, "Johannes Ranke," *CBDAG* 47 (1916): 39.

54. Julius Kollmann, "Die Menschenrassen Europas und die Frage nach der Herkunft der Arier," *CBDAG* 23 (1892): 104.

55. Wilhelm Waldyer, "Eröffnungsrede," *CBDAG* 21 (1890): 79.

56. George W. Stocking, Jr., *Race, Culture, and Evolution: Essays in the History of Anthropology* (Chicago: University of Chicago Press, 1982), 168–69.

57. Wilhelm Waldyer, "Eröffnungsrede," *CBDAG* 21 (1890): 80.

58. Johannes Ranke, "Anthropologie, Urgeschichte, und Ethnologie," in *Die Deutschen Universitäten, für die Universitätsausstellung in Chicago, 1893*, ed. Wilhelm Lexis (Berlin: Asher, 1893), 113.

59. Ranke, for example, developed a system for classifying the volume of the skull. See, for example, Johannes Ranke, "Vergleichung des Rauminhaltes der Rückgrats- und Schädelhöhle als Beitrag zur vergleichenden Psychologie," *Festschrift für Adolf Bastian zu seinem 70. Geburtstag, 26 June 1896* (Berlin: Dietrich Reimer, 1896), 53–62.

60. Julius Kollmann's system of classification combined skull form with hair type to determine varieties. See Johannes Ranke, *Der Mensch*, vol. 2, (1887), 250–51.

61. Rudolf Virchow, "Ueber den prähistorischen Menschen und über die Grenzen zwischen Species und Varietät," *CBDAG* 32 (1901): 85.

62. For an excellent summary of craniometric techniques and debates within the German anthropological community, see Zimmerman, *Anthropology and Anti-Humanism*, 86–94.

63. Stocking, *Race, Culture, and Evolution*, 57–58.

64. Julius Kollmann, "Ueber die Beziehungen der Vererbung zur Bildung der Menschenrassen," *CBDAG* 29 (1898): 116.

65. Rudolf Virchow, "Meinungen und Thatsachen in der Anthropologie," *CBDAG* 30 (1899): 81.

66. Rudolf Virchow, "Rassenbildung und Erblichkeit," in *Festschrift für Adolf Bastian zu seinem 70. Geburtstag, 26 June 1896* (Berlin: Dietrich Reimer, 1896), 43.

67. Ranke, *Der Mensch*, vol. 2 (1887), 236.

68. Felix von Luschan, "Physische Anthropologie, Sommer Semester 1889," File "Allgemeine Phys. Anthropologie," NL Luschan.

69. Virchow, "Rassenbildung und Erblichkeit," 3.

70. Franz Boas, "Rudolf Virchow's Anthropological Work," 39–40.

71. Rudolf Virchow, "Ueber einige Merkmale niederer Menschenrassen am Schädel und über die Anwendung der statistischen Methode in der ethnischen Cranologie," *ZfE* 12 (1880): 1.

72. Rudolf Virchow, "Ueber Schädelform und Schädeldeformation," *CBDAG* 32 (1901): 137.

73. Julius Kollmann, "Die Menschenrassen Europas und die Frage nach der Herkunft der Arier," *CBDAG* 23 (1892): 104.

74. Ernst Frizzi, "Julius Kollmann," *CBDAG* 50 (1919): 4.

75. Johannes Ranke, "Ueber die individuellen Variationen im Schädelbau des Menschen," *CBDAG* 28 (1897): 142.

76. Quoted in Ranke, *Der Mensch*, vol. 2 (1887), 184.

77. Rudolf Virchow, "Über Zwergrassen," *Correspondenz-Blatt der Deutschen Anthropologischen Gesellschaft* 24 (1893): 116.

78. Ranke, *Der Mensch*, vol. 2, (1887), 65–70, especially 70.

79. Virchow, "Ueber einige Merkmale niederer Menschenrassen am Schädel . . . ,"3.

80. Bastian argued that there were "essentially next to no peoples left on earth who were without historical influences." Cited in Penny, *Objects of Culture*, 23.

81. The archeologist Gustav Kossina, for example, based his Germanic brand of archeology around the turn of the century on the notion that racial borders coincided with the boundaries of language and culture. See Suzanne Marchand, *Down from Olympus: Archaeology and Philhellenism in Germany, 1750–1970* (Princeton, NJ: Princeton University Press, 1996), 181–87.

82. Quoted in Massin, 82.

83. Franz Boas, "Rudolf Virchow's Anthropological Work," 40. The distinction between race, language, and culture in German anthropological circles in the late nineteenth century greatly influenced Boas. Echoing his German mentors, he maintained throughout his early career that that there was no correlation between racial, linguistic, and cultural classifications. See Douglas Cole, *Franz Boas: The Early Years, 1858–1906* (Seattle: University of Washington Press, 1999), 267–68.

84. Rudolf Virchow, "Meinungen und Thatsachen in der Anthropologie," *CBDAG* 30 (1899): 82.

85. Ibid., 82.

86. Rudolf Virchow, "Über das Auftreten der Slaven in Deutschland," *CBDAG* 31 (1900): 109.

87. Virchow, "Rassenbildung und Erblichkeit," 3.

88. Depending on the context, the term *Volk* could refer to the common people, the lower classes, the politically active sectors of society, the notion of *Volkstum* drawn from the Romantic movement, or an ethnic group. The term could also be used as a synonym for nation. In German anthropology, however, it was used to refer to ethnic or linguistic groups. For an explication of nineteenth-century uses of the term *Volk*, see Sheehan, *German Liberalism in the Nineteenth Century*, 27.

89. Julius Kollmann, "Die Menschenrassen Europa's und Asien's," Vortrag gehalten in der zweiten Sitzung der 62. Versammlung Deutscher Naturforscher und Aerzte zu Heidelberg. 21. Sept. (Heidelberg: Universitäts-Buchdruckerei von J. Hörning. 1889), 7.

90. Cole, 268.

91. John Efron, *Defenders of the Race: Jewish Doctors and Race Science in Fin-de-Siècle Europe* (New Haven: Yale University Press, 1994): 25–26; Andrew Zimmerman, "Anti-Semitism as Skill: Rudolf Virchow's *Schulstatistik* and the Racial Composition of Germany," *Central European History* 32 (1999): 409–29. See also George Mosse, *Towards the Final Solution: A History of European Racism* (Madison: University of Wisconsin Press, 1985), 90–93.

92. Rudolf Virchow, "Gesammtbericht über die Statistik der Farbe der Augen, der Haare und der Haut der Schulkinder in Deutschland," *CBDAG* 16 (1885): 91.

93. Boas, "Rudolf Virchow's Anthropological Work," 40.
94. Ranke, *Der Mensch*, vol. 2 (1887), 255, 263.
95. Ibid., 86.
96. Ausschnitt aus dem Vorlesungsverzeichnis Sommerhalbjahr 1908, HAS, Dozenten und Personalakten II 142 (Hamburch).
97. Massin, 97.
98. Virchow, "Ueber einige Merkmale niederer Menschenrassen am Schädel," 3.
99. Günter Hartung, "Völkische Ideologie," in *Handbuch zur 'Völkischen Bewegung, 1871–1918*, eds. Uwe Puschner, Walter Schmitz, and Justus H. Ulbricht (München: K. G. Saur, 1996), 22–41.
100. Fritz Stern, *The Politics of Cultural Despair: A Study in the Rise of the Germanic Ideology* (Berkeley: University of California Press, 1961).
101. For a comprehensive study of the intersections between science and ideology in the pursuit of Indo-European origins, see Stefan Arvidsson, *Aryan Idols: Indo-European Mythology as Ideology and Science* (Chicago: University of Chicago Press, 2006).
102. George Mosse, *The Crisis of Germanic Ideology: Intellectual Origins of the Third Reich* (New York: Grosset and Dunlap, 1964), 90–91. Also see Leon Poliakov, *The Aryan Myth* (New York: Basic Books, 1974), 233–38.
103. Rolf Peter Sieferle, "Rassismus, Rassenhygiene, Menschenzuchtideale," in *Handbuch der Völkischen Bewegung, 1871–1918*, eds. Uwe Puschner, et. al. (München: K. G. Saur, 1996), 436–46.
104. Geoffrey G. Field, *Evangelist of Race: The Germanic Vision of Houston Stewart Chamberlain* (New York: Columbia University Press, 1981), 223.
105. Roger Chickering, *We Men Who Feel Most German: A Cultural Study of the Pan-German League, 1886–1914.* (Boston: George Allen and Unwin, 1984), 236–42.
106. Ranke, *Der Mensch*, vol. 2 (1887), 81.
107. Rudolf Virchow, "Die heutige Probleme der anthropologischen Alterthumsforschung," *CBDAG* 24 (1893): 75.
108. Ranke, *Der Mensch*, vol. 2 (1887), 529–30.
109. Felix von Luschan, "Die anthropologische Stellung der Juden," *CBDAG* 23 (1892): 95.
110. Johannes Ranke, "Die Schädel der altbayerischen Landbevölkerung," *BAUG* 1 (1877): 227.
111. On Germans and Slavs, see Rudolf Virchow, "Über das Auftreten der Slaven in Deutschland," *CBDAG* 31 (1900): 112. On Celts and Germans, see Rudolf Virchow, "Meinungen und Thatsachen in der Anthropologie," *CBDAG* 30 (1899): 82.
112. Rudolf Virchow, "Eröffnungsrede," *CBDAG* 27 (1896): 80.
113. Virchow also became cautious about the Germanic label in his prehistoric archeology, insisting that one could often not prove conclusively which artifacts were German and which were not. He subtly derided Germanophiliacs who wished to identify remnants of ancient German graves at every archeological dig: "If our enthusiasts, the pan-Germanists, come forward to identify every one of these graves as ancient German, it is immaterial [*gleichgültig*]. This claim has no effect; one cannot prove that the grave is Germanic." Rudolf Virchow, "Eröffnungsrede," *CBDAG* (1897): 70.
114. Massin, 92.
115. Peter Pulzer, *The Rise of Political Anti-Semitism in Germany and Austria* (Cambridge, MA: Harvard University Press, 1964), 72–119.
116. Rudolf Virchow, "Die Gründung der Berliner Universität und der Übergang aus dem philosophischen in das naturwissenschaftliche Zeitalter," in L. J. Rather, *A Commen-*

tary on the Medical Writings of Rudolf Virchow (San Francisco: Normal Publishing, 1990), 196–97.

117. Rudolf Virchow, "Eröffnungsrede," *CBDAG* 27 (1896): 80.

118. Luschan, "Die Anthropologische Stellung der Juden," 100.

119. See Luschan, "Die Anthropologische Stellung der Juden," 96.

120. Rudolf Pöch to Felix von Luschan, March 15, 1917, file Pöch, NL Luschan.

121. Massin, 90.

122. For example, Ludwig Woltmann, a popularizer of Nordic and Aryan racial theories founded a journal called the *Politisch-Anthropologische Revue* in 1902.

123. Massin, 93–94.

124. Hilkea Lichtsinn, *Otto Ammon und die Sozialanthropologie* (Frankfurt am Main: Peter Lang, 1987), 88–116.

125. Massin, 132.

126. Ludwig Wilser, "Die Rassen der Steinzeit," *CBDAG* 32 (1901): 187.

127. Felix von Luschan, "Anthropological View of Race," in *Papers on Inter-Racial Problems,Ccommunicated to the First Universal Races Congress*. London: P. S. King, 1911, 23.

128. Massin, 114–20.

129. "Ausserordentliche Sitzung von 13. October, 1902: Gedächtniss-Feier für Rudolf Virchow" *ZfE* 34 (1902): 323.

130. Stephen Jay Gould, *Ever Since Darwin: Reflections in Natural History* (New York: W. W. Norton, 1977), 34–38. Darwin's later work, particularly *The Descent of Man*, did include passages that indicated progressive thinking and suggestions that some races were superior to others. In *Descent*, Darwin cited Schaffhausen on the correlation between brain size, civilization, and facial expression. See Charles Darwin, *The Descent of Man and Selection in Relation to Sex*, 2nd ed. (New York: A. L. Burt, 1874), 225.

131. Gustav Schwalbe, "Ueber eine umfassende Untersuchung der physisch-anthropologischen Beschaffenheit der jetzigen Bevölkerung des Deutschen Reiches," *CBDAG* 34 (1903): 75.

132. Otto Reche, "Längen-Breitenindex und Schädellänge," *AA* 38 (1911): 90.

133. On the wider trend, see H. Stuart Hughes, *Consciousness and Society: The Reorientation of European Social Thought, 1890–1930* (New York: Knopf, 1961), 33–66.

134. See Lisauer's response at the end of Ranke's talk on the Frankfurt agreement. Johannes Ranke, "Zur Frankfurter Verständigung und über Beziehungen des Gehirns zum Schädelbau," *CBDAG* 22 (1891): 115–21, here 118.

135. Massin, 107–11.

136. Massin, 109.

137. See Rudolf Virchow, "Zur Frankfurther Verständigung," *CBDAG* 22 (1891): 121–24; Johannes Ranke, "Zur Frankfurter Verständigung und über Beziehungen des Gehirns zum Schädelbau," *Correspondenz-Blatt der Deutschen Anthropologischen Gesellschaft* 22 (1891): 115–21.

138. Otto Reche, "Längen-Breitenindex und Schädellänge," *Archiv für Anthropologie* 38 (1911): 74–90.

139. Franz Boas, "Instability of Human Types," in *The Shaping of American Anthropology, 1883–1911: A Franz Boas Reader*, ed. George W. Stocking, Jr. (New York: Basic Books, 1974), 214–18. See also Franz Boas, "Changes in Immigrant Body Form," in *The Shaping of American Anthropology, 1883–1911: A Franz Boas Reader*, ed. George W. Stocking, Jr. (New York: Basic Books, 1974), 202–14.

140. Johannes Ranke, *Der Mensch*, 3rd ed., vol. 1, (Leipzig: Verlag des Bibliographischen Instituts, 1911), 176.

141. Hermann Klaatsch to Felix von Luschan, July 3, 1908, File Klaatsch, NL Luschan.

142. Luschan, "Anthropological View of Race," 22.

143. Eugen Fischer, *Die Rehobother Bastards und das Bastardierungsproblem beim Menschen* (Jena: Fischer, 1913).

144. Proctor, "From Anthropologie to Rassenkunde," 146.

145. Theodor Mollison, "Die Geltung des Mendelschen Gesetzes beim Menschen," *Sonderabdruck aus Die Naturwissenschaften: Wochenschrift für die Fortschritte der Naturwissenschaften, der Medizin, und der Technik*, Heft 24 (June 13, 1913): 572–78.

146. See Joseph Deniker, *Les Races de l'Europe: L'indice cephalique en Europe . . .* (Paris, Au secrétariat de l'Association, 1899). See also William Z. Ripley, *The Races of Europe: A Sociological Study* (New York: D. Appleman and Company, 1899).

147. Gustav Schwalbe, "Ueber eine umfassende Untersuchung der physisch-anthropologischen Beschaffenheit der jetzigen Bevölkerung des Deutschen Reiches," *CBDAG* 34 (1903): 75.

148. Schwalbe, "Ueber eine umfassende Untersuchung . . ." *CBDAG* 34 (1903): 74.

149. Quoted in Niels C. Lösch, *Rasse als Konstrukt: Leben und Werk Eugen Fischers* (Frankfurt am.Main: Peter Lang, 1997), 101–2.

150. Lösch, 102.

151. Otto Reche, "Zur Anthropologie der jüngeren Steinzeit in Schlesien und Böhmen," *AA* 35 (1909): 220–37.

152. Franz Schwerz, "Untersuchungen über das Wachstum des Menschen," *AA* 38 (1911): 1.

153. Ernst Frizzi, "Über die so-genannten 'Homo-Alpinus'," *CBDAG* 38 (1907): 172–73.

154. Jan Czekanowski, "Beiträge zur Anthropologie von Polen," *AA* 38 (1911): 187–95.

155. Schwalbe, "Ueber eine umfassende Untersuchung . . . .," 74.

156. See Fischer's comment at the end of E. Tschepourkovsky, "Zwei Haupttypen der Grossrussen, ihre geographische Verbreitung und ethnische Provenienz," *CBDAG* 41 (1910): 84–85.

157. Michael S. Titelbaum and Jay Winter, *The Fear of Population Decline* (New York: Academic Press, 1985), 13–31, 47–57; Also see Daniel J. Kevles, *In the Name of Eugenics: Genetics and the Uses of Human Heredity* (New York: Alfred A. Knopf, 1985).

158. Robert N. Proctor, *Racial Hygiene: Medicine under the Nazis* (Cambridge, MA: Harvard University Press, 1988), 15.

159. See, for example, Wilhelm Schallmeyer, *Über die drohende körperliche Entartung der Kulturmenschheit und die Verstaatlichung des ärtzlichen Standes* (Berlin: Heuser, 1891); Alfred Ploetz, *Die Tüchtigkeit unsrer Rasse und der Schutz der Schwachen: Ein Versuch über Rassenhygiene und ihr Verhältnis zu den humanen Idealen, besonders zur Sozialismus* (Berlin: S. Fischer, 1895).

160. Weindling, *Health, Race, and German Politics*, 125.

161. Ibid., 137.

162. Sheila Faith Weiss, *Race Hygiene and National Efficiency: The Eugenics of Wilhelm Schallmeyer* (Berkeley: University of California Press, 1987), 1–6.

163. Massin, 136.

164. Weindling, *Health, Race, and German Politics*, 143.

165. *Verzeichnis der Vorlesungen an der Königlichen-Friedrich-Wilhelms Universität zu Berlin im Sommer-Semester 1910* (Berlin: Universitäts-Buchdruckerei, 1910), 65. In obituaries after Luschan's death, journalists noted that he gave the first-ever lecture on racial

hygiene at the university in Berlin around 1910. See Osw. Erdmann-Müller, "Felix von Luschan," *Aufwärts: Christliches Tageblatt,* Mar. 15, 1924.

166. Georg Thilenius to Felix von Luschan, July 7, 1910, File Thilenius, NL Luschan.

167. "44. Hauptversammlung der deutschen Anthropologischen Gesellschaft" *Fränkischer Kurier,* Aug. 4, 1913.

168. "44. Deutscher Anthropologentag," *Nürnberger Zeitung und Korrespondent,* Aug. 5, 1913, 7.

169. Kevin Repp, "'More Corporeal, More Concrete': Liberal Humanism, Eugenics, and German Progressives at the Last Fin de Siécle," *Journal of Modern History* 72 (2000): 683–730.

170. For an excellent discussion of Luschan's contradictions, see John David Smith, "W. E. B. Du Bois, Felix von Luschan, and Racial Reform at the Fin de Siécle," *Amerikastudien/American Studies: A Quarterly* 47 (2002): 23–38.

171. Emphasis in original. Felix von Luschan, untitled lecture notes, "Definitionen zur Social-Anthropologie," Box 15: Sozial Anthropologie, NL Luschan.

172. When the International Racial Hygiene society inserted a plank into its platform in 1909 saying that all members had to be members of the "white race," Luschan critiqued this view by asking how the group would define the category. Luschan's marginal notes. "Einladung zu einer Generalversammlung der Internationalen Gesellschaft für Rassen-Hygiene am 14. März 1909," File Ploetz, NL Luschan.

173. Felix von Luschan, "Die gegenwärtigen Aufgaben der Anthropologie," Sept. 20, 1909, Box 14: Sozial Anthropologie 1, NL Luschan.

174. Gustav Schwalbe, "Ueber eine umfassende Untersuchung . . . ," *CBDAG* 34 (1903): 83.

175. Martin's work is still influential. The most recent edition of the *Lehrbuch* was published in 1988, and physical anthropologists still refer to it for technical direction.

176. Rudolf Martin, *Lehrbuch der Anthropologie in systematischer Darstellung* (Jena: Gustav Fischer, 1914), 1.

177. Martin, *Lehrbuch,* 7.

178. Felix von Luschan, "Rassen und Völker" in *Deutsche Reden in schwerer Zeit: Gehalten von den Professoren an der Universität Berlin,* vol. 3 (Berlin: Ulrich von Wilamowitz-Moellendorff [u.a.] Hrsg. von d. Zentralstelle für Volkswohlfahrt u. d. Verein für volkstümlicher Kurse von Berliner Hochschulern, 1915), 349–50.

179. Martin, *Lehrbuch,* 9.

180. Ferdinand Birkner, *Die Rassen und Völker der Menschheit* (Berlin: Allgemeine Verlags-Gesellschaft, 1913), 358.

181. "Felix von Luschan zum 60. Geburtstag," *Berliner Tageblatt,* Aug. 11, 1914.

182. Felix von Luschan, "Zur Anthropologie der Preußen," *Berliner Tageblatt,* June 7, 1914.

183. Birkner, *Die Rassen und Völker der Menschheit,* 358.

184. "Felix von Luschan zum 60. Geburtstag," *Berliner Tageblatt,* Aug. 11, 1914.

185. Rudolf Martin, "Germanen, Kelten, und Slaven," *Die Umschau* 20 (1916): 201–4.

186. Armin Geus, *Johannes Ranke (1836–1916): Physiologe, Anthropologie und Prähistoriker* (Marburg: Lahn, 1987), 14.

187. Ferdinand Birkner, "Johannes Ranke," *CBDAG* 47 (1916): 38.

188. Martin, *Lehrbuch,* 22.

189. Felix von Luschan, "Zur Anthropologie der Preußen."

190. "Felix von Luschan zum 60. Geburtstag," *Berliner Tageblatt,* Aug. 11, 1914.

191. Luschan, "Zur Anthropologie der Preußen."

192. Ibid.
193. F. Birkner, "Johannes Ranke," *CBDAG* 47 (1916): 38.
194. Rudolf Martin, "Germanen, Kelten, Slaven," 204.
195. "Die neue anthropologische Sammlung des Staates," *Bayerischen Kourier*, July 19, 1912.
196. Johannes Ranke, "Die Somatisch-anthropologische Abteilung der anthropologischen Sammlung des Staates," *Sitzungsberichte der K. Bayeriche Akademic der Wissenschaften, Math.-Physische Klasse* (1912): 390.
197. Ibid., 390.
198. Ibid., 389.
199. Johannes Ranke to Generalkonservatorium der wissenschfatlichen Sammlungen des Staates, Nov. 15, 1908, BHSTA, MK 11820.
200. "Die neue anthropologische Sammlung des Staates," *Bayerischen Kourier*, July 19, 1912.

CHAPTER THREE

1. Felix von Luschan to Rektor der Handelshochschule Berlin, May 22, 1914, HU, F. v. Luschan Personal-Akten, UK-L252, Bd. 1, Bl. 5.
2. "Proceedings of Societies: Anthropology at the British Association for the Advancement of Science, 1914," *Man: A Monthly Record of Anthropological Science* 14 (1914): 171–75.
3. Felix von Luschan, "In Australien und Amerika," *Berlin Vossische Zeitung*, Jan. 31, 1915.
4. Luschan, "In Australien und Amerika."
5. Felix von Luschan to "Herr Rechnungsrat," "Am Sedantag", 1914, MfVB, I/MfV 193, IIIc, Band 21. It is significant that Luschan dated his letter with "Sedan day," rather than September 1. That date marked the anniversary of the Prussian victory over France in 1870 and remained one of the most patriotic Prussian holidays.
6. Luschan, "In Australien und Amerika."
7. Felix von Luschan to the Kuratorium der Rudolf Virchow Stiftung, Hans Virchow, Aug. 8, 1915, Berliner Gesellschaft für Anthropologie, Ethnologie, und Urgeschichte, Archiv, Rudolf Virchow Stiftung. Many thanks to Dr. Marion Melk-Koch for access to this document.
8. "Verhandlungen der Berliner Gesellschaft für Anthropologie, Ethnologie und Urgeschichte," *ZfE* 47 (1915): 242–70.
9. Albrecht Penck to Felix von Luschan, Feb. 8, 1915, File Penck, NL Luschan.
10. On Luschan's activities in the United States, see John David Smith, "'I Would Like to Study Some Problems of Heredity': Felix von Luschan's Trip to America, 1914–1915," in *Felix von Luschan (1854–1924): Leben und Wirken eines Universalgelehrten*, ed. Peter Ruggendorfer and Hubert D. Szemethy (Wien: Böhlau Verlag, 2009), 141–63.
11. See Michael W. Young, *Malinowski: Odyssey of an Anthropologist, 1884–1920* (New Haven: Yale University Press, 2004), 289–307, 364–66.
12. Wolfgang Mommsen, "German artists, writers, and intellectuals and the meaning of war," in *State, Society, and Mobilization in Europe during the First World War*, ed. John Horne (Cambridge: Cambridge University Press, 1997), 21–38.
13. Margit Szöllösi-Janze, "Science and Social Space: Transformations in the Institutions of *Wissenschaft* from the Wilhelmine Empire to the Weimar Republic," *Minerva* 43 (2005): 353.

14. Fritz Haber's work for the German government under the aegis of the War Chemicals Corporation is perhaps the best example of this phenomenon. See Roger Chickering, *Imperial Germany and the Great War, 1914–1918* (Cambridge: Cambridge University Press, 1998), 38; Rolf-Dieter Müller, "Total War as a Result of New Weapons? The Use of Chemical Agents in World War I," in *Great War, Total War: Combat and Mobilization on the Western Front, 1914–1918*, ed. Roger Chickering and Stig Förster (Cambridge: German Historical Institute and Cambridge University Press), 106–7.

15. Wolfgang U. Eckart, "'The Most Extensive Experiment that the Imagination Can Conceive': War, Emotional Stress, and German Medicine, 1914–1918," in *Great War, Total War: Combat and Mobilization on the Western Front, 1914–1918*, ed. Roger Chickering and Stig Förster (Cambridge: German Historical Institute and Cambridge University Press), 137–39.

16. Paul Forman, "Scientific Internationalism and the Weimar Physicists: The Ideology and Its Manipulation in Germany after World War I," *Isis* 64 (1973): 153–56.

17. "Protokoll der Vorstand und Ausschusssitzung vom 17. August 1914," PSS, Gesellschaft für Anthropologie, Ethnologie und Urgeschichte, Protokollbuch der Münchener Gesellschaft für Anthropologie, Ethnologie und Urgeschichte.

18. "Jahresbericht der Cölner Anthropologischen Gesellschaft," *CBDAG* 47 (1916/17): 19–29.

19. "Verhandlungen der Berliner Gesellschaft für Anthropologie, Ethnologie und Urgeschichte," *ZfE* 46 (1914): 746.

20. Ibid.

21. Christian Andree, "Geschichte der Berliner Gesellschaft für Anthropologie, Ethnologie und Urgeschichte, 1869–1969," in *Festschrift zum Hundertjährigen Bestehen der Berliner Gesellschaft für Anthropologie, Ethnologie und Urgeschichte*, eds. Hermann Pohle and Gustav Mahr (Berlin: Verlag Bruno Hessling, 1969), 113.

22. Vorsitzende der Berliner Gesellschaft to Minister der geistlichen, Unterrichts.- und Medizinal-Angelegenheiten, September 23, 1915, GStA PK, I HA, Rep 76 Vc, Sekt. 1, Tit. 11, Teil I, Nr 4 Band 4, Bl. 105.

23. "Kassenbericht der Deutschen Anthropologischen Gesellschaft," *CBDAG* 47 (1916/17): 8–9.

24. Christian Andree, "Geschichte der Berliner Gesellschaft für Anthropologie, Ethnologie, und Urgeschichte, 1869–1969," 113–14.

25. "Verhandlungen der Berliner Gesellschaft für Anthropologie, Ethnologie und Urgeschichte," *ZfE* 49 (1917): 141–42.

26. "Verhandlungen der Berliner Gesellschaft für Anthropologie, Ethnologie und Urgeschichte," *ZfE* 47 (1915): 434.

27. Letter and Stiftungsurkunde from Hans Virchow to Polizei-Präsidenten von Berlin, Herr von Borries, June 20, 1903, GStA PK, I HA, Rep 76 Vc, Sekt. 1, Tit. 8, Nr. 5.

28. Christian Andree, "Geschichte der Berliner Gesellschaft für Anthropologie, Ethnologie und Urgeschichte, 1869–1969," 113. See also "Verhandlungen der Berliner Gesellschaft für Anthropologie, Ethnologie und Urgeschichte," *ZfE* 50 (1918): 258–59.

29. Johann Albrecht, Herzog zu Mecklenburg, to Präsident der Deutschen Kolonialgesellschaft, Aug. 31, 1914, BAL, R1001/6629, Bl. 5.

30. "Verhandlungen der Berliner Gesellschaft für Anthropologie, Ethnologie und Urgeschichte," *ZfE* 48 (1916): 94.

31. "Verhandlungen der Berliner Gesellschaft für Anthropologie, Ethnologie und Urgeschichte," ZfE 46 (1914): 747.

32. Ferdinand Birkner, Nachruf für Rudolf Martin, July 7, 1925, LMU, E-II-N, Personalakte Rudolf Martin, Bl. 4.

33. See, for example, circular from Generaldirektor der Königlichen Museen to the employees of the Königlichen Museen, Aug. 21, 1916, MfVB, I/MfV 035, Ia, Band 10.

34. Junker to Sedrich, Aug. 6, 1917, MfVB, I/MfV 271, XII, Band 6.

35. Georg Thilenius, "Lebenslauf," HAS, 361–6, Hochschulwesen, Dozenten und Personalakten IV 1030 (Thilenius), Bl. 16.

36. Georg Thilenius, "Bericht über das dritte Vierteljahr 1914," Oct. 3, 1914, MfVH, B 4,10. Also see Georg Thilenius, "Bericht über das 4. Vierteljahr 1914," Dec. 31, 1914, MfVH, B 4,10.

37. George Thilenius to Generaldirektor der. Kgl. Museen, circulated to all departments of Berlin MfV. Jan. 18, 1918, MfVB, I/MfV 195, IIIc, Band 23. See also G. Thilenius, "Lebenslauf," HAS, 361–6. Hochschulwesen, Dozenten und Personalakten IV 1030 (Thilenius). Bl. 32–33.

38. Eugen Fischer, "Die Zerstörung der Freiburger anatomischen Sammlung," CBDAG 47 (1916/17): 73–74.

39. Forman, "Scientific Internationalism and the Weimar Physicists," 153.

40. Daniel J. Kevles, "'Into Hostile Camps': The Reorganization of International Science in World War I," Isis 62 (1971): 48.

41. Paul Forman, "Scientific Internationalism and the Weimar Physicists," 153–56.

42. Suzanne Marchand, Down from Olympus: Archaeology and Philhellenism in Germany, 1750–1970 (Princeton, NJ: Princeton University Press, 1996), 237.

43. Marchand, 237–38.

44. "40. Allgemeine Versammlung der Deutschen Anthropologischen Gesellschaft," Posener Tageblatt, Aug. 3, 1909.

45. Felix von Luschan, "Zur Anthropologie der Preußen," Berliner Tageblatt, June 7, 1914.

46. Felix von Luschan, "Anthropological View of Race," in Papers on Inter-Racial Problems,Ccommunicated to the First Universal Races Congress (London: P. S. King, 1911), 13–24.

47. "Die internationale Wissenschaft im Kriege: Eine Umfrage der Vossichen Zeitung," Berlin Vossische Zeitung, Morgen Ausgabe, Apr. 23, 1916.

48. Rudolf Martin, "Nationale oder internationale Wissenschaft," Die Umschau 14 (1915): 306.

49. "Verhandlungen der Berliner Gesellschaft für Anthropologie, Ethnologie und Urgeschichte," ZfE 46 (1914): 747.

50. Georg Thilenius to Oberschulbehörde, Hamburg, June 20, 1918, HAS, 363–4 Kultusverwaltung Personalakten 37 (Georg Thilenius).

51. "Verhandlungen der Berliner Gesellschaft für Anthropologie, Ethnologie und Urgeschichte," ZfE 47 (1915): 373–82. Also see "Organisches und Kulturelles in der Menschheitsentwicklung: Aus der Anthropologische Gesellschaft," Berliner Tageblatt, Oct. 22, 1915.

52. Report from philosophische Fakultät, Sketion II, to akad. Senat, July 17, [1917], LMU, OC-N 10a. See also Karl von den Steinen to Felix von Luschan, Oct. 29, 1916, File Steinen, NL Luschan.

53. Adolf Heilborn, "Ein Attentat auf die Wissenschaft," Vossische Zeitung, Nov. 17, 1914. See also "Sympathiekundgebung für Otto Hauser," Berliner Zeitung, Apr. 21, 1915.

54. "Verhandlungen der Berliner Gesellschaft für Anthropologie, Ethnologie und Urgeschichte," ZfE 47 (1915): 94.

55. Jürgen von Ungern-Sternberg and Wolfgang von Ungern-Sternberg, *Der Aufruf "An der Kulturwelt": das Manifest der 93 und die Anfänge der Kriegspropaganda im Ersten Weltkrieg* (Stuttgart: Franz Steiner Verlag, 1996): 156–64.

56. Mommsen, "German Artists, Writers, and Intellectuals and the Meaning of War," 29.

57. Bernhard von Brocke, "Wissenschaft und Militarismus: der Aufruf der 93 'An die Kulturwelt!' und der Zussammenbruch der internationalen Gelehrtenrepublik im Ersten Weltkrieg,"in *Wilamowitz nach 50 Jahren*, eds. William M. Calder III, Hellmut Flashar, and Theodor Lindken (Darmstadt: Wissenschaftliche Buchgesellschaft, 1985), 666–78.

58. Ungern-Sternberg, 72.

59. Ibid., 72, 186.

60. Wilhelm von Waldeyer-Hartz, *Lebenserinnerungen* (Bonn: Friedrich Cohen, 1920), 235.

61. Quoted in Bernhard von Brocke, 664.

62. See Ungern-Sternberg, 136–43.

63. Hermann Kellermann, ed. *Der Krieg der Geister: Eine Auslese deutscher und ausländischer Stimmen zum Weltkriege 1914* (Weimar: Alexander Duncker Verlag, 1915), 28–29.

64. "Verhandlungen der Berliner Gesellschaft für Anthropologie, Ethnologie und Urgeschichte," *ZfE* 46 (1914): 747.

65. Eugen Fischer, "Die Zerstörung der Freiburger anatomischen Sammlung," *CBDAG* 47 (1916/17): 73–74.

66. Klaus Schwabe, *Wissenschaft und Kriegsmoral: Die deutschen Hochschulehrer und die politischen Grundfragen des Ersten Weltkrieges* (Göttingen: Mutterschmidt-Verlag, 1969), 38.

67. Albrecht Penck to Felix von Luschan, Feb. 8, 1915, File Penck, NL Luschan.

68. Penck to Luschan, Feb. 8, 1915, File Penck, NL Luschan.

69. Penck to Luschan, Feb. 8, 1915, File Penck, NL Luschan.

70. Marchand, *Down from Olympus*, 232.

71. Felix von Luschan, "Rassen und Völker" in *Deutsche Reden in schwerer Zeit: Gehalten von den Professoren an der Universität Berlin* (Berlin: Ulrich von Wilamowitz-Moellendorff [u.a.] Hrsg. von der Zentralstelle für Volkswohlfahrt und dem Verein für volkstümliche Kurse von Berliner Hochschullehrern, 1915), 3: 366.

72. "Rassen und Völker," *Berliner Tageblatt*, Nov. 3, 1915.

73. Arthur Keith, "Presidential Address: The Bronze Age Invaders of Britain," *Journal of the Royal Anthropological Insitute of Great Britain and Ireland* XLV (1915): 22.

74. Kuno Waltemath, "Sind Deutsche und Engländer Stammverwandt?" *Die Umschau* 21 (1917): 193.

75. The German writer Kuno Waltemath suggested that Keith's views were not accepted by all of his colleagues. See Kuno Waltemath, "Sind Deutsche und Engländer Stammverwandt?" 193.

76. Felix von Luschan, untitled lecture notes, "Sozial Anthropologie 2," File "Definitionen zur Social-Anthropologie," NL Luschan, 5.

77. "Sitzungsberichte der Anthropologischen Gesellschaft in Wien: Jahrgang 1915/16," *MAGW* 46 (1916): 9.

78. Ibid.

79. Sitzungsberichte der Anthropologischen Gesellschaft in Wien: Jahrgang 1915/16," *MAGW* 46 (1916): 9.

80. Ludwig Wilser, *Die Überlegenheit der germanischen Rasse: zeitgemässe Betrachtungen* (Stuttgart: Strecker und Schröder, 1915), v–vi.

81. Ludwig Wilser, "Die Rasse der Kriegführenden," *Natur* 6 (1915): 82.

82. Karl Felix Wolff, "Der gegenwärtige Krieg ein unbewußter Rassenkrieg," *Leipzig Neuste Nachrichten*, Sept. 14, 1915.

83. F. Helmke, "Der wahre Sinn des Völkerkampfes" *Rheinisch-Westfälische Zeitung*, Mar. 28, 1915.

84. Such were the views of the writer Emil Ludwig, reported (and critiqued) in "Rassen-krieg," *Vorwärts*, Sept. 8, 1914.

85. Professor Dr. Haupt, "Der wahre Sinn des Völkerkampfes," *Rheinisch-Westfälische Zeitung*, Mar. 24, 1915.

86. G. B. Dietrich, "Rasse und Weltkrieg," *Deutsche Tageszeitung*, Mar. 15, 1915.

87. Quoted in Michael Jeismann, *Das Vaterland der Feinde: Studien zum nationalen Feind-begriff und Selbstverständnis in Deutschland und Frankreich, 1792–1918*, (Stuttgart: Klett-Cotta), 311.

88. Ludwig Wilser, *Die Überlegenheit der germanischen Rasse*, vii.

89. Wolff, "Der gegenwärtige Krieg ein unbewußter Rassenkrieg."

90. Josef Stolzing, "Rasse und Weltkrieg," *Politisch- Anthropologische Monatschrift*, 14 (Apr. 1915): 15–27. Josef Stolzing, "Rasse und Weltkrieg," *Politisch- Anthropologische Monatschrift*, 16 (May 1915): 17.

91. G. B. Dietrich, "Rasse und Weltkrieg."

92. Wolff, "Der gegenwärtige Krieg ein unbewußter Rassenkrieg."

93. Kuno Waltemath, "Sind Deutsche und Engländer stammverwandt?" *Die Umschau* 22 (Jan. 1918): 41.

94. Ludwig Wilser, "Die Rasse der Kriegführenden," 84.

95. Ibid.

96. Fritz Lenz, "Nordische Rasse in der Blutmischung unserer östlichen Nachbarn," *Ost-europäische Zukunft* II (Jan. 1917): 17–22.

97. R. Martin, "Germanen, Kelten, und Slaven," *Die Umschau* 20 (1916): 201.

98. F. Birkner, "Johannes Ranke," *CBDAG* 47 (1916/17): 38.

99. Martin, "Germanen, Kelten, und Slaven," 201.

100. Luschan, "Rassen und Völker," 362–63.

101. Rudolf Martin, "Germanen, Kelten, Slaven," 204.

102. Eugen Fischer, "Die Herkunft der Buren," *Die Umschau* 18 (1914): 1053.

103. Ibid., 1053–54.

104. At the 1913 meeting of the German Anthropological Society, Luschan gave a talk on the relationship between the peoples of Asia Minor and the "alpine population" of Southern Europe. In 1917, before an explicitly political group, the Committee to Pro-tect the Rights of the Mohammedan Turkish-Tartar Peoples of Russia, Luschan gave a short lecture on the "relationships of the Tatar population in Russia." See Wilhelm Waldeyer-Hartz to Felix von Luschan, Jan. 12, 1916. File: Waldeyer, NL Luschan.

105. "Württembergischer Anthropologischer Verein: Bericht über 1914 (zweite Hälfte) bis 1916," *CBDAG* 47 (1916/17): 6–8.

106. Felix von Luschan, Untitled Handwritten Manuscript," in file "Allgemeine Phys. Anthropologie," NL Luschan. There is a great likelihood that this unpublished handwritten manuscript is the text of the talk that Luschan gave at the Württemberg Anthropological Society. It contains some of the same phrasing as the report on the talk in the *Correspondenzblatt*, and Luschan's mention of the Turks as allies of Ger-many indicates that it was written during the war.

107. Wadie Jwaideh, *The Kurdish National Movement: Its Origins and Development* (Syracuse, NY: Syracuse University Press, 2006), 125–26.

108. *Amtliches Verzeichnis der einstündigen Abendvorlesungen*, Handelshochschule Berlin, Sommersemester 1916, HU, Bestand Handelshochschule Berlin, Akte 293.

109. *Verzeichnis der Vorlesungen an der Königlichen-Friedrich-Wilhelms Universität zu Berlin im Sommer-Semester 1917* (Berlin: Universitäts-Buchdruckerei, 1917), 49.

110. Felix von Luschan, untitled typed manuscript, in file "Allgemeine Phys. Anthropologie," NL Luschan.

111. "Preisausschreiben zur Erlangung deutscher Rassenbilder," *Dresdener Nachrichten*, Oct. 15, 1914.

112. Ibid.

113. Ibid.

114. R. Erdberg to Felix von Luschan, Oct. 18, 1915. File: Zentralstelle für Volkswohlfahrt, NL Luschan.

115. Wilhelm Waldeyer-Hartz and R. von Erdberg, "Vorwort," *Deutsche Reden in schwerer Zeit: Gehalten von den Professoren an der Universität Berlin* (Berlin: Ulrich von Wilamowitz-Moellendorff [u.a.] Hrsg. von der Zentralstelle für Volkswohlfahrt und dem Verein für volkstümliche Kurse von Berliner Hochschullehrern, 1915), 3: vii.

116. Wilhelm Waldeyer, "Die im Weltkriege stehenden Völker in anthropologischer Betrachtung," in *Deutsche Reden in schwerer Zeit: Gehalten von den Professoren an der Universität Berlin* (Berlin: Ulrich von Wilamowitz-Moellendorff [u.a.] Hrsg. von der Zentralstelle für Volkswohlfahrt und dem Verein für volkstümliche Kurse von Berliner Hochschullehrern, 1915), 3: 313.

117. Ibid., 314.

118. Ibid., 330, 339–40.

119. Ibid., 326.

120. "Sitzungsberichte der Anthropologischen Gesellschaft in Wien: Jahrgang 1915/16" *MAGW* 46 (1916): 9.

121. R. Erdberg to Felix von Luschan, Oct. 18, 1915. File: Zentralstelle für Volkswohlfahrt, NL Luschan.

122. Felix von Luschan, untitled lecture notes, "Sozial Anthropologie 2," file "Definitionen zur Social-Anthropologie," NL Luschan, 1–7.

123. Felix von Luschan, "Rassen und Völker," in *Deutsche Reden in schwerer Zeit: Gehalten von den Professoren an der Universität Berlin* (Berlin: Ulrich von Wilamowitz-Moellendorff [u.a.] Hrsg. von der Zentralstelle für Volkswohlfahrt und dem Verein für volkstümliche Kurse von Berliner Hochschullehrern, 1915), 3: 363–64.

124. Ibid., 365.

125. Ibid., 379.

126. Ibid., 377.

127. Ibid., 377.

128. Ibid., 381.

129. On Frobenius, see Dewitt Clinton Durham, "Leo Frobenius and the Reorientation of German Ethnology, 1890–1930" (Ph.D. dissertation, Stanford University, 1985); Suzanne Marchand, "Leo Frobenius and the Revolt Against the West," *Journal of Contemporary History* 32, no. 2 (1997): 153–70.

130. "Unsere farbigen Gefangenen, Vortrag von Leo Frobenius," *Berlin Vossische Zeitung*, May 2, 1917.

131. Ibid.

132. Leo Frobenius, *Der Völkerzirkus unserer Feinde* (Berlin: Eckhart-Verlag, 1916), 13.

133. Ferdinand Birkner, "Nachruf für Rudolf Martin," July 7, 1925, LMU, E-II-N, Personalakte Rudolf Martin.

134. Rudolf Martin to Rektorat der Universität München, Nov. 28, 1921, BHSTA, MK 11820.

135. Rudolf Martin, "Die Körperentwicklung Münchener Volksschulkinder in den Jahren 1921, 1922, und 1923," *Sonderdruck aus dem Anthropologischen Anzeiger* I (1924), 85.

136. Ibid.

CHAPTER FOUR

1. Richard B Speed, III, *Prisoners, Diplomats, and the Great War: A Study in the Diplomacy of Captivity* (New York: Greenwood Press, 1990), 7.

2. Georg Buschan, "Krieg und Anthropologie," *Deutsche Medizinische Wochenschrift* 26 (1915): 773.

3. Rudolf Pöch, "Anthropologische Studien an Kriegsgefangenen," *Die Umschau* 20 (1916): 989.

4. Buschan, 773.

5. Felix von Luschan, *Kriegsgefangene, ein Beitrag zur Völkerkunde im Weltkriege: Einführung in die Grundzüge der Anthropologie* (Berlin: Dietrich Reimer [Ernst Vohsen], 1917), 1-2.

6. Pöch, "Anthropologische Studien an Kriegsgefangenen," 989.

7. Wilhelm Doegen, ed. *Unter Fremden Völkern: eine neue Völkerkunde* (Berlin: Otto Stohlberg, Verlag für Politik und Wirtschaft, 1925).

8. Although both physical anthropologists and ethnologists conducted studies in the camps, this chapter is primarily concerned with physical anthropology.

9. "Sitzungsberichte der Anthropologischen Gesellschaft in Wien: Jahrgang 1915/16," *MAGW* 46 (1916): 10-11.

10. Ibid.

11. Rudolf Pöch, "I. Bericht über die von der Wiener Anthropolgischen Gesellschaft in den k. u. k. Kriegsgefangenlagern veranlaßten Studien," *MAGW* 45 (1915): 219.

12. Rudolf Pöch, "III. Bericht über die von der Wiener Anthropologischen Gesellschaft in den k. u. k. Kriegsgefangenenlagern veranlaßten Studien," *MAGW* 47 (1917): 77.

13. Buschan, "Krieg und Anthropologie," 773.

14. Rudolf Martin, "Anthropologische Untersuchungen an Kriegsgefangene," *Die Umschau* 19 (1915): 1017.

15. Something of a self-promoter, Doegen claimed after the war that the idea of a wartime phonographic commission was more or less his idea, since he had long dreamed of founding a state language museum that would include "the voices, the languages, and the music of all peoples of earth on gramophone recordings." Wilhelm Doegen, "Einleitung," in *Unter Fremden Völkern: eine neue Völkerkunde* (Berlin: Otto Stohlberg, Verlag für Politik und Wirtschaft, 1925), 9.

16. Meinhof to Bürgermeister von Melle, October 9, 1915, HAS, 361-5 II Hochschulwesen II W a 8, Bl. 1.

17. Felix von Luschan to Egon von Eickstedt, July 30, 1915. File Eickstedt, NL Luschan.

18. Egon von Eickstedt to Felix von Luschan, August 8, 1915, File Eickstedt, NL Luschan.

19. Georg Thilenius, "Bericht über das erste Vierteljahr 1915," Apr. 1, 1915, B 4, 11. See also Georg Thilenius, "Bericht über das II. Halbjahr 1918," Jan. 15, 1918, MfVH, B 4, 13.

20. Meinhof to the Oberschulbehörde, Sektion für Wissenschaftlichen Anstalten, Apr. 3, 1916, HAS, 361-5 II Hochschulwesen II, W a 8, Bl. 15.
21. Meinhof to Bürgermeister von Melle, Oct. 9, 1915, HAS, 361-5 II, Hochschulwesen II, W a 8, 1.
22. C. Stumpf to Felix von Luschan, Dec. 28, 1916. File Stumpf, NL Luschan.
23. Report [from Hamburg Oberschulbehörde], Oct. 18, 1915, HAS, 361-5 II Hochschulwesen II, W a 8, Bl. 2.
24. Kriegsministerium to Minister der geistlichen und Unterrichts-Angelegenheiten, Mar. 23, 1915, GStA PK, I HA, Rep 76 Vc Sekt. 1, Tit. 11, Teil VA, Nr. 1, Bd. 20, Bl. 236.
25. Doegen, *Unter Fremden Völkern*, 9.
26. Ibid., first plate in the volume.
27. Memo from General Friedrich, [no date visible], HSTA Dresden, Stellvertretende Generalkommando, XIX Armeekorps, Nr. 23890. Thanks to Katja Mitze for access to this document.
28. Bernhard Struck to Felix von Luschan, May 7, 1916, and Oct. 7, 1916. File B. Struck, NL Luschan.
29. Theodor Mollison to Felix von Luschan, Aug. 12, 1915, File Mollison, NL Luschan.
30. Thilenius to von Melle, Bürgermeister, June 13, 1917, HAS, 361-5 II Hochschulwesen II, W a 8, Bl. 25.
31. Thilenius to Oberschulbehörde, Oct. 19, 1918, HAS, 361-5 II Hochschulwesen II, W a 8, Bl. 38.
32. While Thilenius lobbied to have his own people included in the projects, he also subtly worked to keep others in the discipline from participating. By denying Georg Buschan access to the anthropological instruments of the Hamburg Museum, Thilenius effectively kept this independent scholar, who was unaffiliated with a museum or a university, from conducting his own anthropological studies in the camps. G. Buschan to G. Thilenius, June 1, 1917. G. Buschan to G. Thilenius, June 15, 1917, MfVH, D 2, 186.
33. Pöch to Luschan, Aug. 29, 1915. File Pöch, NL Luschan. Over the course of the war, Pöch wrote a series of articles that described the standard measurement schema and recording methods that both German and Austrian anthropologists were to use in the camps. See Rudolf Pöch, "I. Bericht . . ." *MAGW* 45 (1915): 219–35. Rudolf Pöch, "II. Bericht über die von der Wiener Anthropologischen Gesellschaft in den k. u. k. Kriegsgefangenenlagern veranlaßten Studien," *MAGW* 46 (1916): 107–31. Rudolf Pöch, "III. Bericht über die von der Wiener Anthropologischen Gesellschaft in den k. u. k. Kriegsgefangenenlagern veranlaßten Studien," 47 (1917): 77–100. Pöch, "IV. Bericht über die von der Wiener Anthropologischen Gesellschaft in d. k. u. k. Kriegsgefangenlagern veranlaßten Studien," *MAGW* 48 (1918): 146–61.
34. Rudolf Pöch, "III. Bericht," 79.
35. Pöch, "Anthropologische Studien an Kriegsgefangenen," 989.
36. Rudolf Pöch, Review of O. Stiehl's "Unsere Feinde," *MAGW* 47 (1917): 122.
37. Pöch, "Anthropologische Studien an Kriegsgefangenen," 990.
38. Martin, "Anthropologische Untersuchungen an Kriegsgefangene," 1017.
39. Stephen Jay Gould writes that the title of his classic work on nineteenth-century biological determinism, *The Mismeasure of Man*, was no accident: "My title . . . notes the reality of a truly sexist past that regarded males as the standard for humanity and therefore tended to mismeasure men, while ignoring women." Stephen Jay Gould, *The Mismeasure of Man*, rev. ed. (New York: W. W. Norton, 1996), 20.

40. Speed, 65. See also Daniel J. McCarthy, *The Prisoner of War in Germany* (New York: Moffat, Yard and Company, 1917), 45–46.

41. As the war dragged on and shortages gripped the German home front, many of the prisoners suffered from malnutrition and disease. Speed, 66. Also see Robert Jackson, *The Prisoners, 1914–18* (New York: Routledge, 1989), 8–54.

42. "Sitzungsberichte der Anthropologischen Gesellschaft in Wien: Jahrgang 1915/16," *MAGW* 46 (1916): 11.

43. Daniel J. McCarthy, *The Prisoner of War in Germany*, 281–94.

44. Speed, 76.

45. Goffman's model of the "total institution" is problematic because it does not allow for the agency of the inmates, but his description of the interactions between inmates and staff in such institutions as prisons and asylums is useful here. Erving Goffman, *Asylums: Essays on the Social Situations of Mental Patients and Other Inmates* (New York: Anchor Books, 1961).

46. Hans Fischer, *Die Hamburger Südsee-Expedition: über Ethnographie und Kolonialismus* (Frankfurt am.Main: Syndikat, 1981), 125–38.

47. Ibid., 98.

48. Martin, "Anthropologische Untersuchungen an Kriegsgefangene," 1017.

49. Fischer, *Die Hamburger Südsee-Expedition*, 132.

50. Pöch, "Anthropologische Studien an Kriegsgefangenen," 989.

51. Ibid.

52. Pöch, "III. Bericht," 92.

53. On the cards and the format of the studies, see Rudolf Pöch, "II. Bericht," 125–26.

54. Pöch, "Anthropologische Studien an Kriegsgefangenen," 990.

55. Pöch to Luschan, Feb. 27, 1918, File Pöch, NL Luschan.

56. Eickstedt to Luschan, Jan. 11/12, 1916. File Eickstedt, NL Luschan.

57. Eickstedt to Luschan, March 18, 1916. File Eickstedt, NL Luschan.

58. Eickstedt to Luschan, April 3, 1916. File Eickstedt, NL Luschan.

59. Luschan to Eickstedt, July 30, 1915. File Eickstedt, NL Luschan.

60. See Egon von Eickstedt, "Rassenelemente der Sikh," *ZfE* 52 (1920/21): 317–94.

61. Eickstedt to Luschan, Dec. 31, 1915. File Eickstedt, NL Luschan.

62. Eickstedt to Luschan, June 9, 1916. File Eickstedt, NL Luschan.

63. Eickstedt to Luschan, June 8, 1916. File Eickstedt, NL Luschan.

64. Eickstedt to Luschan, Jan. 15, [1916]. File Eickstedt, NL Luschan.

65. Eickstedt to Luschan, Dec. 6, 1916. File Eickstedt, NL Luschan.

66. Doegen's ethnological team collected songs and tales from Russian soldiers of German descent in German POW camps. Adolf Lane, "Deutsche Bauernkolonien im alten Russland," in *Unter Fremden Völkern: Eine neue Völkerkunde*, ed. Wilhelm Doegen (Berlin: Otto Stollberg Verlag für Politik und Wirtschaft, 1925), 267–74.

67. Otto Reche, "Zur Anthropologie der jüngeren Steinzeit in Schlesien und Böhmen," *AA* 35 (1908): 230.

68. Günther Spannus, "Otto Reche als Völkerkundler" in *Kultur und Rasse*, eds. M. Hesch and G. Spannus (München: J. F. Lehmann, 1939), 251.

69. Reche to Luschan, July 2, 1917. File Reche, NL Luschan.

70. Reche to Luschan, Jan. 8, 1918. File Reche, NL Luschan.

71. Emphasis added. Reche to Hamburg Oberschulbehörde, Mar. 13, 1918, HAS, 361–5 II Hochschulwesen II W a 8, Bl. 31–32.

72. Vejas Gabriel Liulevicius, *War Land on the Eastern Front: Culture, National Identity, and German Occupation in World War I* (Cambridge: Cambridge University Press, 2000).

73. Georg Thilenius, "Museum für Völkerkunde: Bericht für das Jahr 1917," MfVH, D 4,44, Bl. 1–5.

74. Reche to Hamburg Oberschulbehörde, Mar. 13, 1918, HAS, 361–5 II Hochschulwesen II W a 8, Bl. 31–32.

75. Reche to Oberschulbehörde, Mar. 13, 1918.

76. Stephen Beller, "The Tragic Carnival: Austrian Culture in the First World War," in *European Culture and the Great War: The Arts, Entertainment, and Propaganda*, eds. Aviel Roshwald and Richard Stites (Cambridge: Cambridge University Press, 1999), 127–30.

77. Pöch, "I. Bericht," 220.

78. "Sitzungsberichte der Anthropologischen Gesellschaft in Wien: Jahrgang 1918/19," *MAGW* 48 (1919): 24.

79. Pöch, "III. Bericht," 97–100.

80. Pöch contributed a collection of anthropological photographs to the popular "war exhibit" in Vienna that included several racial portraits of Italian POWs alongside images of the Dual Monarchy's other principal enemies, Serbs and Russians. There is a further discussion of this exhibit in the next chapter. See Sitzungsberichte der Anthropologischen Gesellschaft in Wien: Jahrgang 1916/17," *MAGW* 47 (1917): 57.

81. "Anthropologie in Kriegsgefangenenlagern," *Berlin Vossische Zeitung*, Apr. 16, 1916.

82. Pöch, "I. Bericht," 224.

83. Ibid.

84. Pöch, "Anthropologische Studien an Kriegsgefangenen," 990.

85. Josef Weninger, "Über die Verbreitung von vorderasiatischer Rassenmerkmale," *MAGW* 48 (1918): 43.

CHAPTER FIVE

1. Rudolf Pöch, "I. Bericht über die von der Wiener Anthropologischen Gesellschaft in den k. u. k. Kriegsgefangenlagern veranlaßten Studien," *MAGW* 45 (1915): 221.

2. For an ethnographic analysis of photography and life in Brandenburg POW camps during the war, see Margot Kahleyss, *Muslime in Brandenburg: Kriegsgefangene im Ersten Weltkrieg, Ansichten und Absichten* (Berlin: Museum für Völkerkunde, 1998). See also Margot Kahleyss, "Muslime als Gefangene," *Rundbrief Fotografie* 7 (1995): 43–45.

3. Melissa Banta and Curtis M. Hinsley, *From Site to Sight: Anthropology, Photography, and the Power of Imagery* (Cambridge: Peabody Museum Press, 1986), 57–71.

4. Lorraine Daston and Peter Galison, "The Image of Objectivity," *Representations* 40 (1992): 81.

5. Elizabeth Edwards, "Photographic Types: The Pursuit of Method," *Visual Anthropology* 3 (1990): 235–37.

6. Frank Spencer, "Some Notes on the Attempt to Apply Photography to Anthropometry during the Second Half of the Nineteenth Century," in *Anthropology and Photography, 1860–1920*, ed. Elizabeth Edwards (New Haven: Yale University Press, 1992), 99–106.

7. Zimmerman, *Anthropology and Antihumanism in Imperial Germany*, 94–99.

8. Theodor Mollison, "Die Verwendung der Photographie für die Messung der Körperproportionen des Menschen," *AA* 37 (1910): 305–21. See also Rudolf Martin, *Lehrbuch der Anthropologie in systematischer Darstellung* (Jena: Gustav Fischer, 1914): 34–43. There were also critics within the anthropological community who emphasized the limitations and distortions of photography, but even these men allowed

that the camera had scientific uses. See, for example, Otto Schlaginhaufen, "Die Stellung der Photographie in der anthropologischen Methodik und die Pygmäenfrage in Neuguinea," *ZfE* 47 (1915): 53–58.

9. Rudolf Pöch, "IV. Bericht über die von der Wiener Anthropologischen Gesellschaft in den k. u. k. Kriegsgefangenlagern veranlaßten Studien," *MAGW* 48 (1918): 156.

10. Pöch, "IV Berich," 151.

11. See Rudolf Pöch, "IV. Bericht," 150–57.

12. See Allan Sekula, "The Instrumental Image: Streichen at War," in *Photography Against the Grain: Essays and Photo Works, 1973–1983* (Halifax: Press of the Nova Scotia College of Art and Design, 1984).

13. Edwards, "Photographic Types," 235.

14. Roslyn Poignant, "Surveying the Field View: The Making of the RAI Photographic Collection," in *Anthropology and Photography, 1860–1920* ed. Elizabeth Edwards (New Haven, Yale University Press, 1992), 42–73.

15. George Mosse, *Toward the Final Solution: A History of European Racism* (Madison: University of Wisconsin Press, 1978), 17–35.

16. Rudolf Pöch, "IV. Bericht," 155. See the images of Russian POWs (Tafel I and II) in Rudolf Pöch, "III. Bericht über die von der Wiener Anthropologischen Gesellschaft in den k. u. k. Kriegsgefangenlagern veranlaßten Studien," *MAGW* 47 (1917): Tafel I and II.

17. Rudolf Pöch, "I. Bericht über die von der Wiener Anthropologischen Gesellschaft in den k. u. k. Kriegsgefangenlagern veranlaßten Studien," *MAGW* 45 (1915): 225–26. Also see Pöch, "IV. Bericht," 157.

18. Edwards, "Photographic Types," 241.

19. Wilhelm Doegen, ed. *Unter Fremden Völkern: Eine neue Völkerkunde* (Berlin: Otto Stollberg Verlag für Politik und Wirtschaft, 1925), plate opposite 128.

20. Eickstedt to Luschan, May 4, 1916, File Eickstedt, NL Luschan.

21. Egon von Eickstedt, "Die Rasse beim Menschen," *Die Umschau* 26 (1922): 6.

22. Pöch, "III. Bericht," 79.

23. Pöch gave instructions to this effect in his "I. Bericht," 226.

24. The translation of the German term "wissenschaftlich" is problematic because a *Wissenschaft* refers to any organized body of knowledge, not just to the natural sciences. The term is usually rendered into English as "scientific," but it can also mean "academic" or "scholarly." In the context of Luschan's essay and his other comments, however, there is little doubt that the best translation of the term in this case is indeed "scientific." Felix von Luschan, *Kriegsgefangene, ein Beitrag zur Völkerkunde im Weltkriege: Einführung in die Grundzüge der Anthropologie* (Berlin: Dietrich Reimer, Ernst Vohsen, 1917), 2.

25. Zimmerman, "Anthropology and the Place of Knowledge in Berlin," 194–212.

26. Luschan, *Kriegsgefangene*, 2.

27. Eickstedt to Luschan, May 4, 1916. File Eickstedt, NL Luschan.

28. Luschan, *Kriegsgefangene*, plates 55/56.

29. Struck to Luschan, Mar 14, 1916. File H. Struck, NL Luschan.

30. Eickstedt to Luschan, Mar 3, 1919. File Eickstedt, NL Luschan.

31. Egon von Eickstedt, "Rassenelemente der Sikh," *ZfE* 52 (1920/21): 317–94.

32. Allan Sekula, "The Body and the Archive," *October* 39 (Winter 1986): 3–64. For more on photography and power, see John Tagg, *The Burden of Representation: Essays on Photographies and Histories* (Amherst: University of Massachusetts Press, 1988).

33. Jennifer Green-Lewis, *Framing the Victorians: Photography and the Culture of Realism* (Ithaca, NY: Cornell University Press, 1996), 200–201.

34. Pöch, "IV. Bericht," 156.

35. Ibid., 150.

36. Doegen, *Unter Fremden Völkern*, plate opposite 65.

37. Eickstedt to Luschan, Mar. 1, 1916, File Eickstedt, NL Luschan.

38. Eickstedt to Luschan, May 20, 1916. File Eickstedt, NL Luschan.

39. Kriegsministerium to Königlichen stellvertretenden Generalkommandos des Garde-korps, III, VI, VII, X, und XI. Armeekorps, Nov. 17, [1915], HSTA Dresden, Stellver-tretende Generalkommando, XIX Armeekorps, Nr. 23889. Thanks to Katja Mitze for access to this document.

40. Kriegsministerium to Königliche Inspektion der Kriegsgefangenenlager des XIV. Armeekorps, Dec. 10, 1915, HSTA Dresden, Stellvertretende Generalkommando, XIX Armeekorps, Nr. 23892. Thanks to Katja Mitze for access to this document.

41. Pöch, "Anthropologische Studien an Kriegsgefangenen," 991.

42. Eickstedt, "Die Rasse beim Menschen," 4–8; Egon von Eickstedt, "Betrachtungen über den Typus der Menschen," *Umschau* 26 (1922): 446–53.

43. "Unsere Kriegsgefangene," *Vossische Zeitung*, Nov. 4, 1917.

44. The *Norddeutsche Allgemeine Zeitung* reported that Africans at the front had been seen wearing necklaces made of ears from German soldiers. The *Berlin Lokal Anzeiger* reported that African troops were "human slaughterers" who followed behind the advancing French lines to murder the wounded. Africans were often portrayed as cannibals, while Asian troops were considered a "yellow danger" and a threat to European civilization. See "Die Farbigen und ihre Greuel," *Norddeutsche Allgemeine Zeitung*, Nov. 8, 1918; "Neger als Menschenschlächter," *Berlin Lokal Anzeiger*, Mar. 9 1917; Govenneur von Puttkammer, "Der Krieg und die Rassenfrage," *Der Tag*, Sept. 20, 1914; Georg Irmer, "Englands Verrat an der weißen Rasse," *Kreuz-Zeitung*, Oct. 10, 1914. See also Dr. Wygodzinski, "Weiß, Gelb, Schwarz," *Der Tag*, Sept. 5, 1914.

45. A. H. Korbitz, "Typen aus den deutschen Kriegsgefangenlagern," *Zur Guten Stunde* 2 (1916): 600.

46. Ibid.

47. Ibid.

48. A. Alexander Backhaus, *Die Kriegsgefangenen in Deutschland: Gegen 250 Wirklichkeits-aufnahmen aus deutschen Gefangenenlagern*, ed. Walter Stein (Siegen, Leipzig, Berlin: H. Montanus, 1915), 22.

49. Backhaus, 23.

50. Doegen, *Unter Fremden Völkern*, plate accompanying 40–64.

51. Ibid., plate opposite 81.

52. Heinrich Lüders, "Die Gurkhas," in *Unter Fremden Völkern: Eine neue Völkerkunde*, ed. Wilhelm Doegen (Berlin: Otto Stollberg Verlag für Politik und Wirtschaft, 1925), 127.

53. James R. Ryan, *Picturing Empire: Photography and the Visualization of the British Empire* (London: Reaktion Books, 1997), 147–55.

54. Doegen, *Unter Fremden Völkern*. See, for example, the plates opposite 273.

55. Doegen's ethnological team collected songs and tales from Russian soldiers of Ger-man descent in German POW camps, but no photographs or anthropological data appear in the writing devoted to them. Adolf Lane, "Deutsche Bauernkolonien im alten Russland," in *Unter Fremden Völkern: Eine neue Völkerkunde*. ed. Wilhelm Doe-gen (Berlin: Otto Stollberg Verlag für Politik und Wirtschaft, 1925), 274.

56. Wilhelm Doegen, *Kriegsgefange Völker: Der Kriegsgefangenen Haltung und Schicksal in Deutschland* Bd. 1 (Berlin: Verlag von Dietrich Reimer, 1919), iii.

57. Wilhelm Doegen to Minister für Wissenschaft, Kunst und Volksbildung, July 5, 1922, GStA PK, I HA, Rep 76 Vc Sekt. 1, Tit XI, Teil VII. Nr. 41, Bd. 2, Bl. 297–302.

58. Wilhelm Doegen, Kuratorium zur Verbreitung des Werkes "Kriegsgefangene Völker," to Minister für Wissenschaft, Kunst und Volksbildung, Sept. 28, 1922, GStA PK, I HA, Rep 76 Vc Sekt. 1, Tit XI, Teil VII. Nr. 41, Bd. 2, Bl. 288–89.

59. Platen, Reichswehrministerium to Appel [also Reichswehrministerium], Hanover, Sept. 29, 1922, GStA PK, I HA, Rep 76 Vc Sekt. 1, Tit XI, Teil VII. Nr. 41, Bd. 2., 286.

60. Wilhelm Doegen, Rechstudienkommissar für Kriegsgefangenenwesen und Direktor des Lautabteilung an der Preussischen Staatsbibliothek, to Ministerium für Kunst, Wiss., und Volksbildung, Dec. 22, 1920, GStA PK, I HA, Rep 76 Vc Sekt. 1, Tit XI, Teil VII, Nr. 41, Bd. 2, Bl. 178.

61. "Die farbige Hilfsvölker unsrer Feinde," *Deutsche Kriegsnachrichten*, Sept. 4, 1918.

62. Pöch, "Anthropologische Studien an Kriegsgefangenen," 990.

63. Maureen Healy, *Vienna and the Fall of the Habsburg Empire: Total War and Everyday Life in World War* (Cambridge: Cambridge University Press, 2004), 87–121.

64. "Sitzungsberichte der Anthropologischen Gesellschaft in Wien: Jahrgang 1915/16, "*MAGW*, 46 (1916): 37.

65. "Sitzungsberichte der Anthropologischen Gesellschaft in Wien: Jahrgang 1916/17," *MAGW* 47 (1917).

66. Ibid., 57.

67. Sander Gilman, *Jew's Body* (New York: Routledge, 1991), 38.

CHAPTER SIX

1. Luschan to Bode, Nov. 7, 1919, MfVB, I/MfV 99, IV, Band 1.

2. "Festsitzung zur Feier des 50 jährigen Bestehens der Gesellschaft am 29. November, 1919, nachmittags 4 Uhr, im Hörsaale des Museums für Völkerkunde," *ZfE* 51 (1919): 276.

3. Ibid., 276.

4. Christian Andree, "Geschichte der Berliner Gesellschaft für Anthropologie, Ethnologie und Urgeschichte, 1869–1969," in *Festschrift zum Hundertjährigen Bestehen der Berliner Gesellschaft für Anthropologie, Ethnologie und Urgeschichte*, eds. Hermann Pohle and Gustav Mahr (Berlin: Verlag Bruno Hessling, 1969), 116.

5. "Festsitzung zur Feier des 50 jährigen Bestehens der Gesellschaft . . ." *ZfE* 51 (1919): 276, 278.

6. Robert Proctor points out this terminological shift in "From Anthropologie to *Rassenkunde* in the German Anthropological Tradition," in *Bones, Bodies, Behavior: Essays on Biological Anthropology*, ed. George Stocking (Madison: University of Wisconsin Press, 1988), 138–79.

7. Luschan to Boas, Jan. 18, 1920. Franz Boas Collections, file Felix von Luschan, American Philosophical Society.

8. Rudolf Martin to Boas, Nov. 28, 1919. Franz Boas Collections, file Rudolf Martin, American Philosophical Society.

9. Rudolf Martin to Boas, Feb. 10, 1920. Franz Boas Collections, file Rudolf Martin, American Philosophical Society.

10. Circular from Junker to Museum für Völkerkunde staff, Feb. 6, 1919, MfVB, I/MfV 271, XII, Band 6.

11. "Verhandlungen der Berliner Gesellschaft für Anthropologie, Ethnologie und Urge-schichte," *ZfE* 50 (1918): 299.

12. Christian Andree, "Geschichte der berliner Gesellschaft . . . 1869–1969," 118.

13. Willy Foy to Felix von Luschan, Dec. 3, 1920. File Foy, NL Luschan.

14. Christian Andree, "Geschichte der berliner Gesellschaft . . . 1869–1969," 114.

15. "Sitzungsberichte der Anthropologischen Gesellschaft in Wien: Jahrgang 1918/19," *MAGW* 48 (1919): 24–25.

16. Felix v. Luschan to Egon von Eickstedt, Oct. 22, 1918. File Eickstedt, NL Luschan.

17. K. bayerische Staats-Mininsterium des Innern to Verwaltung der wissenschaftlichen Sammlungen des Staates, Dec. 2, 1918, BHSTA, MK 11820.

18. Rudolf Martin to Franz Boas, Nov. 28, 1919. Franz Boas Collections, Rudolf Martin, American Philosophical Society.

19. Egon von Eickstedt to Franz Boas, May 7, 1920. Franz Boas Collections, von Eick-stedt, American Philosophical Society.

20. Hans Virchow to the Minister für Wissenschaft, Kunst und Volksbildung, May 1, 1921. GStA PK, I HA, Rep 76 Vc, Sekt. 1, Tit. 11, Teil I, Nr 4 Band 4, Bl. 129–30.

21. Minister für Wissenschaft, Kunst und Volksbildung to Hans Virchow, May 19, 1921, GStA PK, I HA, Rep 76 Vc, Sekt. 1, Tit. 11, Teil I, Nr 4 Band 4, Bl. 131.

22. Andree, 121.

23. Ibid.

24. Ibid., 122.

25. For example, the smaller Frankfurt Society for Anthropology, Ethnology, and Prehis-tory reported in 1925 that its finances had been "badly damaged" by the inflation. "Frankfurter Gesellschaft für Anthropologie, Ethnologie und Urgeschichte: Program für das Jahr 1925/26," GStA PK, I HA, Rep 76 Vc, Sekt. 1, Tit. 11, Teil I, Nr 4 Band 4, Bl. 141.

26. "Verhandlungen der Berliner Gesellschaft für Anthropologie, Ethnologie und Urge-schichte," *ZfE* 50 (1918): 254.

27. "An die deutschen Universitäten," *CBDAG* 50 (1919): 37.

28. Ibid., 38.

29. Ibid., 37.

30. Karl Weule to Minsterialrat Prof. Dr. Richter, Nov. 15, 1922, HU, Phil. Fak. 1472, Bl. 421.

31. Ethnologists had other advantages as well. As demands for greater representation in the German university system continued, ethnologists also acknowledged that they already had a stable institutional home in German *Völkerkunde* museums. In the call for more professorships in *Völkerkunde* that accompanied the general appeal of the German Anthropological Society in 1919, the ethnologist Augustin Krämer bemoaned the underrepresentation of his discipline at German universities but also noted, "If *Völkerkunde* has bloomed upwards despite the full neglect of the universities, it is thanks to our museums, which collect and work through the objects of *Naturvölker* that at one time one saw only as curiosities. Augustin Krämer, "Die Völkerkunde als notwendiges Lehrfach an den Universitäten," *CBDAG* 50 (1919): 42.

32. Eugen Fischer, "Die Notwendigkeit anthropologischer Lehrstühle an den Universitä-ten," *CBDAG* 50 (1919): 39.

33. "An die deutschen Universitäten," *CBDAG* 50 (1919): 37; Fischer, "Die Notwendig-keit anthropologischer Lehrstühle an den Universitäten," *CBDAG* 50 (1919): 38.

34. Fischer, "Die Notwendigkeit anthropologischer Lehrstühle . . . ," 38.

35. F. W. K. Müller to General Verwaltung der Staatliche Mussen, Mar. 15, 1922, MfVB, I/MfV 68, Ic, Band 16, 1290/21.

36. Felix v. Luschan to Otto Reche, Feb. 5, 1922, File Reche, NL Luschan.

37. Bernhard Struck to Felix von Luschan., Oct. 7, 1916. File B. Struck, NL Luschan.

38. Felix von Luschan to Otto Reche, Feb. 5, 1922. File Reche, NL Luschan.

39. Felix von Luschan, "Rudolf Virchow als Anthropologe," *Virchows Archiv für pathologische Anatomie und Physiologie*, Sonderabdruck aus Band 235 (Berlin: Julius Springer Verlag, 1921), 438.

40. Bernard Struck to Felix von Luschan, Marc.22, 1922. File B. Struck, NL Luschan.

41. "Für die Völkerkunde spricht also alles für eine reinliche Scheidung von der Anthropologie, nicht zuletzt auch ihre Jugend und die damit in Zusammenhang stehende Unabgebautheit ihres riesigen Arbeitsfeldes." Karl Weule to Minsterialrat Prof. Dr. Richter, Nov. 15, 1922, HU, Phil. Fak. 1472, Bl. 422.

42. Georg Thilenius, "Die Museen für Völkerkunde," in *Die Kunstmuseen und das Deutsche Volk*, hrgs. vom Deutschen Museumsbund (Munich: Kurt Wolf Verlag, 1919), 190.

43. Georg Thilenius, "Lebenslauf," HAS, 361–6, Hochschulwesen, Dozenten und Personalakten IV 1030 (Thilenius), Bl. 32–33.

44. Karl Weule to Minsterialrat Prof. Dr. Richter, Nov. 15, 1922, HU, Phil. Fak. 1472, Bl. 420.

45. Ministerium für Wissenschaft, Kunst und Volksbildung to Felix von Luschan, HU, Phil. Fak. 1470, Bl. 299.

46. Felix von Luschan to the Dekan der philosophischen Fakultät, Berlin, Mar. 1, 1923, HU, Phil. Fak. 1472, Bl. 425.

47. Eugen Fischer to Felix von Luschan, May 20, 1921. File Fischer, NL Luschan.

48. Eduard Seler proposed the ethnologist Walter Lehmann, and Karl Weule recommended several ethnologists including Lehmann and Fritz Krause. Seler to Dekan of the Phil. Fak., June 16, 1922, HU, Phil. Fak. 1470, Bl. 326; Karl Weule to Minsterialrat Prof. Dr. Richter, Nov. 15, 1922, HU, Phil. Fak. 1472, Bl. 423.

49. Felix von Luschan to Dekan der philosophischen Fakultät, Nov. 1, 1922, HU, Phil. Fak. 1472, Bl. 418.

50. Walter Scheidt, "Die Stellung der Anthropologie zur Völkerkunde, Geschichte, und Urgeschichte," *AA* 20 (1925): 138.

51. Ibid., 139.

52. Robert Proctor points out that the term *Rassenkunde* has no exact English equivalent. "Racial science" is a rough approximation, but does not fully express the German sense of the term. See Proctor, "From Anthropologie to Rassenkunde," 148.

53. Scheidt, "Die Stellung der Anthropologie zur . . . Urgeschichte," 139–141.

54. Walter Scheidt, *Allgemeine Rassenkunde: Als Einführung in das Studium der Menschenrassen* (München: J. F. Lehmann, 1925), 341.

55. Eugen Fischer, review of *Lehrbuch der Anthropologie in systematischer Darstellung* by Rudolf Martin, in *Zeitschrift für Morphologie und Anthropologie* 17 (1914/15): 435–55; Eugen Fischer, review of *Lehrbuch der Anthropologie* by Rudolf Martin, in *Zeitschrift für Morphologie und Anthropologie* 30 (1932): 432–33.

56. Jens Paulsen, "Ueber die neue Richtung in der Anthropologie," *AA* 21 (1928): 59.

57. Bernard Struck to Felix von Luschan, Nov. 12, 1922. File B. Struck, NL Luschan.

58. Georg Thilenius, "Zur 50. allgemeinen Versammlung der Deutschen Gesellschaft für Anthropologie, Ethnologie, und Urgeschichte." Typewritten draft of article for the *Lehrer Zeitung*, June 18, 1928, MfVH, D 5,21.

59. Paulsen, 57.

60. Rudolf Martin, *Lehrbuch der Anthropologie in systematischer Darstellung* (Jena: Gustav Fischer, 1914), 9.

61. Egon von Eickstedt, "Die Rasse beim Menschen," *Umschau* 26 (1922): 4.

62. Eugen Fischer, "Rassenprobleme in Spanien," *Spanien: Zeitschrift für Auslandskunde* 1 (1919): 24.

63. Otto Reche, "Die Menschenrassen der Gegenwart und der vorgeschichtliche Mensch," in *Einführung in der Biologie*, 5th ed., eds. Karl Kraepelin and C. Schäffer (Leipzig: B. G. Teubner, 1921), 314.

64. Otto Reche, "Rasse und Sprache," *AA* 46 (1921): 218.

65. Michael Hesch, "Otto Reche als Rassenforscher," in *Kultur und Rasse: Otto Reche zum 60. Geburtstag*, eds. Michael Hesch und Günther Spannaus (München/Berlin: J. F. Lehmann, 1939), 11.

66. On Reche's career, see Katja Geisenhainer, *"Rasse ist Schicksal": Otto Reche, ein Leben als Anthropologe und Völkerkundler* (Leipzig: Evangelische Verlagsanstalt, 2002).

67. "Sitzungsberichte der Anthropologischen Gesellschaft in Wien: Jahrgang 1918/19," *MAGW* 48 (1919): 38.

68. Egon von Eickstedt, "Menschenkundliche Zeitforderungen," *Die Deutsche Politik* 6 (1921): 573.

69. Fischer, "Die Notwendigkeit anthropologischer Lehrstühle . . . ," 39.

70. Walter Scheidt, "Rassenbiologie und Familienanthropologie," *Deutschlands Erneuerung* 7 (1923): 47.

71. Scheidt's *Habilitation* lecture made the case for a genetic conception of race. "Einladung [zur Probevorlesung]," June 12, 1923, LMU, OC-N 10a.

72. Walter Scheidt, "Die Stellung der Anthropologie zur . . . Urgeschichte," *AA* 20 (1925): 144.

73. Quoted in Hans Fischer, *Völkerkunde im Nationalsozialismus* (Berlin: Dietrich Reimer, 1990), 35.

74. Scheidt, "Die Stellung der Anthropologie zur . . . Urgeschichte," 144.

75. Fischer, *Völkerkunde im Nationalsozialismus*, 35.

76. Egon von Eickstedt, "Betrachtungen über den Typus der Menschen," *Umschau* 26 (1922): 446.

77. Reche, "Die Menschenrassen der Gegenwart und der vorgeschichtliche Mensch," 314.

78. Thilenius to Hochschulbehörde, July 21, 1926, HAS, 361–5 II Hochschulwesen II, W c 13, Bl. 9–15.

79. Ibid.

80. Walter Scheidt to Felix von Luschan, Dec. 29, 1923, File Scheidt, NL Luschan.

81. Ibid.

82. Georg Thilenius, *Das Hamburgische Museum für Völkerkunde* (Berlin: Georg Reimer, 1916), 19.

83. Thilenius to Hochschulbehörde, Aug. 1, 1924, MfVH, B 4, 2.

84. Scheidt, "Die Stellung der Anthropologie . . . ," 145.

85. Walter Scheidt to Felix von Luschan, Dec. 29, 1923, File Scheidt, NL Luschan.

86. Later, in the 1930s, Thilenius expressed his disappointment with Scheidt's method of combining the two disciplines. Rather than utilizing ideas from *Völkerkunde*, Thilenius claimed that Scheidt approached the study of culture from a purely biological standpoint, ignoring the artifacts of material culture that were the centerpieces of ethnological work. Thilenius complained that during his tenure at the museum, Scheidt had not interested himself in the ethnological methods of his colleagues at all, even

though he was "housed under the same roof for years." G. Thilenius to Dr. Doering, July 12, 1935, MfVH, B 4,151.

87. G. Thilenius to Dr. Doering, July 12, 1935, MfVH, B 4,151.

88. Thilenius to Hochschulbehörde Hamburg, June 13, 1928, HAS, Dozenten und Personalakten IV 1184 (Scheidt), Beiakte 3, Bl. 2.

89. Walter Scheidt, "*Rassenkunde*, Völkerkunde und Völkerbiologische Forschungs- und Lehraufgaben," in *Festschrift zum Fünfzigjährigen Bestehen des Hamburgischen Museums für Völkerkunde* (Hamburg: Selbstverlag des Museums für Völkerkunde, 1928), 75–109, here 107.

90. "Entwurf zum 10. Jahresbericht 1917/1927," Feb. 28, 1928, MfVH, D 4,44.

91. [No title], *Hamburger Nachrichten*, May 15, 1928.

92. Ibid.

93. For more on the comparison of the two exhibits, see Andrew D. Evans, "Race Made Visible: the Transformation of Museum Exhibits in Early-Twentieth-Century German Anthropology." *German Studies Review* 31/1 (2008): 87–108.

94. Ferdinand Birkner, Nachruf für Rudolf Martin, July 13, 1925, LMU, E-II-N, Personalakte Rudolf Martin.

95. Proctor, "From *Anthropologie* to *Rassenkunde* . . . ," 149.

96. See the introduction to Walter Scheidt, *Allgemeine Rassenkunde: Als Einführung in das Studium der Menschenrassen* (München: J. F. Lehmann, 1925), xi. Also see 342–44.

97. Felix von Luschan, *Völker, Rassen, Sprachen* (Berlin: Welt Verlag, 1922), v.

98. Ibid., 187–88.

99. Felix von Luschan, "Rudolf Virchow als Anthropologe," *Virchows Archiv für pathologische Anatomie und Physiologie*, Sonderabdruck aus Band 235 (Berlin: Julius Springer Verlag, 1921), 419.

100. "Rasse und Volkstumsfragen in der Deutschkundlichen Woche: Rasse und Leitung, Prof. Eugen Fischer spricht," *Danzige Allgemeine Zeitung*, Oct. 11, 1933.

101. "An die deutschen Universitäten," *CBDAG* 50 (1919): 37.

102. Ibid.

103. Egon von Eickstedt, "Menschenkundliche Zeitforderungen," *Die Deutsche Politik* 6 (1921): 572–73.

104. Fischer, "Die Notwendigkeit anthropologischer Lehrstühle . . . ," 38.

105. Scheidt, "Die Stellung der Anthropologie . . . Urgeschichte," 145.

106. Felix von Luschan, *Völker, Rassen, Sprachen* (Berliner: Welt Verlag, 1922), 157.

107. Abschrift, Hauptausschuß der Notgemeinschaft der Deutschen Wissenschaft, Dec. 10, 1928, HAS, Dozenten und Personalakten IV 1184 (Scheidt), Personalakte, Bl. 29.

108. Thilenius to Hochschulbehörde, July 21, 1926, HAS, 361–5 II Hochschulwesen II, W c 13, Bl. 10.

109. While four European races were generally the norm in German typologies that featured the Nordic race before the war, the Frenchman Joseph Deniker included six in his work of 1899, including the "Nordic," "Eastern," "Iberian," "Western," "Mediterranean," and "Dinaric." See Martin, *Lehrbuch der Anthropologie*, 22.

110. Egon von Eickstedt, "Die Rasse beim Menschen," *Die Umschau* 26 (1922): 5.

111. Reche, "Die Menschenrassen der Gegenwart und der vorgeschichtliche Mensch," 324–25.

112. Luschan, *Völker, Rassen, Sprachen*, 157.

113. Felix von Luschan, "Zur Anthropologie der Preußen," *Berliner Tageblatt*, June 7, 1914.

114. Egon von Eickstedt, "Die Rasse beim Menschen," *Umschau* 26 (1922): 4–5, 8.
115. Egon von Eickstedt, "Menschenkundliche Zeitforderungen," *Die Deutsche Politik* 6 (1921): 574.
116. Eickstedt, "Die Rasse beim Menschen," 5.
117. Reche, "Die Menschenrassen der Gegenwart und der vorgeschichtliche Mensch," 318.
118. Johannes Ranke, Review of *Rasse und Kultur*, by Friedrich Hertz, AA 43 (1916): 73.
119. Proctor, "From Anthropologie to Rassenkunde . . . ," 148.
120. Walter Scheidt to Felix von Luschan, Dec. 29, 1923. File Scheidt, NL Luschan.
121. Felix von Luschan, *Kriegsgefangene, ein Beitrag zur Völkerkunde im Weltkriege: Einführung in die Grundzüge der Anthropologie* (Berlin: Dietrich Reimer Ernst Vohsen, 1917), 318.
122. Martin, *Lehrbuch der Anthropologie*, 3.
123. Scheidt, *Allgemeine Rassenkunde*, 58.
124. Franz Boas, "What is a Race?" *The Nation* 120 (1925): 89.
125. Bernhard Struck to Felix von Luschan, Mar. 3, 1916. File B. Struck, NL Luschan.
126. Felix von Luschan to Bernard Struck, May 22, 1922. File B. Struck, NL Luschan.
127. Eugen Fischer to Felix v. Luschan, Nov. 9, 1917, File Fischer, NL Luschan.
128. Scheidt wrote, "I think of Gobineau and predecessors Thierry and Edwards, of Chamberlain, Schemann, and the school of political anthropology that follows him. The scientific contestability need not be especially emphasized here. A complete rejection of the, in my opinion, useful core contained within [these writings] would be just as wrong as their absolute recognition." See Walter Scheidt, "Die Stellung der Anthropologie zur . . . Urgeschichte," 145.
129. Reche, "Die Menschenrassen der Gegenwart und der vorgeschichtliche Mensch," 318.
130. Otto Reche, "Vorwort der Herausgebers," in Ludwig Woltmann, *Politische Anthropologie*, I. Band (Leipzig: Justus Dörner, 1936), 25–33; Otto Reche, "Vorwort der Herausgebers," in Ludwig Woltmann, *Die Germanen und die Renaissance in Italian*, II. Band (Leipzig: Justus Dörner, 1936), 7–21.
131. It is worth noting that the timing of the acceptance of *völkisch* thought in Germany was in direct contrast to that of the anthropological communities in other countries. In 1925, for example, a group of prominent American anthropologists including Franz Boas and Edward Sapir wrote a series of articles for a popular American periodical designed to puncture the myth of Nordic superiority and refute the writings of theorists like Gobineau, Chamberlain, Günther, and others. It is significant that a similar debate was not occurring within the German anthropological community. See, for example, Franz Boas, "What is Race?" 89–91; Melville J. Herskovits, "Brains and the Immigrant," *The Nation* 120 (1925), 139–41; Edward Sapir, "Let Race Alone," *The Nation* 120 (1925), 211–13; Harry Elmer Barnes, "The Race Myth Crumbles," *The Nation* 120 (1925), 515–17.
132. John Keegan, *The First World War* (New York: Vintage Books, 1998), 7.
133. Robert Weldon Whalen, *Bitter Wounds: German Victims of the Great War, 1914–1939* (Ithaca, NY: Cornell University Press, 1984), 41.
134. "Krieg und Volksvermehrung," *Berliner Tageblatt*, Apr. 14, 1915.
135. Eugen Fischer, "Die Notwendigkeit anthropologischer Lehrstühle . . ." 38.
136. Ibid.
137. Felix von Luschan, "Einige Aufgaben der Sozial-Anthropologie," *Die Schwester* 4 (Jan. 1921): 26.

138. Felix von Luschan to Herr Generaldirektor d. Staatliche Museen, Mar. 29, 1919, MfVB, I/MfV 67, Ic, Band 15. 367/19.

139. Egon von Eickstedt, "Menschenkundliche Zeitforderungen," *Die Deutsche Politik* VI (1921): 576.

140. Luschan, "Einige Aufgaben der Sozial-Anthropologie," 1.

141. Rudolf Martin to Rektorat der Ludwig Maximilians-Universität, Feb. 22, 1924, BHSTA, MK 11820.

142. Rudolf Martin to Rektorat der Ludwig Maximilians-Universität, München, July 17, 1924, BHSTA, MK 11820.

143. Rudolf Martin, "Die Körperentwicklung Münchener Volksschulkinder in den Jahren 1921, 1922, und 1923," *Sonderdruck aus dem Anthropologischen Anzeiger* I (1924): 85.

144. Rudolf Martin, "Die Körperbeschaffenheit der deutschen Turner," *Monatsschrift für Turner, Spiel und Sport* 2 (1924): 53–61.

145. Ferdinand Birkner, Nachruf für Rudolf Martin, July 7, 1925, LMU, E-II-N, Personalakte Rudolf Martin.

146. Rudolf Martin to Rektorat der Universität München, Nov. 28, 1921, BHSTA, MK 11820.

147. Rudolf Martin to Rektorat der Universität München, July 17, 1924, BHSTA, MK 11820.

148. Rudolf Martin, "Die Körperentwicklung Münchener Volksschulkinder in den Jahren 1921, 1922, und 1923," *Sonderdruck aus dem Anthropologischen Anzeiger* I (1924): 78.

149. Rudolf Martin to Rektorat der Universität München, July 17, 1924, BHSTA, MK 11820.

150. Rudolf Martin to Rektorat der Universität München, Feb. 22, 1924, BHSTA, MK 11820.

151. "Biologische Familienforschung," *Münchner Neuste Nachrichten*, Feb. 6, 1923.

152. Ibid.

153. Letter (Abschift) from Dekanat der medizinischen Fakultät to Adademischer Senat der Universität München, Dec. 18, 1922, LMU, Sen. 548, Hygiene, a.o. Prof. für Rassenhygiene.

154. Eugen Fischer, "Zweck und Aufgaben eines Forschungsinstituts für Anthropologie, menschliche Erblichkeitslehre und Eugenik," GStA PK, I HA, Rep 76 Vc Sekt. 2, Tit. 23A, Nr. 144, Bd. 1, Bl. 52.

155. Eugen Fischer, untitled section in the larger article, "Er den nordiske race domt til undergang?" redigert av Dr. John Alfr. Mjoen. *Det Nye Nord.* (May 1922): 100.

156. Egon von Eickstedt, "Menschenkundliche Zeitforderungen," *Die Deutsche Politik* 6 (1921): 577.

157. Ibid.: 575–76.

158. Eugen Fischer, "Zweck und Aufgaben eines Forschungsinstituts für Anthropologie, menschliche Erblichkeitslehre und Eugenik," GStA PK, I HA, Rep 76 Vc Sekt. 2, Tit. 23A, Nr. 144, Bd. 1, Bl. 53.

159. Eugen Fischer, "Ein Forschungsinstitut für Anthropologie und menschliche Erblichkeitslehre," May 15, 1926, GStA PK, I HA, Rep 76 Vc Sekt. 2, Tit. 23A, Nr. 144, Bd. 1, Bl. 21.

160. Fischer, "Zweck und Aufgaben eines Forschungsinstituts für Anthropologie, menschliche Erblichkeitslehre und Eugenik," Bl. 53.

161. Eugen Fischer, "Ein Forschungsinstitut für Anthropologie und menschliche Erblich-keitslehre," May 15, 1926, GStA PK, I HA, Rep 76 Vc Sekt. 2, Tit. 23A, Nr. 144, Bd. 1, Bl. 19.

162. Eugen Fischer, "Zweck und Aufgaben eines Forschungsinstituts für Anthropologie, menschliche Erblichkeitslehre und Eugenik," GStA PK, I HA, Rep 76 Vc Sekt. 2, Tit. 23A, Nr. 144, Bd. 1, Bl. 55.

163. Adolf von Harnack, Präsident der Kaiser-Wilhelm-Gesellschaft zur Förderung der Wissenschaften to Minister für Wissenschaft, Kunst und Volksbildung, June 21, 1926, GStA PK, I HA, Rep 76 Vc Sekt. 2, Tit. 23A, Nr. 144, Bd. 1, Bl. 43.

164. Eugen Fischer, "Zweck und Aufgaben eines Forschungsinstituts für Anthropologie, menschliche Erblichkeitslehre und Eugenik," GStA PK, I HA, Rep 76 Vc Sekt. 2, Tit. 23A, Nr. 144, Bd. 1, Bl. 57.

165. Eugen Fischer, "Ein Forschungsinstitut für Anthropologie und menschliche Erblich-keitslehre," May 15, 1926, GStA PK, I HA, Rep 76 Vc Sekt. 2, Tit. 23A, Nr. 144, Bd. 1, Bl. 22.

166. See, for example, the appendix "Mitarbeiter-Verzeichnis des KWI" in Niels Lösch, *Rasse als Konstrukt: Leben und Werk Eugen Fischers* (Frankfurt am Main: Peter Lang, 1997), 562–76.

CONCLUSION

1. Mollison to Verwaltung der wissenschaftlichen Sammlungen des Staates, Mar. 15, 1933, Bay. HSTA, MK/VI 1056—Anthropologische Staatssammlung, 1927–51 [no Blatt numbers].

2. Mollison, Anthropologisches Insitut, to Staatsminister für Unterricht und Kultus Gauleiter Adolf Wagner, Feb. 9, 1937, Bay. HSTA. MK/VI 1057—Anthropologi-sches Staatssammlung, Vorstand und wissenschaftl. Personal, 1927–57 [no Blatt numbers].

3. Mollison to Verwaltung der wissenschaftlichen Sammlungen des Staates, Apr. 29, 1935, Bay. HSTA. MK/VI 1056—Anthropologische Staatssammlung, 1927–51 [no Blatt numbers].

4. Fritz Reim to Herrn Ministerpräsident Ludwig Siebert. Aug. 29, 1935. Bay. HSTA. MK/VI 1056—Anthropologische Staatssammlung, 1927–51 [no Blatt numbers].

5. Fritz Reim to Ludwig Siebert. Aug. 29, 1935.

6. Mollison to Verwaltung der wissenschaftlichen Sammlungen des Staates. April 29, 1935. Bay. HSTA. MK/VI 1056—Anthropologische Staatssammlung, 1927–51 [no Blatt numbers].

7. Fritz Reim to Ludwig Siebert. Aug. 29, 1935.

8. Ibid.

9. Fritz Reim to Ludwig Siebert, Aug. 29, 1935.

10. Ibid.

11. Proctor, "From Anthropologie to Rassenkunde," 160–61.

12. *Kultur und Rasse: Otto Reche zum 60. Geburtstag*, eds. Michael Hesch und Günther Spannaus (München/Berlin: J. F. Lehmann, 1939).

13. Quoted by Katja Geisenhainer, "Otto Reche's Verhältnis zur sogenannten Rassenhy-giene," *Anthropos* 91 (1996): 500.

14. Michael Hesch, "Otto Reche als Rassenforscher," *Kultur und Rasse: Otto Reche zum 60. Geburtstag*, eds. Michael Hesch and Günther Spannaus (München/Berlin: J. F. Lehmann, 1939), 9.

15. Proctor, "From Anthropologie to Rassenkunde," 161.

16. Egon von Eickstedt, "An Anthropology of the Whole," *This is Race: An Anthology Selected from the International Literature on the Races of Man* ed. Earl W. Count (New York: Henry Schuman, 1950), 541.

17. Proctor, "From Anthropologie to *Rassenkunde* . . . " 161.

18. Rektor der Hansischen Universität to Prof. Dr. Mattiat, Reichs- und Preussisches Ministerium für Wissenschaft, Erziehung, und Volksbildung, Feb. 15, 1936. HAS Dozenten und Personalakten IV 1184 (Scheidt), Bl 19.

19. Gretchen E. Schafft, *From Racism to Genocide: Anthropology in the Third Reich* (Urbana: University of Illinois Press, 2004), 73–75.

20. Michael Burleigh and Wolfgang Wippermann, *The Racial State: Germany*, 23–28.

21. Zimmerman, *Anthropology and Anti-Humanism in Imperial Germany*, 10–11, 242–43.

22. H. Glenn Penny and Matti Bunzl, "Introduction: Rethinking German Anthrpology, Colonialism, and Race," in *Worldly Provincialism: German Anthropology in the Age of Empire* (Ann Arbor: University of Michigan Press, 2003), 1–2.

23. Michael Gordin, et. al., "Ideologically Correct Science" in *Science and Ideology: A Comparative History*, ed. Mark Walker (New York: Routledge, 2003), 35.

24. Michael Gordin, et. al., "Ideologically Correct Science."

BIBLIOGRAPHY

ARCHIVES AND SPECIAL COLLECTIONS

Archiv der Berliner Gesellschaft für Anthropologie, Ethnologie, und Urgeschichte
Archiv der Humboldt Universität zu Berlin
Archiv des Museums für Völkerkunde, Berlin
Archiv des Museums für Völkerkunde, Hamburg
Bayerisches Hauptstadtsarchiv, Munich
Bundesarchiv Lichterfelde, Berlin
Franz Boas Collections, American Philosophical Society
Geheimes Staatsarchiv Preußischer Kulturbesitz, Berlin
Ludwig-Maximilian Universitätsarchiv, München
Nachlaß Felix Luschans, Handschriftenabteilung, Staatsbibliothek zu Berlin–Preußischer
    Kulturbesitz
Nachlass Wilhelm von Bode, Zentralarchiv, Staatliche Museen Preussischer Kulturbestiz
Prähistorische Staatssammlung, Museum für Vor- und Frühgeschichte, München
Staatsarchiv der Freien und Hansestadt Hamburg

PERIODICALS

Anthropos
Archiv für Anthropologie
Beiträge zur Anthropologie und Urgeschichte Bayerns
Correspondenz-Blatt der Deutschen Anthropologischen Gesellschaft
Deutsche Medizinische Wochenschrift
Die Deutsche Politik
Deutschlands Erneuerung
Die Gartenlaube
Journal of the Royal Anthropological Institute of Great Britain and Ireland
Man: A Monthly Record of Anthropological Science
Mitteilungen der Anthropologischen Gesellschaft Wien
Monatsschrift für Turner, Spiel und Sport
Natur
Politisch-Anthropologische Monatschrift
Die Umschau

Zeitschrift für Ethnologie
Zeitschrift für Morphologie und Anthropologie
Zur Guten Stunde

PUBLISHED PRIMARY SOURCES

Das 25 Jährige Jubiläum der Münchener Gesellschaft für Anthropologie am 16. März, 1895. K. Hof und Universitätsdruckerei Dr. C. Wolf und Sohn, 1895.

Backhaus, A. Alexander. *Die Kriegsgefangenen in Deutschland: Gegen 250 Wirklichkeitsaufnahmen aus deutschen Gefangenenlagern.* Edited by Walter Stein. Siegen, Leipzig, Berlin: H. Montanus, 1915.

Barnes, Harry Elmer. "The Race Myth Crumbles." *The Nation* 120 (1925): 515–17.

Bastian, Adolf. *Alexander von Humboldt: Festrede.* Berlin: Weigandt und Hempel, 1869.

———. *Der Mensch in der Geschichte: Zur Begründung einer psychologischen Weltanschauung.* Osnabruck: Biblioverlag, 1860.

Birkner, Ferdinand. *Die Rassen und Völker der Menschheit.* Berlin: Allgemeine Verlag, 1913.

Blumenbach, Johann Friederich. *The Anthropological Treatises of Johann Friedrich Blumenbach.* London: Longman, 1865.

Boas, Franz. "Changes in Immigrant Body Form." In *The Shaping of American Anthropology, 1883–1911: A Franz Boas Reader,* edited by George W. Stocking, Jr., 202–14. New York: Basic Books, 1974.

———. "Instability of Human Types." In *The Shaping of American Anthropology, 1883–1911: A Franz Boas Reader,* edited by George W. Stocking, Jr., 214–18. New York: Basic Books, 1974.

———. "Rudolf Virchow's Anthropological Work." In *The Shaping of American Anthropology, 1883–1911: A Franz Boas Reader,* edited by George W. Stocking, Jr., 36–42. New York: Basic Books, 1974.

———. "What is a Race?" *The Nation* 120 (1925): 89–91.

Buschan, Georg. "Krieg und Anthropologie." *Deutsche Medizinische Wochenschrift* 26 (1915): 773.

"Charakterköpfe aus dem Gefangenlager in Ohrdruf," *Die Gartenlaube* (1915): 469.

Darwin, Charles. *The Descent of Man and Selection in Relation to Sex.* 2nd ed. New York: A. L. Burt, 1874.

Deniker, Joseph. *Les Races de l'Europe: L'indice cephalique en Europe.* Paris: Au secrétariat de l'Association, 1899.

Doegen, Wilhelm. *Kriegsgefangene Völker: Der Kriegsgefangenen Haltung und Schicksal in Deutschland.* Bd. 1. Berlin: Verlag von Dietrich Reimer, 1919.

———, ed. *Unter Fremden Völkern: Eine neue Völkerkunde.* Berlin: Otto Stollberg Verlag für Politik und Wirtschaft, 1925.

Eickstedt, Egon von. "An Anthropology of the Whole." In *This is Race: An Anthology Selected from the International Literature on the Races of Man,* edited by Earl W. Count, 537–45. New York: Henry Schuman, 1950.

———. "Menschenkundliche Zeitforderungen." *Die Deutsche Politik* 6 (1921): 572–76.

Fischer, Eugen. "Er den nordiske race domt til undergang?" *Det Nye Nord.* (May 1922): 100.

———. "Rassenprobleme in Spanien." *Spanien: Zeitschrift für Auslandskunde* 1 (1919): 24.

———. *Die Rehobother Bastards und das Bastardierungsproblem beim Menschen.* Jena: Fischer, 1913.

Frobenius, Leo. *Der Völkerzirkus unserer Feinde.* Berlin: Eckhart-Verlag, 1916.

Herskovits, Melville J. "Brains and the Immigrant." *The Nation* 120 (1925): 139–41.

Hesch, M., and Günter Spannus, eds. *Kultur und Rasse: Otto Reche zum 60. Geburtstag.* München: J. F. Lehmann, 1939.

Johnston, H. H. "Dr. Weule's Expedition to German East Africa." *Journal of the Royal African Society* 8 (1909): 383–86.

Keith, Arthur. "Presidential Address: The Bronze Age Invaders of Britain." *Journal of the Royal Anthropological Institute of Great Britain and Ireland* XLV (1915): 12–22.

Kellermann, Hermann, ed. *Der Krieg der Geister: Eine Auslese deutscher und ausländischer Stimmen zum Weltkriege 1914.* Weimar: Alexander Duncker Verlag, 1915.

Kollmann, Julius. "Die Menschenrassen Europa's und Asien's." Vortrag gehalten in der zweiten Sitzung der 62. Versammlung Deutscher Naturforscher und Aerzte zu Heidelberg. 21. September, 3–11. Heidelberg: Universitäts-Buchdruckerei von J. Hörning, 1889.

Königliche Museen zu Berlin. *Führer durch das Museum für Völkerkunde.* 5th ed. Berlin: W. Spemann, 1892.

———. *Führer durch das Museum für Völkerkunde,* 14th ed. Berlin: Georg Reimer, 1908.

Königliches Museum für Völkerkunde in Berlin. *Anleitung für ethnographische Beobachtungen und Sammlungen in Afrika und Oceanien.* Berlin: Unger, 1904.

Korbitz, A. H. "Typen aus den deutschen Kriegsgefangenlagern." *Zur Guten Stunde* 2 (1916): 597–600.

Lenz, Fritz. "Nordische Rasse in der Blutmischung unserer östlichen Nachbarn." *Osteuropäische Zukunft* II (January, 1917): 17–22.

Luschan, Felix von. "Anthropological View of Race." In *Papers on Inter-racial Problems, Communicated to the First Universal Races Congress.* London: P.S. King, 1911.

———. "Einige Aufgaben der Sozial-Anthropologie." *Die Schwester* 4 (Jan. 1921): 1–7, 24–27.

———. *Kriegsgefangene, ein Beitrag zur Völkerkunde im Weltkriege: Einführung in die Grundzüge der Anthropologie.* Berlin: Dietrich Reimer [Ernst Vohsen], 1917.

———. "Rassen und Völker." In *Deutsche Reden in schwerer Zeit: Gehalten von den Professoren an der Universität Berlin,* 349–81. Vol. 3. Berlin: Ulrich von Wilamowitz-Moellendorff [u.a.], 1915.

———. "Rudolf Virchow als Anthropologe." *Virchows Archiv für pathologische Anatomie und Physiologie.* Sonderabdruck auf Band 235. Berlin: Julius Springer Verlag, 1921.

———. *Völker, Rassen, Sprachen.* Berlin: Welt Verlag, 1922.

Martin, Rudolf. *Lehrbuch der Anthropologie in systematischer Darstellung.* Jena: Gustav Fischer, 1914.

———. "Die Körperbeschaffenheit der deutschen Turner." *Monatsschrift für Turner, Spiel und Sport* 2 (1924): 53–61.

———. "Die Körperentwicklung Münchener Volksschulkinder in den Jahren 1921, 1922, und 1923." *Sonderdruck aus dem Anthropologischen Anzeiger* I (1924): 85.

Melle, Werner von. *Dreißig Jahre Hamburger Wissenschaft, 1891–1921.* Hamburg: Kommissionsverlag von Broschek, 1923.

Mollison, Theodor. "Die Geltung des Mendelschen Gesetzes beim Menschen." *Sonderabdruck aus Die Naturwissenschaften: Wochenschrift für die Fortschritte der Naturwissenschaften, der Medizin, und der Technik.* 24 (June 13, 1913): 572–78.

"Proceedings of Societies: Anthropology at the British Association for the Advancement of Science, 1914." *Man: A Monthly Record of Anthropological Science* 14 (1914): 171–75.

Ploetz, Alfred. *Die Tüchtigkeit unsrer Rasse und der Schutz der Schwachen: Ein Versuch über Rassenhygiene und ihr Verhältnis zu den humanen Idealen, besonders zur Sozialismus.* Berlin: S. Fischer, 1895.

Ranke, Johannes. "Anthropologie, Urgeschichte, und Ethnologie." In *Die Deutschen Universitäten, für die Universitätsausstellung in Chicago, 1893,* edited by Wilhelm Lexis, 112–25. Berlin: Asher, 1893.

———. *Der Mensch.* 2 vols. Leipzig: Verlag des Bibliographischen Institues, 1886–87.

———. "Die Somatisch-anthropologische Abteilung der anthropologischen Sammlung des Staates." *Sitzungsberichte der K. Bayeriche Akademie der Wissenschaften, Mathematische.-Physische Klasse* (1912): 389–90.

———. "Vergleichung des Rauminhaltes der Rückgrats- und Schädelhöhle als Beitrag zur vergleichenden Psychologie." *Festschrift für Adolf Bastian zu seinem 70. Geburtstag, 26 June 1896,* 53–62. Berlin: Dietrich Reimer, 1896.

Reche, Otto. "Die Menschenrassen der Gegenwart und der vorgeschichtliche Mensch." In *Einführung in der Biologie.* 5th ed. Edited by Karl Kraepelin and C. Schäffer, 313–27. Leipzig: B. G. Teubner, 1921.

———. "Vorwort der Herausgebers." In *Politische Anthropologie,* by Ludwig Woltmann, 25–33. Bd. I. Leipzig: Justus Dörner, 1936.

———. "Vorwort der Herausgebers." In *Die Germanen und die Renaissance in Italien,* by Ludwig Woltmann, 7–21. Bd. II Leipzig: Justus Dörner, 1936.

Ripley, William Z. *The Races of Europe: A Sociological Study.* New York: D. Appleman and Company, 1899.

Schallmeyer, Wilhelm. *Über die drohende körperliche Entartung der Kulturmenschheit und die Verstaatlichung des ärtzlichen Standes.* Berlin: Heuser, 1891.

Sapir, Edward. "Let Race Alone." *The Nation* 120 (1925): 211–13.

Scheidt, Walter. *Allgemeine Rassenkunde: Als Einführung in das Studium der Menschenrassen.* München: J.F. Lehmann, 1925.

———. "Rassenbiologie und Familiananthropologie." *Deutschlands Erneuerung* 7 (1923): 47.

———. "Rassenkunde, Völkerkunde und Völkerbiologische Forschungs- und Lehraufgaben." In *Festschrift zum Fünfzigjährigen Bestehen des Hamburgischen Museums für Völkerkunde,* 75–109. Hamburg: Selbstverlag des Museums für Völkerkunde, 1928.

Thilenius, Georg. *Das Hamburgische Museum für Völkerkunde.* Berlin: Georg Reimer, 1916.

———. "Die Museen für Völkerkunde." In *Die Kunstmuseen und das Deutsche Volk,* hrgs. vom Deutschen Museumsbund, 185–97. Munich: Kurt Wolf Verlag, 1919.

Verzeichnis der Vorlesungen an der Königlichen Friedrich-Wilhelms-Universität zu Berlin. Berlin: Universitäts-Buchdruckerei, 1914–19.

Virchow, Rudolf. "Rassenbildung und Erblichkeit." In *Festschrift für Adolf Bastian zu seinem 70. Geburtstag, 26 June 1896,* 1–43. Berlin: Dietrich Reimer, 1896.

Waldeyer, Wilhelm. "Die im Weltkriege stehenden Völker in anthropologischer Betrachtung." In *Deutsche Reden in schwerer Zeit: Gehalten von den Professoren an der Universität Berlin,* 313–46. Vol. 3. Berlin: Ulrich von Wilamowitz-Moellendorff [u.a.], 1915.

———. *Lebenserinnerungen.* Bonn: Friedrich Cohen, 1920.

Walsh, James J. *Makers of Modern Medicine.* New York: Fordham University Press, 1915.

Weule, Karl. *Negerleben in Ostafrica: Ergebnisse einer ethnologischen Forschungsreise.* Leipzig: Brockhaus, 1908.

Wilser, Ludwig. "Die Rasse der Kriegführenden." *Natur* 6 (1915): 82–85.

———. *Die Überlegenheit der germanischen Rasse: Zeitgemässe Betrachtungen.* Stuttgart: Strecker und Schröder, 1915.

———. "Das Völkergemisch unserer Feinde." *Die Gartenlaube* (1915): 72–76.

SECONDARY SOURCES

Ackerknecht, Erwin. *Rudolf Virchow: Doctor, Statesman, Anthropologist.* Madison: University of Wisconsin Press, 1953.

Andree, Christian. "Geschichte der Berliner Gesellschaft für Anthropologie, Ethnologie und Urgeschichte, 1869–1969." In *Festschrift zum Hundertjährigen Bestehen der Berliner Gesellschaft für Anthropologie, Ethnologie und Urgeschichte,* edited by Hermann Pohle and Gustav Mahr, 9–140. Berlin: Verlag Bruno Hessling, 1969.

———. *Rudolf Virchow als Prähistoriker.* 2 vols. Cologne: Böhlau Verlag, 1976.

Arblaster, Anthony. *The Rise and Decline of Western Liberalism.* Oxford: Basil Blackwell, 1984.

Arvidsson, Stefan. *Aryan Idols: Indo-European Mythology as Ideology and Science.* Chicago: University of Chicago Press, 2006.

Ash, Mitchell G. "Wissenschaft und Politik als Ressourcen für einander." In *Wissenschaften und Wissenschaftspolitik: Bestandaufnahmen zur Formationen, Brüchen und Kontinuitäten im Deutschland des 20. Jahrhunderts,* edited by Rüdiger vom Bruch und Brigitte Kaderas, 32–51. Stuttgart: Franz Steiner Verlag, 2002.

Banta, Melissa, and Curtis M. Hinsley. *From Site to Sight: Anthropology, Photography, and the Power of Imagery.* Cambridge: Peabody Museum Press, 1986.

Bellamy, Richard, ed. *Victorian Liberalism: Nineteenth-century Political Thought and Practice.* New York: Routledge, 1990.

Beller, Stephen. "The Tragic Carnival: Austrian Culture in the First World War." In *European Culture and the Great War: The Arts, Entertainment, and Propaganda,* edited by Aviel Roshwald and Richard Stites, 127–61. Cambridge: Cambridge University Press, 1999.

Ben-David, Joseph. *The Scientist's Role in Society: A Comparative Study.* Englewood Cliffs, NJ: Prentice Hall, 1971.

Berner, Margit. "Forschungs-'Material' Kriegsgefangene: Die Massenuntersuchungen der Wiener Anthropologen an gefangenen Soldaten, 1915–1918." In *Vorreiter der Vernichtung? Eugenik, Rassenhygiene, und Euthanasie in der österreichischen Diskussion vor 1938,* edited by Heinz Eberhard Gabriel and Wolfgang Neugebauer, 167–98. Wien: Böhlau Verlag, 2005.

———. "Die 'rassenkundlichen' Untersuchungen der Wiener Anthropologen in Kriegsgefangenenlagern 1915–1918." *Zeitgeschichte* 30 (2003): 124–36.

Beyerchen, Alan. "On the Stimulation of Excellence in Wilhelmian Science." In *Another Germany: A Reconsideration of the Imperial Era,* edited by Jack R. Dukes and Joachim Remak, 139–68. Boulder, London: Westview Press: 1988.

Blackbourne, David, and Geoff Eley. *The Particularities of German History: Bourgeois Society and Politics in Nineteenth-century Germany.* Oxford: Oxford University Press, 1984.

Boyd, Byron A. *Rudolf Virchow: The Scientist as Citizen.* New York: Garland Publishing, 1991.

Brocke, Bernhard von. "Wissenschaft und Militarismus: Der Aufruf der 93 'An die Kulturwelt!' und der Zusammenbruch der internationalen Gelehrtenrepublik im Ersten Weltkrieg." In *Wilamowitz nach 50 Jahren,* edited by William M. Calder III, Hellmut Flashar, and Theodor Lindken, 649–719. Darmstadt: Wissenschaftliche Buchgesellschaft, 1985.

Bruch, Rüdiger von. "The Academic Disciplines and Social Thought." In *Imperial Germany: A Historigraphical Companion*, edited by Roger Chickering. Westport: Greenwood Press, 1996.

Bruckner, Sierra. "Spectacles of (Human) Nature: Commercial Ethnography between Leisure, Learning, and *Schaulust*." In *Worldly Provincialism: German Anthropology in the Age of Empire*, edited by Matti Bunzl and H. Glenn Penny, 127–55. Ann Arbor: University of Michigan Press, 2003.

———. "The Tingle-Tangle of Modernity: Popular Anthropology and the Cultural Politics of Identity in Imperial Germany." Ph.D. diss., University of Iowa, 1999.

Bunzl, Matti. "Franz Boas and the Humboldtian Tradition." In *Volksgeist as Method and Ethic: Essays on Boasian Ethnography and the German Anthropological Tradition*, edited by George Stocking, Jr., 17–78. Madison: University of Wisconsin Press, 1996.

Burleigh, Michael, and Wolfgang Wippermann. *The Racial State: Germany, 1933–1945*. Cambridge: Cambridge University Press, 1991.

Buschmann, Rainer. "Colonizing Anthropology: Albert Hahl and the Ethnographic Frontier in German New Guinea." In *Worldly Provincialism: German Anthropology in the Age of Empire*, edited by H. Glenn Penny and Matti Bunzl, 230–55. Ann Arbor: University of Michigan Press, 2003.

Chickering, Roger. *Imperial Germany and the Great War, 1914–1918*. Cambridge: Cambridge University Press, 1998.

———. *We Men Who Feel Most German: A Cultural Study of the Pan-German League, 1886–1914*. Boston: George Allen and Unwin, 1984.

Churchill, Frederick B. "Rudolf Virchow and the Pathologist's Criteria for the Inheritance of Acquired Characteristics." *Journal of the History of Medicine and Applied Sciences* 31 (1976): 117–48.

Cahan, David. *An Institute for an Empire: The Physikalisch-Technische Reichsanstalt, 1871–1918*. Cambridge: Cambridge University Press, 1989.

Cohen, William B. *The French Encounter with Africans: White Responses to Blacks, 1530–1880*. Bloomington: Indiana University Press, 1980.

Cole, Douglas. *Franz Boas: The Early Years, 1858–1906*. Seattle: University of Washington Press, 1999.

Dannheimer, Hermann. "90 Jahre Prähistorische Staatssammlung München." *Bayerische Vorgeschichtsblätter* 40 (1975): 1–33.

Daston, Lorraine, and Peter Galison. "The Image of Objectivity." *Representations* 40 (1992): 81–128.

Daum, Andreas. *Wissenschaftspopularisierung im 19. Jahrhundert: Bürgerliche Kultur, naturwissenschaftliche Bildung, und die deutsche Öffentlichkeit, 1848–1914*. München: R. Oldenbourg, 1998.

Durham, Dewitt Clinton. "Leo Frobenius and the Reorientation of German Ethnology, 1890–1930." Ph.D. diss., Stanford University, 1985.

Eckart, Wolfgang U. "'The Most Extensive Experiment that the Imagination Can Conceive': War, Emotional Stress, and German Medicine, 1914–1918." In *Great War, Total War: Combat and Mobilization on the Western Front, 1914–1918*, edited by Roger Chickering and Stig Förster, 133–49. Cambridge: German Historical Institute and Cambridge University Press, 2000.

Edwards, Elizabeth. "Photographic Types: The Pursuit of Method." *Visual Anthropology* 3 (1990): 235–58.

Efron, John. *Defenders of the Race: Jewish Doctors and Race Science in Fin-de-Siècle Europe*. New Haven: Yale University Press, 1994.

Evans, Andrew D. "Anthropology at War: Racial Studies of POWs during World War I." In *Worldly Provincialism: German Anthropology in the Age of Empire*, edited by H. Glenn Penny and Matti Bunzl, 198–229. Ann Arbor: University of Michigan Press, 2003.

———. "Capturing Race: Anthropology and Photography in German Prisoner-of-War Camps during World War I." In *Colonialist Photography: Imag(in)ing Race and Place*, edited by Eleanor Hight and Gary Sampson, 226–56. New York: Routledge, 2002.

———. "A Liberal Paradigm? Race and Ideology in Late Nineteenth Century German Physical Anthropology." *Ab Imperio: Studies of New Imperial History and Nationalism in the Post-Soviet Space* 8 (1/2007): 113–38.

———. "Race Made Visible: The Transformation of Museum Exhibits in Early-Twentieth-Century German Anthropology." *German Studies Review* 31/1 (2008): 87–108.

Fiedermutz-Laun, Annemarie. *Der Kulturhistorische Gedanke bei Adolf Bastian: Systematisierung und Darstellung der Theorie und Methode mit dem Versuch einer Bewertung des Kulturhistorischen Gehaltes auf dieser Grundlage.* Wiesbaden: Franz Steiner Verlag, 1970.

Field, Geoffrey G. *Evangelist of Race: The Germanic Vision of Houston Stewart Chamberlain.* New York: Columbia University Press, 1981.

Fischer, Hans. *Die Hamburger Südsee-Expedition: Über Ethnographie und Kolonialismus.* Frankfurt a.M: Syndikat, 1981.

———. *Völkerkunde in Nationalsozialismus: Aspekte der Anpassung, Affinität, und Behauptung einer wissenschaftlichen Disziplin.* Berlin: Reimer Verlag, 1990.

Forman, Paul. "Scientific Internationalism and the Weimar Physicists: The Ideology and Its Manipulation in Germany after World War I." *Isis* 64 (1973): 151–80.

Gasman, Daniel. *The Scientific Origins of National Socialism: Social Darwinism in Ernst Haeckel and the German Monist League.* New York: American Elsevier Publishing Company, 1971.

Geisenhainer, Katja. "Otto Reche's Verhältnis zur sogenannten Rassenhygiene." *Anthropos* 91 (1996): 495–512.

———. *"Rasse ist Schicksal": Otto Reche, ein Leben als Anthropologe und Völkerkundler.* Leipzig: Evangelische Verlagsanstalt, 2002.

Geus, Armin. *Johannes Ranke (1836–1916): Physiologe, Anthropologie und Prähistoriker.* Marburg: Lahn, 1987.

Gilman, Sander. *Jew's Body.* New York: Routledge, 1991.

Gingrich, Andre. "After the Great War: National Reconfigurations of Anthropology in Late Colonial Times." In *Doing Anthropology in Wartime and War Zones: World War I and the Cultural Sciences in Europe*, eds. Monique Scheer, Reinhard Johler, and Christian Marchetti. Bielefeld: Transcript Verlag, 2010.

———. "The German Speaking Countries: Ruptures, Schools, and Non-traditions: Reassessing the History of Sociocultural Anthropology in Germany." In *One Discipline, Four Ways: British, German, French, and American Anthropology*, Fredrik Barth et al., 61–153. Chicago: University of Chicago Press, 2005.

———. "Liberalism in Imperial Anthropology: Notes on an Implicit Paradigm in Continental European Anthropology before World War I," *Ab Imperio: Studies of New Imperial History and Nationalism in the Post-Soviet Space* 8 (1/2007): 224–39.

Goffman, Erving. *Asylums: Essays on the Social Situations of Mental Patients and Other Inmates.* New York: Anchor Books, 1961.

Gordin, Michael et al. "Ideologically Correct Science." In *Science and Ideology: A Comparative History*, edited by Mark Walker, 35–65. New York: Routledge, 2003.

Gothsch, Manfred. *Die deutsche Völkerkunde und ihr Verhältnis zum Kolonialismus: Ein Beitrag zur kolonialideologischen und kolonialpraktischen Bedeutung der deutschen Völkerkunde in der Zeit von 1870 bis 1945*. Hamburg: Institute Institut für Internationale Angelegenheiten der Universität Hamburg, 1983.

Gould, Stephen Jay. *Ever Since Darwin: Reflections in Natural History*. New York: W. W. Norton, 1977.

———. *The Mismeasure of Man*. New York: W. W. Norton, 1981.

Green-Lewis, Jennifer. *Framing the Victorians: Photography and the Culture of Realism*. Ithaca, NY: Cornell University Press, 1996.

Grosse, Pascal. "Turning Native? Anthropology, German Colonialism and the Paradoxes of the Acclimitization Question, 1885–1914." In *Worldly Provincialism: German Anthropology in the Age of Empire*, edited by H. Glenn Penny and Matti Bunzl, 179–97. Ann Arbor: University of Michigan Press, 2003.

Hartung, Günter. "Völkische Ideologie." In *Handbuch zur Völkischen Bewegung, 1871–1918*, edited by Uwe Puschner, Walter Schmitz, and Justus H. Ulbricht, 22–41. München: K. G. Saur, 1996.

Healy, Maureen. *Vienna and the Fall of the Habsburg Empire: Total War and Everyday Life in World War*. Cambridge: Cambridge University Press, 2004.

Hiltner, Gerhard. *Rudolf Virchow: Ein weltgeschichtlicher Brennpunkt im Werdegang von Naturwissenschaft und Medizin*. Stuttgart: Verlag Freies Geistesleben, 1970.

Hoßfeld, Uwe. *Geschichte der biologischen Anthropologie in Deutschland*. Stuttgart: Franz Steiner Verlag, 2005.

Hughes, H. Stuart. *Consciousness and Society: The Reorientation of European Social Thought, 1890–1930*. New York: Knopf, 1961.

Iggers, George G. *The German Conception of History: The National Tradition of Historical Thought from Herder to the Present*. Middletown, CT: Wesleyan University Press, 1968.

Jackson, Robert. *The Prisoners, 1914–18*. New York: Routledge, 1989.

Jeismann, Michael. *Das Vaterland der Feinde: Studien zum nationalen Feindbegriff und Selbstverständnis in Deutschland und Frankreich, 1792–1918*. Stuttgart: Klett-Cotta, 1992.

Jelavich, Peter. "German Culture in the Great War." In *European Culture in the Great War: The Arts, Entertainment, and Propaganda, 1914–1918*, edited by Aviel Roshwald and Richard Stites, 31–57. Cambridge: Cambridge University Press, 1999.

Johanson, Donald, and Maitland A. Edey. *Lucy: The Beginnings of Humankind*. New York: Simon and Schuster, 1981.

Johnson, Jeffrey Allan. *The Kaiser's Chemists: Science and Modernization in Imperial Germany*. Chapel Hill: University of North Carolina Press, 1990.

Jwaideh, Wadie. *The Kurdish National Movement: Its Origins and Development*. Syracuse, NY: Syracuse University Press, 2006.

Kahleyss, Margot. *Muslime in Brandenburg: Kriegsgefangene im Ersten Weltkrieg: Ansichten und Absichten*. Berlin: Museum für Völkerkunde, 1998.

———. "Muslime als Gefangene." *Rundbrief Fotographie* 7 (1995): 43–45.

Keegan, John. *The First World War*. New York: Vintage Books, 1998.

Kelly, Alfred. *The Descent of Darwin: The Popularization of Darwinism in Germany, 1860–1914*. Chapel Hill: University of North Carolina Press, 1981.

Kevles, Daniel J. *In the Name of Eugenics: Genetics and the Uses of Human Heredity*. New York: Alfred A. Knopf, 1985.

———. "'Into Hostile Camps': The Reorganization of International Science in World War I." *Isis* 62 (1971): 47–60.

Koepping, Klaus-Peter. *Adolf Bastian and the Psychic Unity of Mankind: The Foundations of Anthropology in Nineteenth-Century Germany*. St. Lucia: University of Queensland Press, 1983.

Kuklick, Henrika. "The British Tradition." In *A New History of Anthropology*, edited by Henrika Kuklick, 52–78. Oxford: Blackwell, 2008.

———. "Continuity and Change in British Anthropology, 1914–1919." In *Doing Anthropology in Wartime and War Zones: World War I and the Cultural Sciences in Europe*, edited by Monique Scheer, Reinhard Johler, and Christian Marchetti. Bielefeld: Transcript Verlag, 2010.

Kuhn, Thomas S. *The Structure of Scientific Revolutions*. 3rd ed. Chicago: University of Chicago Press, 1996.

Lange, Britta. "Ein Archiv von Stimmen: Kriegsgefangene unter ethnographischer Beobachtung." In *Original/Ton: Zur Mediengeschichte des O-Tons*, edited by Harun Maye, Cornelius Reiber, Nikolaus Wegmann, 317–42. Constance: UVK, 2007.

Lewerentz, Annette. "Die Berliner Gesellschaft für Anthropologie, Ethnologie, und Urgeschichte und ihre Bedeutung für die Berliner Museen." *Mitteilungen der Berliner Gesellschaft für Anthropologie, Ethnologie, und Urgeschichte* 21 (2000): 111–28.

———. "Forschungsprojekte und staatliche Förderung: Die Berliner Gesellschaft für Anthropologie, Ethnologie, und Urgeschichte und die preußischen Ministerien biz zum Ersten Weltkrieg." *Mitteilungen der Berliner Gesellschaft für Anthropologie, Ethnologie, und Urgeschichte* 20 (1999): 45–64.

———. "Die Rudolf Virchow Stiftung der Berliner Gesellschaft für Anthropologie, Ethnologie, und Urgeschichte: Ein Einblick in einige ihrer Forschungsprojekte." *Mitteilungen der Berliner Gesellschaft für Anthropologie, Ethnologie, und Urgeschichte* 21 (2000): 93–110.

Lichtsinn, Hilkea. *Otto Ammon und die Sozialanthropologie*. Frankfurt am Main: Peter Lang, 1987.

Lindfors, Bernth, ed. *Africans on Stage: Studies in Ethnological Show Business*. Bloomington: Indiana University Press, 1999.

Liulevicius, Vejas Gabriel. *War Land on the Eastern Front: Culture, National Identity, and German Occupation in World War I*. Cambridge: Cambridge University Press, 2000.

Lorimer, Douglas A. "Race, Science, and Culture: Historical Continuities and Discontinuities, 1850–1914." In *The Victorians and Race*, edited by Shearer West, 12–33. Aldershot: Scolar Press, 1996.

Lösch, Niels. *Rasse als Konstrukt: Leben und Werk Eugen Fischers*. Frankfurt am.Main: Peter Lang, 1997.

McCarthy, Daniel J. *The Prisoner of War in Germany*. New York: Moffat, Yard, and Company, 1917.

McClelland, Charles E. *The German Experience of Professionalization*. Cambridge: Cambridge University Press, 1991.

———. *State, Society and University in Germany, 1700–1914*. Cambridge: Cambridge University Press, 1980.

MacLeod, Roy M. "Introduction." In *Science and the Pacific War: Science and Survival in the Pacific, 1939–1945*, edited by Roy M. MacLeod, 1–9. Dordrecht: Kluwer Academic Publishers, 2000.

Maner, Brent. *The Search for a Buried Nation: Archaeology in Central Europe, 1750 to the Present*. Ph.D. diss., University of Illinois at Champaign-Urbana, 2001.

Marchand, Suzanne. *Down from Olympus: Archaeology and Philhellenism in Germany, 1750–1970*. Princeton, NJ: Princeton University Press, 1996.

———. "Leo Frobenius and the Revolt against the West," *Journal of Contemporary History* 32, no. 2 (1997): 153–70.

Marchand, Suzanne, and David F. Lindenfeld, eds. *Germany at the Fin de Siécle: Culture, Politics, Ideas.* Baton Rouge: Louisiana State University Press, 2004.

Massin, Benoit. "From Virchow to Fischer: Physical Anthropology and Modern Race Theories in Wilhelmine Germany." In *Volksgeist as Method and Ethic: Essays on Boasian Ethnography and the German Anthropological Tradition,* edited by George Stocking, Jr., 79–154. Madison: University of Wisconsin Press, 1996.

Metcalf, Thomas R. *Ideologies of the Raj.* Cambridge: Cambridge University Press, 1995.

Mogilner, Marina. "Doing Anthropology in a Russian Military Uniform." In *Doing Anthropology in Wartime and War Zones: World War I and the Cultural Sciences in Europe,* edited by Monique Scheer, Reinhard Johler, and Christian Marchetti. Bielefeld: Transcript Verlag, 2010.

Mommsen, Wolfgang. "German Artists, Writers, and Intellectuals and the Meaning of War." In *State, Society, and Mobilization in Europe during the First World War,* edited by John Horne, 21–38. Cambridge: Cambridge University Press, 1997.

Mosse, George. *The Crisis of Germanic Ideology: Intellectual Origins of the Third Reich.* New York: Grosset and Dunlap, 1964.

———. *Towards the Final Solution: A History of European Racism.* Madison: University of Wisconsin Press, 1978.

Mühlmann, Wilhelm E. *Geschichte der Anthropologie.* Frankfurt am Main: Athenaum Verlag, 1968.

Müller, Rolf-Dieter. "Total War as a Result of New Weapons? The Use of Chemical Agents in World War I." In *Great War, Total War: Combat and Mobilization on the Western Front, 1914–1918,* edited by Roger Chickering and Stig Förster, 95–111. Cambridge: German Historical Institute and Cambridge University Press, 2000.

Neil, Edmund. "Political Ideologies: Liberalism, Conservatism, Socialism." In *A Companion to Nineteenth-Century Europe,* edited by Stefan Berger, 211–23. Malden, MA: Blackwell, 2006.

Nye, Robert A. "The Rise and Fall of the Eugenics Empire." *The Historical Journal* 36 (1993): 687–700.

Nyhart, Lynn. *Biology Takes Form: Animal Morphology and the German Universities, 1800–1900.* Chicago: University of Chicago Press, 1995.

Parkin, Robert. "The French-Speaking Countries." In *One Discipline, Four Ways: British, German, French, and American Anthropology,* Fredrik Barth et al., 157–253. Chicago: University of Chicago Press, 2005.

Penny, H. Glenn. "Bastian's Museum: On the Limits of Empiricism and the Transformation of German Ethnology." In *Worldly Provincialism: German Anthropology in the Age of Empire,* edited by H. Glenn Penny and Matti Bunzl, 86–126. Ann Arbor: University of Michigan Press, 2003.

———. "The Civic Uses of Science: Ethnology and Civil Society in Imperial Germany." *Osiris* 17 (2002): 228–52.

———. "Fashioning Local Identities in an Age of Nation-Building: Museums, Cosmopolitan Visions, and Intra-German Competition." *German History* 17 (1999): 489–505.

———. *Objects of Culture: Ethnology and Ethnographic Museums in Imperial Germany.* Chapel Hill: University of North Carolina Press, 2002.

———. "Traditions in the German Language." In *A New History of Anthropology,* edited by Henrika Kuklick, 79–95. Oxford: Blackwell, 2008.

Pflanze, Otto. *Bismarck and the Development of Germany.* 3 vols. Princeton, NJ: Princeton University Press, 1990.

Pick, Daniel. *Faces of Degeneration: A European Disorder, 1848–1918.* Cambridge: Cambridge University Press, 1989.

Poignant, Roslyn. "Surveying the Field View: The Making of the RAI Photographic Collection." In *Anthropology and Photography, 1860–1920,* edited by Elizabeth Edwards, 42–73. New Haven: Yale University Press, 1992.

Poliakov, Léon. *The Aryan Myth: A History of Racist and Nationalist Ideas in Europe.* Translated by Edward Howard. New York: Basic Books, 1974.

Proctor, Robert. "From Anthropologie to Rassekunde in the German Anthropological Tradition." In *Bones, Bodies, Behavior: Essays on Biological Anthropology,* edited by George Stocking, 138–79. Madison: University of Wisconsin Press, 1988.

———. *Racial Hygiene: Medicine under the Nazis.* Cambridge, MA: Harvard University Press, 1988.

———. *Value-Free Science? Purity and Power in Modern Knowledge.* Cambridge, MA: Harvard University Press, 1991.

Pulzer, Peter. *The Rise of Political Anti-Semitism in Germany and Austria.* Cambridge, MA: Harvard University Press, 1964.

Querner, H. "Zur Geschichte der Anthropologie." *Anthropologische Anzeiger* 44 (1986): 281–97.

Rather, L. J. *A Commentary on the Medical Writings of Rudolf Virchow.* San Francisco: Normal Publishing, 1990.

Reader, John. *Missing Links: The Hunt for Earliest Man.* Boston: Little, Brown, 1981.

Repp, Kevin. "'More Corporeal, More Concrete': Liberal Humanism, Eugenics, and German Progressives at the Last Fin de Siécle." *Journal of Modern History* 72 (2000): 683–730.

Ringer, Fritz. *The Decline of the German Mandarins: The German Academic Community, 1890–1933.* Cambridge, MA: Harvard University Press, 1969.

Ruggiero, Guido de. *The History of European Liberalism.* Translated by R. G. Collinwood. London: Oxford University Press, 1927.

Ryan, James R. *Picturing Empire: Photography and the Visualization of the British Empire.* London: Reaktion Books, 1997.

Ryding, James N. "Alternatives in Nineteenth-Century Ethnology: A Case Study in the Sociology of Science." *Sociologus* 25 (1975): 1–28.

Sachse, Carola, and Mark Walker. "Introduction: A Comparative Perspective." In *Osiris Politics and Science in Wartime: Comparative International Perspectives on the Kaiser Wilhelm Institute* 20 (2005): 1–20.

Schlenther, Ursula. "Zur Geschichte der Völkerkunde an der Berliner Universität von 1810–1945." *Wissenschaftliche Zeitschrift der Humboldt Universität Berlin* 9 (1959/60): 67–79.

Schott, Lothar. "Zur Geschichte der Anthropologie an der Berliner Universität." *Wissenschaftliche Zeitschrift der Humboldt Universität Berlin* Math.-Naturwissenschaftliche Reihe 10 (1961): 57–65.

Schafft, Gretchen E. *From Racism to Genocide: Anthropology in the Third Reich.* Urbana: University of Illinois Press, 2004.

Schwabe, Klaus. *Wissenschaft und Kriegsmoral: Die deutschen Hochschulehrer und die politischen Grundfragen des Ersten Weltkrieges.* Göttingen: Mutterschmidt-Verlag, 1969.

Sekula, Allan. "The Body and the Archive." *October* 39 (Winter 1986): 3–64.

————. "The Instrumental Image: Streichen at War." In *Photography against the Grain: Essays and Photo Works, 1973–1983*. Halifax: Press of the Nova Scotia College of Art and Design, 1984.

Sheehan, James J. *German History, 1770–1866*. Oxford: Oxford University Press, 1989.

————. *German Liberalism in the Nineteenth Century*. Chicago: University of Chicago Press, 1978.

Sibeud, Emmanuelle. "The Metamorphosis of Ethnology in France, 1839–1930." In *A New History of Anthropology*, edited by Henrika Kuklick, 96–110. Oxford: Blackwell, 2008.

Sieferle, Rolf Peter. "Rassismus, Rassenhygiene, Menschenzuchtideale." In *Handbuch der Völkischen Bewegung, 1871–1918*, edited by Uwe Puschner et al., 436–46. München: K. G. Saur, 1996.

Silverman, Sydel. "The United States." In *One Discipline, Four Ways: British, German, French, and American Anthropology*, Fredrik Barth, et al., 257–347. Chicago: University of Chicago Press, 2005.

Smith, John David. "W. E. B. Du Bois, Felix von Luschan, and Racial Reform at the Fin de Siècle." *Amerikastudien/American Studies: A Quarterly* 47 (2002): 23–38.

Smith, Woodruff D. "Colonialism and Colonial Empire." In *Imperial Germany: A Historiographical Companion*, edited by Roger Chickering, 430–53. Westport, CT: Greenwood Press, 1996.

————. *The German Colonial Empire*. Chapel Hill: University of North Carolina Press, 1978.

————. *European Imperialism in the 19th and 20th Centuries*. Chicago: Nelson Hall, 1982.

————. *Politics and the Sciences of Culture in Germany, 1840–1920*. New York: Oxford University Press, 1991.

Smolka, Wolfgang J. *Völkerkunde in München: Voraussetzungen, Möglichkeiten, und Entwicklungslinien ihrer Institutionalisierung, ca. 1850–1933*. Berlin: Duncker and Humboldt, 1994.

Soloway, Richard. *Demography and Degeneration: Eugenics and the Declining Birth Rate in Twentieth-Century Britain*. Chapel Hill: University of North Carolina Press, 1990.

Speed, Richard B., III. *Prisoners, Diplomats, and the Great War: A Study in the Diplomacy of Captivity*. New York: Greenwood Press, 1990.

Spiegal-Rosing, Ina, and Ilse Schwidetzky, eds. *Maus und Schlange: Untersuchungen zur Lage der deutschen Anthropologie*. München: R. Oldenburg, 1982.

Spencer, Frank. "Some Notes on the Attempt to Apply Photography to Anthropometry during the Second Half of the Nineteenth Century." In *Anthropology and Photography, 1860–1920*, edited by Elizabeth Edwards, 99–106. New Haven: Yale University Press, 1992.

Stepan, Nancy. *The Idea of Race in Science: Great Britain, 1800–1960*. Hamden: Archon Books, 1982.

Stern, Fritz. *Einstein's German World*. Princeton, NJ: Princeton University Press, 1999.

————. *The Politics of Cultural Despair: A Study in the Rise of the Germanic Ideology*. Berkeley: University of California Press, 1961.

Stocking, George W., ed. *Bones, Bodies, Behavior: Essays on Biological Anthropology*. Madison: University of Wisconsin Press, 1988.

————. *Colonial Situations: Essays on the Contextualization of Ethnographic Knowledge*. Madison: University of Wisconsin Press, 1991.

————. *Ethnographer's Magic and Other Essays in the History of Anthropology*. Madison: University of Wisconsin Press, 1992.

———. *Functionalism Historicized: Essays on British Social Anthropology.* Madison: University of Wisconsin Press, 1984.

———. *Race, Culture, and Evolution: Essays in the History of Anthropology.* Chicago: University of Chicago Press, 1982.

———. *The Shaping of American Anthropology, 1883–1911: A Franz Boas Reader.* New York: Basic Books, 1974.

———. *Volksgeist as Method and Ethic: Essays on Boasian Ethnography and the German Anthropological Tradition.* Madison: University of Wisconsin Press, 1996.

Szöllösi-Janze, Margit. "Science and Social Space: Transformations in the Institutions of Wissenschaft from the Wilhelmine Empire to the Weimar Republic." *Minerva* 43 (2005): 339–60.

Tagg, John. *The Burden of Representation: Essays on Photographies and Histories.* Amherst: University of Massachusetts Press, 1988.

Thode-Arora, Hilke. *Für fünfzig Pfennig um die Welt: Die Hagenbeckschen Völkerschauen.* New York: Campus, 1989.

Titelbaum, Michael S., and Jay Winter. *The Fear of Population Decline.* New York: Academic Press, 1985.

Tuchman, Arleen Marcia. "Institutions and Disciplines: Recent Work in the History of German Science." *Journal of Modern History* 69 (1997): 298–319.

Ungern-Sternberg, Jürgen von, and Wolfgang von Ungern-Sternberg. *Der Aufruf "An der Kulturwelt": Das Manifest der 93 und die Anfänge der Kriegspropaganda im Ersten Weltkrieg.* Stuttgart: Franz Steiner Verlag, 1996.

Walker, Mark. Introduction to *Science and Ideology: A Comparative History,* edited by Mark Walker, 1–16. New York: Routledge, 2003.

Wehler, Hans-Ulrich. *The German Empire, 1871–1918.* Leamington Spa: Berg, 1985.

Weindling, Paul. *Health, Race, and German Politics between National Unification and Nazism, 1870–1945.* Cambridge: Cambridge University Press, 1989.

West, Shearer. Introduction to *The Victorians and Race,* edited by Shearer West, 1–9. Aldershot: Scolar Press, 1996.

Whalen, Robert Weldon. *Bitter Wounds: German Victims of the Great War, 1914–1939.* Ithaca, NY: Cornell University Press, 1984.

Young, Michael W. *Malinowski: Odyssey of an Anthropologist, 1884–1920.* New Haven: Yale University Press, 2004.

Zimmerman, Andrew. *Anthropology and Antihumanism in Imperial Germany.* Chicago: University of Chicago Press, 2001.

———. "Anthropology and the Place of Knowledge in Imperial Berlin." Ph.D. diss., University of California, San Diego, 1998.

———. "Anti-Semitism as Skill: Rudolf Virchow's Schulstatistik and the Racial Composition of Germany." *Central European History* 32 (1999): 409–29.

INDEX

Lightning Source UK Ltd.
Milton Keynes UK
UKOW04f1527210214

226920UK00001B/132/P